NAPOLEON
THE FINAL VERDICT

NAPOLEON IN HIS STUDY, WEARING THE UNIFORM
OF THE *GRENADIERS À PIED*, IMPERIAL GUARD.
PRINT AFTER DELAROCHE.

NAPOLEON
THE FINAL VERDICT

Philip J. Haythornthwaite

James R. Arnold – Ian Castle – Guy C. Dempsey, Jr

Tim Hicks – J. David Markham – Peter Tsouras

Andrew Uffindell

FOREWORD BY DAVID G. CHANDLER

ARMS AND
ARMOUR

Arms and Armour Press
An Imprint of the Cassell Group
Wellington House, 125 Strand, London WC2R 0BB

Distributed in the USA by Sterling Publishing
Co. Inc., 387 Park Avenue South, New York,
NY 10016-8810.

British Library Cataloguing-in-Publication Data:
a catalogue record for this book is available from
the British Library

ISBN 1-85409-342-8

Designed and edited by DAG Publications Ltd.
Designed by David Gibbons; edited by Michael Boxall;
printed and bound in Great Britain.

CONTENTS

FOREWORD, 7
by David G. Chandler

INTRODUCTION, 9
by Philip J. Haythornthwaite

PART ONE: THE EVIDENCE

The Early Years and First Commands, 13
by J. David Markham

The Years of Legend, 1805–1809, 45
by Ian Castle

The Peninsular War: A Reputation Tarnished, 83
by Guy C. Dempsey, Jr.

The Russian Campaign: A Reputation Damaged, 111
by Philip J. Haythornthwaite

Abdication, Exile and Return, 143
by J. David Markham

Waterloo: A Reputation Destroyed, 161
by Andrew Uffindell

CONTENTS

St. Helena: Controversy to the End, 191
by Tim Hicks

PART TWO: THE ASSESSMENT

Napoleon and his Men, 213
by James R. Arnold

Napoleon's Art of War, 247
by Philip J. Haythornthwaite

Napoleon and his Words, 285
by Peter G. Tsouras

POSTSCRIPT, 305
by Philip J. Haythornthwaite

INDEX, 314

FOREWORD

by David G. Chandler
MA (Oxon), D.Litt, FRHist.S

N APOLEON – THE FINAL VERDICT IS, OF COURSE, NO MORE 'FINAL' than Francis Fakuyama's celebrated volume *The End Of History and the Last Man* (1992) – but is rather a challenge to its readers to review their own conclusions on the 'great, bad man' (as Clarendon called Cromwell).

To the outsider, and even – it has to be said – to some historians, it is inexplicable that a man – Napoleon Bonaparte – who commanded his nation's military forces for only a couple of decades could have caused so much to be written about him in the years following his death and, two centuries on, still merit such study and re-assessment. After all, the doubters will say, his was not an unsullied career, devoid of personal or professional blemish; he was no paragon of military astuteness or virtue.

Such opinions surely miss the point. Napoleon Bonaparte was a one-off, and will remain so in comparison with any who have followed him, and most who preceded him. As we enter the 200th anniversaries of the early events in his remarkable career, a new generation of younger historians – professionals and enthusiastic amateurs alike – are eagerly sifting the evidence in the bid to determine just how it was that this diminutive man could have achieved such status. His early training, his first commands, his early successes and his response to unexpected setbacks, the road which took him from his Corsican roots to become Emperor of France, all being freshly examined. His later Peninsular and Russian excursions, subsequent loss of reputation and regard, and the humiliation of exile will continue to fascinate not only students of strategy but those intrigued by the trials of command and the effect of power on personality and decision-making. The Hundred Days – triumphant return to a position of influence, then further defeats and a final flight into captivity – will remain the most avidly examined three months in European (or even world?) history. Even his death still stirs controversial debate and re-assessment.

The very nature of the man, the power he exercised, his influence on a continent and the legacy he left, all demand that he remain a focal point of military and political study.

In this volume a group of British and American military historians review Napoleon Bonaparte's career and assess his performance in crucial aspects of his military life. I have personally known six of them, and the other two by repute. It is refreshing to find an admixture of interpretations and reports, a variety of viewpoints, for it enables the reader to grow with the book, gauge his own opinions and place the Emperor where he wishes in the context of the era during which he operated and in world history.

The book contributes significantly to the continuing evaluation of a remarkable life; it helps to clarify and expand on many important factors. It will not complete the reader's quest, for there may yet come another ten thousand works on the subject to double the output already published, but it will surely stimulate further energetic analysis and discussion and that in itself makes it worthwhile whether the reader agrees with or alternatively denounces, the following chapters. And if the latter case obtain, may he echo Voltaire: 'I disapprove of what you say, but I will defend to the death your right to say it.'

So it will be for YOU – the reader – to decide the value of the most recent ideas of these eight able writers. 'What is truth? said jesting Pilate; and would not stay for an answer,' mused Francis Bacon. Surely our readers can do better than that, at least in their own minds. But ultimately, of course, as the celebrated Dutchman Professor Pieter Geyl ('one of the great historic minds of our time' according to A. J. P. Taylor in the *New Statesman*) wrote in his 1944 book entitled *Napoleon: For and Against*. 'The argument goes on'. And so, doubtless it will, for many decades if not millennia to come.

David G. Chandler,
November, 1996

INTRODUCTION
Philip J. Haythornthwaite

W HEN A LIFE, A CAREER, IS SO MICROSCOPICALLY ANALYSED AS
that of the subject of this book it is inevitable that, however
glorious and significant the achievements, faults and imperfections will be discovered. No mortal man can survive such lengthy and
determined assessment without his reputation being tarnished and his
qualities questioned. This book describes and discusses one of the most
important lives that has been lived, and has as its main aim the presenta-
tion of evidence to assist its reader to reach a verdict, perhaps a final verdict, on that life.

On 15 August 1769 a Corsican lawyer and his formidable wife celebrated
the birth of a second son. Although the family had some social standing it
was, on the face of it, an unremarkable household but it was to provide, in
addition to this new son, a further four offspring who would rise to high
office or seat of power including three who became kings of their own
states, as a consequence of the triumphs of their brother. This son was
named Napoleon and twenty years later he was witnessing the outbreak of
the French Revolution and setting out on a military career which would
begin with success at the siege of Toulon and suffer very few setbacks during victorious campaigns in Italy, Austria and Egypt. Before the campaigns
of 1805–7 against the Austrians, Prussians and Russians, Napoleon
Bonaparte had already proclaimed himself Emperor, and even his first battlefield reverse – at Aspern-Essling in May 1809 – did little to dent a reputation that all Europe now revered or feared.

It was at this point, however, that he became more theoretical in his
approach to his nation's military affairs, more distant from the sharp end of
battle action. Affairs of state kept him in Paris and there were plenty of
ambitious subordinates ready to receive delegated responsibility. From then
on some historians observe a weakening of military realism in the interest
of personal ambition, national supremacy and rampant adventurism.
Certainly the Peninsula theatre – which he visited only once – and his ill-
fated trek to Moscow betrayed looser management and indecision, and lost
him armies. Despite a more vigorous approach and subsequent reward in

the early months of 1814, the die was cast and defeat outside Paris in March brought the humiliation of abdication and exile.

As Napoleon himself had written, 'if courage is the first character of the soldier, perseverance is the second', and this 'good man' was not to be kept down. While his European enemies relaxed in the knowledge of his incarceration on Elba, the deposed Emperor gathered men together and sailed for France. He found the forces sent to block his return were still open to his persuasive leadership, and within days he was back in a Paris from which Louis XVIII had fled.

Now the European allies were forced hurriedly to re-form in order to meet the freshly enthused if numerically weak French Army. The huge battleground, south of Brussels, which saw the forces of Wellington and Blücher confront Napoleon's *l'Armée du Nord*, was to enter history as the venue for the most studied military action in history. It was here that the great Commander's amazing career ended, where he lost a battle so badly that he could not recover credibility or power, where he 'met his Waterloo'. Although narrowly escaping capture on the field, his surrender, second abdication and exile followed shortly afterwards.

Even deposed and finally absent from power, Napoleon had news to make with his last six years, on the remote island of St. Helena, adding controversy about the cause of his death.

Napoleon died on 5 May 1821, and from that day his life and work has been assessed and re-assessed in the minutest detail. Most will agree we shall never see a greater soldier; many will rate him the greatest of all. His career and abilities encompassed more than the military sphere; as head of state his influence extended throughout French society, and into wider Europe: politician, statesman, administrator, legislator. Some will describe him as a flawed genius; few will deny he had genius. 'Had I succeeded, I should have died with the reputation of the greatest man that ever lived,' Napoleon was reported as saying. But the 'final verdict' on Napoleon must not be imposed on the historian and military enthusiast, he must apply his own criteria and draw his own conclusion. The contributors to this book seek only to help that process.

NAPOLEON IN ITALY.
PRINT AFTER RAFFET.

THE EARLY YEARS
AND FIRST COMMANDS
J. David Markham

NAPOLEON WAS BORN AT AJACCIO, CAPITAL OF THE ISLAND OF
Corsica, on 15 August 1769. His parents, Carlo and Letizia, were of
the minor nobility, what would today be essentially middle class.
Letizia was a strong woman who kept her family together during the difficult times in Corsica after Carlo died, and was determined that her children
achieve success. She strongly encouraged Napoleon in his career. Napoleon
confirmed her importance with his words 'As to my mother, she deserves all
kind of veneration.'[1]

Although he died while Napoleon was only fifteen, Carlo played an important role both in the development of Napoleon's value system and in providing some very specific opportunities for his career development. Carlo
was a lawyer and a Corsican patriot. Swearing to die for Corsica's freedom,
he was among the first to support the Corsican patriot Pasquale di Paoli.
Carlo's willingness to take to the hills and risk all for a deeply held belief
must have had a tremendous effect on Napoleon, albeit later in time. At the
same time, he served as an excellent example of good common sense. When
he decided that the Corsican cause was hopeless, he was smart enough to
establish good relations with the French, thereby protecting his family and
enabling himself to continue to work 'from within' for the betterment of the
Corsican situation under French rule.[2]

Napoleon's father was also wise enough to take advantage of the opportunity to provide free education for his sons. This involved furnishing evidence of four generations in the island, and the payment of a fee to the
appropriate official. Evidence of *noblesse* (nobility) was also necessary to
obtain royal scholarships.

One of the earliest important players in the development of Napoleon's
career was Louis Charles René, comte de Marbeuf. Marbeuf was the French
civil and military commander who took over when the French gained control of Corsica. He became very popular with Corsicans, and a good friend
to Carlo, in whose house he had stayed earlier in his Corsican assignment.
Marbeuf developed a strong attraction for Letizia, Carlo's young wife. It
appears that this never developed into anything more than a distant love.

Marbeuf was 64 with a mistress, Letizia 20 with a husband, but his infatuation with her caused him to go out of his way to help the Bonapartes.[3] Marbeuf and Letizia spent a great deal of time together and many people assumed that there was more to the relationship than just the long walks for which they were noted. Indeed, some have held that Marbeuf may well

HOUSE WHERE NAPOLEON WAS BORN. PRINT AFTER ERIC PAPE.

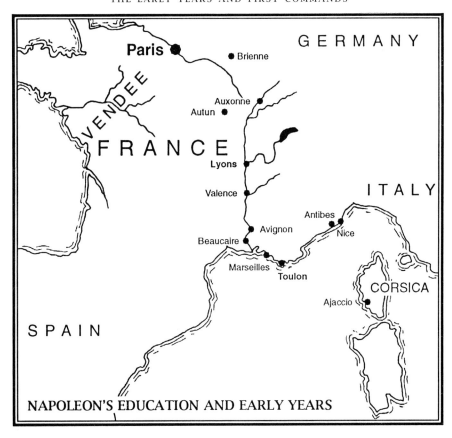

NAPOLEON'S EDUCATION AND EARLY YEARS

have been Napoleon's father. Dorothy Carrington's exhaustive research tends to dispel this gossip, and she strongly questions those who assume that there was at least an affair between the two.[4]

Marbeuf told Carlo of the availability of royal scholarships for boys who aspired to the military or the Church, and for girls at Madame de Maintenon's school at Saint-Cyr. Marbeuf made all the arrangements, even lodging Napoleon's elder brother Joseph at the college of Autun (where Marbeuf's nephew was bishop) at his own expense.

Napoleon had been accepted for the military school at Brienne, but had first to wait for his certificates of nobility. While waiting, he stayed with Joseph, again at Marbeuf's expense. Marbeuf also paid for the seminary education of Letizia's half-brother and Napoleon's uncle, Giuseppe Fesch, the future cardinal. Before all this happened, Carlo had planned for Napoleon and Joseph to study law in Pisa. Napoleon as a lawyer would no doubt have ranked with the best, but ironically the *Code Napoléon* might never have been written!

CARLO. ENGRAVING BY R. A. MULLER AFTER GIRODET.

LETIZIA. ENGRAVING BY T. JOHNSON.

NAPOLEON AT SCHOOL AT BRIENNE. PRINT AFTER M. REALIER-DUMAS.

Marbeuf's influence and financial support made it possible for Napoleon to enter the *Ecole militaire de Brienne* in 1779. He was a very promising student, though his Corsican accent, his unusual name, and the fact that he was a 'foreigner' led to some harassment from his fellow students and a fair level of social isolation. The insults offered to him because of his Corsican origins led him to become especially proud of that heritage, and of the Corsican 'freedom fighter' Paoli.[5] He studied hard and excelled in history, geography, and mathematics. His historical interests lay mainly in ancient heroes, especially Caesar, on whom he seems to have based many of his later actions. Napoleon wanted to serve in the navy, but his teachers decided that his best aptitude lay in the artillery. After five years of study, he graduated in 1784, at the age of fifteen.

Napoleon's nomination to the *Ecole militaire de Paris* (Military School of Paris), the French equivalent of West Point and Sandhurst, was signed by Louis XVI. There he was affronted by the snobbery of the higher level French nobility in attendance. An excellent student, he graduated in May 1785, two years early, and was one of a select few to pass the test for admission to the artillery. On 1 September 1785, aged sixteen, he was appointed a lieutenant in the French Royal Artillery's *Régiment La Fère*. He spent the next year at Valence learning his trade and studying history and other subjects. Throughout his entire life he would be an avid reader, and would often discuss the military campaigns of past masters of the art.

During the 1780s France was in turmoil, and social disturbances were common. In August 1786 Napoleon was sent to Lyons to quell such a disturbance. While there he turned his efforts to writing. He wrote a prize-winning essay and began to write a history of his native Corsica.

The French military system of the late 18th century was very different from today's equivalent. It was possible, for example, to obtain frequent and

NAPOLEON AS A YOUNG OFFICER, WORKING IN HIS STUDY.
PRINT AFTER FRANÇOIS FLAMENG.

extensive leaves of absence for seemingly any reason at all. Of course, abuse of these opportunities could get one into trouble. Such was the case with Napoleon. For the next several years he alternated between duty assignments and leaves of absence in Corsica. He had strong feelings about the future of Corsica and spent extensive leaves there in order to become involved in Corsican politics and to visit his family.

By 1789 Napoleon was stationed at Auxonne as an artillery officer and student at the artillery school there. He took an avid interest in, and developed a reputation as a Republican supporter of, the Revolution. On 15 September 1789 he returned on leave to Corsica where he completed his history of the island and wrote an address to the French National Assembly asking that Corsica be declared a part of France. His and others' efforts met with success, Paoli returned as their new leader, and the young Bonaparte was on the winning side.

In February of 1791 Napoleon returned to duty at Auxonne, and was stationed at Valence when Louis XVI made his unfortunate flight to Varennes on 20 June 1791. The King, who had made some moves in support of the Revolution, had begun to fear for the survival of the monarchy. He hoped to join with royalist and Austrian military forces and force some changes in the new constitution. Louis was recognised by the postmaster at Varennes, and was captured and returned to Paris. This event shattered the hopes of the people that the King truly supported the Revolution, and marked the end of any hope for his continuance in power. The people lost faith in their government, and radical factions prepared to make their moves.

The King's flight to Varennes radicalised Napoleon's political beliefs. He participated in the swearing of the national oath on 3 July 1791 and evidently took the ceremony very seriously:

> 'Until then, I doubt not that if I had received orders to turn my guns against the people, habit, prejudice, education, and the King's name would have induced me to obey. With the taking of the national oath it became otherwise; my instincts and my duty were thenceforth in harmony.'[6]

Napoleon soon became restless, and political opportunities in Corsica beckoned. In September 1791 he took yet another leave to Corsica, joining his brother Louis. His immediate commander had refused him leave (Napoleon had been back in service only some seven months after his lengthy leave of absence), but Lieutenant-General baron du Teil, the director of the School of Artillery at Auxonne, gave him permission. The two had become friends when Napoleon was stationed there, and du Teil did much to encourage his development. Du Teil, through his brother Jean, a noted specialist in artillery tactics, would have much influence on Napoleon's later career opportunities as well.

While in Corsica Napoleon supported the radical Jacobin[7] cause and became politically active in the move to make Corsicans free French citizens. To avoid charges of desertion from his French unit, he obtained an appointment from the French Minister of War as an adjutant-major assigned to Corsica, and was then elected a lieutenant-colonel in the Corsican military, thereby avoiding the risk of court-martial and forfeiture of his French rank.

Returned to power in Corsica, Paoli was becoming supportive of the royalist and clerical factions that opposed the Revolution. This did not sit well with the revolutionary Bonaparte. In religious riots that followed, his troops were forced to fire on Corsican citizens, a move that decreased Napoleon's popularity with Paoli's many supporters. It was clearly time to return to France.

Napoleon was a revolutionary, but was appalled by two major events that involved the mob of Paris. On 20 June 1792, thousands crowded into the courtyard of the Tuileries Palace in Paris. Louis XVI watched and listened from a window as speaker after speaker insulted and threatened him, but this was the mere shadow of what was to come. On 10 August the Paris mob stormed the Tuileries. Fearing for his safety, Louis fled to the National Assembly. Soldiers of the Swiss Guard, under orders from Louis not to resist, were slaughtered. Napoleon witnessed this event, and ever after feared the power of the mob.

Meanwhile, Napoleon was able to get his irregular absences excused, and was promoted to captain retroactive to 6 February 1792. His precautions taken in Corsica to safeguard his return to French military service had worked. Once again boldness and political astuteness had marched hand in hand to further his career.

In September 1792, aged 23, Napoleon returned to Corsica and was still there when Louis XVI was executed in Paris on 21 January 1793. Napoleon attempted to gain power in Corsican politics, but a final break with Corsican patriot Paoli forced his return to France on 11 June 1793. In Corsica Napoleon had met the Corsican lawyer Antonio Cristoforo Saliceti (1757–1809). Twelve years his senior, Saliceti would figure prominently in Napoleon's career. A politician of Jacobin persuasion who represented the Third Estate of Corsica at the Estates General convened in 1789, Saliceti made it possible for Paoli to return from exile in England. But his support of Paoli waned, and he was eventually sent to Corsica to try to bring him under control, and actively to support the increasingly radical Revolution. Saliceti's mission ultimately failed, which led to a hasty departure from Corsica for both Saliceti and Napoleon, but Saliceti would figure strongly in Napoleon's career for many years to come.

Saliceti eventually returned to Paris where he served as a member of the Convention, as the ruling legislative body of France was then called. In 1793 he gave valuable assistance to the Bonaparte family, appointing Napoleon's elder brother Joseph as Comptroller of Army Supplies. He also made Napoleon's uncle Fesch military storekeeper at le Beausset, near Toulon, and Napoleon's younger brother Lucien military storekeeper at St-Maximin, where Lucien became president of the Jacobin club. These appointments to other members of the Bonaparte family indirectly assisted Napoleon, as his family's influence and prestige would be important factors at crucial moments of his career.

In 1793 Napoleon reported for duty to the 12th Company of the Fourth Artillery Regiment at Nice. The commanding officer was none other than General Jean du Teil, brother of baron du Teil who had had such a high opinion of Napoleon when he was at Auxonne. The baron's feelings carried over to his brother in Nice, and Napoleon once again had a friend in command authority. General du Teil assigned Napoleon to Avignon to organise ammunition supplies. While there, Napoleon wrote *Le Souper de Beaucaire* (*Supper at Beaucaire* [a town in France]). This short piece was a defence of the Revolution and a call for an end to civil war, that is to say internal opposition to the Revolution. Napoleon advocated support for the Jacobin government and a call to arms against outside invaders. He decried the possibility of a civil war and took the side of the extremely pro-revolutionary Montagnards in the National Assembly against the less radical Girondins and the Royalists. These three political factions were engaged in a struggle for control of the government and the future of France.

In the story Napoleon also promoted the concept that light cannon are at least as good in the field as heavier guns. This reflected his own opinion, but also that of General du Teil, an expert in the use of mobile artillery.[8]

As one might expect, the representatives of that revolution looked favourably on such writing. Saliceti and his fellow commissioner Gasparin had it printed and published, and it became a major literary document of the Revolution. It is important to note not only that Saliceti and Gasparin favoured *Le Souper de Beaucaire*, but it impressed the Committee of Public Safety[9] and the Robespierre brothers[10] as well.

Clearly, not everyone in France supported the Jacobin government. Civil war was rampant in much of the country, as counter-revolutionaries attempted to regain control from the radical Montagnard faction. In 1793 the city of Toulon revolted and admitted the British Royal Navy into its harbour. Napoleon had been assigned to join the Army of France in Italy, but as luck would have it, his duties took him to Toulon. On 7 September 1793, he left Avignon with an ammunition convoy. On his way to Nice he stopped to visit friends and family in the community of le Beausset. Uncle Fesch was storekeeper of military supplies there. Another person worth visiting was his old friend Saliceti.

Saliceti was a member of the Convention. During these troubled days in France, Convention members were often sent throughout France to take personal charge of military affairs, or at least to see to it that the 'will of the people' was being followed. Under certain circumstances, the 'will of the people' could include removal of a general from command and a one way trip to Paris and the guillotine. Convention members serving in this capacity were called members *en mission*, Commissioners, or Representatives of the People. To many military commanders, they were no doubt called 'trouble'. Clearly a man like Saliceti was a good man to have on your side. And Saliceti had proven himself to be on the side of the Bonapartes.

The meeting between Saliceti and Napoleon at le Beausset went very well. Saliceti had a great deal of admiration and loyalty for his friend and was in need of an artillery commander. He offered Napoleon the job, knowing that Paris would agree, since Napoleon was very highly regarded there thanks to *Le Souper de Beaucaire*, thanks to Baron du Teil, and thanks to the general recognition of Napoleon's talent that was just beginning to develop. Napoleon immediately accepted the position. His younger brother Lucien was at the meeting, and is said to have remarked on the possible good fortune this appointment might mean.[11] No doubt Lucien's presidency of the Jacobin Club of Toulon augmented Napoleon's claim to 'political correctness'.[12]

Napoleon had a number of friends and supporters close to Toulon. Commissioner Fréron was stationed in the south of France, and worked with Saliceti and the other commissioners. He was favourably predisposed toward Napoleon, as he had had an affair with Napoleon's sister Pauline. Another commissioner in the area was Stanislas Gasparin. While not so directly connected to Napoleon personally, he was a fellow Corsican and, with Fréron, was supportive of Saliceti's efforts to promote their Corsican captain.

The other two commissioners were giants of the time, and prominent in Napoleon's development. Paul Barras had proven to be one of the most important early members of the Revolutionary leadership. He was a witness to the taking of the Bastille and a friend of the important Revolutionary leader Mirabeau. Barras was one of the first members of the Jacobin club, having correctly determined the direction of the day. He was to join Saliceti as a 'Representative of the People', his main task being to keep an eye on General Carteaux at Toulon.

The final member of this group of 'representatives of the people' was Augustin Robespierre. A revolutionary in his own right, his power and influence came largely from the fact that he was the brother of Maximilien Robespierre, the head of the Committee of Public Safety, and virtual dictator of France. For now, at least, the Robespierres were virtually unchallenged in their authority within the revolutionary government, though, of course, they were clearly challenged by uprisings such as that of the citizens of Toulon.

SIEGE OF TOULON SHOWING POSITION OF FRENCH BATTERY. PRINT AFTER JUNG.

Napoleon and Augustin became friends, and Augustin became a strong supporter of this young captain, this revolutionary who had penned the strong defence of his and his brother's revolution, *Le Souper de Beaucaire*. In time, Napoleon also became friends with the third Robespierre, Charlotte.[13]

By October 1793 Napoleon's benefactors at Toulon were all pretty much well in place: Saliceti, Gasparin, Barras, Fréron and Robespierre. By now Napoleon had become a major figure. Indeed the fact that Napoleon had gained his appointment from the Commissioners gave him much more standing with the military commanders than had he been appointed through the more traditional channels.

Two other figures who were to become important later were also at Toulon. André Masséna was serving in a diversionary army north of Toulon. And Sergeant Andoche Junot had become Napoleon's secretary, and would serve him for the rest of his life. Junot was very impressed with the young Napoleon, and immediately decided to attach himself to his fortunes. He wrote to his father in 1794: 'He is one of those men of whom Nature is sparing, and whom she does not throw upon the earth but with centuries between them.'[14]

Napoleon requested that a general officer from the artillery be assigned to the Toulon campaign. It was his hope that in such an officer he would have someone willing to listen to him. He got even better than that. The man appointed was none other than General Jean du Teil who, as we know, greatly admired Napoleon. Moreover du Teil was not well and not really capable of running the show. So, with the full support of the commissioners, du Teil let Napoleon pretty much have his way. And when, in November, General Jacques Coquille Dugommier assumed overall command, and took an immediate liking to Napoleon, the days of the British in Toulon were numbered.

Napoleon's letter requesting an artillery general officer is an indication of just how secure he must have felt, given the level of his support. In his letter to the Committee of Public Safety of 25 October 1793, he says in part:

'I have had to struggle against ignorance, and the passions it gives rise to ... The first step I will propose to you is to send to command the artillery an artillery general who can, if only by his rank, demand respect and deal with a crowd of fools on the staff with whom one has constantly to argue and lay down the law in order to overcome their prejudices and make them take action which theory and practice alike have shown to be axiomatic to any trained officer of this corps. The Commander of Artillery, Army of the South, BUONAPARTE.[15]

SIEGE OF TOULON. CONTEMPORARY PRINT.

Napoleon insisted that rather than a frontal assault on the city, the key to victory was control of the heights, called by the British 'Little Gibraltar'. His plan worked: the British were driven out and Toulon returned to government control. Napoleon had not only been the military brains behind this success, he was constantly in the thick of the action and in great danger. Indeed, he suffered a bayonet wound that could have cost him his leg. At St. Helena he said that his greatest personal danger occurred at Toulon and, during the first Italian Campaign in 1796, at Arcola.

The siege of Toulon lasted some three months, but its success was a great victory for the Jacobin government, and it marked the first major foray into the limelight for Napoleon. Past and future came together for him at Toulon. His contacts from past efforts – Saliceti, Robespierre, du Teil – and his recent contacts, Barras and Dugommier, gave him the support he needed to succeed. His future was there as well: André Masséna and Sergeant Andoche Junot.

A victory is always important, but *credit* for a victory is of equal importance. There had been a large number of killings of civilians when the French
army entered Toulon, and there were substantial recriminations, including
some against General Dugommier.[16] Napoleon, however, was lauded by all
concerned. The first line in his letter to Citizen Duphin, Assistant to the
Minister of War, says it all: 'I promised you brilliant successes and, as you
see, I have kept my word.'[17] His official dossier was glowing. Saliceti and
Gasparin wrote very positive reports on his actions: 'The Representatives of
the People, bearing in mind the zeal and intelligence of which Citizen
Buonaparte has given proof, have decided to recommend his promotion to
the rank of Brigadier-General.'[18] That promotion came on 22 December
1793, when Napoleon was twenty-four. Dugommier had added his praise in
a letter to the Minister of War: 'I have no words to describe Buonaparte's
merit: much technical skill, an equal degree of intelligence and too much
gallantry, there you have a poor sketch of this rare officer.'[19] As a result of
Dugommier's praise, Napoleon made his first appearance in the French
newspaper *Le Moniteur* on 7 December 1793.[20]

Napoleon was appointed Inspector of Coastal Defences and, in 1794,
Artillery Commander to the Army of Italy under General Pierre Dumerbion.
Napoleon had long hoped for an opportunity to drive the Austrians out of
Italy, but to promote his plan he needed support in high places. As it happened, the Representatives of the People in that area were Citizen Ricord
and, fortuitously, Citizen Augustin Robespierre. Augustin's support gave
Napoleon the chance for some limited success in Italy, and another star
after his name. He developed an overall strategy, and specifically planned
the attacks on Oneglia and Saorgio. Ultimately, Paris insisted on a defensive
policy in Italy, preferring the action to be farther north at the Rhine. Even
this reflected Napoleon's belief that the conquest of Germany was the key
to control of Europe.[21]

With the fall of Maximilien Robespierre in the *coup d'état* of 9 *Thermidor*
(27 July 1794), Napoleon was arrested and held at the Château d'Antibes.
The government had finally had enough of the mass killings of the Terror,
and Robespierre, his brother Augustin, the infamous Saint-Just and others
of the powerful Committee for Public Safety had been arrested and sent to
the guillotine. Napoleon was accused of having proposed the reconstruction
of what the citizens of Marseilles considered their Bastille (in reality an
important military fortress), and of treason in a secret mission to Genoa,[22]
but his real problem was his closeness to the recently executed Augustin

Robespierre. Interestingly, Napoleon's old friend Saliceti was placed in charge of the investigation. It is unclear as to the precise motives for this turn of events, other than the possibility that Saliceti was simply trying to provide cover for himself and, perhaps, Napoleon as well.

During his fifteen days of house arrest, Napoleon spent his time in study and the development of military ideas. Had he been closer to Paris he might have met an untimely end, but instead he was found innocent of any wrong-doing and released after two weeks. One reason for his release was his own spirited defence. On 12 August 1794 he wrote to the Representatives of the People:

'You have caused me to be arrested. I have been dishonoured without trial; or rather I have been tried without being heard ... Since the com-mencement of the revolution, have I not been seen fighting against domestic enemies, or, as a soldier, fighting against foreigners? I have sacrificed living in my département; I have abandoned my property; I have lost all for the Republic.'[23]

Another reason may well have been the words written in a report by General Pierre Dumerbion, Napoleon's most recent commander. 'Officers of his abil-ity are rare' and 'Our success has been due to the intelligent suggestions of the commander of the Artillery,' he wrote after the aborted Italian cam-paign.[24]

Napoleon's letter to Ambassador Tilly, the French representative to Genoa, was no doubt intended to give Saliceti and others some cover should they desire (as they probably did) to find Napoleon innocent and, most importantly, politically correct. In it he says in part 'I was slightly affected by the fate of the younger Robespierre, whom I liked and believed honest; but had he been my father I would have stabbed him myself had he aspired to tyranny.'[25]

Napoleon had dodged a bullet, but he had remained calm and optimistic. He wrote to his friend Junot that while men might be treating him unfairly, 'my conscience is the tribunal before which I submit my conduct'.[26] Shortly thereafter he moved to Marseilles where most of his family now lived. Under the direction of Saliceti, he prepared the plans that led to the French victo-ry at Dego in September 1794, as well as an invasion to drive the British out of Corsica. He was opposed to naval operations against the British fleet, and the disastrous campaign proved him right. As he was on record as having advised against it, and was supported by his many friends, this did not harm his career.

In the spring of 1795 Napoleon was ordered to put down an uprising in the Vendée,[27] and was given command of an infantry brigade. He felt insulted at having been removed from the artillery, and had no interest in fighting against French citizens. Instead of obeying his orders, he took a long sick leave and eventually, accompanied by Junot and Marmont, went to Paris to plead his case, while Junot contributed money to live on. Napoleon's protests gained him little, however, until in a last desperate attempt to avoid the Vendée he pleaded his cause to the recently appointed Minister of War, Louis-Gustave Le Doulcet, comte de Pontécoulant. During the interview he also put forward his ideas for getting the Austrians out of Italy. Pontécoulant was impressed, forwarded his ideas up the ladder, and appointed Napoleon to the *Bureau Typographique* (a General Staff organisation), where he rubbed noses with many high officials both at work and on the social scene. This latter included the salons of Madame de Staël and Madame Notre-Dame de Thermidor, who introduced Josephine to Barras. It also included Madame Tallien, at whose salon Napoleon and Josephine may well have first met.

The interview with Pontécoulant was important. Earlier, Napoleon had tried exactly the same thing with the former War Minister Aubry, who had received him coldly. If Aubry had remained Minister of War, Napoleon probably would not have received this nice appointment to the *Bureau Typographique* . His friends might still have been able to keep him out of the Vendée, but who knows what direction his career might have taken? An appointment away from Paris would have kept him out of the limelight and, of course, away from Barras and Josephine.

Another interesting 'what if' is the matter of Napoleon's desire to go to Turkey. Unhappy at his reception by Aubry, he actually requested assignment to Constantinople, to help modernise the Turkish artillery. This was not, in fact, an unreasonable idea. One can only begin to imagine the effect on history if some officer in the War Ministry had approved the request in a timely manner![28]

The French government, headed by the Directory of five members, had lost a great deal of popularity, largely as a result of its efforts to keep itself in power. A new constitution had established a new Legislative Assembly, but the existing Convention decreed that two-thirds of the new representatives to the Legislative Assembly must come from the Convention's existing membership. This self-perpetuating decree was unpopular with many people who had hoped either to reform the government or replace it. In Paris there was a revival of royalist sentiment, and many people hoped to re-establish a monarchy. By early October the Convention was under siege by royalist sympathisers and elements of the Paris mob, headquartered at the church of St. Roch. They were supported by a large force of the National Guard. The Directory and the Convention were desperate to find a general to lead their troops in defence of the government. Paul Barras, one of the Directors, was put in charge of protecting the Convention. With Fréron's encouragement, he appointed Napoleon to put down the uprising.

Napoleon was in complete command of the situation. The insurgents far outnumbered the defenders commanded by General Bonaparte. To improve

NAPOLEON'S 'WHIFF OF GRAPESHOT', 13TH *VENDÉMIAIRE* (1795), HE DEFENDS THE CONVENTION AGAINST ROYALIST SYMPATHISERS. PRINT AFTER F. DE MYRBACH.

the odds, Napoleon sent Captain Murat to procure cannon which were then sited near the Tuileries Palace in such a way as to command all avenues of approach. The insurgents attacked, and with his famous 'whiff of grapeshot' Napoleon crushed the revolt on *13 Vendémiaire, an IV* (5 October 1795). After defeating the royalists' last stand at St. Roch, Napoleon dispatched troops to disarm Paris and restore order.

Accepting an assignment which would lead to the slaying of Frenchmen had been yet another political gamble, because even in victory he could have earned the enmity of many. Once again, however, the gamble paid off, and his career was enhanced. By the end of the month he had been placed in command of the Army of the Interior. He was 26 and already at what would be the peak of most careers.

During this period of Napoleon's life he became involved in one of the great romances of history. It is unclear exactly how Napoleon first met Josephine, though it is likely that they had been introduced to each other at one of the numerous social functions hosted by Paul Barras. Hortense, Josephine's daughter from her first husband, relates the following story:

'Following the riots on 13th Vendémiaire a law was passed forbidding any private citizen to have weapons in his house. My brother, unable to bear the thought of surrendering the sword that had belonged to his father, hurried off to see General Bonaparte, who at that time was in command of the troops stationed in Paris. He told the General he would kill himself rather than give up the sword. The General, touched by his emotion, granted his request and at the same time asked the name of his mother, saying he would be glad to meet a woman who could inspire her son with such ideals.'[29]

Josephine is then said to have visited Napoleon to express her gratitude at his generosity, and Napoleon is said to have fallen head over heels in love. Whether or not this story is true, it is clear that at about this time Napoleon began to see Josephine as the woman for him. He had previously expressed an interest in marriage, and had hoped to find a woman who would provide some financial security and social standing. While stationed at Marseilles he had been involved with Desirée Clary, whose sister Julie had married Napoleon's brother Joseph. Desirée's father was rich, which would certainly have suited Napoleon, but when Napoleon left Marseilles for Paris, the relationship languished.[30]

Josephine had been married to Alexandre de Beauharnais, an aristocrat who had lost his head to the guillotine. Indeed, she only avoided that fate

JOSEPHINE AS EMPRESS. ENGRAVING BY H. WOLF AFTER GÉRARD.

herself thanks to the timely fall of Robespierre. She became the mistress of Barras, and moved in the very highest circles of French society. Barras soon tired of her and, conveniently enough, Napoleon soon became enamoured of her. Although Josephine was reluctant at first, the romance flourished. Josephine at thirty-two was six years older than Napoleon, did not have the wealth that he might have anticipated, and was opposed by most of Napoleon's family, but when Napoleon was appointed General of the Army in Italy, they married on 9 March 1796.

His new army was ragtag, demoralised, and short of just about everything, but from the very beginning Napoleon proved himself capable of
great things. He brought with him what is often said to have been one of the
greatest collections of military minds to serve together at one time.[31] It consisted of such luminaries as Chief of Staff Alexandre Berthier, and aide-de-
camp Colonel Joachim Murat, as well as Junot, Marmont and his own brother Louis. Napoleon's inspirational address to his troops is a classic:

'Soldiers! You are hungry and naked; the government owes you much,
but can give you nothing. Your patience and courage, displayed among
these rocks, are admirable, but that brings you no glory ... I will lead you
into the most fertile plains on earth. Rich provinces, wealthy cities, all
will be at your disposal; there you will find honour, glory and riches ...'[32]

Napoleon was determined to split the alliance of the Piedmontese and the
Austrians and, in the process, take his troops into the 'fertile plains' that
would provide a much needed source of food. After sweeping aside the over-
extended Austrian forces of General Beaulieu, Napoleon defeated the
Piedmontese at the battles of San Michele, Ceva and Mondovi in late April.
His tactics of concentrating his forces against the centre and then defeating
the various elements of the enemy's forces in detail would serve him well
for the rest of his career.

In May 1796, Napoleon's forces defeated the Austrian rearguard at Lodi.
While not an engagement of the utmost importance, it did open the way to

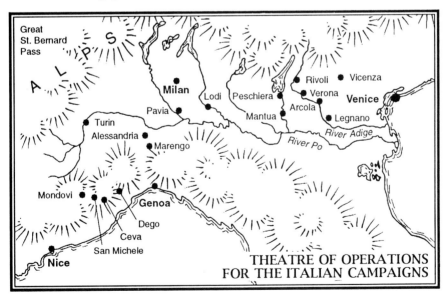

THEATRE OF OPERATIONS
FOR THE ITALIAN CAMPAIGNS

Milan. More importantly it seems to have created a change in Napoleon's attitude to his future. At St. Helena he wrote:

'It was only on the evening of Lodi [10 May 1796] that I believed myself a superior man, and that the ambition came to me of executing the great things which so far had been occupying my thoughts only as a fantastic dream.'[33]

Two other victories in this campaign have become a part of the Napoleonic legend. In November he fought a three-day battle centred on the bridge at Arcola. Both sides took heavy losses, but eventually Napoleon was able to prevail. He led his troops personally on the bridge, and was, in fact, almost pushed into the river!

In January of 1797, the Austrians made a determined effort to push back the French forces. Napoleon met them at Rivoli, and won a major victory. He

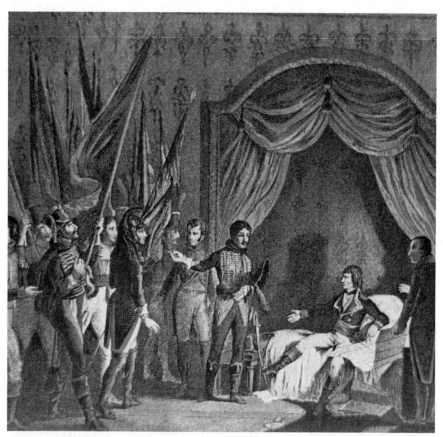

NAPOLEON IS PRESENTED WITH CAPTURED COLOURS AT MILLESIMO, 14 APRIL 1796. PRINT AFTER ROEHN.

BATTLE OF LODI: THE FRENCH STORM THE BRIDGE. PRINT AFTER LEJEUNE.

NAPOLEON PERSONALLY AIMS A CANNON AT LODI. PRINT AFTER F. DE MYRBACH.

then turned and defeated an Austrian army moving up from the south, and the Austrians' fate in Italy was sealed.

In the space of one year he had completely defeated the Austrian army occupying Italy and had achieved the Peace of Campo Formio, which gained France some significant territory and peace with her last continental adversary. He also gained the release by the Austrians of General Lafayette.[34] General Bonaparte was now established as a true national hero and France's greatest soldier. More importantly, he had met his first complete military challenge with overwhelming success. He had brought glory and riches to France and great confidence to himself.

The riches were probably more important to the Directory than the glory, because the government was still in great financial difficulties. Napoleon was politically astute enough to recognise this, and was careful to send a steady stream of booty to Paris. He also endeared himself to his men, not only through his great leadership and personality, but by paying them in hard currency for the first time in memory.

Glory, however, also figured in his political and military strategy. Glory helped inspire his troops to fight. Equally important, his victories gave him a degree of national popularity that both threatened the Directory and protected him from political harm.

An important component of the Treaty of Campo Formio was Napoleon's establishment of the Cisalpine Republic. This was far beyond the scope of his orders and constituted a challenge to the Directory and, indeed, the very structure of Europe. By expanding French influence beyond her 'natural' borders, he ran the risk of continual war. Yet once again his gamble paid political dividends; he was seen by French citizens as a liberator of the oppressed, and carrier of the Revolution to Europe.[35] Napoleon, it should be said, was not content simply to establish the new republic. He provided a constitution and organised a government whose members were nominated by himself.

Back in Paris in December 1797, he was given a hero's welcome by both the government and the people. He was then put in charge of planning an invasion of England. The Directory, meanwhile, was not interested in having an idle, popular general hanging about Paris for long. When he became convinced that an invasion of England was out of the question, both he and the Directory searched for another appropriate campaign. Talleyrand, whose scheming would be both a boon and a bane throughout Napoleon's career, suggested the ancient French dream of wounding England by conquering

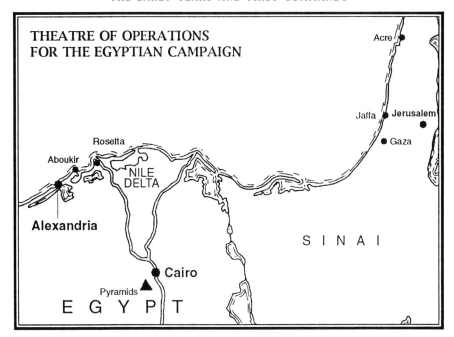

THEATRE OF OPERATIONS FOR THE EGYPTIAN CAMPAIGN

Acre

Jaffa   Jerusalem

Gaza

Rosetta

Aboukir

NILE DELTA

Alexandria

S I N A I

Cairo

Pyramids

E   G   Y   P   T

Egypt. Both the Directory and Napoleon quickly approved the idea, and in May 1798 he launched the Egyptian campaign.

The Egyptian campaign was reminiscent of those of Alexander the Great. Napoleon was not content simply to bring with him a substantial military force. He also brought a large number of scientists with their own equipment, libraries, and hopes for the development of a greater understanding of what was at the time the mysterious Egypt. While there, this team would record everything that they found, and artists would create images that would become the basis for a virtual Egyptian stylistic frenzy in France that would last many years. Their greatest accomplishment would be the discovery of the Rosetta Stone, though it would ultimately end up in British hands and be translated by the Frenchman Jean-François Champollion in 1822.

The battle of the Pyramids on 21 July 1798, captured Cairo and was a great victory, but the destruction of the French fleet at Aboukir Bay on 2 August 1798 left Napoleon isolated from France and ultimately prevented the total success of the campaign, which dragged on for the next year. He gained control of Egypt and moved on to conquer Syria. An outbreak of bubonic plague brought death and despair to his troops, though it did provide another heroic image for Napoleon's legend when he visited his plague-stricken soldiers at Jaffa, captured in March 1799. This heroic image was somewhat offset by his ordering the execution of several thousand prisoners. To be fair to Napoleon, it must be said that they had broken their parole and that he did not have the resources to provide for their care as prisoners. Also, some of Napoleon's men had been treated harshly by the enemy.[36]

After an unsuccessful siege of some six weeks, Napoleon was forced to abandon his efforts to capture the fortress of Acre and he returned to Cairo with a much depleted army. He had sent for reinforcements, but they were not forthcoming. In July he defeated an invading Turkish army at the land battle of Aboukir near Alexandria.

His Egyptian campaign had been less than an overwhelming success, and hearing of French defeats in Germany and Italy, Napoleon longed to be where the real action was. Fearing too for his political future, in October 1799 he returned to Paris where he received a cool reception by the Directory because he had technically deserted his army. The populace, however, considered him a great hero, and the government, which was in chaos, was in no position to take action against a General who had the support of the army and of the people.

Before Napoleon could deal with affairs of state, he had to deal with affairs of the heart. Throughout the Italian campaign he had been deeply in love with Josephine, who had finally joined him there. During the year in Egypt, however, he heard of a continuing affair between Josephine and a young officer named Charles. Worse, he heard of a great deal of profiteering by Josephine, who was heavily involved in the provision of military supplies. Although heartbroken by these stories, he was able to soothe his hurt by having an affair of his own with the blonde young wife of one of his soldiers. Nevertheless, he returned to France determined to divorce Josephine. After a difficult evening, she and her children, Hortense and Eugène, were able to persuade him to abandon those plans. He never lost his love for Josephine, but their relationship was never quite the same again.

France's enemies had formed the Second Coalition against her, and the internal affairs of the government were in turmoil. There had been a series of destabilising *coups d'état* as the Republicans attempted to strengthen their control over the government. The Revolution, to say nothing of the nation, was in great danger. Stability was needed, and in the planned *coup d'état de Brumaire* (9-10 November 1799) Napoleon was to become one of three ruling Consuls. Sieyès, a member of the Directory who sought its overthrow, and the other instigators of this latest coup needed a popular General to neutralise the army and inspire the people to support their new leaders.

This was a *coup* that very nearly didn't take place. All appeared to be in order, with the appropriate troops commanded by loyal generals (including Murat), and with Napoleon's brother Lucien installed as President of the Council of Five Hundred. Delays and confusion led to a tricky situation, however. Napoleon ultimately attempted to appeal to the Council in person, but made the mistake of suggesting that if necessary he would resort to the use of force. When he later returned to the Council, he was physically attacked and had to be rescued by several soldiers.

This was enough of an outrage to encourage the soldiers under his command to move on the Council, many of whom took the opportunity to depart by way of the windows! Those that were left provided for a provisional executive government of three Consuls, including Napoleon, Sieyès and Ducos (another member of the Directory).

Napoleon was to have been their tool, but he quickly moved to consolidate his power. He was offered a meaningless position, but insisted on becoming First Consul, with the Second and Third Consuls reduced to a consultative role. Napoleon became, in fact, the new leader of France.[37]

To seize power during such a period of instability was risky. This was, after all, just the latest in a string of governmental take-overs. Napoleon agonised over the decision:

'It was a service that I did not like; but when I considered that if the
convention were overturned, l'étranger [the foreigner] would triumph;
that the destruction of that body would seal the slavery of the country,
and bring back an incapable and insolent race, those reflections and
destiny decided that I should accept of it.'[38]

Yet now Napoleon's full political abilities were brought to bear. Secure in the knowledge that his army would support him and that he was a national hero, he convinced the rest of the government that only he could save the nation and the Revolution. Indeed, he told Las Cases on St. Helena:

'I closed the gulf of anarchy and cleared the chaos. I purified the Revolution ...'[39] In February 1800, by a vote of 3 million to 1,500, the people of France confirmed him as First Consul when they ratified the new constitution.

The coming months and years would see a whirlwind of activity. Napoleon unified the nation, restored financial integrity to the government, and reformed all levels of government. And everywhere, there was Bonaparte, hard at work, usually upwards of eighteen hours a day. Herbert Fisher in his book *Bonapartism* tells us:

NAPOLEON AS FIRST CONSUL. ENGRAVING BY T. JOHNSON AFTER INGRES.

'Napoleon brought to the task of government exactly that assemblage of qualities which the situation required, an unsurpassed capacity for acquiring technical information in every branch of government, a wealth of administrative inventiveness which has never been equalled, a rare power of driving and draining the energies of man, a beautiful clear-ness of intellect which enabled him to seize the salient features of any subject, however tough, technical and remote, a soldierly impatience of verbiage in others combined with a serviceable gift of melodramatic elo-quence in himself; above all, immense capacity for relevant labour.'[40]

It may be that Napoleon's greatest strength was that once he established a goal he never wavered from pursuit of that goal. This could, on occasion, lead to excess, but it is one reason for his tremendous success.

During the Revolution, the financial situation in France had been chaotic, and she was deeply in debt. Napoleon immediately raised millions of francs from foreign bankers and a national lottery, then set about reforming the entire tax system. Taxes had been collected by part-time workers: Napoleon created a special cadre of collectors, eight for each *département* (adminis-trative region of France). These officials were required to pay as much as 5 per cent of expected revenue in advance, thus improving the cash flow. Napoleon's improvements in the income tax system led to the elimination of virtually all debt and put the country on sound financial footing. He also added taxes on wine, playing-cards, carriages, salt and tobacco.

Perhaps his greatest and longest lasting financial achievement was the establishment of the Bank of France, which allowed France to eliminate high interest rates for its own loans and brought stability to the financial situation. Within a year the débâcle that had been France's finances was no more.

Napoleon's most famous domestic accomplishment was his legal work. France had not been completely unified all that long, and the system of laws that had emerged was an unbelievable tangle. There were countless region-al codes, courts, case law, almost 15,000 decrees (often contradictory), and other documents. Napoleon once wrote 'we are a nation with 300 books of laws yet without laws'. It is true that Napoleon did not write the entire 'revi-sion', but he did preside at most of the meetings of lawyers, and he got his way on numerous points, especially in the civil code. This code reflected the needs of the middle class, who had most benefited from the Revolution and who needed assurances that their gains would last. He codified their right to keep lands gained as a result of the Revolution, thus ensuring that one of their most important gains would be maintained. And contrary to his image

41

as anti-female, women gained property and family rights significantly beyond what they had during the Revolution or before.

The *Code* provided for other things as well, of course, including the right of men to enter any trade, craft, profession or religion they chose. It was a judicial compromise between democratic ideals and the monarchy. Because of Napoleon's personal and powerful interest, for the first time in French history there was a critical unity of law. It is, therefore, completely appropriate that this system of laws became known as the *Code Napoléon*, and it is in many ways his most lasting legacy.

Governmental and fiscal reform is often necessary, but seldom produces results that are immediately apparent. Such was the case with Napoleon. To give his reforms time to act, he knew that he had to provide France with more victories against foreign aggressors in order to maintain his high level of popularity. His choice of operations was once again Italy. He drew up his plans to oust the Austrians from Italy, and sent his armies forward. In May 1800 he crossed the Great Saint Bernard Pass in the Alps, and 'descended like a thunderbolt' on the Austrians and into a new page of Napoleonic history.

Napoleon's rise to power resulted from many factors. His determination, intelligence, and sheer force of will were certainly important characteristics. There can be no doubt that family, luck and the influence of powerful friends also played an important role. Of great importance was his willingness to take significant risks – political as well as military – and his ability to foresee the consequences of his actions. Yet perhaps as much as anything else, Napoleon was a product of the Revolution and the turbulence brought about by a decade of instability, constant change and war. Such a situation is ripe for the advancement of those who are willing to seize opportunities and exploit them, and Napoleon proved capable of this from the very beginning.

NOTES

1. Las Cases, comte de. *Mémorial De Sainte Hélène* (Journal of the Private Life and Conversations of The Emperor Napoleon at St. Helena), Boston, 1823, vol. IV (7), p. 39.

2. Ratcliffe, Bertram. *Prelude to Fame: An Account of the Life of Napoleon Bonaparte From His Arrival in France to the Battle of Montenotte*, London, 1981, p. 7. The general reader may well enjoy this author's 'Formative Moments for Napoleon', in *Military History* ,vol. 8, No. 4, December 1991, pp. 12 *et seq.*

3   Cronin, Vincent. *Napoleon Bonaparte: An Intimate Biography*, New York, 1972, p. 27.

4. *Napoleon and His Parents: On the Threshold of History*, New York, 1990. See

especially chapters Four and Five for very detailed accounts of this period of Napoleon's life. Carrington seems convinced that there was no sexual relationship between Letizia and Marbeuf, though even she is forced to admit that it is impossible to be certain. She is much more convinced that Marbeuf could not have been Napoleon's father, because he was out of the country at the presumed time of conception.

5. Carrington, Dorothy. *Napoleon and his Parents*, New York, 1990, pp. 142-3.
6. Sloan, William Milligan. *Life of Napoleon Bonaparte*, New York, 1896 vol. I, p. 89.
7. There were several political factions competing for control of the Revolution, and members of the Jacobin Club were the most radical and anti-monarchist.
8. Wilkinson, Spenser. *The Rise of General Bonaparte* , Oxford, 1930, p. 18.
9. The Committee of Public Safety was the main executive governing body of France, and was responsible for sending many people to the guillotine.
10. Maximilien Robespierre was the head of the Committee of Public Safety, and his brother Augustin was also an important political figure.
11. Ratcliffe, *op. cit.*, p. 25.
12. Ibid., p. 4.
13. Ibid., p. 64.
14. Alison, Sir Archibald. *History of Europe From the Commencement of the French Revolution in MDCCLXXXIX to the Restoration of the Bourbons in MDCCCXV* , mixed ed., 10 vols., Edinburgh and London, 1843, vol. 5, pp. 12-13.
15. Napoleon I, Emperor of the French. *Correspondance de Napoléon Ier; Publiée par ordre de l'empereur Napoléon III.* Paris, 1858-69 [Hereinafter *Correspondance.*], vol. I, p. 1: 'Au Comité Salut Public' (25 octobre 1793). Partially tr. in John Eldred Howard (ed. and tr.), *Letters and Documents of Napoleon, Volume One: The Rise to Power*, London, 1961, p. 40.
16. The citizens who had surrendered Toulon to the British were, after all, considered as traitors by supporters of the Revolutionary government.
17. *Correspondance*, vol. I, p.12 (24 décembre 1793): 'Je t'avais annoncé brillants succès, et tu vois que je te tiens parole.' Partially tr. in Howard, *op. cit.*, p. 44.
18. Ratcliffe, *op. cit.*, p. 45.
19. Cronin, *op. cit.*, p. 77.
20. Beyle, Marie Henri (Stendhal). *A Life of Napoleon*, tr. Roland Gant, London, 1956, p.12 fn.
21. Markham, Felix. *Napoleon* , New York, 1963, p. 13.
22. Chandler, David G. *The Campaigns of Napoleon.*, New York, 1966, p. 34.
23. Bingham, D. A. *A selection from the Letters and Despatches of the First Napoleon, with Explanatory Notes, In Three Volumes.*, London, 1884, vol. I, p. 40.
24. Ratcliffe, *op. cit.*, p. 68.
25. Bingham, *op. cit.*, vol. I, p. 41.
26. *Correspondance*, vol. I, p. 35, 'A Junot' (12 au 19 août 1794). '... ma conscience est le tribunal où j'évoque ma conduite'.
27. This region of France was very pro-monarchist and posed a direct military threat to the Revolution in what was no less than a civil war.
28. Bussey, George Moir. *History of Napoleon Illustrated by Horace Vernet.* 2 vols, London, 1840, vol. II, p. 34.
29. Hortense, queen consort of Louis, king of Holland. *The Memoirs of Queen*

Hortense. Pubd. by arrangement with Prince Napoleon, ed. Jean Hanoteau, tr. Arthur K. Griggs, New York, 1927, vol. I, p. 26.

30. In a touch of irony, Desirée eventually married General Bernadotte, who later turned against Napoleon. They became the King and Queen of Sweden.

31. Chandler, *op. cit.*, pp. 55-7.

32. Britt, Albert Sidney. *The Wars of Napoleon*, Wayne, NJ, 1985, p. 6.

33. Markham, *op. cit.*, p. 28.

34. A hero of the War of American Independence, Lafayette had supported the Revolution but tired of its excesses. In 1792 he tried to join the Austrians, but was instead imprisoned for some five years.

35. See Markham, Felix. *Napoleon and the Awakening of Europe*, London, 1954, 1965 edn, pp. 29-33; Markham, *op. cit.*, pp.49-54; Ludwig, Emil, *Napoleon* , York, 1926, pp. 81-4, 100-7.

36. Markham, *op. cit.*, p. 51. Prisoners, and sometimes envoys, were often beheaded.

37. Markham, *op. cit.*, p. 65.

38. O'Meara, Barry E. *Napoleon in Exile; or, A Voice From St. Helena. The Opinions and Reflections of Napoleon on the Most Important Events in His Life and Government, in His Own Words.*,Philadelphia, 1822, vol. II. p. 228. The French word *l'étranger* is in the text.

39. Las Cases, *op. cit.*, vol. II, pp. 3, 102.

40. Fisher, Herbert. *Bonapartism: Six Lectures Delivered at the University of London*, London, 1913, pp. 41-2.

BIBLIOGRAPHY

Bingham, D. A. *A Selection from the Letters and Despatches of the First Napoleon, with explanatory notes*, 3 vols., London, 1884.

Bonaparte, Napoleon. *Correspondance de Napoléon 1er, publiée par ordre de l'empereur Napoléon III*, Paris, 1858–69.

Britt, Albert Sidney. *The Wars of Napoleon*, Wayne, NJ, 1985.

Carrington, Dorothy. *Napoleon and his Parents: On the Threshold of History*, New York, 1990.

Chandler, David G. *The Campaigns of Napoleon*, New York, 1966.

Cronin, Vincent. *Napoleon Bonaparte: an Intimate Biography*, New York, 1972.

Hortense, Queen Consort of Louis, King of Holland. *The Memoirs of Queen Hortense*. Published by arrangement with Prince Napoleon, ed. Jean Hanoteau, tr. Arthur K. Griggs, New York, 1927.

Las Cases, comte de. *Mémorial de Sainte-Hélène*. Journal of the Private Life and Conversations of the Emperor Napoleon at St. Helena, Boston, 1823.

Markham, Felix. *Napoleon*, New York, 1963.

O'Meara, Barry E. *Napoleon in Exile: or, A Voice from St. Helena. The Opinions and Reflections of Napoleon on the Most Important Events in His Life and Government, in His Own Words*, Philadelphia, 1822.

Ratcliffe, Bertram. *Prelude to Fame: An Account of the Life of Napoleon Bonaparte From His Arrival in France to the Battle of Montenotte*, London, 1981.

Wilkinson, Spenser. *The Rise of General Bonaparte*, Oxford, 1930.

THE YEARS OF LEGEND,
1805 – 1809
Ian Castle

A T THE DAWN OF THE NEW CENTURY, NAPOLEON, NEWLY CON-
firmed AS First Consul, prepared for the work ahead. France was
weary of war and looked forward to an extended period of peace.
Napoleon also desired peace, eight years of constant war abroad and rebel-
lion in the west of France having dangerously weakened the economy. Time
was needed to bring about a programme of effectual reforms to return stability to France. But his efforts to make peace with Britain and Austria failed
and the war of the Second Coalition, which had begun the previous year,
continued into 1800. An appeal to the French people that peace could only
be obtained with 'money, steel and men' was received with enthusiasm and
in June Napoleon led his army to a somewhat fortunate victory over the
Austrians at Marengo in northern Italy. In Bavaria a further victory by a
French army under Moreau at Hohenlinden later that year brought the war
to an end, the peace negotiations culminating with the Peace of Lunéville.
With Austria's defeat the Second Coalition collapsed and Britain stood alone
against France. In March 1802 calm finally descended across Europe with
the conclusion of the Peace of Amiens. But the peace was illusory and over
the next seven years Emperor Napoleon, as he became in December 1804,
was to lead the army from victory to victory and build his reputation as one
of the truly great generals of history.

In 1805 the formation of the Third Coalition, which allied Britain, Austria,
Russia and Sweden against Napoleon, finally brought an end to Europe's
thin veneer of peace. In fact as early as May 1803, only fourteen months
after signing the Peace of Amiens, Britain and France had re-opened naval
hostilities. Now, angered by acts of French provocation the Coalition determined to return the map of Europe, and France in particular, to its pre-
Revolutionary borders.

In response to the resumption of war with Britain Napoleon determined
to crush his implacable opponents and began to assemble *l'Armée
d'Angleterre* along the Channel coast. Whether he really intended to carry
out the invasion has been debated over the years, but the failure of the
French Navy to present him with the opportunity eventually led to the aban-

EMPEROR OF THE FRENCH IN HIS CORONATION ROBES.
ENGRAVING BY H. WOLF AFTER LEFÈVRE.

donment of the plan and the redirection of this formidable army against the forces of the Third Coalition in Europe.

While bivouacked on the coast the army had used the period of peace on land well. Rested, trained and re-organised as *la Grande Armée*, Napoleon was now able to unleash this finely honed weapon against his disjointed opponents. The plans of the Third Coalition were complex. In the north a joint British/Swedish/Russian force was to restore Hanover to its Elector, George III, King of Great Britain. In central Europe an Austrian army, led by Quartermaster-General Mack but nominally under the command of Archduke Ferdinand, was to advance into Bavaria where it would be joined by a large Russian force. In northern Italy Archduke Charles at the head of another Austrian army was to push westwards into Lombardy. The armies of Charles and Mack were linked by yet another force, commanded by Archduke John, operating in the Tyrol. In the extreme south a multi-national force was to invade Naples.

Napoleon's reaction to the impending crisis was swift and decisive. While awaiting his chance to launch the attack against England he began to receive reports of the Allies' plans. Considering this intelligence Napoleon identified the Austrian pushes into Bavaria and northern Italy as the most threatening. But whereas the Austrian high command incorrectly anticipated that Napoleon would make his move against Italy, he had in fact determined to launch a crushing blow against Mack and Ferdinand in Bavaria, designed to eliminate them before Russian support could arrive. While holding forces operated in northern Italy and against Naples, the main army could proceed to deal with the Russians, thereby inflicting defeats upon two of the major parties of the Coalition.

On 25 August the invasion of England was finally abandoned and orders for the advance on Bavaria were issued. I and II Corps, drawn from Hanover and Holland, were to concentrate in Württemberg while the remaining five corps, Murat's cavalry and the Guard, all from the Channel, were to deploy on the Rhine between Mannheim and Strasbourg. With great thoroughness Napoleon ordered a secret reconnaissance of his planned area of operations, specifying a detailed report on the Ulm locality. Across the whole a cloak of secrecy descended that effectively blinded Mack to the disaster that was approaching. On 20 September Napoleon received the news that Mack had occupied Ulm, where he intended to await Russian support. The trap was set and on the night of 24/25 September orders were issued for the crossing of the Rhine and the enveloping of Mack's army. With Murat's cavalry holding

Mack's attention by demonstrating through the Black Forest to the west of Ulm, the remainder of the French Army began to execute the dramatic right wheel which eleven days later brought them to the Danube and across the rear of Mack's isolated force. Stunned into inactivity by the sudden realisation of his predicament, Mack allowed himself to become virtually surrounded. For fourteen days each side probed and manoeuvred while a number of minor actions were fought. Disunity among the Austrian command added further problems to Mack's position, culminating in Archduke Ferdinand's decision to cut his way out of Ulm with a cavalry force on 14 October. Three days later Mack agreed to surrender his force on 25 October if no sign of relief from the Russians, led by Kutusov, were apparent. Napoleon agreed to this clause because he knew that Austria's allies were too far away to intervene. In fact Mack surrendered five days early on 20 October, having being convinced by Napoleon that help was not forthcoming. Napoleon, at the head of his victorious army, stood and watched as 25,000 Austrians marched out of Ulm and into captivity. In fact, without having fought a major battle some 50,000 Austrians had fallen into French hands since the opening of the campaign. The French soldiers, though cold, hungry and tired, acclaimed Napoleon. Having suffered minimal casualties

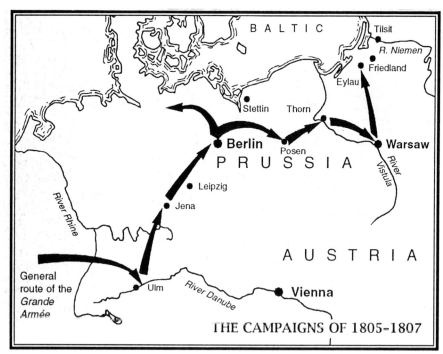

THE CAMPAIGNS OF 1805–1807

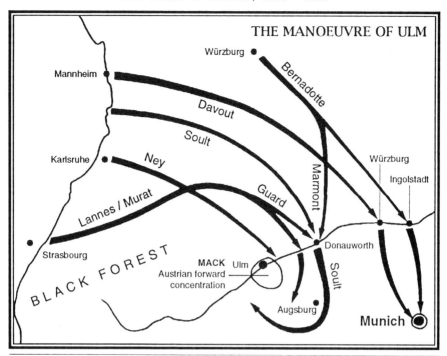

THE MANOEUVRE OF ULM

NAPOLEON ACCEPTS THE SURRENDER OF MACK AT ULM, 1805.
PRINT AFTER E. BOUTIGNY.

the 8th Bulletin of *la Grande Armée* commented 'Never have victories been so complete and less costly.' But the war was not over.

Napoleon was now in a very difficult situation. Although Mack's army had ceased to exist, the Russian forces of Kutusov, Buxhöwden and Bennigsen were approaching the theatre of war; meanwhile Archduke John still occupied the Tyrol and Archduke Charles was slowly withdrawing through northern Italy. In addition the threat of Prussian intervention was becoming more real. Napoleon's rapid march on the Danube had seen Bernadotte's I Corps violate Prussian territory at Ansbach. Angered by this and encouraged by the Tsar, Prussia hesitatingly agreed to mediate for the Allies prior to any actual involvement in the war. To ensure that these numerous adversaries could not unite and overwhelm him, Napoleon again decided on the bold approach. Perhaps a lesser commander, concerned by the effects of a Prussian threat to his flanks, would have withdrawn to the Rhine. But Napoleon purposefully continued eastwards in an attempt to destroy the approaching Kutusov before such a convergence could take place. In appalling weather the French began their advance, but Kutusov, on hearing of Mack's defeat at Ulm, immediately set his force in reverse and began to retreat. Kutusov's intention now was to link up with Buxhöwden, currently in Moravia. Joined by a number of Austrian units, Kutusov conducted an impressive withdrawal, deceiving Napoleon in the process. Napoleon was convinced that Kutusov would retire on Vienna and turn and fight in the area of St. Polten. But Kutusov had no intention of risking his army in the hopeless defence of the Austrian capital and succeeded in getting his army across to the left bank of the Danube at Krems and destroying the bridge behind him. Napoleon was furious that Kutusov had escaped, and was forced to change his plans. Advancing to Vienna, which had been declared an open city, he crossed the Danube and continued the pursuit of the able Russian. But with a combination of skill and trickery Kutusov escaped and was able to rendezvous with the Tsar and Buxhöwden's force in the area of Olmütz. On 23 November Napoleon halted his advance at Brünn, some 45 kilometres south-west of Olmütz, and granted his exhausted army some much-needed rest. The situation which confronted Napoleon was not ideal. At Brünn his army could muster only about 53,000 weary men while at Olmütz a combined Russo-Austrian army was preparing to field 85,000 men against him. From this unlikely position Napoleon was about to achieve his greatest triumph, one in which he not only dictated his own strategy but that of his enemy as well.

French troops had first occupied Brünn four days earlier, on 19 November, and on the 21st French cavalry had skirmished with their Russian counterparts on the road to Olmütz. Napoleon rode up to the French outposts at Wischau later that day and during the return journey to Brünn studied the ground carefully. At one point he turned off the road and surveyed an area more scrupulously than the rest. Then, satisfied, he turned to his staff and said, 'Gentlemen, examine this ground carefully, it is going to be a battlefield.'

Having selected the site for battle, Napoleon set out to inflict his will upon the enemy, lure them into his trap and destroy them. For it was imperative that he inflict total defeat on his opponents to bring the war to an end. If only a partial defeat were obtained the French, exposed at the end of a long and vulnerable line of communications, could find themselves threatened in flank and rear. The forces of the Archdukes Charles and John, having effected a junction on 26 November, were in Hungary to the south and any involvement by Prussia could have cut his line of retreat to the west.

Napoleon now began to lay the bait for the trap. By 25 November Lannes (V Corps) and the Guard were occupying Brünn and the local area, and Soult (IV Corps) was positioned around the village of Austerlitz and on the commanding Pratzen heights above. Murat's Cavalry Reserve were on the Olmütz road, around Wischau. Bernadotte (I Corps) was at Iglau, 80 kilometres north-west of Brünn, and Davout (III Corps) was in Vienna, more than 100 kilometres to the south. Having halted his pursuit and presented the Russians with his widely dispersed position, Napoleon hoped that the enemy would detect his apparent weakness and attack. Then, with the Russo-Austrian army committed to advance he would order Bernadotte and Davout forward by forced marches, adding another 22,000 men to his own army, and fight the battle on his chosen ground.

Further to convince the Allies of his weakness, Napoleon eagerly entered into communications with the Tsar about the possibility of an armistice. General Savary, a member of his staff, was sent to Allied headquarters ostensibly to continue these discussions but in reality to discover Allied intentions. Savary reported back that there was much dissension among the Allied ranks with Emperor Francis and Kutusov recommending caution while the Tsar was being encouraged to take an aggressive stance by a group of young officers on his staff. These men had little respect for their Austrian allies whom they felt had performed badly in the earlier stages of the campaign. More dangerously they had a high opinion of their own abilities and what they could achieve against an apparently weakened and disjointed French army. The war party had its way.

As the ponderous Allied columns prepared to move forward, Napoleon confirmed the illusion of weakness by ordering Soult with IV Corps to withdraw, abandoning the dominating heights of the Pratzen. Finally, the French cavalry outposts hurriedly departed from Wischau as the Allies approached. Now convinced that Napoleon was running scared, the Allies only fear was that he would be able to avoid battle and his ultimate defeat. Meanwhile Napoleon ordered up the corps of Bernadotte and Davout to complete his army. On 1 December the Allied armies occupied the Pratzen heights, recently abandoned by the French, and began to plan the battle that would finally crush the armies of France and bring to an end the years of turmoil that had plagued Europe. The trap was set, the bait taken.

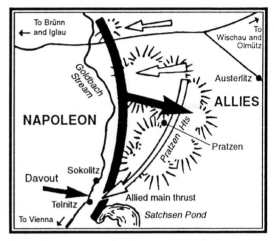

The Allied plan called for a major attack against the extreme right of the French position. By coming down from the Pratzen heights this move offered the opportunity to cut through the French line and after this initial success a turn to the north would force the rest of the army back towards Brünn. With the ground ahead opened in this way, the Allied cavalry would be able to advance through the gap provided and cut the Brünn-Vienna road, severing Napoleon's communications and line of retreat. In support a secondary attack would move against the French left along the Olmütz-Brünn road. But Napoleon had deliberately weakened his right to encourage the Allies to undertake such a move. The threat to his communications was limited because unknown to them he had already opened another line from Brünn to Krems via Iglau. By offering his right Napoleon anticipated that the Allies would weaken their centre enough to allow him to exploit the situation, and by cutting their line of retreat he could throw them into confusion and panic. The weakened forces on the right flank, Legrand's division of IV Corps, which was to bear the brunt of the Allied attack, was to be supported by the anticipated arrival of elements

NAPOLEON AT AUSTERLITZ. PRINT AFTER A. NORTHERN.

of Davout's III Corps during the battle. The true strength of the French centre and left was kept concealed by careful use of the terrain.

During the late afternoon of 1 December it became apparent that the Allies were concentrating a large force against the French right. Napoleon now felt sure of success. Orders were issued to the Corps commanders that night. At about 4 a.m. on 2 December the troops began to move into their appointed positions; a thick mist which had come down during the night hung over the battlefield and aided the secrecy of these movements. The Allies had suffered a night of confusion as units had moved to their form-up areas hindered by the darkness and the mist, and some delays in transmitting orders had not helped matters. But at 7 a.m. three large Allied columns began to descend from the heights following an Advance Guard and moved against the French right. Heavy fighting soon flared up around the villages of Telnitz on the extreme right of the French line and Sokolnitz. Only after two hours of fighting did these strong-points fall into Allied

RUSSIAN ARTILLERY FALLING THROUGH THE ICE AT AUSTERLITZ, 1805.
PRINT AFTER F. DE MYRBACH.

hands. They had achieved their first objective, but Napoleon had been watching their columns gradually bleeding the centre of its strength. At 9 a.m., considering the critical moment had arrived, Napoleon unleashed the divisions of Saint-Hilaire and Vandamme of IV Corps and sent them straight forward towards the summit of the Pratzen. Stunned by this audacious move the Allies hurriedly attempted to recall units about to join the attack on the French right. But the Pratzen heights were the key to the battle and now the French had gained them the die was cast. Three nations now locked in vicious combat, each desperate for victory. Muskets crashed out their volleys, cannon belched forth their deadly fire, hordes of cavalry swept across the battlefield. North of the Pratzen the secondary Allied attack was also the scene of furious fighting while to the south, the first of Davout's divisions had arrived and was helping to strengthen the position where the full might of the Allied attack had ground to a halt. After a titanic struggle, despite the Allies' fierce determination to restore their domination of the Pratzen, their centre was defeated and began to fall back. Having moved his headquarters to the Pratzen, Napoleon now issued the orders that would complete his victory. Leaving Bernadotte to secure the heights Napoleon turned the exhausted victors of the struggle to the south where they threw their weight against the flank and rear of the now isolated columns of the Allied left. Overwhelmed and exhausted, these men turned and made their escape as best they could. On the Allied right the secondary attack had already been forced back, and the Russian commander, Bagration, now ordered its retreat.

Napoleon had won a crushing victory. In October he had eliminated an Austrian army; now six weeks later he had destroyed a largely Russian one. It was the first anniversary of his coronation as Emperor and he had effectively dismantled the Third Coalition. Now no one in Europe doubted the military brilliance of Napoleon.

As Austria sued for peace and the humbled Russian army trudged eastwards, Napoleon, having proved his military might, turned his diplomatic force against Prussia. Having considered joining the Allies in their disastrous campaign, Prussia was now isolated. Napoleon, angered by Prussia's stance, pressurised the King, Frederick William III, into signing an alliance between the two countries. Recognising the impotence of Prussia Napoleon extracted the territories of Ansbach, Cleves and Neuchâtel while forcing Prussia to cut all ties with Britain. In return for this diplomatic humiliation Prussia received Hanover which the French had occupied since 1803.

MEETING OF NAPOLEON AND EMPEROR FRANCIS I OF AUSTRIA AFTER AUSTERLITZ.
ENGRAVING BY M. HAIDER AFTER GROS.

Napoleon now turned his attentions to re-ordering Europe. Having dismantled the Habsburg-controlled Holy Roman Empire he created in its place the Confederation of the Rhine. This grouping of German states would owe allegiance to France and provide a defensive barrier between France and her main European opponents. In addition it was required to provide soldiers for French wars. Then, hoping to bring about some understanding between Britain and France, Napoleon surprisingly offered to return Hanover to its Elector, King George III of Great Britain, only a few months after granting it to Prussia. For Prussia, already humbled by French demands, this was the final straw. Amid increasing dissatisfaction, a group of senior army officers began to advocate war and were supported in their actions by Queen Louise. The vacillating King, facing pressure from all sides, finally agreed that Napoleon had gone too far. On 7 August 1806 the irrevocable decision for war was taken and mobilisation of the Prussian Army began. A few weeks later Russia refused to ratify a peace treaty with France. By October the Fourth Coalition was in place, Prussia's actions receiving support from Russia and Great Britain. On paper the Prussian Army was large, impressive and self-confident, but it had little understanding of the new methods of war evinced by Napoleon and his victorious armies. The lack of a co-ordinated command and control structure ensured confusion and rivalry at Headquarters. The high command endlessly debated the best course of action by which to destroy the French Army and repair the damage done to Prussian esteem. While the army was mobilising no fewer than five plans were put forward. While the Prussians dithered Napoleon's normally efficient network of spies failed to detect their new resolve. When in September he finally got wind of these developments he was greatly surprised by Prussian intentions to challenge him in battle. He wrote to Talleyrand, his Foreign Minister, on 12 September, 'The idea that Prussia could take me on single-handed is too absurd to merit discussion.' Prussia's timing was indeed bad. Had she joined forces with Austria and Russia in the campaign of 1805 perhaps the outcome would have been different. Now, in 1806, Prussia was to enter war alone, mobilising its army while the French Army lay close at hand in southern Germany. This was an army of proven ability, resting on the laurels it had won in the campaign of 1805, brimming with confidence in itself and its leader.

Although Napoleon at first disbelieved Prussian intentions, he soon accepted that the situation was serious and that his new opponents had gained a month's start in its mobilisation programme. Some order was actually becoming apparent as the Prussian forces formed into three armies for the opening of the campaign, numbering in the region of 146,000 men. Although he had little military acumen Frederick William was placed at the head of the army. His senior commander was the Duke of Brunswick who had about 75,000 men forming in the Leipzig/Naumburg area. The Prince of Hohenlohe commanded 42,000 men concentrating around Dresden. This army included about 18,000 men of the Saxon Army which had recently been pressurised into an alliance with Prussia. The third army, of 29,000 men, under General Rüchel formed between Mühlhausen and Göttingen. Additionally, 25,000 men commanded by General Lestocq were grouped far to the east in the area around Posen. The Prussian council of war was unwilling to await Russian assistance and resisted the option to pull the army back to effect an earlier junction with the Russians. After much confusion a plan which involved the concentration of the three armies and a direct push through Erfurt and Würzburg towards the French cantonments around Stuttgart was agreed. Any initial success would threaten French communications. But even as the Prussian Army were about to open the campaign the high command was again thrown into confusion. On 5 October word came in that the French Army was concentrated in the Würzburg-Bamberg area, preparing to march on Saxony, with Napoleon at its head.

As soon as he recognised the seriousness of the developing situation Napoleon alerted the army to the prospect of war. Preparatory orders were issued to each Corps while he awaited intelligence that would reveal the Prussian intentions. Changes of plan promulgated by their high command were leaving him in some confusion, but on 18 September, having received definite news of Prussia's intervention in Saxony, he swung into action. An avalanche of orders stemmed from Paris. By 4 October six corps of the army were to be arrayed between Frankfurt and Amberg. These were joined by the Imperial Guard, Reserve Cavalry and a weak Bavarian Corps. At the end of September Napoleon received information that the Prussians were massing in the Erfurt region. This was more than he had hoped for. He had presumed that the Prussians would defend the line of the River Elbe, east of Erfurt, while awaiting Russian support. Now the opportunity presented itself for him to drive a wedge between the two armies and destroy the Prussians before help could arrive. On 8 October the army began its advance into the passes of the hilly *Thüringerwald*. Six days later the might of the Prussian Army would be crushed and in precipitate retreat.

The Army advanced in three columns, utilising the three passes through the forest. On the left V Corps was followed by VII Corps. In the centre I Corps preceded III Corps, the Reserve Cavalry, the Imperial Guard and Napoleon himself. On the right IV Corps advanced ahead of VI Corps and the Bavarians. Here was Napoleon's celebrated *bataillon carré* in action: on the march every component Corps was able to turn and face the enemy in any direction. While the leading corps held the enemy in position the other corps would advance in support and overwhelm the opposition. Having passed safely through the forest the French continued their advance while Napoleon still searched for clear evidence of the Prussian Army's exact position. On 9 October elements of the central column met and dispersed a

Prussian/Saxon force at Schleiz which opened the road to Gera and Leipzig. On 10 October continuing confusion at Prussian Headquarters had caused Prince Louis Ferdinand to find himself in an exposed position at Saalfeld. Caught by Lannes' V Corps, Louis' heavily outnumbered Prussian/Saxon division was routed and the Prince was killed.

On 11 October Napoleon surmised that a large Prussian force was concentrated to the west of the French advance and a battle close to Erfurt would be the most likely outcome. The following day new orders were issued. The former left-flank column of Lannes (V Corps) and Augereau (VII Corps) now became the Advance Guard and veered left, marching for Jena where there was a crossing over the River Saale. Davout (III Corps) and Bernadotte (I Corps), now forming the right flank, were to continue northwards to Naumburg whence they would be able to support V and VII Corps. Additionally, should the Prussians attempt to avoid battle and retreat northwards, III and I Corps would

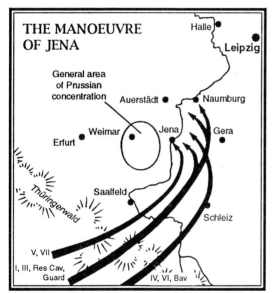

THE MANOEUVRE OF JENA

be in a position to intercept the move. The new left flank was formed by Ney (VI Corps) and the Heavy Cavalry. Most of the Cavalry Reserve were scouting in the direction of Leipzig with Murat. Soult (IV Corps), now forming the rearguard, was positioned around Gera watching for any enemy activity to the north and east of the Army.

The two early reverses suffered by Prussia had done much to undermine their earlier confidence. On 13 October a council of war decided that the main army would immediately withdraw in the direction of Halle. To protect this movement Hohenlohe, supported by Rüchel, would act as a rearguard while Brunswick extracted the main army. Later that day outposts of Lannes' and Hohenlohe's forces made contact just north of Jena. Moving rapidly, Napoleon received Lannes' report and shortly afterwards arrived in the town, agreeing with his subordinate's erroneous conclusion that before them lay the main Prussian Army. Fresh orders

FREDERICK WILLIAM III OF PRUSSIA. ENGRAVING BY T. JOHNSON.

were issued for the concentration of the Army. Ney, Soult, the Guard and the Heavy Cavalry were to move rapidly on Jena to which place Augereau was already ordered. Davout was to strike westwards from Naumburg towards the Salle while Bernadotte was to move to Dornburg on the Salle between Naumburg and Jena where he would be joined by Murat's cavalry. During the night of 13/14 October Lannes' Corps occupied the Landgräfenberg, a hill to the north of Jena, and supported the position with about 40 guns. Further orders were then dispatched to Davout instructing him to cross the Saale and move on Apolda to threaten the rear of the Prussian Army standing before Jena. Not knowing the exact whereabouts of Bernadotte at this time, a postscript was added by Berthier, Napoleon's Chief of Staff, stating that if Davout and Bernadotte were in direct contact they should march together; but it was hoped that Bernadotte was at Dornburg as previously instructed. Davout passed this message on in person to Bernadotte who, making a serious error of judgement, refused to alter his line of march for Dornburg without clear written orders and was missing from the crucial battles about to ensue.

At 6.30 a.m. on 14 October 1806 the battle of Jena opened as Lannes attacked the village of Closewitz, one of a number of small villages, lying to the north of the town. This was a necessary move to create space on the Landgräfenberg for the rapidly approaching supporting corps. Lannes' two infantry divisions met stiff resistance from the Prussian defenders of Closewitz and the neighbouring village of Cospeda. Generalmajor

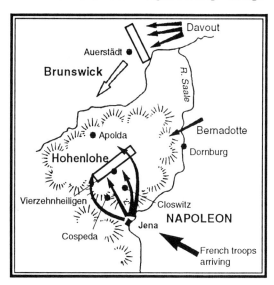

Tauentzien, the Prussian commander, surprised by the strength of the attack, ordered his men back from these villages towards his reserve at the village of Vierzehnheiligen. Here they turned and repulsed the pursuing French. However, realising that the security of the Army's right was under threat as Augereau's Corps began to appear, having advanced to the left of Lannes, Tauentzien turned

MURAT LEADS THE CHARGE AT JENA. PRINT AFTER CHARTIER.

his command again. Moving north-west towards Hohenlohe's main body, he reported that they appeared to be engaged by the whole French army and not a flank guard as the Prince had assumed. Determined to carry out his orders and protect the withdrawal of Brunswick's main army, Hohenlohe ordered forward his remaining troops while an urgent message was sent to General Rüchel to bring his men forward from Weimar in support. In the meantime on the French right the advanced division of Soult's Corps had been heavily engaged with a strong Prussian force which had attacked it after it had passed Closewitz. But the French light infantry tactics proved too much for the Prussians who were eventually forced to retreat. The French line remained relatively static for a while although an unauthorised attack by Ney against the village of Vierzehnheiligen almost ended in disaster. Only quick thinking by Napoleon, who ordered forward two regiments of cavalry and instructed Lannes and Augereau to renew their attacks, saved the situation, and earned Ney a rebuke from his Emperor. It could have been far worse. As Lannes' men stormed through Vierzehnheiligen to Ney's aid and emerged on the other side they were met by a massed volley from the main Prussian line. Taking heavy casualties they were forced to fall back on the village. Had the Prussians followed up, the outcome might have been different. But Hohenlohe kept the line in position, awaiting Rüchel's support. From the safety of the village the French opened a devastating fire on the exposed Prussians who could do little in reply. An attempt by Lannes to break the deadlock failed, but again Hohenlohe refused to follow up. This time with more reason. News was coming in that as a consequence of French pressure against the right he had lost contact with the three Saxon brigades keeping the important road to Weimar open, the road by which Rüchel was to advance. Farther to the south the build-up of fresh French troops was apparent as the final elements of Napoleon's corps arrived to join the battle.

Hohenlohe was about to become hopelessly outnumbered. Until now Napoleon had had about 54,000 men engaged, but with his reserves now in place a further 42,000 were about to enter the fray. Hohenlohe, who had received no reinforcements, had begun with about 39,000 men. At about 12.30 p.m. Napoleon ordered the final advance. On the left Augereau moved against the Saxons on the Weimar road. On the right Soult was to lead his Corps against the Prussians to his front. When these attacks were under way, Lannes and Ney were to smash through the centre, supported by Murat's cavalry ready to exploit the situation. Unable to stand in the face of such an onslaught Hohenlohe ordered a withdrawal which very soon collapsed into a fearful rout as the French cavalry descended on the shaken Prussian masses. Those fugitives that fled towards Weimar soon came up with Rüchel's force that had finally made its appearance. Briefly the pursuing French were brought to a halt, but overwhelmed by superior numbers Rüchel too was forced to retreat in disarray. Napoleon could feel well pleased with himself. He believed he had beaten and put to flight the main Prussian Army. He had inflicted about 10,000 casualties and taken some 15,000 prisoners. He anticipated that more would be added to this toll when the fugitives were intercepted by Davout and Bernadotte whom Napoleon expected to be astride the Prussian line of retreat at Apolda. He was therefore stunned by and initially found it hard to believe the news that was awaiting him on his return to Headquarters that evening. Davout with III Corps had engaged and defeated Brunswick's main army a few miles to the north near the village of Auerstädt. Slowly the truth dawned on him and the enormous misjudgement he had made became clear. While he had employed the main strength of the army against the Prussian rearguard, Davout, with only about 28,000 men, had destroyed Brunswick's army of about 63,000. Napoleon officially recognised Davout's remarkable victory and to him was given the honour of being the first to enter Berlin, the Prussian capital, at the head of III Corps. Bernadotte, however, who had failed to make an appearance on either battlefield and been too late to cut off the Prussians retreating from Jena, was severely reprimanded by Napoleon and narrowly escaped court-martial. In the relentless pursuit of the remnant of the Prussian Army that followed, Bernadotte was noticeable for the energy and zeal he displayed in carrying out his orders. By the time the campaign closed on 10 November the battles of Jena and Auerstädt, and the pursuit that followed, had accounted for almost the entire Prussian Army which only a few weeks before had entered the war with such confidence. But the enormity of the victory did not bring the end of the war. Although Napoleon had destroyed his armies and occupied his capital, King Frederick William, spurred on by his Queen and her supporters, refused to accept the peace as dictated by the Emperor. Russian assurances that their alliance was still intact ensured that the soldiers of *la Grande Armée* would have little time to rest and lick their wounds during the coming winter months.

In France the people had received the news of the Emperor's victory over the Prussian Army with a noticeable lessening of enthusiasm than that which had greeted Austerlitz less than a year before. The people longed for peace. Despite approaches from the Senate the Emperor was determined to continue the war until Russia could be forced to sever its ties with his inveterate enemy Britain, the paymaster of all opposition to Napoleon. Following the destruction of the French/Spanish Navy at Trafalgar in 1805, Napoleon lacked the means with which to plan a new invasion of England. Instead, while still in Berlin, he announced his 'Continental System' which he hoped would destroy Britain's economy by eliminating its overseas trade. He intended to have all Europe's ports closed to British trade and shipping; to bring this plan to fruition Russia would have to submit to his will and be compelled to join the blockade.

64

Napoleon now began to formulate his plans for taking the war to Russia. A war that would carry *la Grande Armée* farther away from France, into the inhospitable terrain of a barren and frozen Poland. The army was in fact in need of rest. It was only some fourteen months since the troops had left their cantonments on the Channel coast, but in that time it had fought the campaigns of Ulm, Austerlitz and Jena-Auerstädt. Many of the best soldiers were dead or wounded, the rest were tired, hungry and sorely in need of new equipment. The first conscripts from the 1806 intake were beginning to arrive now, but in addition Napoleon was forced to call upon Holland and Spain to supply him with fresh troops which he could utilise on his lines of communication. Prussia in turn was forced to supply greatcoats and boots for Napoleon's tattered army.

In an attempt to gain some intelligence of Russia's intentions, Napoleon ordered two reconnaissances eastwards in early November. A few days later he learnt from other sources that the Russians were on the move and deduced that they could be heading for a critical position on the Vistula near Thorn. Determined to secure the line of the Vistula and occupy both Thorn and Warsaw himself, he issued orders for the advance of the army. If all went according to plan he would be able to set up winter quarters along the west bank of the river, and in the spring launch his refreshed troops on a campaign that would destroy the Russian Army.

The advance went very smoothly. Apart from a minor skirmish or two Murat entered Warsaw unopposed on 28 November. On 5 December Lannes occupied Thorn, the city having been abandoned by Lestocq, the commander of the last viable Prussian force in the field. On 20 December Napoleon rejoined the army at Warsaw.

As with the Prussians earlier, Napoleon found it difficult to read Russian intentions. Believing that they were about to retreat from their positions north of Pultusk, about 60 kilometres north of Warsaw, he attempted to encircle his opponents. He predicted that there would be a major battle on the 21 or 22 December, but he was wrong. The Russians were actually moving forward and over the next few days a series of disjointed and inconclusive actions were fought before the Russians again withdrew on 27 December. Napoleon felt that they would turn and fight near the town of Makov but again he was wrong. The Russians continued to retreat. With a general deterioration in the weather and an army that had lost its cohesion in the pursuit, Napoleon at last ordered a halt and the establishment of winter quarters, much to the relief of his men.

65

The Russians meanwhile were keen to continue the campaign, undaunted by the rain, mud and frosts. In mid January General Bennigsen, the newly appointed army commander, advanced westwards, intending to get to the Vistula by carving his way through the extended bivouacs of the most northerly of the French corps, that of Bernadotte. Unfortunately for Bennigsen his men ran into part of Ney's Corps, which had disobeyed specific orders and had advanced northwards in their search for much-needed supplies. With the alarm now sounded Napoleon was stung into action by this unanticipated turn of events. He quickly grasped the situation and began to issue orders which he hoped would bring an early resolution to the campaign. Napoleon's plan to draw Bennigsen on and then unleash the rest of the army on to his flank and rear was thwarted when orders intended for Bernadotte were intercepted by the Russians. Realising how close he was to disaster, Bennigsen immediately halted his advance and called for a concentration of the army at Ionkovo. Unaware that the Russians were privy to his orders, Napoleon searched unsuccessfully for his enemy until they were located on 3 February. Convinced of the need to prevent the Russians from retreating again, he ordered an immediate attack even though the number of available troops was initially limited. The attack started late in the day but by nightfall some progress had been made and more troops were beginning to arrive which made Napoleon feel confident for the following day. But under cover of darkness the Russians silently extricated themselves and withdrew northwards into the freezing night.

The tireless pursuit of the Russians soon continued. In the centre Murat and Soult advanced in the direction of Landsberg. On the right Davout moved on Heilsberg while Ney, on the left, was ordered to prevent a junction between the forces of Bennigsen and the Prussian Lestocq. After a sharp exchange at Hoff the Russian rearguard again fell back and rejoined the main army, which had drawn up on the snow-covered hills to the east of the town of Preussisches-Eylau, on the evening of 6 February 1807.

The French centre, Soult and Murat, reached the outskirts of Eylau during the afternoon of 7 February where they were soon re-united with Augereau and the Guard. French strength was now in the region of 45,000 men, but Napoleon planned for Davout and Ney to march towards Eylau and join the attack. While the French centre held the Russians in position, these two corps, with a combined strength of about 26,000, were to envelop the Russian flanks and gain Napoleon another great victory. The Russians had approximately 67,000 men and a superiority of guns, so it is possible that he did not intend to begin his attack until the following morning when help would arrive. In fact the order calling Ney to Eylau was only sent at about 8 a.m. the next day, but a misunderstanding led to part of the Emperor's baggage arriving in the town of Eylau which Napoleon had not occupied. A Russian patrol attempted to capture the baggage which prompted a French response. The sound of firing alerted the Russians outside the town and soon both sides were feeding more and more men into the ferocious struggle. Some eight hours later the Russians withdrew to their position on the hills, leaving the frozen streets of Eylau choked with the bodies of the fallen. Possibly as many as 8,000 French and Russians had become casualties of this unplanned action.

After a night of sub-zero temperatures the two armies awoke on the morning of 8 February, peering through a howling blizzard. Napoleon had drawn his infantry up with two divisions of Soult (IV Corps) on the left. In the centre Augereau (VII Corps) formed his two divisions one behind the other supported by Murat's Reserve Cavalry. To the right of Augereau stood the remaining division of Soult's corps, Saint-Hilaire's. The Imperial Guard were held behind Eylau, and the extreme left and right of the army were each protected by a brigade of cavalry. Bennigsen's army, drawn up opposite the French, had the divisions of Tutchkov on the right, those of Essen and Sacken in the centre, with Tolstoi's on the left. Behind the centre Doctorov held two divisions in reserve. Cavalry were positioned on the flanks.

The battle opened with an exchange of cannon fire as the snow continued to fall. Intending to distract the Russians from the anticipated advance of Davout (III Corps) against their left, Napoleon ordered Soult, with his two

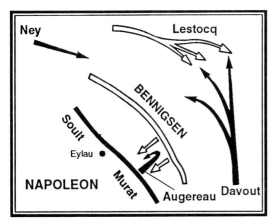

divisions and Lasalle's cavalry brigade, to advance against the Russian right. The Russians reacted, but with more force than he had expected and soon Tutchkov's men were pushing Soult back. At the same time the first of Davout's divisions began to arrive on the Russian left but was immediately assailed by Russian cavalry. Concerned that the Russians would renew their attack on Soult and push him back again, taking Eylau in the process, Napoleon decided on a counter-attack against Tolstoi's men on the Russian left to relieve the pressure. Augereau was ordered to advance with Saint-Hilaire's division on his right, a move Napoleon hoped would gain him time. For with the arrival of all his divisions Davout could then launch himself against an embattled Russian left already deeply embroiled with Augereau. Having begun the battle outnumbered by the Russians, in atrocious weather, Napoleon had denied himself the subtlety of manoeuvre which had served him so well in 1805 and 1806. Now he was forced to use battering-ram techniques to gain time to save a worsening situation. Augereau bravely advanced towards the Russians, but, losing their sense of direction in the raging snowstorm, his men gradually veered to the left. Saint-Hilaire's men soon lost contact with

14TH LINE AT EYLAU. PRINT AFTER L. ROYET.

Augereau but continued their advance; they reached Tolstoi's troops as planned, but were unable to breakthrough on their own. Meanwhile the unfortunate men of Augereau's corps, continuing their advance, suddenly found themselves in front of Sacken's divisions in the centre of the Russian line and confronted by a 70-gun battery. The casualties among Augereau's troops were horrific, perhaps as high as 75 per cent; as a corps it ceased to exist. The Russians began slowly to advance towards the gap created by the destruction of VII Corps while others penetrated into Eylau itself before being expelled. So desperate was the situation that Napoleon only narrowly escaped capture. He now had only one throw of the dice with which to save the situation. Calling forward the Reserve Cavalry to the centre of line, he ordered Murat to lead his almost 11,000 men against the advancing Russian columns. This gallant charge crashed into them, checked their advance and gained the time Davout needed to deploy his corps for battle. Napoleon had regained the initiative. Soult's men were ordered to hold their positions while Murat's returning cavalry were ordered to occupy the weak centre with the survivors of Augereau's corps. Then, at about 1 p.m., Davout advanced against the left of the Russian line and slowly began to push them back until it appeared that the line would break. But just at this crucial moment the Prussians of Lestocq, about 9,000 men, appeared to the north of the battle lines. Receiving word from Bennigsen of the coming battle, Lestocq had evaded Ney and marched on Eylau before the commander of VI Corps had received similar orders. Lestocq bolstered the left of the teetering Russian line and in turn attacked Davout's flank, pushing the French back again. A renewed attack by the Russian right added to Napoleon's discomfort. The eventual arrival of Ney, late in the day, helped stabilise the situation as he moved to support the French left. Darkness then descended on the battle-field and both sides drew back a little, preparing for another freezing night in the snow. Later Bennigsen called his senior commanders together and after much discussion the Russians decided against renewing the battle in the morning and settled on an immediate retreat. The shattered French troops were in no position to pursue.

The Russians had done much to dent Napoleon's aura of invincibility at Eylau. For the first time Napoleon had been checked in battle and although he remained on the field there could be no denying that he had come close to defeat. It has been suggested that he was actually considering retreat himself when the Russians began their own withdrawal. Despite one or two further minor actions, Napoleon deemed it an appropriate time to return his men to winter quarters to give them time to recuperate before spring brought fresh conflict, and with it death or glory.

News of renewed Russian activity prompted Napoleon to re-form the army at the beginning of May in readiness for the resumption of the campaign. But nothing of major significance occurred until the Russians made brief stinging attacks, first against I and IV Corps, and shortly afterwards against VI Corps before retreating again. The French concentrated four corps and engaged the Russians at Heilsberg on 10 June, while two more corps, those of Davout and Mortier (VIII Corps), were to move to the left so as to threaten Russian communications with Königsberg. This important city was currently their centre of operations and the refuge of the Prussian King. Napoleon, though outnumbered, sent his men forward to attack the entrenched Russian position head-on and suffered accordingly. With the French beginning to fall back in the evening, the situation was saved by the timely arrival of Lannes' corps. The French had little to show for the day except some 10,000 casualties. Napoleon did not renew his attack in the morning, but waited for the movement of Davout and Mortier to take effect. With their communications now threatened, Bennigsen's Russians began to withdraw that evening.

Having failed to inflict a serious defeat on his opponents, Napoleon now committed what many would consider a cardinal error – he split his forces. Intending to cut the Russians off from Königsberg, he dispatched Murat and Soult to try to capture the city with Davout providing support. Meanwhile Bennigsen, whose aggressiveness Napoleon had continually failed to recognise, observed an isolated Lannes probing towards the town of Friedland. The forward elements of both forces clashed in the early evening of 13 June 1807 and during the night the Russians began to build-up their forces with the River Alle and the town of Friedland to their rear. It was this disposition that was to determine the outcome of the battle. The Russians soon lost the initiative during the morning because they wasted much time forming their divisions prior to launching an attack. By the time they were ready the situation had dramatically changed and instead of only Lannes confronting them, first Mortier, then Ney, Victor, now commanding I Corps, and the Guard had arrived. Napoleon had about 80,000 men concentrated west of Friedland; confronting him were about 60,000 Russians.

Bennigsen now realised the weakness of his position and was about to order his men to pull back across the Alle during the night when his earlier optimism turned to despair. Napoleon had also quickly recognised the poor position the Russians had occupied and despite opposition from his staff, who wanted to await the arrival of Murat and Davout who had been recalled from Königsberg, he ordered the main assault to take place later that afternoon. Napoleon liked omens. He had won the great victory at Austerlitz on the anniversary of his coronation as Emperor, now he planned to bring about another triumph on the anniversary of the battle of Marengo. At 5.30 p.m. Ney's corps attacked the left of the startled Russian line. Russian attempts to counter-attack with cavalry were repulsed. As Ney's advance began to lose impetus the Russians launched another cavalry attack but this was again beaten back, with assistance from Victor's corps. French artillery then added to Russian distress by creating havoc in the packed lines of infantry. An attempt by Bennigsen to relieve pressure on his left by attack-

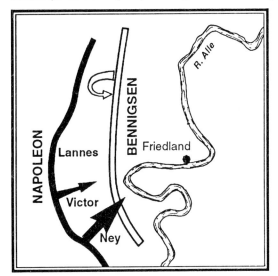

ing with his right failed to bring the desired result. Ney pressed on towards Friedland while Victor hit the flank of the Russian centre as it fell back. Bennigsen was in danger of losing his entire army as three of the four bridges across the Alle were now destroyed, but a ford was discovered just north of the town which allowed the Russians to extricate themselves. But the cost had been high. The Russians had suffered perhaps 18,000 casualties. Napoleon had won his decisive victory. Two days later Soult had occupied Königsberg. The war was over, an armistice was signed on 23 June and at Tilsit between 25 June and 9 July the Fourth Coalition was laid to rest. Russia agreed to join Napoleon's Continental System against Britain while Prussia was further humiliated by losing large tracts of land which became the Kingdom of Westphalia and the Grand Duchy of Warsaw.

The Treaty of Tilsit at last promised peace. The three great powers of Europe, Austria, Prussia and Russia had all opposed France and been decisively beaten. But the army was now no longer the one which had embarked on the campaign of Ulm in 1805. Increasing losses of manpower were now

ARCHDUKE CHARLES. ENGRAVING BY T. W. HARLAND AFTER KELLERHOVEN.

made up by early enrolment of the conscripts of 1808 and by an increasing number of foreign allies – Germans, Italians, Poles, Spanish and Dutch entering French service. In Paris criticism and discontent caused by the effects of the Continental System was increasing. Napoleon had been absent for more than nine months. It was time to return to affairs of state.

Napoleon's fierce determination to deny Britain access to the ports of Europe soon distracted him again however. His ban on British trade was being openly flouted through Portugal. Determined to close this open doorway, Napoleon advanced troops into Portugal through friendly Spain in late 1807. His heavy-handed treatment of Spain the following year, including the placing of his own brother on the throne, would not be tolerated by the people. France became embroiled in a vicious war. In central Europe this did not go unnoticed.

Still smarting from the conditions imposed on her following defeat in 1805, Austria had long yearned for a chance to strike back and regain her former status. Avoiding involvement in 1806 and 1807, she had carefully rebuilt her army and awaited the right moment. With Napoleon now in Spain and thousands of French troops being transferred from Germany and Poland to join him, the Austrians set course for war.

With the rumours of a plot against him in Paris and the growing threat of war with Austria, Napoleon left the army and returned to France. The prospect of yet another war was unpopular in Paris, but in Austria there was an awakening of nationalistic pride and a general enthusiasm for the coming war. With British support the Fifth Coalition came into being. There was a belief that Prussia would add it's strength to this renewed effort but this hope failed to materialise.

The Austrian Army under Archduke Charles crossed the River Inn into Bavaria on 10 April 1809. The French were in confusion. Napoleon, who felt confident that Austria would not advance before 15 April, was in Paris, issuing orders to the army through his Chief of Staff, Berthier. But Berthier was out of his depth. As one earlier commentator eloquently put it, 'Berthier, who was unrivalled in placing the pieces on the board, had no idea how to move them.' When this news reached him Napoleon sprang into action, arriving at the front on 17 April much to Berthier's relief. Restoring order to the army, he immediately planned his response to the Austrian advance. On 20 April at the battle of Abensberg he attacked two Austrian corps and forced them to retreat. Convinced that he had beaten the main army, Napoleon pursued these corps and a third, which attempted unsuccessfully to halt the French advance, back to Landshut. So convinced was he that he ignored repeated reports from Davout who claimed that he was engaged with the main army more than 30 kilometres to the north at Eggmühl (Eckmühl). Not until the early hours of 22 April did Napoleon fully recognise his mistake and dispatch orders for a rapid northwards march by the majority of the men under his command. The resulting victory of Eggmühl was brought about mainly thanks to the aggressive tactics employed by Davout on the previous day. With the Austrian Army now split in two, Napoleon failed to follow one of his own principles of war. Instead of concentrating on destroying either part of the retreating Austrians, he began an advance directly on the Austrian capital, Vienna. On 13 May he entered the city, leading an army reduced to 80,000 men by detachments, knowing little of Austrian movements but believing them to be marching away to the north.

DEFENCE OF THE GRANARY, ESSLING: AUSTRIAN GRENADIERS ATTACK THE FRENCH POSITION. PRINT AFTER F. DE MYRBACH.

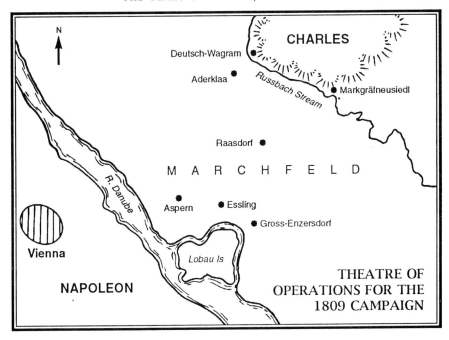

THEATRE OF
OPERATIONS FOR THE
1809 CAMPAIGN

In fact the two sections of the army had now been re-united and were forming for battle on the Marchfeld, north-east of the city, 110,000 strong.

Napoleon at this time had little respect for the Austrian Army. He had
personally beaten it in 1796, 1800 and again in 1805. In the early battles of
this campaign he had seen little to change his opinion. But the army of
Archduke Charles had learnt much from the lessons handed to it by
Napoleon and was about to inflict on him his first defeat.

Eager to get to grips with the Austrians before they retreated out of reach,
Napoleon ordered an urgent bridging of the Danube. Before the surrender
of the city the Austrians had destroyed the bridges, something they had
failed to do in 1805. Ignoring advice that the Danube could be treacherous
at this time of year because of the melting mountain snows upstream,
Napoleon hurriedly constructed a single bridge to transfer his army to the
far bank. The first French troops crossed the flimsy bridge on 20 May and
occupied the villages of Aspern and Essling. Later that day Austrian
attempts to break the bridge with floating obstacles succeeded. This would
be repeated throughout the coming battle and would seriously limit
Napoleon's options. An intelligence report received that night commenting
on the number of enemy campfires visible confirmed Napoleon's suspicions
that he was now facing merely the rearguard. He was wrong. Unseen by

French patrols, the Austrian Army was moving into position to launch its attack the following morning. The breaking of the bridge had hampered his plans for the pursuit. By 1 p.m. on 21 May 1809 he had only three divisions of Masséna's IV Corps, about 9,000 men and 7,000 cavalry between Aspern and Essling. At this point Napoleon learnt the truth of his position. He had under-estimated his opponents; an Austrian Army, some 99,000 strong, was approaching in five converging columns bearing down on his isolated force. The bridge connecting him with the rest of his army had again been broken. Seriously outnumbered, his only hope was to hold the two villages and await support. Throughout the rest of the day the battle for control of Aspern swung one way and then the other in a series of bloody attacks and counter-attacks. It was not until about 6 p.m. that the Austrians began to attack Essling. During the evening phase of the battle French reinforcements were again able to cross the bridge before it collapsed once more. As fighting died

FRENCH INFANTRY DEFEND THE STREETS OF ESSLING.
PRINT AFTER F. DE MYRBACH.

NAPOLEON SUPERVISES CONSTRUCTION OF THE BRIDGE ACROSS THE DANUBE AT LOBAU, AFTER THE REVERSE OF ASPERN-ESSLING (CAUSED BY AN IMPERFECT BRIDGE) AND BEFORE WAGRAM. PRINT AFTER F. DE MYRBACH.

down that night the French retained a foothold in Aspern and control of Essling. The French concentration recommenced during the night and by morning Napoleon had been joined by II Corps and the Guard. With a force of about 71,000 men under command, he chose to switch to the attack. Three of the newly arrived divisions of II Corps were deployed between Aspern and Essling and ordered to smash through the Austrian centre. A heavy concentration of artillery fire halted this forward movement. Despite efforts by the cavalry to relieve the pressure, the infantry had suffered too much and began to edge back. The struggle for the two villages continued throughout the morning until shortly after 1 p.m. when the French defenders were finally ejected from Aspern although those in Essling tenaciously clung on. Archduke Charles now planned his own attack against the French centre, but after beginning to push their line back further the Austrians were halted by their own increasing casualties. With growing disorder in the ranks the French position was weakening all the time and Napoleon was left with no alternative but to begin to withdraw the army back over the Danube. The invincibility of Napoleon had been broken, but he had only himself to blame. Having first under-estimated the resolve of his opponents, the rash crossing of the Danube without adequate reconnaissance and the vulnerability of the single link across the river had combined to bring about his defeat.

Archduke Charles was unwilling to push his advantage and hoped that Napoleon would be prepared to discuss a peaceful settlement. Napoleon, however, was determined to avenge his defeat and began meticulous preparations for a renewed crossing of the Danube. Six weeks after his defeat at Aspern-Essling Napoleon had gathered an army of about 190,000 ready to re-open the campaign. Archduke Charles, still in position on the Marchfeld, had increased his own army to about 138,000. Another colossal struggle was about to take place.

Throughout the night of 4/5 July 1809 the French Army once more crossed the river on to the Marchfeld. Capturing the village of Gross-Enzersdorf early on the morning of 5 July, Napoleon prepared to pivot the army on the village and advance northwards. Ahead of him were three corps and the advance guard of the Austrian Army in a strong position on an escarpment a short distance behind the Russbach stream. Away to the left of the French advance three more corps were preparing for the coming battle. By about 6 p.m. Napoleon had five corps (approx. 105,000 men) drawn up facing the Austrian position between the villages of Deutsch-Wagram and Markgräfneusiedl. An additional corps, Masséna's, was drawn up beyond the village of Aspern protecting the left and rear of the army. Unaware of the true strength of the Austrians facing him, Napoleon chose to launch an attack that night against the escarpment. Although Archduke Charles had presumed that the French would not attack until the morning he had some 83,000 men in position. The badly co-ordinated attack was repulsed all along the line and panic ensued in one section when a group of Saxons opened fire on their own countrymen, believing them to be Austrian. Recognising that the Austrians were in strength and intent on fighting, Napoleon proceeded to plan his main attack for the morning.

With the last of his army reaching the Marchfeld during the night Napoleon was ready to crush the Austrian line. Bringing up all but one division of Masséna's corps to strengthen his attack, he planned to occupy and hold the Austrian corps on the escarpment while relying on Davout to turn

NAPOLEON AT WAGRAM. ENGRAVING BY M. HAIDER AFTER HORACE VERNET.

their left and roll up the line. With only one division to protect his rear, Napoleon was gambling on a quick breakthrough. His opponent, however, had decided to take the initiative. At first light the three Austrian corps away on the French left were to begin an advance against his flank and rear while the corps on the extreme left of their line moved forward to attack Davout. Because of the huge distances involved – the Austrian position extended for about 20 kilometres – the moves were not well co-ordinated. The delayed arrival of the formations scheduled to attack the French left caused Charles to abort the attack against Davout which had gone ahead as planned. Taken by surprise, Napoleon had rushed men to Davout's assistance when firing first broke out, believing fresh troops were attacking his open right flank. But when the Austrian attack withdrew Napoleon returned, with his reserve infantry, to his central position at Raasdorf. Then on the

French left a new threat developed. Unknown to Napoleon, IX Corps had abandoned the forward village of Aderklaa during the night. Eagerly occupied by the Austrians, Napoleon ordered Masséna to recapture it. Having gained initial success, repeated fierce and bloody attacks and counterattacks eventually saw the village back in Austrian hands. Napoleon's position was becoming difficult. The delayed Austrian corps were now making their appearance against his left. Most worrying of all was the sight of the extreme right-hand corps advancing towards his rear where only one division stood in its way. This lone division was soon brushed aside and Austrian VI Corps were in Aspern awaiting to align itself with the rest of the flanking attack before continuing deep into the French rear. With quick thinking Napoleon ordered Davout to commence his attack on the right while he dealt with the crisis on the left. Masséna's men, who were recovering from their failure to recapture Aderklaa, were ordered to march south again to oppose the Austrians at Aspern. To protect this move the cavalry were ordered to throw themselves at the Austrian line across the front of which Masséna would have to march. They sustained terrible casualties but Masséna arrived safely and immediately engaged the Austrians, securing the left of the position. Napoleon plugged the gap created by Masséna's withdrawal by creating a mass artillery battery whose weight of fire forced the Austrian line to draw back.

After some desperate fighting on the right, Davout's corps was beginning to make progress. Believing the time was now right Napoleon ordered a general assault against the Austrian position. Despite heavy casualties, including the virtual destruction of three divisions of the Army of Italy under Macdonald, the French kept up the pressure. So finely balanced was the situation that Napoleon was forced to commit all his reserves except two regiments of the Old Guard. But at about 2 p.m. Archduke Charles reviewed the situation and realised that the battle was swinging away from him. Unwilling to risk the destruction of his army, he gave the order for a phased withdrawal. The French were too exhausted to follow up. So ended the greatest battle of Napoleon's early campaigns. Napoleon caught up with the Austrians again four days later, and while the two sides once more exchanged shot and shell an armistice was agreed that eventually put an end to the war.

Napoleon had won another campaign. For four years he had led his army from victory to victory, but the cracks were beginning to show. This was not the army that had stunned Europe with its bewildering manoeuvres at Ulm and its crushing victory at Austerlitz. That experienced, highly trained and well-organised fighting machine was no more. Four years of almost constant warfare had left huge gaps in the ranks of *la Grande Armée*. By 1809, in order to fill these gaps, the army was no longer French but multi-national. At Wagram the French core formed alongside men from Poland, Corsica, Portugal, Italy, Baden, Hesse-Darmstadt, Bavaria and Saxony. There was less reason for these men to sacrifice their lives for the Emperor. Many of the French soldiers themselves were tiring of constant fighting. With a lessening in the quality and conviction of the army, Napoleon was no longer able to wield it as he had done in 1805 and 1806. By 1807 and in the later stages of 1809 he was reduced to throwing it forward in great numbers hoping to force a result, regardless of casualties. The fate of Augereau's men at Eylau and Macdonald's at Wagram are prime examples. There is little sign of remorse for the sacrifice of his men. Criticism aimed at Napoleon following the losses at Eylau prompted the response, 'What are 2,000 men killed in a big battle'. In fact a gross under-estimate of his casualties but the sentiment is clear. There is no doubt that Napoleon was still the master of battlefield tactics as he proved on the second day at Wagram, but his opponents were learning all the time. Perhaps one of the greatest advantages Napoleon had over his opponents was that he controlled the state and the army with a single hand. The war councils that opposed him were invariably beset with petty jealousies and personal rivalries which weakened their resolve. Napoleon believed in his own infallibility, but cracks that started to appear at Eylau spread much deeper at Aspern-Essling. Never again would he fight a successful campaign, and it would only be a matter of time before the end came. For the lives of those men still to fall it is a pity that it did not come earlier than it did. In the words of Marshal Foch, French army commander in the Great War, 'he [Napoleon] forgot that war is not the highest aim, for peace is above war'.

BIBLIOGRAPHY

Arnold, J. R. *Crisis on the Danube*, London, 1990.
Castle, I. *Aspern and Wagram 1809*, London, 1994.
Chandler, D. G. *Austerlitz 1805*, London, 1990.
– *The Campaigns of Napoleon*, London, 1966 (numerous reprints).
– *Dictionary of the Napoleonic Wars*, London, 1979.
– *Jena 1806*, London, 1993.
Furse, Colonel G. A. *Campaigns of 1805*, Tyne & Wear, 1995 (reprint of 1905 edition).
Gill, J. *With Eagles to Glory*, London and California, 1992.
Macdonnell, A. G. *Napoleon and his Marshals*, London, 1950.

Maude, Colonel F. N. *The Ulm Campaign*, London, 1912.

Maycock, Captain F. W. O. *The Napoleonic Campaign of 1805*, Aldershot, 1912.

Petre, F. L. *Napoleon and the Archduke Charles*, 1909 (reprinted London, 1976).

- *Napoleon's Campaigns in Poland 1806-7*, London, 1901 (reprinted London, 1976).

- *Napoleon's Conquest of Prussia*, London, 1907 (reprinted London, 1977).

Rothenberg, G. E. *Napoleon's Great Adversaries*, London, 1982 (reprinted as *Napoleon's Great Adversary*, Staplehurst, 1995).

Stutterheim, Major General C. *A Detailed Account of the Battle of Austerlitz*, London, 1807 (reprinted Cambridge, 1985).

Thompson, J. M. *Napoleon Bonaparte - His Rise and Fall*, Oxford, 1963.

THE PENINSULAR WAR: A REPUTATION TARNISHED

Guy C. Dempsey, Jr.

NAPOLEON'S ATTEMPT TO CONQUER SPAIN AND PORTUGAL WAS A crucial episode in his reign, but because he spent only a short period of time in the Iberian Peninsula, its story is usually told from other perspectives. The great narratives are ones of triumph focusing on the brilliant achievements of the Duke of Wellington and the British Army or on the heroic resistance of the Spanish and Portuguese people to a foreign invader. From an exclusively Napoleonic viewpoint, however, the story is one of abject failure, a drama made tragic because both the attempt and its adverse outcome for the French were entirely unnecessary and entirely the responsibility of Napoleon. The Emperor's own verdict on his handling of affairs in the Peninsula is consistent with this view: 'That miserable war was my undoing; it divided my forces, multiplied my exertions, [and] attacked my moral ascendancy ... All the circumstances of my disasters can be traced to that fatal [conflict]'.[1]

The story is all the more fascinating because it is accompanied by a stunning reversal of Napoleon's personal fortunes. When he first turned his attention to the Peninsula, he was the most powerful ruler in Europe. He presided over a French Empire which extended from Rome to the frontiers of Holland and from the Rhine to the Pyrenees, and he was at the same time king of the recently created state of Italy and Protector of the Confederation of the Rhine which he had brought into being as the successor organisation to the Holy Roman Empire. Most significantly, he had achieved this power not through 'divine right', but by his own merit. First, he lifted France out of domestic chaos, consolidating and refining the achievements of the Revolution. Then he both defended France and re-established her position as a great power in the battles of Marengo, Austerlitz, Jena/Auerstädt and Friedland, successes which confirmed him as a military genius and forever changed the face of warfare. The other rival powers – the Austrian Empire, the Kingdom of Prussia and the Russian Empire – had all been humbled by him and had become his allies out of fear or self-interest. There was no shadow across his future other than that cast by the intransigent resistance of the British to his domination of the Continent.

From the moment he began to intervene in Spanish and Portuguese affairs, however, his power began to erode. That involvement gave rise to the series of military campaigns which came to be known (by the victors at least) as the Peninsular War, and it was Napoleon's failure to win that struggle, or at least resolve it at an acceptable cost, that contributed, as much as any other single factor, to his forced abdication and exile on a small island in the Mediterranean just over six years later. Of course, there were many points before the final denouement of his Iberian entanglement at which Napoleon had opportunities to change its outcome, but, uncharacteristically, he failed to recognise some of these and failed to exploit the others. Instead, the war in Spain became the 'ulcer' which sapped the physical and psychological strength of France by causing huge numbers of casualties in the French army and by puncturing the myth of Napoleon's invincibility. That ulcer finally became malignant when he took on the exertions of the Russian campaign without first having treated it successfully.

There is no single event which marks the precise beginning of Napoleon's Peninsula entanglement. Like most occurrences of history, it came about as

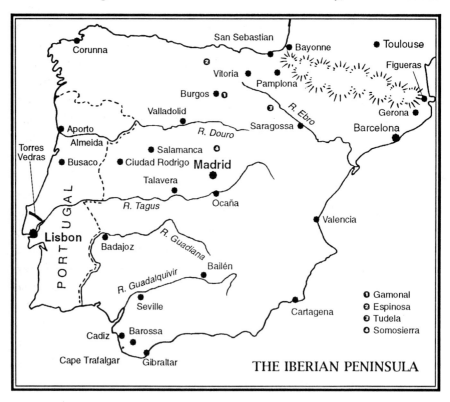

THE IBERIAN PENINSULA

the culmination of many interrelated events which ultimately caused him to perceive that his best interests, and those of France, required him to interfere with the governing of the two Peninsular states. While his interaction with Portugal was strictly military and therefore relatively straightforward, that with Spain was initially political and consequently more complex. It is in this complexity that the origins of Napoleon's worst Peninsular problems can be found.

Although Spain had initially taken up arms against the French Revolution, by the time Napoleon came to power the Treaty of San Ildefonso (1796) had transformed that country into a submissive ally of France who gained little and lost much from the association.[2] The Treaty itself created an offensive and defensive alliance aimed primarily at Britain, but the relationship eventually expanded to encompass such transactions as Spain's cession to France of the Louisiana territory in America in exchange for a new kingdom in Italy (Etruria) for some Bourbon relatives. For France, the advantages of the relationship included the close co-operation of the Spanish navy in French naval strategy and an annual subsidy of gold and silver, but by 1807 these had disappeared because of the annihilation of the main Spanish fleet in the disaster of Trafalgar, and because British control of the seas made it impossible for Spain to import large amounts of specie from its New World colonies.

At the same time, the prestige of the Spanish monarchy had sunk to almost negligible levels under the feeble leadership of King Charles IV. Charles was certainly not the most dynamic representative of the Bourbon family; in fact, hunting was the only activity for which he showed any aptitude or enthusiasm. As for ruling the country, the king and his consort, Queen Maria Luisa, left most governmental decisions in the hands of their favourite courtier, Manuel Godoy, whom they had rewarded with the title 'Prince of Peace'. Godoy, a one-time member of the royal bodyguard, was, at least, probably better qualified than the king in terms of talent and education for the responsibilities allotted to him.[3] His position *vis-à-vis* Napoleon, however, had been compromised when he made the mistake of publicly engaging in anti-French posturing in 1806 when it was thought that Prussia would take the measure of the upstart Emperor. He quickly reversed himself when the news of Napoleon's victories at Jena and Auerstädt reached Madrid, but the damage had been done. Prince Ferdinand of the Asturias, the heir apparent, had no more talent than his father, and few positive character traits other than a bitter hatred of Godoy and of his domination of Ferdinand's parents, but, merely because he represented the possibility of change for the better, he enjoyed a widespread (if undeserved) popularity within the nation. One pro-French contemporary succinctly summed up the Spanish political scene in the following unflattering terms:

'The [Spanish] monarchy was governed by an incapable and weak-minded king, who abandoned the reins of government to the hands of a vain and unprincipled favourite [sic], who was detested by the nation, and who was the lover of a dissolute queen. The heir presumptive to the crown was a prince lacking in qualities of heart as well as of intelligence, false, [and] profoundly hypocritical'.[4]

Under such circumstances, there was little reason for Napoleon to feel anything but contempt for his erstwhile allies, particularly since the Spanish royal family was related to the deposed Bourbons of his own country. Nevertheless, as a pragmatic matter, he was still willing to work within the Spanish alliance when its suited his needs. In the aftermath of the Peace of Tilsit (and of the seizure by the British of the Danish fleet later that summer), these included forcing Portugal to join the Continental System he had created for the purpose of striking at the economy of his arch-enemy, Britain. In order to facilitate achieving that goal, Napoleon negotiated a new agreement with Spain in October 1807.

The resulting Treaty of Fontainebleau gave him Spanish support (and troops) for an invasion of Portugal.[5] In return, the Spaniards received Napoleon's promise to carve out of the conquered country a principality in the south for Godoy and a kingdom in the north which was to be given to Charles's grandson, the infant King of Etruria, in exchange for his agreement to relinquish his Italian realm to Napoleon. The central portion of Portugal, including Lisbon, was reserved for disposition by Napoleon.

The immediate practical results of the co-operation envisaged by the Treaty were impressive. The leading elements of a Spanish-French expeditionary force commanded by General Androche Junot entered Lisbon without opposition on 30 November 1807, and the whole country submitted quietly thereafter to the invaders. The only disappointing note was that the Portuguese king (and his fleet) escaped capture by sailing to Brazil.

At the same time, domestic affairs in Spain were developing in ways which created unusual, and perhaps irresistible, opportunities for Napoleon to meddle in the Spanish royal succession. The first significant event was a request from Ferdinand asking Napoleon to grant him a bride from the extended Bonaparte family.[6] Such marriage propositions were a common feature of European diplomacy in the age of monarchies, but what made this one unusual was that it came from Ferdinand himself and not from his father, the reigning Spanish monarch. There was an obvious motivation for Ferdinand to have taken such a step – by offering to accept the Emperor's choice for his spouse he undoubtedly hoped to curry favour, which could be used in his personal struggle against Godoy's influence. The way in which he chose to do this, however, was contrary to established practice and had the unfortunate effect of drawing Napoleon's attention to the dissensions within the Bourbon family.

When Godoy learned of this and certain other actions by Ferdinand, he saw them as a direct threat to his personal power. In a pre-emptive strike against Ferdinand, he persuaded the king to have his son arrested and publicly accused of treason on the basis of several alleged misdeeds, including his unauthorised communications with Napoleon, a foreign monarch. This 'Affair of Escorial', played out in October and November 1807, ended in a shaky affirmation of the status quo when King Charles accepted a grovelling apology from Ferdinand and sent his son's closest advisers to prison or into exile. As a final ironic twist, after forgiving his son, Charles proceeded to renew, this time in proper form, Ferdinand's request for a Bonaparte bride.[7] (Godoy, presumably, felt less threatened by this idea so long as he was in control of the situation.)

The repercussions of this affair were significant. Ferdinand was confirmed in his hatred of Godoy, and Godoy in his fear of Ferdinand. King Charles and Queen Maria Luisa proved that they were irretrievably under the control of the Prince of Peace. And Napoleon was given another reason to despise the Bourbons and to realise that Spain in its then present governmental state was unlikely ever to become the vigorous ally his ambition required to help him recreate a viable naval threat to Britain.

The next moves were made by Napoleon, but they were not made immediately because he spent the last six weeks of 1807 on a state visit to Italy. That journey gave him some time to reflect on affairs in the Peninsula and to ponder the four obvious alternatives open to him:

1. He could support the existing government of Godoy in return for its greater co-operation in his military and naval plans.
2. He could persuade Charles to create a new pro-French government excluding both Godoy and Ferdinand.
3. He could support Ferdinand against his father and Godoy.
4. He could attempt to put forward some other (possibly non-Bourbon) claimant to the throne.

Although Napoleon had meetings with both Joseph *and* Lucien Bonaparte in December, at which he apparently discussed the possibility of replacing the Spanish king, there is no evidence to suggest that this was the alternative he preferred to all others. Indeed, there is no evidence that he found any one of them to be particularly attractive. But his first actions in the New Year demonstrate that he had definitely reached the conclusion that he could not allow affairs in Spain to remain as they were. Beyond that, however, it seems equally definite that he had not made up his mind about the nature of the change he wanted or the means by which it could be effected.

In the absence of a single, decisive plan of action, Napoleon limited himself to taking a step which could be helpful no matter how he ultimately decided to proceed – he began to build up a military presence in Spain itself. The secret articles of the Treaty of Fontainebleau envisaged that Napoleon could, under certain conditions, send reinforcements through Spain into Portugal should the original invasion force for Portugal be inadequate for its task. He had taken advantage of these provisions back in November to send a reserve force under General Dupont into northern Spain, and there it halted when word was received of Junot's success in Portugal. Now, as the New Year began, he stretched interpretation of the Treaty to breaking point by ordering still another corps, this one commanded by Marshal Adrien Moncey, to advance across the border and occupy towns in Biscay and Navarre while Dupont's force moved on into northern Castile. Perhaps not surprisingly, the progress of these troops towards Portugal was painfully slow, if not non-existent.

Even more alarming from a Spanish point of view was the fact that, shortly thereafter, French troops under General Philippe Guillaume Duhesme began to enter Catalonia as well, accompanied by the vague Imperial explanation that they might be used either to co-operate in the defence of Cadiz against British attack or to participate in a joint Spanish/French assault on Gibraltar. Finally, in mid-February, Napoleon took the stunningly cynical step of authorising the seizure of some of his ally's most important fortresses. While the Spanish government remained paralysed by a combination of fear of Napoleon and greed for a partition of Portugal, Napoleon's forces in short order insinuated themselves into control of San Sebastián, Figueras, Barcelona and Pamplona, the citadel of the latter place being seized by French soldiers who gained entry under cover of a snowball fight.

To cap these developments, Joachim Murat, Grand Duke of Berg and Napoleon's brother-in-law, was named as the Emperor's lieutenant in Spain and ordered to move into Madrid with a strong force which included detachments of the Imperial Guard. The number of French troops that had been introduced into Spain was definitely inadequate for an attempt to seize the throne by force, but it was certainly sufficient to put Napoleon in a position to exert a very real direct influence on Spanish domestic affairs.

The threat posed by the French military presence was enhanced by some ominous direct communications from Napoleon to Charles. On 10 January Napoleon sent two letters to the Spanish monarch. The first gave Napoleon's official response to the Bourbon's request for a bride for Ferdinand: 'Your Majesty will understand that no man of honour would wish to enter into a family alliance with a son dishonoured [by his traitorous activities] unless he has received assurances that the son has re-acquired the full good graces of his father.'[8] The second letter informed Charles that Napoleon thought it premature to make public the terms of the Treaty of Fontainebleau relating to the future of Portugal even though he had already in December taken over the Kingdom of Etruria without taking any steps to organise the Portuguese compensation promised to the ex-ruler of that state.[9]

Some have speculated that the Napoleon's intention at this point was to scare Charles into voluntarily abandoning his throne, leaving a vacuum of authority which Napoleon could fill. The most Napoleon himself would reveal about his intentions is contained in an order dated 8 March to Murat telling him to allay Spanish fears by publishing a proclamation in French and Spanish stating that Napoleon 'has nothing in mind except things which will be useful and advantageous for the Spanish nation, for which he has always had the highest esteem'.[10]

By playing a waiting game, Napoleon was trying to keep all his options open, but in fact all he achieved was to make himself a victim of new circumstances which developed beyond his control. The growing French influence may have paralysed Charles and his government, but it had the opposite effect on the people of Spain and spurred them to unprecedented action. As the political and moral bankruptcy of Charles's regime became more apparent from its pusillanimous behaviour in the face of French aggression, the people placed more of their hopes in Ferdinand and directed more of their anger against Godoy, whom they blamed for the shortcomings of the monarchy. Popular sentiment was probably more nationalistic than revolutionary, but this became a distinction without a difference when the crowd asserted itself on 17 March 1808, at the Royal residence in Aranjuez, twenty-five miles south of Madrid.

There are conflicting stories as to how this episode began, but there is no doubt that rumours of another attack by Godoy on Ferdinand, spread by Ferdinand's own supporters, were an important contributing factor. In any event the local populace stormed into Godoy's residence on the night of the 17th, pillaged its contents and forced its owner into hiding in a corner of his own attic. He remained hidden throughout the next day while a frantic Charles tried to mollify the crowd by dismissing his favourite from all official positions. The crowd, once again egged on by Ferdinand's agents, became even more threatening on the 19th. Godoy was found and dragged from his hiding-place, and demands for abdication of the king were added to those for Godoy to stand trial for his misdeeds. For once Ferdinand acted decisively and offered to protect the lives of Godoy and his parents if Charles would abdicate the throne. The frightened King, overwhelmed by the unprecedented action of his subjects, agreed on the evening of the 19th: 'Since my increasing infirmities make it impossible for me any longer to sustain the burden of the government of my realm, and needing, for the sake of my health to retire into private life in a warmer climate, I am resolved after mature consideration to abdicate my crown to my much loved son, the Prince of the Asturias.' [11]

This unexpected development finally caused Napoleon to make up his mind about the best course of action to pursue with respect to Spain. The choice he made was to overthrow the Bourbon monarchy and to put a member of his own family on the throne of Spain. He announced his decision by writing to his brother, King Louis of Holland, offering him the position. The matter-of-fact tone of Napoleon's letter, including the casual way he suggests the possibility of swapping one throne for another, accentuate the supreme arrogance of what he had determined to achieve:

'My Brother,
The King of Spain has just abdicated, the Prince of Peace has been put in prison and an insurrection has broken out in Madrid ... Since I am certain that I cannot achieve a solid peace with England without creating a great movement on the continent, I have resolved to place a French prince on the throne of Spain. The climate in Holland does not agree with you. Moreover, Holland is never going to arise again from its ruins ... Under these circumstances, I am thinking of you for that throne. Tell me categorically your opinion of this project ...' [12]

This idea did not lead to immediate action, however, because Napoleon could not make it public before he received a reply from Louis. Until that moment arrived, he had to continue to play a waiting game. He decided that the key to this approach was to act as if the events at Aranjuez had never occurred. He therefore ordered Marshal Murat, who entered Madrid on 23 March, to withhold official recognition from Ferdinand even after the new monarch, calling himself Ferdinand VII, returned to the capital on the 24th, receiving a tumultuous welcome from his subjects and taking up the reins of government. Murat also sent agents to seek out King Charles, who required little prompting to sign an official protest against his abdication (because it had been extorted by the violence of the mob controlled by his son) and to accept French protection for his personal safety. Despite the importance of Murat's role at this stage of events, Napoleon, as demonstrated by the letter excerpts quoted below, cynically withheld his true intentions from his representative in Spain:

'Events have been singularly complicated by the affair of March 19 ... What are the best measures to be taken? Shall I go to Madrid? Shall I play the part of grand protector and decide between the father and the son? It seems to me difficult to allow Charles IV to reign. His government and his favourite are so unpopular that they could not survive three months.

'Ferdinand is the enemy of France, and that is why he is being made the king. To place him on the throne would play into the hands of the parties who for the last twenty-five years have desired the annihilation of France. A family alliance [i.e., a French queen] would be a feeble tie .... I am of the opinion that nothing must be hurried, that it will be a good thing to be guided by the events that will follow...

' You will behave with courtesy and consideration towards the King, the Queen and Prince Godoi [sic]. You will insist that the same honours are paid to them as formerly, and you will pay them these honours yourself. You will act in such a way that the Spaniards will not be able to suspect what line of action I intend to adopt, and this will be a matter of no difficulty, seeing that I myself am in ignorance on this point.' [13]

In the face of this hostile stance by the French, Ferdinand could and should have secured his own future by confidently asserting his rights without reference to what Napoleon thought or said, but he was mesmerised by the power of the French ruler and lacked the self-confidence to believe that his subjects would follow him without some overt sign that he enjoyed the support of the Emperor. Napoleon was consequently able to use Ferdinand's confusion and weakness to stall developments until he could achieve the outcome he now desired. Through Murat and General Jean Savary, another Imperial representative sent to Madrid, Napoleon was able to make Ferdinand believe that his best hope for success was a personal audience with his fellow monarch. As a result, on 10 April 1808, Ferdinand headed north from Madrid to seek a meeting with 'his intimate friend and august ally' in which he could 'maintain, renew and tighten the bonds of harmony, intimate friendship and advantageous alliance' already existing between Spain and France.[14]

This decision was one of the worst Ferdinand could have made, because moving north put him within the French zone of occupation. He then compounded his difficulties by naïvely taking a positive view of the letter from Napoleon which reached him at Vitoria, ominously addressed not to the King of Spain, but to the Prince of the Asturias. In that missive, Napoleon promised Ferdinand everything he wanted, but only subject to conditions which Napoleon knew could never be met:

'I say to Your Royal Highness, to the Spanish people and to the whole world: If the abdication of King Charles was purely voluntary, and was not forced by the insurrection and unrest at Aranjuez, then I will have no difficulty in giving it effect and recognising Your Royal Highness as the king of Spain. I therefore wish to speak to you about this point.'[15]

Napoleon even had the effrontery to state in the letter that one of his reasons for withholding recognition was a concern that, in the 'eyes of Europe and of posterity', the coincidence of Charles' abdication taking place while there were French troops in Spain would be viewed as evidence that Napoleon had plotted the overthrow of his ally and friend.

Even at this point, Ferdinand could have changed the course of history by fleeing the clutches of the French as many of his counsellors urged him to do. Instead, after some hesitation, like a moth drawn to the destructive flame Ferdinand agreed to go on to a meeting with Napoleon on French soil at Bayonne. Of course he had no idea that his parents had already been called to that same destination or that Napoleon would soon write to them: 'I have not recognised and will never recognise the Prince of the Asturias as the king of Spain.'[16] To make his duplicity complete, Napoleon had at the same time sent word to King Joseph of Naples, who had taken his brother Louis' place as the leading family candidate for the Spanish throne, to hold himself in readiness for an imminent summons.[17]

It is obvious from these letters that Napoleon was still focused on changing Spain's dynasty, but they do not reveal anything more about his motives.

Ferdinand's craven and pathetic behaviour throughout the weeks of his temporary reign demonstrate that he was not ideal royal material, but he was the undisputed choice of his subjects. Moreover, that same behaviour must have suggested to Napoleon that the mere threat of dethronement would have caused Ferdinand to grant any demand which the Emperor cared to make (including, possibly, territorial concessions), in which case any national backlash would have been borne by Ferdinand, and not by Napoleon. The straightforward alternative would, therefore, have been to support the new monarch, with all his faults.

Napoleon chose a more drastic course and he did so in spite of warnings from Spanish advisers that he was in danger of converting the 'child's play' of dealing with Ferdinand into a 'labour of Hercules' if he sought to impose a new king on the Spaniards.[18] The clearest statement of Napoleon's reasons for his choice is to be found in a document which is ostensibly a report to him from his Foreign Minister Jean-Baptiste Champagny, but which is known to have been heavily edited by Napoleon. This report stresses that the submission of Spain was necessary to bring about peace with Britain, but it also contains echoes of an argument that it was manifest destiny for the France and Spain to be joined as a single state:

'Spain has the necessary maritime resources [for war against Britain] which have been lost for her and for France. The country requires a good government to renew these resources ... so that Your Majesty can use them against the common enemy to arrive at last at that state of peace which humanity demands and of which all Europe has such a great need. *Everything which leads to this result is legitimate* [emphasis added]. The interests of France and those of continental Europe do not permit Your Majesty to neglect the sole means by which the war against England can be pursued with success.

'The work of Louis XIV must be begun again .... Your Majesty can ... neither re-establish a dethroned king, nor sanction the revolt of his son, nor abandon Spain to its fate.'

The report ends with a call for Napoleon to take the 'bold', but tactfully unnamed, action which 'justice authorises and the troubles of Spain demand'.

Even after the Bourbons arrived in Bayonne (Ferdinand on 21 April and his parents on the 30th) there remained a great deal of work to be done by Napoleon in order to make the results of his 'bold action' as legitimate and orderly as possible. As far as appearances went, what he had in mind was not the overthrow of the Bourbons, but rather their lawful replacement by a new dynasty. To achieve the desired result he had to revise at least two points of recent history. First he had to resurrect King Charles as the legal ruler of Spain. Secondly he had to persuade Charles to abdicate again, this time in favour of himself. Both these revisions turned out to be relatively easy to achieve.

The old king genuinely felt he had been unfairly treated at Aranjuez and had already published a formal protest against his son's subsequent actions. When they were re-united at Bayonne, Charles demanded the formal return of his crown. Ferdinand resisted for a short while, but he quickly gave in when news of the 2 May riots in Madrid raised the possibility of his again being tried for treason (this time on the grounds that the riots were insti- gated by his partisans). On 6 May he wrote a letter to Charles ceding all his rights to the throne. What Ferdinand apparently did not know was that Charles had already decided on the 5th that he was willing to forego volun- tarily the difficult job of ruling a country in favour of a pampered existence in exile for himself, his wife and his beloved servant, Godoy. He therefore signed another act of abdication, this time in favour of Napoleon, which stipulated only that the territorial integrity of the kingdom be maintained and Catholicism be recognised as the state religion:

> 'Art. 1. His Majesty King Charles, having throughout his life been con-
> cerned only with the well-being of his subjects ... has resolved to cede
> ... all of his rights to the throne of Spain and the Indies to His Majesty
> the Emperor Napoleon, the sole person who can re-establish order
> given the point to which affairs have arrived ....'[20]

Napoleon was so concerned about ensuring the legality of the change in the ruling family that he also demanded, and received, from Ferdinand a second document, dated 10 May, in which the Prince affirmed his adherence to the abdication of Charles in return for the grant to Ferdinand of certain estates and revenues in France.

At the conclusion of this remarkable sequence of events, one point was clear – the throne of Spain had been surrendered to Napoleon. Moreover, the legality of the transfer of power had been observed through the abdication of Ferdinand in favour of Charles and that of Charles in favour of Napoleon, so that in theory all the existing elements of the Spanish government, includ- ing its administrators, soldiers and sailors, were bound to obey the com- mands of the new ruler. But practice is sometimes different from theory, and in this case the difference was dramatic. Blinded by his own ego and by the pathetic behaviour of the Bourbons, Napoleon completely miscalculated the extent to which the people of Spain would remain loyal to the old (and, in his eyes, reprehensible) regime and react violently to the cavalier way in which he had dealt with their king and his heir. While he proceeded to invest Joseph with all the trappings of the power to rule Spain, including a new constitution, the power itself was being claimed and used by revolutionary councils, or *juntas*, which acted spontaneously as news of the events of Bayonne spread throughout the country during May and June.

Napoleon evidently did not understand either the extent or the revolutionary nature of these developments. Remaining at Bayonne, he continued to give orders as if there were nothing more to be concerned about than a few scattered riotous incidents similar to the one which had been handled so easily by the French soldiers in Madrid on 2 May. He had 80,000 or so troops in Spain to maintain order, but the specific objectives he assigned to particular forces betrays an ignorance of the resistance they might encounter. On 18 May, for instance, he ordered General Pierre Dupont to march to Cadiz with a force of only 9,000 French troops, plus 8,000 Swiss mercenaries in the service of Spain. The unrealistic nature of this order was accentuated by an accompanying direction to Junot to detach a brigade from his small force in Portugal and send it overland to the same destination. On 30, May he detached Marshal Adrien Moncey and 9,000 troops from Madrid with orders to subdue the city of Valencia, and he shortly afterwards dispatched another force to deal with the insurrection at Saragossa.

The consequences of Napoleon's under-estimation of Spanish resistance were especially damaging because the quality of the French troops in Spain was even lower than their quantity. Napoleon had decided early on that the forces he needed for the Peninsula could be formed without disturbing the concentration of troops he had in Germany and Poland because they were destined only for police work and garrison duty. He therefore drew them from second-line components of his army, although he took care to include a few experienced units from his own Imperial Guard. Only a few complete line battalions were used, and these came mostly from posts within France and had not served with the *Grande Armée*.

Far more numerous were the so-called 'provisional' regiments, infantry and cavalry units created by throwing together companies and battalions of established regiments into new operational groups. Such formations contained some veterans, but their efficiency was limited by the fact that the sub-units were unfamiliar with one another and that there was a complete absence of any cohesion or *esprit de corps*. The remainder of the French forces consisted primarily of conscripts from recent classes (including the all-conscript Reserve Legions) and foreigners. Under stress, the defects of such motley formations would become swiftly apparent.

Throughout the month of June the political developments were favourable for the French; Joseph was officially proclaimed King of Spain and Emperor of the Indies and numerous Spanish dignitaries rallied to the new regime. But the military situation began to deteriorate as soon as the Spanish authorities loyal to Ferdinand were able to put substantial forces into the field. Dupont got as far as the city of Cordoba in Andalusia, which his undisciplined troops sacked on 7 June. The savagery of their behaviour helped to beget the escalating brutality which was to characterise much of the fighting between the French and their Spanish enemies in the years to come. Dupont's advance then stalled, however, as opposition built up in front of him and closed in on his communications with Madrid. Moncey succeeded in reaching Valencia, but was easily repulsed with heavy losses on 28 June and only escaped back to Madrid through a combination of good luck and Spanish incompetence. The French had no difficulty in clearing the main lines of communication between Madrid and France, but significant resistance developed both at Saragossa in Aragon and Gerona in Catalonia, in each case tying down a relatively large French force.

In the face of such news, one might have expected some decisive new action on the part of Napoleon, but he maintained the status quo, neither calling for significant reinforcements nor curtailing the dispersion of the French forces nor taking a more active command in the field. It may be that he honestly believed that these upheavals were temporary and that the situation would stabilise once Joseph was established on his throne and the machinery of government was able to re-assert control of outlying regions. In any event, the military situation took a turn for the better in July when Marshal Jean-Baptiste Bessières routed the Spanish Army of Galicia at Medina del Rio Seco on the 14th. This victory literally cleared the way for Joseph to make his entry into Madrid on the 20th, cheered on by the encouraging words of his brother: 'You should not find it extraordinary to have to conquer your kingdom. Both Philip V and Henry IV were obliged to conquer theirs. Be cheerful, don't let anything bother you, and don't doubt for an instant that things will soon turn out better than you can imagine.'[21]

As evidenced by this letter, Napoleon thought that things were going well, although he continued to be concerned about Dupont's situation. However, the worst case he could imagine for that force was merely a tactical withdrawal, so he did not see any need to send immediate reinforcements to the south. 'If Dupont suffers a setback it will be a matter of little consequence. It will have no result other than to cause him to retreat across the mountains back towards Madrid.'[22] What happened instead, of course, was the unthinkable. A combination of mistakes by Dupont and his subordinates and bold manoeuvres by his opponents left the bulk of the French forces in Andalusia surrounded by insurgent Spanish forces. They might have been able to fight free at the cost of heavy casualties and great loss of equipment, but the incentive to do so was removed when the Spaniards offered very favourable terms for capitulation and repatriation of his troops to France. On 18 July, General Dupont opted for surrender. *or 23 Jul 1808·*

Taking into consideration only the facts known to Dupont at the time, his decision was certainly a reasonable one from a military point of view, especially since he could not have foreseen that the Spaniards would not honour the terms of surrender. From a political and psychological point of view, however, the effects of his capitulation at Bailén were devastating for the French. The Spanish triumph validated the resistance being shown to the French, encouraged its spread to hitherto unaffected areas of the country and gave Britain a chance to accord formal recognition to the Supreme *Junta* formed by the insurgents. It also destroyed King Joseph's confidence and led him to a precipitous departure from Madrid only eleven days after he had arrived. That action in turn caused the defection of many of the ministers, generals and other government officials who had initially acquiesced in the change of dynasty. Once he began to retreat, Joseph found it very hard to stop. Even though the Spanish pursuit was lethargic at best, Joseph was unable to hold a position along the River Douro and, much to his brother's disgust, ultimately fell back all the way to the line of the River Ebro in northern Spain.

Napoleon himself took the disaster at Bailén as a personal insult: 'Dupont has dishonoured himself and he has dishonoured my armies. Ineptitude, cowardice and madness determined his operations at the end of July and has upset all my Spanish affairs.'[23] In theory, at least, this reversal of fortune might have caused Napoleon to reconsider the political course he had embarked upon in Spain. In practice, he was pre-occupied with this affront and was only interested in preparing to avenge it on the field of battle. News of Bailén reached Napoleon on 2 August. Within days another 100,000 Imperial soldiers had been ordered to Spain. This time there would be no miscalculation of the resources required for the task to hand: the new troops would come in the form of veteran units led by some of his best combat commanders – Marshals Michel Ney, Jean Soult, Claude Victor and Jean Lannes. His resolve to strike a military blow to restore French prestige was further hardened when a British expeditionary force landed in Portugal in August and quickly defeated General Junot and his troops. Only the negotiation of favourable surrender terms, which included a swift voyage back to France, mitigated the effect of the British triumph.

During the late summer and early autumn a false calm prevailed in the Peninsula. The insurgent armies were very slow to pursue Joseph, and when they reached the Ebro the initial result was only some indecisive manoeuvring and skirmishing. The French were content to wait for their reinforcements and otherwise put the time to use for training and repairing the effects of their retreat. On 7 September, Napoleon reorganised his Army of Spain into a reserve and six field corps, each commanded by one of his marshals. He then took advantage of the hiatus to organise and attend the celebrated conference at Erfurt which brought together all the crowned heads of Europe. There he made the diplomatic arrangements which freed him to focus on his planned onslaught against the Spanish insurgents. By late October he was back in Paris confidently addressing the Legislative Corps:

NAPOLEON AT SOMOSIERRA. PRINT AFTER HORACE VERNET.

'In a few days I will be leaving to place myself at the head of my army and, with the help of God, I will crown the King of Spain in Madrid and plant my Eagles over the forts of Lisbon.'[24] Soon afterwards the Spaniards launched an ill-advised offensive which was easily defeated by the French, but, except for a successful, though unauthorised, advance by Marshal François Joseph Lefebvre, they did not pursue their advantage because they were waiting for Napoleon. By the time he arrived at Bayonne on 3 November, he had formulated a plan of campaign which would sweep the enemy before him and was ready to put it into action. Less than a month later, the main Spanish armies had been routed at the battles of Gamonal, Espinosa, Tudela and Somosierra, and Napoleon was at the gates of Madrid.

In the long run, the ease with which Napoleon swept away the Spanish opposition was to have very serious negative consequences for the French, because it confirmed his contempt for Spanish military ability and made him forever after unsympathetic when the subordinates he left behind in the Peninsula had difficulties in dealing with threats from Spanish regular or guerrilla forces. In the short term, however, it gave Napoleon a remarkable opportunity to repair some of the damage which Bailén had inflicted on the new regime he was sponsoring. With his troops poised to assault the Spanish capital, Napoleon could have chosen to be magnanimous to both his brother and the Spanish people, by allowing Joseph to take the leading role in the forthcoming events and, perhaps, even to extend an amnesty to his misguided subjects who had temporarily forgotten their allegiance to him. Instead, Joseph was kept intentionally in the background while Madrid surrendered and Napoleon asserted his right of conquest to make any dispositions he saw fit. The last lines of Napoleon's proclamation of 7 December to the Spanish people suggest an ego inflated to dangerous proportions:

'I have destroyed everything which could stand in the way of your prosperity and grandeur; I have freed you from the shackles oppressing you; I have given you a liberal constitution and a moderate monarchy in place of an absolute monarchy ... But if all my efforts are in vain and you do not respond to the confidence I have placed in you, I will be forced to treat your country like a conquered province and place my brother on another throne. I will then put the crown of Spain on my own head and make the wicked respect me, because God has given me the strength and the will to surmount all obstacles.'[25]

Given such a clear statement that he would never be considered more than a lackey of the Emperor, Joseph made an effort to abdicate: 'I am shamed in the eyes of my supposed subjects. I beg Your Majesty to accept my renunci-ation of all the rights you have given me to the throne of Spain. I will always prefer honour and honesty to power so dearly bought.'[26] Napoleon merely brushed his brother's protests aside, and Joseph never pressed the point.

Following the surrender of Madrid, Napoleon clearly thought that the suc-cessful outcome of the campaign was a foregone conclusion, but he had momentarily forgotten one key piece of the Peninsular military puzzle – the British force under the command of Sir John Moore. While the Emperor made plans for easy marches of conquest to Cadiz and Lisbon, Moore moved boldly into Spain from Portugal and formulated a plan to strike at Marshal Soult's isolated corps. When news of this unexpected action reached Napoleon on 19 December he was galvanised into action and set nearly 80,000 troops in motion to trap and crush the army which his hated British enemy had so foolishly put within his reach. To do so, however, meant that he had to postpone other elements of his plans and put the French forces in central Spain on the defensive, giving the Spanish armies a much-needed breathing space.

Despite some heroic marching by the French, including a crossing of the Sierra de Guadarrama mountains in a blizzard, Moore managed to keep his small force out of the Emperor's reach. At the little town of Benavente, the British even managed to inflict an embarrassing skirmish defeat on the Mounted Chasseurs of the Imperial Guard, who lost their commander as a captive. Just after that incident, a more significant event occurred – Napoleon received firm news that the war faction in Austria was gaining the upper hand. The Emperor kept up the pursuit in person for another two days, but then withdrew to Valladolid, leaving Marshal Soult to complete the job of driving the British into the sea.

The prospect of war with Austria convinced Napoleon that he had to leave the Spain until that situation was resolved. It was obviously crucial for him to make appropriate and realistic arrangements for the completion of the recon-quest of the Peninsula in his absence. He was unable to do so, however, because he was labouring under two important misconceptions about the nature of the task that remained. First, he believed that organised Spanish resistance had already effectively ended so that only minor opposition would be encountered from the insurgents in the future – 'My business in Spain is finished.'[27] Second, he believed that the British would be very hesitant to send another force to Spain after the thrashing he had administered to Moore – 'The English escaped me by only a single march ... If even half of them make it to their ships (which I doubt), they will embark without horses or munitions and they will be well exhausted, demoralised and embarrassed.'[25] In light of these beliefs, it is not surprising that plans based on them were wholly unrealistic. Marshal Soult was given less than one month to march from Corunna and reconquer Lisbon, and that accomplishment was then to be the signal for Joseph to launch an invasion of Andalusia. The pacification of Valencia was scheduled to begin after Saragossa was retaken, an event Napoleon was certain would occur before the end of February.

Before his departure, Napoleon created one further handicap for the army he left behind – he failed to give it a leader. King Joseph was officially designated as the Emperor's deputy, but in practice his authority was undermined from the start by the lack of respect shown to him by his own brother. Moreover, Napoleon reinforced the insubordinate tendencies of the marshals commanding the various army corps by communicating orders directly to them and by authorising them to report in return directly to Marshal Berthier, and not to the King. As a last straw, he remained the source of all honours and compensation for meritorious service, so his subordinates were always more interested in his assessment of their actions rather than Joseph's.

Under the circumstances, it is perhaps surprising that the French armies in the Peninsula achieved as much as they did during the remainder of 1809, despite the defeat of Soult at Oporto and of Joseph himself at the battle of Talavera. In an overall sense, however, they were merely marking time, waiting for the conclusion of the war against Austria and the moment when Napoleon could turn his full attention to the situation in Spain. His presence would certainly have ended the squabbling among the various French commanders which paralysed efforts towards military co-operation and would probably have solved most of the morale problems caused by the growing isolation of the army in Spain. After his defeat of Austria, Napoleon dispatched large numbers of reinforcements to the Peninsula and even began to make concrete preparations to go there himself. But by the end of the year his attention had certainly wandered, perhaps in part because of the decisive French victories at the battles of Oçana (19 November) and Alba de Tormes (28 November), but more likely because of his preoccupation with divorcing Empress Josephine and finding a new Habsburg bride.

Joseph and Marshals Soult and Victor, for once acting in concert, took advantage of Wellington's inactivity in Portugal and Napoleon's distraction with domestic affairs to launch on their own an invasion of Andalusia which

JOSEPH, KING OF SPAIN. ENGRAVING BY L. RADOS AFTER J. B. BOSIO.

turned into the second most successful French operation of the war. Starting from Madrid in early January 1810, they rolled over the feeble opposition provided by the remaining forces of the insurgent government directing the Spanish war effort and flooded into southern Spain. It may be that history would have been changed if the French had been able to seize the island city of Cadiz in their initial offensive surge, but by the time the French forces had assembled near the city, this strategic site had received a garrison sufficient to protect it from all but the luckiest, or most determined, assault. This left the French no choice but to hazard a siege, but that effort was almost certainly doomed from the outset by British command of the sea. Troops and supplies could enter Cadiz at will and so it became the symbolic bastion of Spanish resistance and the impregnable home of the acting Spanish government.

Despite this ultimately serious setback, the conquest of Andalusia was a brilliant military achievement. But even as Joseph basked in the glow of a triumphal procession through his new territories, Napoleon took two more actions which helped to undermine French prospects for any further success in the Peninsula. First, on 8 February 1810, despite his promises to preserve the territorial integrity of the Kingdom ceded to him by Charles, Napoleon decreed the formation of four (later increased to six) military territories to be administered by French generals having exclusive military, civil and financial authority. By doing so, Napoleon hoped to make the war in Spain more financially self-sustaining for his treasury, but his flagrant disregard for Spanish sovereignty destroyed once and for all the credibility of the Bonaparte regime in Spain as an independent state. Moreover his diversion of Joseph's revenues into his own coffers pushed the new king's government irrevocably towards bankruptcy.

Second, in the course of 1810 Napoleon gave a formal blessing to the *de facto* decentralisation of military authority in Spain by reorganising the various corps of the Army of Spain into several regional armies, all of which received their orders directly from him and not from King Joseph.[30] This arrangement perpetuated the problems of divided command and of orders from the Emperor which were out of date before they were read by their recipients. The new armies of Portugal, Aragon, Catalonia, the North, the Centre and the '*Midi*', or South, together with the Imperial garrison troops of the military governments, totalled close to 270,000 men. However, these forces were rarely able to act in an effective co-operative fashion because of the self-interested behaviour of the French commanders and the increasing difficulty of concentrating large bodies of troops in a single geographic location without advance assembly of supplies on a scale which was usually beyond the scope of French logistical capabilities.

Napoleon's plan for the 1810 campaign of the French forces was strategically sound but generally unrealistic; he simply under-estimated the manifold problems which his commanders in the field would face in carrying it out. The most obvious strength of the plan was its focus on driving the British out of the Peninsula, a job which was entrusted to Marshal André Masséna, possibly the best general in the French army after Napoleon. The invasion of Portugal was handicapped from the start, however, because Napoleon neglected to organise any effective co-ordination between Masséna's movements and those of the other French armies, and because the French had no information about the impregnable fortifications which Sir Arthur Wellesley had created for the British around Lisbon. Masséna made some mistakes along the way, but it is doubtful that even Napoleon in person could have forced his way through the lines of Torres Vedras which stymied the French Army of Portugal. Elsewhere, the conquest and pacification of Catalonia, Aragon and Andalusia continued with overall success, but as long as the British Army remained intact and undefeated, this success could not be sustained. Meanwhile, the guerrilla movement continued to grow and to exact a steadily increasing physical, psychological and emotional toll from the French forces.

It is startling that a man of Napoleon's perspicacity could not recognise that many of the French problems were ones of his own making. His correspondence is replete with criticism of his Peninsula subordinates and disbelief about the way in which events constantly had an unexpected and unfavourable outcome, but only rarely could he see that these irritating results were the near inevitable result of the faulty system for running the war which he himself had created. One such moment of awareness occurred in late 1810 when he realised that Spanish affairs might require a political rather than a purely military solution. He therefore actually authorised Joseph to take affirmative steps to reach some accommodation with the 'rebel' government. He even told his brother that he would give up his territorial claims if it would bring peace: 'if ... the insurgents are really ready to enter into agreements [concerning the recognition of Joseph as king], His Majesty will consent to the integrity of Spain because it will free up the majority of his troops and finish a war which may yet still cost much [French] blood.'[31] The Spanish government was not receptive to this overture.

The situation in the Peninsula would almost certainly have improved if Napoleon had gone back to Spain and taken personal command of his armies there, but Napoleon the man continued to have more important matters to attend to. In 1810 he was occupied with his marriage to the young Austrian princess, Marie-Louise, and by the beginning of 1811 she was six months' pregnant, possibly carrying the male heir which had been the main objective of his remarriage exercise. The birth of his son in March 1811 raised again the theoretical possibility of a return to Spain, but there is no evidence that he ever seriously considered that option, perhaps because he feared the adverse consequences which could result if he went to Spain and was unable to bring about the decisive victory which would then be expected.

Napoleon instead continued to direct matters from afar. This would have been an unsatisfactory arrangement under the best of circumstances, but it became almost entirely unworkable as Spanish guerrilla activity disrupted the flow of communications. Napoleon was using out of date information to make military decisions which then became even more stale and, in some cases, even harmful because of the delay between the time they were made and the time they could be implemented.

An example of the latter situation is provided by the events of December 1811 to January 1812. Pleased with the successes of Marshal Louis Gabriel Suchet and his Army of Aragon on the eastern side of the Peninsula, Napoleon decided to strip troops away from the Army of Portugal to support an offensive by Suchet against the city of Valencia. As soon as Wellington became aware of this development, he was emboldened to attempt the siege of Ciudad Rodrigo, the key fortress guarding the northern border between Spain and Portugal. Marshal August Marmont's depleted army was not strong enough to attempt a relief expedition, and Wellington was consequently able to capture the town and, as a bonus, the entire French siege train which had been stored there for the winter. Meanwhile the detached troops had made such a late start because of delays in receipt and execution of orders that they were not a factor at all in Suchet's capture of Valencia.

Throughout these middle years of the Peninsular War, Napoleon continually had three broad options open to him to bring the struggle to an end: 1. he could seek to make peace with the Spaniards alone (which might include still another change of the Spanish monarch); 2. he could seek a military resolution of the war by pouring more men and resources into Spain, or 3. he could seek peace with Britain, which would either bring peace with the Spaniards in its wake or leave him free to deal with them from a position of overwhelming strength. Instead of pursuing any one of these with vigour, however, he tried all three, with varying degrees of enthusiasm, but never with an all-out effort to achieve success. In 1809, 1810 and 1811, this lack of focus was unfortunate, but not fatal. In 1812 it led the greatest soldier in history to commit the most basic of military mistakes – he committed himself intentionally to fighting a two-front war, with the two fronts separated by the full expanse of Europe.

Once Napoleon decided to go to war with Russia, the Peninsular War became unwinnable (at least until he had achieved a successful outcome against the Tsar Alexander). Nevertheless, it had certainly not become an inevitably losing proposition so long as the French developed a holding strategy which could be viable despite the diminishing number of French troops available to carry it out. In that regard, the year did not start well. In late January, Napoleon eliminated all possibility of reconciliation with the insurgents by formally annexing the province of Catalonia to France.[32] He then took the positive step of reconfirming Joseph as the commander in charge of all the armies in Spain, but he failed to take even the minimal precaution of sending a direct personal order to each army commander to obey his brother. Instead, the information about Joseph's new role was passed on to his erstwhile subordinates in a haphazard manner that effectively encouraged the army leaders to continue to ignore Joseph, and each other, as much as possible.[32] There was also no practical reorganisation of the command structure of the armies in Spain which would give this delegation some real teeth in so far as local command and control were concerned.

As for a substantive holding strategy, by a remarkable coincidence one had already been formulated by Marshal Jean-Baptiste Jourdan, the ageing hero of the French Revolutionary Wars who was now King Joseph's chief of staff.[34] By taking a common-sense look at the events of the preceding years, he realised that the British army under Wellington had been able to exert an influence on events in the Peninsula out of proportion to its actual size because it was relatively concentrated and relatively mobile. He equally realised that the French army lacked those attributes because it was committed to the task of holding an unrealistic amount of territory, an approach that negated its absolute superiority of numbers. These realisations led him in turn to the conclusion that it was absolutely essential for the French to create a mobile reserve to counter the British threat, even if that meant the French had to evacuate Andalusia voluntarily in order to free the Army of the South for field operations. 'Only disaster can result if things remain as they are and Lord Wellington marches with all his forces on either the Army of the South or the Army of Portugal.'[35]

Given what actually happened in 1812, Jourdan's analysis was unusually prophetic. However, even before it could be presented to the Emperor for consideration, Joseph received the last set of orders Napoleon had dictated for Spain before he turned his full attention to the invasion of Russia. They could not have been less helpful. Joseph was emphatically ordered to hold all the territory then under French control and he was even encouraged to seek to expand his geographic holdings if possible.[36] Given the character of Joseph, these orders removed all possibility of his following Jourdan's advice on his own responsibility. As Jourdan had predicted, when Wellington moved against Marshal Marmont during the summer, the French were unable to concentrate in time to prevent the Army of Portugal from suffering a catastrophic defeat at Salamanca. As if the wisdom of Jourdan's plan had not been clear enough at the outset, this defeat led to the invol- untary evacuation of Andalusia, and the resulting concentration of forces enabled the French to send Wellington packing back to Portugal.

The French success in the autumn of 1812 temporarily obscured the fact that a fundamental change had taken place in the balance of power in the Peninsula, but Wellington's spring offensive in 1813 quickly clarified that state of affairs. Napoleon was, by this time, preoccupied with trying to re- assert control of the military and political situation in central Europe, but he still found time to interfere in Spanish affairs in a manner detrimental to his own best interests. He had now become obsessed with the need to defeat the guerrilla bands which had grown into armies and which were wreaking havoc on his communications. He therefore sent order after order commit- ting significant elements of the French field armies to punitive expeditions within the occupied territories. In the event, they had only limited success against the guerrillas and some detachments had still not rejoined Joseph's main army before the battle of Vitoria was fought.

Disaster often brought out the best of Napoleon's genius , and so in the aftermath of Vitoria he moved quickly and decisively to stabilise the military situation in Spain. Marshal Soult, who had been briefly recalled to the *Grande Armée*, was swiftly sent back to the Peninsula with a mandate to disband the separate French armies and weld them into a single fighting force. Even then, however, Napoleon did not give him command over Suchet's Army of Aragon, so there was still an important lack of co-ordination in the French war effort. When Soult's attempts to re-take the offensive failed and he was even unable to prevent the British from pushing their way to the border of France and beyond, Napoleon decided that drastic political measures were also in order.

Napoleon's last-ditch gamble was patently unrealistic. What he optimistically proposed was a new treaty with the captive Ferdinand which would restore that prince to the throne of Spain and provide for the evacuation of all remaining French forces.[37] In return, Ferdinand was expected to enter into a new alliance with Napoleon and expel all the British troops from his soil. He was also offered the hand of Joseph's daughter in marriage, a gesture which accentuated the desperate situation of the French. After extensive negotiation Ferdinand signed the Treaty of Valençay (but rejected the proffered bride) in December 1813. It still had to be ratified by the acting government, however, and that body unanimously rejected it in February 1814. The Spaniards were not about to lose through diplomacy what the British, Portuguese and Spanish armies had won on the battlefield.

Of all the episodes of Napoleon's career, his entanglement in Spain is one of the least honourable and least successful, as well as one of the most tragic, because it could have been so easily avoided. Spain was an ally, not an enemy when Napoleon decided that the best interests of France required a change in its government. Assuming for the sake of argument that Napoleon's conclusion was valid, it is impossible to justify his related decision to pass over less drastic alternative ways of achieving that change and settle instead on a replacement of the Bourbon dynasty by one from his own family. Napoleon could certainly not have specifically foreseen that his decision would lead to a revolt of the entire population of Spain, or that the insurgent army would inflict a stunning defeat on his armies at Bailén, or that Britain would send an army to support its age-old Spanish enemy, or that the British Army would find a uniquely qualified general who would lead it to victory in the ensuing six years of campaigns, but his actions betray a complete indifference to consequences which could also be interpreted as evidence that Napoleon had reached a level of self-confidence in his decision-making close to megalomania. The only justification Napoleon himself ever put forward for his actions was that his ends would have justified his means if things had turned out differently:

'I admit that I started off on the wrong foot in this whole [Spanish] business. Its immorality must have seemed too patent, its injustice too cynical; the whole thing remains very ugly, since I lost out. For, having failed, my attempt is revealed in its hideous nakedness, stripped of all grandeur and of the many beneficial reforms I contemplated. And yet posterity would have commended my deed [the overthrow of the Bourbons] if it had succeeded, and rightly so, perhaps, on account of its great and happy results: such is the fate of things on this earth, and thus they are judged.'[38]

Because it failed, Napoleon's seizure and disposition of the Spanish throne brings to mind the famous epigram relating to his execution of the Duc d'Enghien: 'It was worse than a crime – it was a blunder.'[39] Napoleon was a man of such prodigious talents that the blunder was certainly remediable, but only if he were willing to admit past mistakes and able to recognise the geographic and physical limitations of what he could accomplish as a single human being. For Napoleon after Tilsit, that possibility did not exist.

NOTES

1. Las Cases, comte de. *Mémorial de Sainte-Hélène*, ed. G. Walter, 2 vols., Paris, 1956, Notes for 6 May 1816, vol. 1, p. 584.
2. The text of the Treaty of San Ildefonso is set out in John Hall Stewart, *A Documentary Survey of the French Revolution*, New York, 1951, Document 143, pp. 678–82.
3. The relationship among Charles, Luisa and Godoy is explained and put in perspective in the chapter entitled 'A Study in Decadence' in Gabriel Lovett, *Napoleon and the Birth of Modern Spain*, 2 vols., New York, 1965, vol. 1, pp. 1–46.
4. Méneval, C.-F. de. *Memoirs of Napoleon Bonaparte*, 3 vols., New York,1910, vol. 2, pp. 501–2.
5. The text of the Treaty of Fontainebleau can found in Charles Oman, *A History of the Peninsular War*, 7 vols., 1902–30, vol. 1, appendix 2.
6. Méneval, *op. cit.*, vol. 2, pp. 489–90, 499–500.
7. Lovett, *op. cit.*, vol. 1, p. 86.
8. Napoleon to Charles IV, 10 January 1808, in Napoleon, *Correspondance de Napoléon 1er*, 32 vols., Paris, 1864, No. 13443, vol. 16, p. 237.
9. Napoleon to Charles IV, 10 January 1808, *Correspondance*, vol. 16, No. 13444, p. 237.
10. Napoleon to Murat, 8 March 1808, *Correspondance*, vol. 17, p. 397.
11. Quoted in Glover, Michael. *The Legacy of Glory*, New York, 1971, p. 19.
12. Napoleon to Louis Bonaparte, 27 March 1808, *Correspondance* [no official number], vol. 16, p. 500.
13. Méneval, *op. cit.*, vol. 2, pp. 507–10. Some authorities, including Méneval, think that this document was a draft which was never sent to Murat, but the editors of Napoleon's *Correspondance* decided it was authentic and included it in their work: vol. 16, p. 450, n. 1.
14. Lovett, *op. cit.*, vol. 1, pp. 109–10.
15. Napoleon to Ferdinand, 16 April 1808, *Correspondance*, No. 13750, vol. 17, pp.10–12.
16. Napoleon to Charles IV, 29 April 1808, *Correspondance*, No. 13793, vol. 17, p. 17.
17. Napoleon to Joseph, 18 April 1808, *Correspondance*, No. 13763, vol. 17, pp. 23–5.
18. Las Cases, *op. cit.*, Notes of June 1816, vol. 1, p. 783.
19. Report to the Emperor, 24 April 1808, *Correspondance*, No. 13776, vol. 17, pp. 33–7.

20. The text of the abdication document is set out in Oman, *op. cit*, vol. 1, appendix VII, p. 617.
21. Napoleon to Joseph, 19 April 1808, *Correspondance*, No. 14218, vol. 17, p. 407.
22. Notes for General Savary, 13 July 1808, *Correspondance*, No. 14192, vol. 17, pp. 379-83.
23. Napoleon to Soult, 23 August 1808, *Lettres Inèdites de Napoléon Ier*, ed. Léon Lecestre, 2 vols., Paris, 1897, No. 341, vol. 1, pp. 234-5.
24. Speech, 25 October 1808, *Correspondance*, No. 14413, vol. 18, p. 21.
25. Proclamation to the Spanish People, 7 December 1808, *Correspondance*, No. 14537, vol. 18, pp. 103-4.
26. Joseph to Napoleon, 8 December 1808, *Mémoires et Correspondance Politique et Militaire du Roi Joseph*, ed. A. Ducasse,10 vols., Paris, 1854, vol. 5, p. 281; quoted in Glover, *op. cit.*, p. 66.
27. Napoleon to Jérôme, 16 January 1809, *Correspondance*, No. 14731, vol. 18, p. 237.
28. Napoleon to Caulaincourt, 14 January 1809, *Lettres Inédites*, No. 397, vol. 1, pp. 269-70.
29. Melito, comte A.-F. Miot de. *Mémoires*, 3 vols., Paris, 1873-4, vol. 3, p. 170; see also, Napoleon to Berthier, 8 February 1810, *Correspondance*, No. 16229, vol. 20, p. 195.
30. Jourdan, Marshal Jean-Baptiste. *Mémoires militaires du Maréchal Jourdan (Guerre d'Espagne)*, ed. Marshal Grouchy, Paris, nd, p. 301.
31. Napoleon to Champagny, 7 November 1810, *Correspondance*, No. 17111, vol. 21, p. 262.
32. Napoleon to Berthier, 25 January 1812, *Correspondance*, No. 18452, vol. 23, p. 186.
33. Napoleon to Berthier, 16 March 1812, *Correspondance*, No. 18583, vol. 23, pp. 313-14.
34. 'Mémoire sur les Armées d'Espagne', 28 May 1812, in Jourdan, *op. cit.*, pp. 386-94.
35. Ibid., p. 393.
36. Ibid., pp. 395-6.
37. This gambit of Napoleon's is described at length in Oman, op. cit., vol. 7, pp. 297-313.
38. Las Cases, *op. cit.*, Notes of June 1816, vol. 1, p. 785, as translated in J. Christopher Herold (ed.), *The Mind of Napoleon*, New York, 1965, p. 278.
39. This epigram is ordinarily attributed either to Talleyrand or to Fouché, but according to *Bartlett's Familiar Quotations*, 14th edn., 1968, it was uttered by Antoine Boulay de la Meurthe.

BIBLIOGRAPHY

Bonaparte, Joseph. *Mémoires et Correspondance politiques et militaires du Roi Joseph*, ed. A Ducasse, 10 vols., Paris, 1854.
Bonaparte, Napoleon. *Correspondance de Napoléon 1er*, 32 vols., Paris, 1854.
Glover, Michael. *The Legacy of Glory*, New York, 1971.
Jourdan, Jean-Baptiste. *Mémoires militaires du Maréchal Jourdan (Guerre d'Espagne)*, ed. vicomte Grouchy, Paris, nd.
Las Cases, comte de. *Mémorial de Sainte-Hélène*, ed. G. Walter, 2 vols., Paris, 1956.
Lovett, Gabriel. *Napoleon and the Birth of Modern Spain*, 2 vols., New York, 1965.
Méneval, C.-F. de. *Memoirs of Napoleon Bonaparte*, 3 vols., New York, 1910.
Oman, Sir Charles. *A History of the Peninsular War*, 7 vols., Oxford, 1902-30.

THE RUSSIAN CAMPAIGN:
A REPUTATION DAMAGED
Philip J. Haythornthwaite

AT THE MID-POINT OF THE YEAR 1812 NAPOLEON'S MILITARY strength was at its peak, his army the greatest to have been seen in Europe for many centuries. To the world at large and even among his enemies, it appeared that he was following the same path as he had trodden before, the combination of personal military skill and splendid army producing victory against all odds and regardless of the opposition. The British *Royal Military Chronicle*, in the issue published when Napoleon's success in the 1812 campaign had reached its zenith, could only explain his triumphs in terms of his being the instrument of Divine providence:

'It is unmanly to deceive ourselves with false hopes. The Battle of Borodino, and the consequent occupation of Moscow, will be followed up by tremendous consequences. Where, indeed, will the successes of this man end? Let no one, however, entertain a doubt, but that all eventually will be right. Buonaparte has been here (as most probably in all his other successes), the agent and instrument of a Power, who for his own wise purposes leads him by the hand; and allows him the use and enjoyment of a temporal prosperity, as one of the incidental consequences concurring with his own ultimate designs. The temporal exaltation of an agent of this kind, and the seeming consequent irregularity in the economy of rewards and punishments, cannot be brought into comparison with the good of the general purpose. The felicity and glory are personal, they are those of the man and the individual, whilst the good wrought through his instrumentality, is perhaps a change in the whole system of the world; the regeneration of those principles and elements, upon which society stands, and by which it is held together. No one can lament, more than ourselves, that the talents of this man are so miserably abused, to the destruction, rather than to the benefit, of the human race; but, it is in the highest degree absurd, it is even vulgar and low-minded, to deny that he really possesses them, and to conceal from ourselves what he really is. He is a man of most magnificent mind.'[1]

No doubt the readers of this passage, with all its grudging praise, would have been relieved had they known that by the time it was published, not

TSAR ALEXANDER I. ENGRAVING BY T. W. HARLAND AFTER BOLK.

only was success in the campaign slipping from Napoleon's grasp, but that his decline had already begun.

Following the victory over Austria in 1809, Napoleon was engaged personally in no further campaigning until 1812; he did not return to the Iberian peninsula, where his war was being carried on by his marshals. France and Russia had been at peace since the signing of the Treaty of Tilsit in July 1807, but at least as far as the Russians were concerned, it was an uneasy peace. The breakdown of the Treaty was a gradual affair, with tension increasing until war was inevitable. Certainly Russia resented the imposition of peace, made in the aftermath of French victory, while Napoleon realised that Tsar Alexander was not prepared to remain subservient. Russia became increasingly uneasy about the Grand Duchy of Warsaw, created and supported by France; there were suspicions of French intrigue in the Balkans against Russia's interests; the appointment of Bernadotte as Crown Prince of Sweden suggested that Russia was being surrounded by enemies sympathetic to France (though in fact it was towards Napoleon that Bernadotte would prove hostile); and the Tsar felt personally affronted by Napoleon's seizure of the lands of the Duke of Oldenburg, who had married the Tsar's sister. Britain's continuing hostility towards Napoleon was also a catalyst in the change from peace to war. Russian evasion of the 'Continental System' (Napoleon's attempt to cripple British trade by denying it access to European markets) presented Napoleon with an increased challenge from Russia; and Britain, currently bereft of allies in Europe save those of the Iberian peninsula, was always ready to support any nation which exhibited hostility towards France.

Franco-Russian tension increased as the Tsar became increasingly less compliant; in April 1812 he was sufficiently bold as to suggest that he might address Napoleon's economic grievances in exchange for a French evacuation of Prussia, compensation for the Duke of Oldenburg and the creation of a neutral zone between the French and Russian empires. To none of these could Napoleon have been expected to accede; so to strengthen his military position the Tsar negotiated Bernadotte's neutrality and concluded a cessation of hostilities with the Turkish Empire, thus releasing Russian resources to meet any French threat. Russia's diplomatic efforts culminated in an alliance with Britain, although this was only cemented after the opening of hostilities with France.

It was not the Tsar who initiated hostilities, however; indeed, despite what appears to have been Napoleon's belief, he was probably anxious to resolve differences by other means, but was prepared for a military trial of strength if necessary. The ultimate responsibility for the Russian war lies with Napoleon, although he later professed to have been an unwilling participant. His pronouncements from exile on St. Helena are hardly a reliable guide to what had actually happened – for example, he once remarked that he had triumphed at Waterloo, only to be thrown down again, and claimed that in relation to 1812, 'to annul with a word every charge that can be brought against me, I may say that this famous war, this bold enterprise, was perfectly involuntary on my part. I did not wish to fight; neither did Alexander; but being once in presence, circumstances urged us on, and fate accomplished the rest.'[2] He also claimed that the campaign 'should have been the most popular of any in modern times. It was a war of good sense and true interests; a war for the repose and security of all ... I had no wish to obtain any new acquisition; and I reserved for myself only the glory of

NAPOLEON WATCHES THE *GRANDE ARMÉE* CROSSING THE NIEMEN TO LAUNCH
THE 1812 CAMPAIGN. PRINT AFTER J. GIRODET.

doing good, and the blessings of posterity ... l never acted more disinterest-edly, and never better merited success';[3] and that had it been successful, his reorganisation of Europe would have been complete, with himself 'the ark of the old and the new covenant, the natural mediator between the old and the new order of things'.[4]

Whatever the truth of such assertions, Napoleon *did* initiate the 1812 campaign, though it was true that conquest of territory was not his aim; by launching an invasion of such power to enable him to overcome any pre-dictable resistance, he intended to force the Tsar to make peace upon French terms, after smashing the Russian field army. Historically, the omens for his task were not propitious: Sigismund III of Poland had captured Moscow in 1610, only to have his garrison massacred in 1612, and an inva-sion of Russia had been the downfall of Charles XII of Sweden in 1709. Nevertheless, although negotiations continued until the outbreak of war, Napoleon assembled a host which fully deserved its title of *la Grande Armée*, both in size and from its multi-national composition. Its troops came from all the territories under French control – the Empire itself had recently been extended to incorporate the Netherlands – and from those states which owed allegiance to Napoleon, including the two principal Italian states (the Kingdom of Italy, whose sovereign was Napoleon himself, and Naples, ruled by his brother-in-law Joachim Murat), and the mass of German states which formed the Confederation of the Rhine (*Rheinbund*). Contingents came from as far afield as Portugal and Spain (troops from the latter drawn from supporters of Joseph Bonaparte as King of Spain) and the Balkans. Some of the non-French elements of the *Grande Armée* might not have been enthusiastic at the prospect of campaigning against Russia, but despite any lack of political conviction, most of the German contingents were composed of reliable soldiers, while the Poles of the Grand Duchy of Warsaw forces probably regarded with enthusiasm the prospect of engaging their traditional enemy. In general, it was not the calibre of the individual members of the *Grande Armée* that was a primary cause of the failure of the expedition, but rather the situations in which they were placed.

Napoleon organised his immense force into three principal formations, plus supports. The main army under his own command comprised the Imperial Guard and three *corps d'armée*: I, under Davout, almost all French; II, under Oudinot, mostly French but with one largely Swiss division; III, under Ney, two divisions mostly French and one of Württembergers. This army was accompanied by the I and II Corps of reserve cavalry under

Nansouty and Montbrun respectively, mostly French but I having one Polish brigade and II one Polish and one Prussian. The total strength of Napoleon's own army was about 217,000. To provide immediate support, two additional armies were formed, commanded by Napoleon's stepson Eugène de Beauharnais, Viceroy of Italy, and Napoleon's brother Jérôme, King of Westphalia. Eugène's Army of Italy comprised his own IV Corps (two divisions primarily French, one Italian), Gouvion Saint-Cyr's Bavarian VI Corps, and Grouchy's III Cavalry Corps (French but for one Bavarian-Saxon brigade); total strength was about 80,000. Jérôme's army comprised his own Westphalian VIII Corps, Poniatowski's Polish V Corps, Reynier's Saxon VII Corps, and Latour-Maubourg's IV Cavalry Corps of one Polish and one Saxon-Polish-Westphalian division; in all about 79,000 strong. The flanks of this main body were protected by two allied contingents: on the left flank, Macdonald's X Corps, about 32,000 strong, mainly Prussian with a division of Polish, Bavarian and Westphalian troops; and on the right flank Schwarzenberg's Austrian reserve corps, about 34,000 strong. This immense force, more than 440,000 in number, was supported by a second line intended to serve as a source of replacements, including Victor's IX Corps (one French division and two composed of Polish and various *Rheinbund* contingents), and Augereau's XI Corps (various French and *Rheinbund* units, and a division of Neapolitans). The total of these and the various supporting formations and garrisons was about 225,000 men.

This mighty army was the largest that Napoleon had ever led, and indeed its very size was one of its shortcomings; such a host was impossible for one

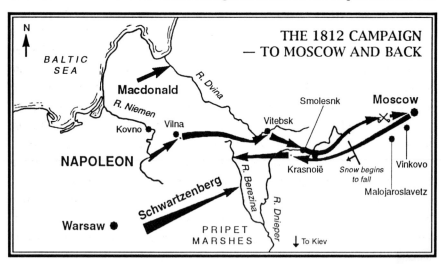

man to command in person, and thus Napoleon had to rely on the some-times dubious skills of his subordinates to put into practice the directions he issued. The fact that few of his subordinates had ever been allowed to exercise much initiative in independent command compounded the diffi-culties of scale and distance. An additional problem lay in the need to sup-ply so great a host; the traditional 'living off the land' of the French armies early in the period had proved not to work adequately, so an enormous sys-tem of supply depots and transportation had to be organised. This might have been the most complex system that Napoleon had yet managed, but when put to the test it was found wanting, so that hunger, disease and the failure to provide protective clothing against the Russian winter caused more damage to the army than did the enemy.

Nevertheless it was with high spirits and higher expectations that the campaign began, following the final attempts at negotiation which probably neither side expected to succeed. Napoleon's plan was aimed as usual at the destruction of the enemy field army, and two principal Russian forces cov-ered the border across which the invasion would be mounted. In the north was the 'First West Army' of the Russian minister of war, Mikhail Barclay de Tolly, about 127,000 strong; and farther south the 'Second West Army', 48,000 strong or more, under Peter Bagration, whose dislike of Barclay as a 'foreigner' (he was a Livonian of Scots-German ancestry) served to compli-cate relations and co-operation between the two. Covering the Russian left flank, south of the Pripet marshes, was Tormassov's 'Third West Army', still assembling, about 45,000 strong, and other forces included Admiral Pavel Tchitchakov's 35,000-strong Army of the Danube, marching northwards.

Napoleon's initial intention was deliver a rapid and devastating blow to wreck much of the Russian army. He intended to demonstrate to the south of the area of main operations, to persuade the Russians to concentrate against the perceived threat, while his own main army penetrated deep into Russian territory and concentrated around Vilna, and then while holding back his own right wing, to execute a giant wheel to the right, enveloping the Russians and assailing their flank and rear, compelling them to fight on his terms. His plans were not fixed unalterably, for other options were open; but this bold scheme he believed could result in complete success, in as few as twenty days after the initiation of hostilities. That it did not succeed was due partly to the scale of the operation, too great even for Napoleon to over-see in all necessary details, and partly to the behaviour of the Russians who did not react as expected.

The leading elements of the *Grande Armée* crossed the River Niemen into Russian territory on 23 June 1812. The advance was somewhat slower than Napoleon's usual speed of operations, partly because of the huge quantity of baggage and supplies accompanying the army, and partly as a consequence of unusual caution on the part of the commander; from the very beginning the restricted mobility of the army had begun to frustrate his planning. Equally frustrating was the Russian refusal to be trapped by overwhelming forces, Barclay retiring in front of Napoleon and Bagration before Davout and Jérôme. An attempt to trap Bagration came to nothing when Davout (as authorised) attempted to take command of Jérôme's corps to accomplish the movement; Jérôme, who had not been informed of Davout's authority, was so incensed that he departed for Westphalia, leaving his command without orders, and thus Bagration escaped. A further opportunity to engage the Russians occurred some days later (26 July) when it appeared that Barclay was preparing to fight at Vitebsk. Napoleon declined to attack immediately to allow more of his troops to come up; by the time he ordered the advance (28 July) he discovered that Barclay, having learned that Davout was still interposed between himself and Bagration, thus depriving him of support, had resumed his retreat.

Instead, Barclay retired on Smolensk, to which city Bagration also directed his march; the union of the two Russian armies was a considerable reverse for Napoleon who expected that they could have been kept apart and defeated in turn; the failings in the *Grande Armée*'s system of command and mobility had squandered a promising position. Napoleon now planned a great enveloping movement aimed at cutting the route from Smolensk to Moscow, forcing Barclay to fight; but this also miscarried when Murat, commanding the cavalry, was halted on 14 August by a small Russian force (9,500 strong) under General Neverovski at Krasnoïë, southwest of Smolensk, Murat making piecemeal cavalry attacks which permitted the Russians to hold their ground and then retire on Smolensk. Somewhat surprisingly Napoleon now halted his march for a day to regroup; this gave the Russians time to escape from the intended trap, and to garrison Smolensk with General Raevski's corps. Napoleon then chose not to manoeuvre the Russians out of the position, which was probably what Barclay most feared, but to make a frontal attack on the city. For two days (16–17 August) the Russians held out, until Barclay ordered a withdrawal; the attacks on Smolensk had achieved nothing for Napoleon except a loss of about 10,000 men (the Russians lost slightly more). An attempt to

ON THE MARCH IN RUSSIA, 1812: PINO'S DIVISION OF EUGÈNE'S IV CORPS.
PRINT AFTER ALBRECHT ADAM.

engage Barclay as he withdrew failed because of the slow progress and ignoring of orders by General Andoche Junot, Jérôme's successor in command of VIII Corps.

While these operations were proceeding on the main battle-front, the *Grande Armée*'s flanking forces were engaged in holding off Russian forces to the north and south; in the north, Oudinot and Gouvion Saint-Cyr held their flank against General Ludwig Wittgenstein's troops, while to the south Reynier, with the assistance of Schwarzenberg's Austrians, kept Tormassov's Third West Army in check.

Napoleon had to re-assess his situation following the capture of Smolensk. Having failed to bring about the decisive battle he desired, his choice was either to consolidate at Smolensk, even if that meant waiting until spring for a renewal of the campaign, or follow the retreating Russians in the direction of Moscow, with all the implications for the stretching of the *Grande Armée*'s supply lines. The former option was contrary to Napoleon's original intentions for the campaign, but the latter was fraught with hazard. Even at this stage of the campaign, the hit-and-run tactics of the Cossacks had proved capable of disrupting the *Grande Armée*'s routine to a degree

KUTUSOV. ENGRAVING AFTER R. KER PORTER.

out of all proportion to the military threat they posed: fear of the Cossacks exerted a malign influence over the confidence of Napoleon's troops, and their threat, real and imagined, would increase as the lines of communication stretched ever farther.

The degree to which the Russians deliberately lured Napoleon onwards is uncertain; probably there was no fixed plan, the manoeuvres of the Russians being determined by circumstances, but whatever the case, it proved hugely destructive to his cause. In addition to battle casualties, the *Grande Armée* had been weakened considerably by sickness and the loss of cavalry and draught horses, and every step eastwards produced further losses. Nevertheless the Russian position was regarded as sufficiently perilous for the Tsar to recall a commander whom he openly disliked, the old, fat and somewhat immobile General Mikhail Kutusov, to succeed Barclay in overall command and redress the worst consequences of the Barclay-Bagration antipathy. Shrewd, experienced and popular with his soldiers, Kutusov assumed command of the combined Russian forces on 29 August.

But before then Napoleon had decided to resume his advance. In retrospect it seems a great gamble; but at the time there were good reasons for it. Although he could have rebuilt and re-equipped his army while wintering in Smolensk, so too could the Tsar, and there might have been political consequences arising from such a delay: the Prussian and Austrian regimes, though both contributing troops to the *Grande Armée*, were at best lukewarm in their support of Napoleon, and the delay of a season might well convince them that his star was sinking, allowing their old animosities to supplant French power as the determining factor for their present conduct. Furthermore, even though the Russians had avoided battle so far, Napoleon believed that they would have to make a stand somewhere before Moscow, 280 miles to the east, giving him the opportunity he desired to execute the crushing blow which would force the Tsar to concede defeat. Consequently, on 25 August the *Grande Armée* resumed its march deeper into enemy territory. It proved hostile in more ways than one: food and fodder were destroyed by the Russians to deny them to the *Grande Armée*, and the Russian population was as implacably hostile to the invaders as were the people of occupied Spain. Napoleon's army was still mighty, but the force he led to Moscow was nothing like the 'paper' strength which he had deployed at the beginning of the campaign: he left Smolensk with some 156,000 men and 587 guns. In four weeks, he said, they would be in Moscow, and in six would have peace, on terms he would dictate.

For once in the campaign, Napoleon's wish was turned into reality, at least as far as the opportunity of battle was concerned. Kutusov established a defensive position on a ridge near the little town of Borodino, on the River Moskowa, about two-thirds of the way between Smolensk and Moscow. The position was strengthened by fieldworks erected by the Russian engineers, but their strength of more than 120,000 men was inferior to the approximately 130,000 Napoleon had available for the battle; but they had a superiority in artillery, some 640 guns. One of the fieldworks, the Shevardino Redoubt (named after the village near which it was situated), was too far in advance of the main position to be sustainable; but it gave the *Grande Armée* a taste of what they might expect if they were to attack Kutusov's main position.

Napoleon arrived in the vicinity of Borodino on 5 September, and as the redoubt would hinder both a frontal attack, or a flanking movement against the Russian left wing where their position was weakest, an assault was delivered which captured Shevardino. A Russian counter-attack re-possessed it, but a renewed assault succeeded and the Russians retired to their main position after a fierce struggle. Both sides spent the following day preparing for the expected battle, but the inaction of the *Grande Armée* may have been in part thanks to the indisposition of its commander. Ill health had afflicted Napoleon at times, and was especially inconvenient at such moments, when the activity of his previous campaigns was required; with command centred so crucially on his own person, any illness or lethargy could prove critical. (In this case, at least according the Philippe de Ségur, Napoleon was suffering from a dry cough and great thirst, the assuaging of which complicated the recurrence of an old complaint, the retention of urine. Ségur's classic account of the 1812 campaign, written with the authority of one who served in it as a general, was held by pro-Bonapartists to be unduly critical of Napoleon, to the extent that Ségur even fought a duel with General Gourgaud, so should be treated with some caution).

Napoleon had a number of options for the impending battle. The most audacious plan was proposed by Davout: that he take his own corps and that of Poniatowski, and make a circuitous march around the Russian left flank, to fall upon their rear early next morning, while Napoleon occupied the Russians with a frontal attack. The plan was declined, and when Davout persisted, 'Napoleon, impatient of contradiction, sharply replied with this exclamation, "Ah! You are always for turning the enemy; it is too dangerous a manoeuvre!" The Marshal, after this rebuff, said no more: he then returned to his post, murmuring against a prudence which he thought unseasonable, and to which he was not accustomed; and he knew not to what cause to attribute it, unless the looks of so many allies, who were not to be relied on, an army so reduced, a position so remote, and age, had rendered Napoleon less enterprising than he was'; at least, according to Ségur.[5] A decline in Napoleon's spirit of enterprise is not the only reason which might be advanced for his rejection of this potentially successful manoeuvre. Dividing his army, when faced with an enemy of approximate parity in numbers, might have been unduly hazardous; his troops were tired, which might have slowed Davout's speed of march; and the appearance of a French force in their rear could have had one of two effects on the Russians: they might have ignored it and still stood and fought, or they might have retired again, thus again depriving Napoleon of the decisive battle which he had so long sought. Neither of these might have been worth the risk of an elaborate flanking manoeuvre.

By declining such a tactic, however, Napoleon committed his army to a brutal frontal assault upon an enemy intent on holding firm at all costs. Early on the morning of 7 September he issued a proclamation to the army, of fairly typical rhetoric, and which Ségur described as 'simple, grave, and frank ... This harangue will some day be deemed admirable: it was worthy of the commander and of the army; it did honour to both'; and, wrote Ségur, it mentioned glory, 'the only passion to which he could appeal in these deserts: "Soldiers! Here is the battle which you have so ardently desired. The victory will now depend upon yourselves; it is needful for us; it will give us abundance, good winter-quarters, and a speedy return home! Behave as you did at Austerlitz, at Friedland, at Vitebsk, and at Smolensk, and afford to remotest posterity occasion to cite your conduct on that day: let it be said of you, 'He was in that great battle under the walls of Moscow.'"'[6]

The battle which began at 6 a.m. on 7 September was what the Duke of Wellington would have described as a 'pounding match'; though it was more than just a frontal assault by the *Grande Armée*, in that Napoleon planned a tactical outflanking movement against the Russian left (on the battlefield, not the flank-march envisaged by Davout), conducted by Poniatowski's V Corps, and to concentrate the army's efforts against the centre and left centre of the Russian position; but otherwise Borodino was largely a series of attempts to batter in the Russian line, an attritional contest enormously costly to both sides. If Kutusov remained largely immobile during the action, trusting Barclay and Bagration to conduct the tactical battle, Napoleon also appeared rather ill and weary, lacking the fire which he had been wont to exhibit of old. The troops of both sides were slaughtered in enormous numbers, and their commanders as well: Bagration received a mortal wound, Montbrun was killed by a shell-splinter, and General Auguste de Caulaincourt, an Imperial aide and brother of Napoleon's Master of the Horse, was killed leading the cavalry charge which finally drove the Russians from the 'Great Redoubt' in the centre of their position. This penetration of the Russian line brought forth one of a number of calls throughout the day for Napoleon to commit his last reserve, the Imperial Guard, to deliver the *coup de grâce*. Conscious that he was in a hostile land, far from support, he refused: 'And if there should be another battle tomorrow, where is my army?'[7]

This caution – perhaps unusual considering Napoleon's earlier campaigns – ensured that Borodino would not produce the decisive result that he had sought; but given the circumstances it was an understandable decision. By evening, although the Russians had given ground along their front, and had

NAPOLEON AMID THE RUINS OF MOSCOW. PRINT AFTER ALBRECHT ADAM.

suffered the same prolonged butchery that had devastated the *Grande Armée*, the survivors of their gallant regiments still held firm. The battle subsided from sheer exhaustion, and Kutusov began to withdraw. Estimates of the casualties ranged from about 44,000 Russians to between 30,000 and 50,000 of the *Grande Armée*; and no decision had been reached. The appearance of the battlefield was enough to chill even the most hardened campaigner; one remarked that there appeared to be more dead than living, and so thickly was the field strewn with casualties that only with difficulty was Napoleon able to pick his way among the heaps of slain and wounded. During this melancholy tour of the field, one of the horses of Napoleon's staff trod upon a wounded man, who cried out; Napoleon's emotions, which had remained impassive throughout the day, broke out as he reprimanded the rider and showed concern for the unfortunate who had been stepped upon. One of the staff remarked that it was only a Russian, whereupon Napoleon rejoined angrily, 'After a victory there are no enemies, but only men!'[8]

Kutusov extricated a sizeable part of his army in good order, and was soon increased in strength as stragglers rejoined and reinforcements arrived; but on 13 September he announced that he would not fight again before Moscow, and abandoned it to the enemy, remarking that the loss of the city did not signify the loss of Russia, and that his concern was for the preservation of the army. There was no pursuit after the battle, the *Grande Armée* being in no state to mount anything so energetic; rather, they followed the Russians and duly entered Moscow late on 14 September. They found the city almost deserted, evacuated on the orders of Governor Rostopchin. The French and their allies had little chance to settle in to their new quarters before much of the city was burned, parts perhaps by accident but others upon the orders of Rostopchin, the very ultimate in the 'scorched earth' policy designed to deny the invaders any supplies or fodder. Enough of the city remained inhabitable, however, to accommodate the 95,000 survivors of the *Grande Armée*, and it was this fact which proved more decisive than the burning of the rest.

Having defeated the Russian army (as he saw it), and captured Moscow, Napoleon was convinced that the Tsar would make peace; so he remained there with his army as the days drew into weeks and the season began to change, awaiting the expected response to his attempts at negotiation. The Tsar, however, remained impassive, as every day brought a strengthening of the Russian position and a weakening of that of the *Grande Armée*. Napoleon can be criticised for remaining so long in Moscow, as his strategic and logistical position deteriorated, but in fairness he was faced with a difficult choice: unless the Russians came to terms, he could either stay there until the spring, an option fraught with difficulty, the length of his supply-lines being a major concern, and probably indefensible against a major Russian effort; he could winter somewhere else in Russia, perhaps at Smolensk or to the south around Kiev, which would present similar problems; he could attempt another battle, but there was no guarantee that the Russians would fight, and in any case his own troops were tired and in need of reinforcement; or he could retreat, which would be an admission of failure. While Napoleon considered, and awaited the expected reply from the Tsar, winter drew closer and his position became ever more parlous. His inactivity was seen by some as indecision, and he was criticised for his attitude to the *Grande Armée*'s situation. Montesquiou Fezensac, who had recently taken command of the 4th Line following the death of its previous colonel (Massy) at Borodino, was one who believed that Napoleon did not appreciate the true difficulty of the situation, and that the orders he issued were contradictory or unrealistic, especially concerning the lack of supplies and horses: 'Napoleon would see nothing – would hear nothing; and his generals only received the most extraordinary orders in answer to their remonstrances'.[9]

After much understandable hesitation, and following the return of a second unsuccessful diplomatic mission to the Tsar, Napoleon was forced to admit that his situation in Moscow was untenable; he decided to retire upon the now well-stocked depots at Smolensk, not by the route originally taken but by swinging south, into territory not yet eaten bare by his army, even if this meant another pitched battle with Kutusov. During the abortive attempts at negotiation, an unofficial truce had existed; but on 18 October, the day on which Napoleon decided upon his course of action, Kutusov surprised and cut-up some of Murat's cavalry at Vinkovo.

On 19 October Napoleon left Moscow at the head of his army, the 95,000-strong force swollen to unmanageable proportions by a train of wagons bearing all the movable booty that could be carried away from the unburned sector of Moscow, which disordered the line of march and severely slowed its progress. Napoleon headed south, intending to make a sweeping manoeuvre to approach Smolensk from that direction, and to garner the resources of the unspoiled country through which they would pass; but on 24 October the vanguard, Eugène's IV Corps, was halted and engaged by part of Kutusov's army at Malojaroslavets. The position was contested fiercely, the Russians retiring when Napoleon came up with the remainder of the army, but though he was left in possession of the field, he suffered a strategic defeat; or allowed himself to be defeated, for Kutusov had ordered that he should not be engaged again if the advance proceeded. Instead, Napoleon waited a day to re-organise, was almost captured or killed by Cossacks when reconnoitring on 25 October, and then decided to abandon his plan for a southern sweep, choosing instead to withdraw to Smolensk by the route over which the army had marched to Moscow, over a terrain stripped bare. This decision may have marked the most crucial point in the campaign; indeed, perhaps in Napoleon's career.

RETREAT FROM MOSCOW. PRINT AFTER CHARLET.

From this point, the retreat from Moscow can be said to have begun in earnest, involving a process of unremitting and increasing torment as the *Grande Armée* disintegrated; slowly at first, and then – chaos. The Russians held back from a full-scale attack, though in addition to constant hit-and-run raids by Cossacks, supplemented by 'flying columns' of hussars and a vengeful peasantry that missed no opportunity to butcher helpless stragglers, some telling blows were delivered against the main body of the *Grande Armée*, notably against Davout's I Corps near Viasma on 3 November. On this occasion Eugène was able to provide reinforcements, and no further serious attempt was made to divide the retreating army; perhaps Kutusov realised that it was easier to harass it and let it disintegrate from exhaustion, than suffer the inevitable casualties of a major battle. Elsewhere, however, Russian forces were more threatening. In the north Wittgenstein's command was pressing against the northern boundary of the

NAPOLEON INTERROGATES RUSSIAN PEASANTS DURING THE RETREAT FROM MOSCOW. PRINT AFTER VERESCHAGIN.

128

Grande Armée's sphere of operations, requiring Victor's IX Corps (intended as a general reserve) to support Saint-Cyr; and in the south, Tchitchakov's Russians were pressing northwards. If these forces were not held in check, they could unite and block Napoleon's path home.

Such strategic considerations would probably have been lost upon the diminishing army trudging wearily westwards, for their concern was reduced to the most basic matter of survival. Exhaustion and starvation were trials severe enough, but after the first snowfall on 5 November cold made the situation many times worse. The combination of these factors, plus the harassment of the Cossacks, destroyed the army as discipline broke down and much of the army was transformed into a mass of fugitives, each one intent only on procuring enough food to prolong the agony of life for another day, or to secure warm clothing to survive the falling temperatures. To achieve these objectives, the plight of comrades, women and children was ignored, the weak were killed for morsels of food, the dying stripped for scraps of clothing. All the horrors imaginable became reality on this dreadful march of death; and yet there remained contingents of stalwart men who clung around their Colours, maintaining discipline enough to prevent the wholesale massacre of the crowd of fugitives and camp-followers by the marauding Cossacks and their assistants. Ney and the remnant of his corps won immortal fame in forming the rearguard.

Had these been the only troops available to Napoleon, the converging forces of Wittgenstein and Tchitchakov, intent on uniting to hold the line of the River Berezina over which the *Grande Armée* would have to pass, would have brought about the total annihilation of the Moscow army; but as Napoleon fell back he encountered the forces which had been holding his rear areas, principally the corps of Oudinot and Victor. The reaction of these units to the sight of the shambling mass of scarecrows coming back from Moscow serves to exemplify the plight of Napoleon's troops: 'a train of spectres covered with rags, with female pelisses, pieces of carpet, or dirty cloaks, half burnt and holed by the fires, with nothing on their feet but rags of all sorts ... faces black with dirt and hideously bristly beards, unarmed, shameless, marching confusedly, with their heads bent, their eyes fixed on the ground, and silent, like a troop of captives. But what astonished them more than all, was to see the number of colonels and generals scattered about and isolated, who seemed only occupied about themselves, and to think of nothing but saving the wrecks of their property, or their persons; they were marching pell-mell with the soldiers, who did not notice them, to whom they had no longer any commands to give, and of whom they had nothing to expect, all ties between them being broken, and all ranks effaced by the common misery. The soldiers of Victor and Oudinot could not believe their eyes.'[10]

The stores at Smolensk did not provide the expected succour, the vanguard having devoured them and left nothing for the rest; every yard of the route was marked by the bodies of those who had died from malnutrition, cold or exhaustion. A Russian attack was beaten off at Krasnoïe, and in late November Napoleon arrived at the Berezina, to find his way barred. The advance elements of Tchitchakov's army which had seized the crossing were eventually driven off, but not before they had destroyed the bridge across the river: Napoleon was marooned on the far bank. For all the destruction caused by the severity of the weather, it was

CROSSING THE BEREZINA; RETREAT FROM MOSCOW. PRINT AFTER RAFFET.

perhaps the mildness of the early winter which proved crucial, conceivably persuading Napoleon to tarry longer than he ought in Moscow, and now, although the weather remained bitter for the half-starved fugitives, it was not so cold as to freeze the Berezina sufficiently to allow the army to cross on the ice. Expecting colder weather, Napoleon had ordered the army's pontoon train to be burned some way back on the road from Moscow, convinced that it would not be needed. The army's saviour now proved to be the commander of the pontoon train, General Jean-Baptiste Eblé, who on his own initiative had preserved two forges, charcoal and sufficient tools to permit his engineers to construct two ramshackle bridges over the Berezina. Heroically, with efforts almost superhuman, and despite the frequent breakdown of the bridges, the pontoneers kept the pathway to safety open sufficiently for most of the survivors of the *Grande Armée* to cross, while Victor and Oudinot, aided by the few elements of Napoleon's force still capable of organised resistance, kept at bay the converging armies of Wittgenstein and Tchitchakov. On the morning of 29 November, to hinder Russian pursuit, Eblé was ordered to destroy the bridges, marooning on the far bank many thousands of fugitives. Those elements of the *Grande Armée* least affected by the retreat from Moscow, Oudinot's II and Victor's IX Corps, lost probably more than half their number in the fighting around the Berezina crossing; the mighty army was destroyed almost totally.

On 5 December 1812 Napoleon left the remnant of his army to return to Paris; to criticise him for abandoning his followers would be unjust. There was little left for him to command, and his own efforts would plainly be better directed towards organising a new army to combat what was to become an irresistible tide of opposition. Taking advantage of what had been a defeat of monumental proportions, the bulk of Macdonald's corps, Prussians under Johann Yorck, defected to the Russians even before the King of Prussia had officially switched from unwilling co-operation to outright hostility to his old enemy. Another justification for Napoleon's quitting the army was the abortive *coup d'état* in Paris in October, in which the mentally unstable General Claude Malet had endeavoured to supplant the empire with a republican revolt. He was overthrown in hours (and executed, with some accomplices), but the number of officials who had not acted against him immediately perhaps suggested that Napoleon had been too long away from the centre of his empire. The shreds of the *Grande Armée* quit Russia when Ney followed the remnant of his rearguard, perhaps 2,000 strong, across the Niemen at Kovno, the Marshal himself supposedly the last Frenchman to leave enemy soil.

In material terms, including prisoners, Napoleon probably lost about 570,000 troops in the Russian campaign. He was able to re-create his armies for the campaigns of 1813-14, but all too many of the members of these were under-age recruits or invalids and pensioners, and he was never again able to restore his cavalry to the force it had been; the cream of his experienced men had been lost, together with a vast arsenal of cannon. Perhaps more damaging was the psychological blow which had been dealt to his empire, for the scale of the defeat was immense, and those states which had been beaten into submission took the opportunity for revenge, most significantly Austria and Prussia.

Later, Napoleon maintained that he was blameless: 'Was I defeated by the efforts of the Russians? No! My failure must be attributed to pure accident, to absolute fatality. First a capital was burnt to the ground, in spite of its inhabitants and through foreign intrigues; then winter set in with such unusual suddenness and severity that it was regarded as a kind of phenomenon. To these disasters must be added a mass of false reports, silly intrigues, treachery, stupidity, and, in short, many things that will perhaps one day come to light, and which will excuse or justify the two great errors I committed in diplomacy and war; namely, to have undertaken such an enterprise, leaving on my flanks, which soon became my rear, two cabinets of which I was not master, and two allied armies, which, on the least check would become my enemies ...[11] I had undertaken the expedition to fight against armed men, not against nature in the violence of her wrath. I defeated armies, but I could not conquer the flames, the frost, stupefaction, and death! I was forced to yield to fate![12]

The actual reasons for the defeat are many, not least the grave miscalculation that a number of limited successes and temporary territorial acquisition would compel the Russians to negotiate; their will to resist, and the efforts made by the population as a whole, had not been envisaged. Impressive though his army was, Napoleon commanded contingents which mirrored the lack of enthusiasm and commitment of their political leaders, and although the supplies needed for the campaign were probably adequate, the means of transporting them most certainly was not, so that the *Grande Armée* starved at a time when there were full magazines at the rear. Napoleon claimed that if Moscow had not been burned he would have wintered there and defeated the Russians in the spring, though this was itself

MARSHAL NEY AND THE REARGUARD, RETREAT FROM MOSCOW.
PRINT AFTER A. YVON.

doubtful; and as for blaming the weather, it is noteworthy that the retreat was well under way before the first snows, and that the winter wrought havoc upon a force which had already failed in its objective. His own actions can be seen as contributing markedly to the defeat, in the decision to extend his supply-lines in pursuit of bringing about a decisive engagement, in delaying in Moscow for so long, and for altering the course of the withdrawal after Malojaroslavets, when proper reconnaissance would have revealed that the Russians were not again preparing to bar his route. It is easy to be critical in retrospect; the decisions which now appear in error were less clear at the time. More fundamental were failings which became evident in this campaign perhaps more than before: Napoleon's practice of concentrating command entirely in his own hands, which led to the suppression of his subordinates' initiative, was revealed as a weakness when it was necessary for them to take independent decisions. The whole task of controlling so huge an army was too great an undertaking for any one general, even Napoleon at the height of

133

his powers; which, in 1812, he was not, at times exhibiting a degree of physical limitation which was not evident earlier.

Despite the scale of the defeat in Russia, which might have demoralised another commander, the 1812 campaign did not signify the end of Napoleon's empire, although it undoubtedly began the process of military decline. Far from being psychologically crushed by his recent catastrophe, he returned to Germany in 1813 with a new army, to reinforce the troops already there. This new army may have been 200,000 strong, but it was very inexperienced; for the remainder of the war Napoleon had to resort to the mobilisation of classes of conscripts before they were officially due, resulting in very young soldiers (the 'Marie-Louises', named after Napoleon's empress) with imperfect training and equipment. As Napoleon had grown

NAPOLEON IN 1813. PRINT AFTER RAFFET.

weaker, so his enemies had become stronger; in addition to the Russians, Prussia and Sweden united to oppose him, followed by Austria on 12 August 1813, and they were joined by an increasing number of German states which had been loyal to Napoleon as members of the *Rheinbund*, but which now took the opportunity to throw off what many regarded as a foreign yoke. The common German name for the following campaign – the *Befreiungs-kriege* or 'War of Liberation' – appropriately summarises the popular senti-ments which turned against Napoleon in Germany. Furthermore, at the same time he was still maintaining the fight in the Peninsular War, a division of resources which further weakened his efforts in the east.

Napoleon's intention in 1813 was probably to inflict a serious defeat upon the Russians in northern Germany, frightening Prussia back into his own camp, and by victory stiffening the resolution of those German states which still supported him; but his resources were insufficient in both numbers and ability, for the new levies were inca-pable of the sustained feats of marching as of old, and the cavalry arm was very weak. Such factors hindered Napoleon in exploiting divi-sions and uncertainties with-in the Allied command.

THEATRE OF OPERATIONS FOR THE 1813 CAMPAIGN

Nevertheless, the 1813 campaign commenced with Napoleon apparently restor-ed to something like his old ability. On 2 May, Wittgenstein surprised Ney's corps near Lützen; Napoleon moved to his aid and defeated the enemy with his counter-attack, but his success was limited because of a shortage of cav-alry, making effective pursuit impossible. Another limited victory was gained over Wittgenstein at Bautzen (20–21 May), and from 4 June to 16 August Napoleon negotiated an armistice in order to gain time in which to train his young soldiers. During this period his enemies themselves increased in strength, notably by the addition of Austrian forces to the Allied armies, and from this point Napoleon was strategically on the defen-sive, against an enemy which outnumbered him considerably. No matter how he might delay it by limited successes, only one outcome was likely; and

SCHWARZENBERG. PRINT AFTER MANSFELD.

again Napoleon suffered from the inability of his subordinates to hold their own, his own actions being counter-balanced by the defeats of his generals.

At the end of the armistice Napoleon was faced by three armies: that of Bohemia, commanded by the Austrian Karl Schwarzenberg; of Silesia, led by the old Prussian General Gebhard Blücher, Wittgenstein's replacement; and Bernadotte's Army of the North. Napoleon turned back an attack by Schwarzenberg at Dresden, then counter-attacked and defeated him (26-27 August), only for Schwarzenberg to be allowed to escape; and amid the defeat of Napoleon's subordinates, the *Rheinbund* began to collapse in earnest as one of the most important states, Bavaria, withdrew in October and joined the opposition. The climax of the campaign came on 16-19 October at Leipzig, in the 'Battle of the Nations', in which Napoleon attempt-ed to hold at bay all his opponents, Blücher, Schwarzenberg and Bernadotte,

NAPOLEON AT LEIPZIG. LITHOGRAPH BY MOLTE AFTER GRENIER.

BATTLE OF LEIPZIG. PRINT AFTER F. DE MYRBACH.

accompanied by their principal monarchs (the Tsar, the Emperor of Austria and King Frederick William III of Prussia); as if to emphasise the scale of the forces ranged against him, there was even a token British contingent in the presence of a rocket troop. Napoleon held his defensive perimeter around Leipzig until the position was hopeless, and then managed to escape the intended trap with much of what survived from his army; but it was a defeat of major proportions, and involved the loss of one of Napoleon's last important allies: the Saxon forces changed sides during the battle. As Napoleon retired towards the Rhine, his erstwhile Bavarian allies attempted to block his path; he defeated them at Hanau (30–31 October) but continued to withdraw. The war in Germany was lost; what followed was an attempt to preserve France itself.

In November 1813 the Allies made overtures of peace, based on the principle that France be restricted to her 'natural frontiers'; but this offer was withdrawn and replaced by an insistence on the restoration of the frontiers of 1792, which Napoleon found unacceptable (as, perhaps, the Allied powers had foreseen). Three armies began to converge: Bernadotte's Army of the North was to isolate French garrisons in northern Germany (notably Davout at Hamburg), and to advance into the Netherlands; Blücher's Army of Silesia would advance into Lorraine; Schwarzenberg's Army of Bohemia, more than 200,000 strong, would cross the upper Rhine. The ultimate objective was Paris, and in addition to these, Austrian and Neapolitan forces were to advance from Italy, and Wellington's Peninsular army over the Pyrenees.

Against such overwhelming numbers, Napoleon's attempts to resist, with the often ill-trained and ill-equipped troops at his disposal, was ultimately futile; but in the few weeks of the campaign in the defence of France in 1814, he demonstrated that he had not lost his old skill and vigour. In his attempts to prevent the unification of the Allied armies, he won a number of impressive victories, defeating isolated enemy formations in detail; but his subordinates were unable to emulate his successes, and the numbers ranged against him were too great. Against Blücher and the Army of Silesia, Napoleon fought successful actions at Brienne (29 January) and La Rothière (30 January) and, in a series of manoeuvres which demonstrated his old abilities, on successive days won actions at Champaubert, Montmirail, Château-Thierry (10–12 February), and Vauchamps (14 February). These temporarily repelled the Army of Silesia; he then switched his attention to Schwarzenberg, throwing him back at Montereau (18 February), before again turning on Blücher whose troops had reached to within 25 miles of Paris.

Napoleon pushed back Blücher at Craonne (7 March) but was himself driven back after he attacked at Laon (9-10 March), his enemy having been rein-forced by elements of Bernadotte's army. In his absence, Schwarzenberg had defeated Marshal Macdonald at Bar-sur-Aube (27 February), and continued to advance. Napoleon crushed an isolated corps at Rheims (13 March) and attempted to strike at Schwarzenberg's line of communications, but was repulsed at Arcis-sur-Aube (20-21 March), Napoleon's last battle in the defence of France. Schwarzenberg defeated the forces of Marshals Mortier and Marmont at La Fère-Champenoise (25 March) and on 28 March united with Blücher. Frustrating Napoleon's strategy by ignoring his threat to their communications, they pushed on to Paris; Marmont and Mortier were forced back to Montmartre, and after Marmont agreed to an armistice, Paris sur-rendered on 31 March. This was the final blow against which Napoleon could not respond; it brought to an end the penultimate stage of his mili-tary career.

Despite his ultimate failure, the campaign of 1814 demonstrated that Napoleon was still capable of exercising his strategic and tactical skill as of old; indeed, it was largely by the force of his will that the fight was sustained so long, against such odds. But his sense of purpose, which sustained him personally throughout this period, led him to under-estimate the enormity of the problem and the abilities of the forces ranged against him, and to delude himself that he could still triumph by force of arms. Although the true situation is defined more clearly in retrospect, perhaps Napoleon should have realised the extent of the exhaustion of his empire and accept-ed the terms which the Allies were prepared to offer, rather than fight on in a vain hope of victory, and lose everything. By prolonging the war, irrespec-tive of how well he performed himself, Napoleon brought about much death and destruction which might have been avoided; for not even his revitalised military skill could have postponed the inevitable for long.

NOTES

1. *Royal Military Chronicle*, November 1812, pp. 7-8.
2. Las Cases, comte de. *Memoirs of the Life, Exile and Conversations of the Emperor Napoleon*, London, 1836, vol. IV, p. 109.
3. Ibid., vol. IV, pp. 19-20.
4. Ibid., vol. III, p. 165.
5. Ségur, comte P. de. *History of the Expedition to Russia undertaken by the Emperor Napoleon in the Year 1812*, London, 1825, vol. I, p. 321.
6. Ibid., vol. I, pp. 324-5.
7. Ibid., vol. I, p. 344.

8. Ibid., vol. I, p. 358.
9. Fezensac, duc de. *A Journal of the Russian Campaign of 1812*, ed. Colonel W. Knollys, London, 1852, p. 64.
10. Ségur, *op. cit.*, vol. II, p. 284.
11. Las Cases, *op. cit.*, vol. IV, p. 109.
12. Ibid., vol. III, pp. 164–5.

BIBLIOGRAPHY

Austin, Paul Britten. *1812: The March on Moscow*, London, 1993 (narrative using eye-witness accounts, with extensive bibliography).
- *1812: Napoleon in Moscow*, London, 1995 (as above).
- *1812: The Great Retreat*, London 1996 (as above).
Bourgogne, A. J. B. F. *The Memoirs of Sergeant Bourgogne 1812–13*, trans. and ed. P. Cottin and M. Hénault, London, 1899; reprinted with introduction by David G. Chandler, London, 1979.
Brett-James, A. *1812*, London, 1966 (eye-witness accounts, with extensive bibliography).
- *Europe against Napoleon*, London, 1970 (eye-witness accounts of the Leipzig campaign).
Chandler, D. G. *The Campaigns of Napoleon*, London, 1967.
Clausewitz, General C. von. *The Campaign of 1812 in Russia*, 1843; reprinted with introduction by G. F. Nafziger, London, 1992.
Coignet, J.-R. *The Note-Books of Captain Coignet, Soldier of the Empire*, intr. by the Hon. Sir John Fortescue, London, 1929.
Delderfield, R. F. *Imperial Sunset: the Fall of Napoleon*, London, 1969.
- *The Retreat from Moscow*, London, 1967.
Duffy, C. *Borodino and the War of 1812*, London, 1972.
Esposito, V. J., and Elting, J. R. *Military History and Atlas of the Napoleonic Wars*, London, 1964 (superb collection of maps).
Fezensac, duc de. *A Journal of the Russian Campaign of 1812*, ed. and intr. by Colonel W. Knollys, London, 1852.
Horward, D. D. (ed.). *Napoleonic Military History: A Bibliography*, London, 1986 (includes valuable bibliography and commentary, especially 'The Russian Campaign', G. F. Jewsbury; 'The Rise of German Nationalism and the Wars of Liberation', M. W. Gray; and 'The Collapse of Empire', J. R. Elting.
Labaume, E. *Circumstantial Narrative of the Campaign in Russia*, London, 1814.
Marbot, A.-M. *The Memoirs of Baron de Marbot*, ed. A. J. Butler, London, 1913.
Nafziger, G. F. *Napoleon's Invasion of Russia*, Novato, California, 1988 (important study with extensive statistical material).
Olivier, D. *The Burning of Moscow*, London, 1964.
Palmer, A. *Napoleon in Russia*, London, 1967.
Petre, F. L. *Napoleon at Bay, 1814*, London. 1914; reprinted with introduction by D. G. Chandler, London, 1977.
Pflugk-Harttung, J. von. *1813–15: Illustrierte Geschichte der Befreiungskriege*, Stuttgart, n.d. (1913), (includes many contemporary illustrations).
Quennevat, J.-C. *Atlas de la Grande Armée*, Paris, 1966.
Rehtwisch, T. *Die Grosse Zeit: Ein Jahrhundertbuch*, Leipzig, 1913 (includes many contemporary illustrations, including eye-witness depictions of the 1812 campaign by

Albrecht Adam and Christian Faber du Faur).

Roeder, H. *The Ordeal of Captain Roeder*, trans. and ed. H. Roeder, London, 1960.

Ségur, comte Philippe de. *History of the Expedition to Russia undertaken by the Emperor Napoleon in the Year 1812*, London, 1825.

Verestchagin, V. *1812: Napoleon I in Russia*, intr. R. Whitcing, London, 1899 (by the notable Russian historical painter).

Vossler, H. A. *With Napoleon in Russia*, trans. W. Wallich, London, 1969 (with illustrations by Christian Faber du Faur).

Walter, Jakob. *The Diary of a Napoleonic Foot Soldier*, ed. M. Raeff, Windrush Press, Gloucestershire and Doubleday, New York, 1991.

Wilson, Sir Robert. *General Wilson's Journal 1812-14*, ed. A. Brett-James, London, 1964.

- *Narrative of Events during the Invasion of Russia by Napoleon Bonaparte, and the Retreat of the French Army*, ed. Revd. H. Randolph, London, 1860.

- *Private Diaries of Travels ... with the European Armies in the Campaigns of 1812, 1813, 1814*, ed. Revd. H. Randolph, London, 1861.

ABDICATION, EXILE
AND RETURN

J. David Markham

I N THE CAMPAIGN OF 1813–14, NAPOLEON NEITHER DEFEATED HIS enemies nor accepted early offers to retain his throne. In March 1814 he was faced with a dilemma. With his army at Vitry, some 100 miles east of Paris, he felt he was in a position to move about rather freely, as the Allies had begun to move towards Paris. He might well have consolidated his forces, added new soldiers from various fortresses, declared a levée en masse (draft) and attacked retreating Allied forces near Saint-Dizier.[1] Expecting to be joined by Marmont and Mortier, he might possibly have been able to operate successfully against increasingly overwhelming odds. When it became clear, however, that Marmont was being pushed toward Paris and that his marshals would not stand

'1814'. PRINT AFTER MEISSONIER.

for the loss of Paris without any effort to prevent it, he began a race against the Allies for his capital city.[2] He placed his last hopes in a desperate defence of Paris, hoping to sandwich the Allies between the defenders of Paris and his own forces. As he later told Montholon, 'they [the Allies] would never have given battle on the left bank of the Seine with Paris in their rear'.[3]

As the Allied troops drew closer to Paris, King Joseph and the Regency Council that governed in the absence of the Emperor, decided that a letter from Napoleon calling for the Empress Marie-Louise and the King of Rome to withdraw from Paris in the event of a military threat to the capital should now take effect. Thus, against the better judgement of those who felt that she could help inspire the troops to defend their city and save it for the Emperor's return, the imperial party left Paris, while Joseph stayed to direct its defence.

The withdrawal of the Empress and her party proved a major blow to the morale of the citizens of Paris. Napoleon's step-daughter Hortense noted that the National Guard was 'completely discouraged', and that the citizens were 'indignant at this family that seemed to be abandoning them in the hour of adversity'.[4]

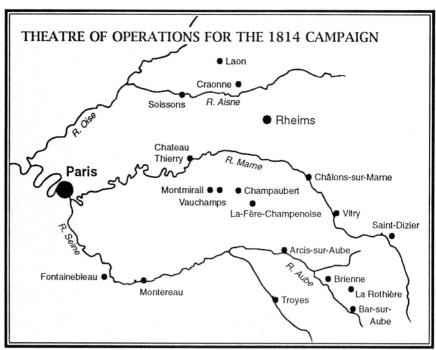

THEATRE OF OPERATIONS FOR THE 1814 CAMPAIGN

MARIE-LOUISE AND THE KING OF ROME. ENGRAVING BY C. STATE AFTER GÉRARD.

1814 CAMPAIGN: NAPOLEON AIMS A CANNON AT MONTEREAU.
PRINT AFTER E. LAMY.

The good citizens of Paris were not interested in making additional sacrifices. After Marie-Louise and the King of Rome were sent to safety, the Parisians busied themselves with their own version of a defence. 'Instead of volunteering to build redoubts, they moved any valuable furniture to the country. Instead of chipping in with money, they buried their *napoléons* in their gardens.'[5] The sadness that Napoleon must have felt is surely reflected in the Sixteenth Bulletin of 5 April 1814 which reads in part: 'The occupation of the capital by the enemy is a misfortune which deeply afflicts the heart of His Majesty, from which, however, there is nothing to apprehend.'[6]

To be fair, the Parisians were being constantly bombarded with reports that the Prussians or, worse, the Cossacks, were determined either to burn Paris to the ground in revenge for Moscow or to undertake an orgy of looting and violence. The English newspapers published reports of such threats, and they were repeated in the Parisian newspapers. If the French publication of these rumours was intended to encourage the citizens to fight even harder, they had quite the opposite effect.[7]

146

The defence of Paris was quickly thought to be impossible, and soon Joseph and most of the government left the city. Unfortunately for Napoleon, Talleyrand, who by now had decided that the Empire was finished and was prepared to seek terms with the Allies for the restoration of the Bourbons, was able to stay behind, where he could conspire with the Allies for the ultimate overthrow of Napoleon.

When Napoleon arrived, he was several hours too late. Paris had fallen, and the best he could do was retire to Fontainebleau to await further developments or, as it happened, his fate. He was, of course, livid. Caulaincourt describes his reaction:

'What cowardice! Surrender! Joseph has ruined everything. Four hours too late! ... If I had come four hours sooner, all would have been saved,' he added in sorrowful tones.[8]

1814 CAMPAIGN: DEFENCE OF THE CLICHY GATE, PARIS.
PRINT AFTER HORACE VERNET.

Under the influence of Talleyrand, the legislative body established a provisional government with Talleyrand at its head. While Napoleon prepared for further military action at Fontainebleau, Talleyrand conspired to deprive him of his political support and to prepare the way for the return of the monarchy that so many had died to remove.

If there were any hope of a military victory for Napoleon, it was dashed with the defection of Marshal Marmont's VI Corps, with its 11,000 troops. Marmont, who fancied that he was saving France, simply marched his soldiers over to the Allied forces. This strengthened the unwillingness of the marshals to continue to rally the troops; led by Marshal Ney they informed Napoleon that they, and their men, were no longer willing to fight. Rebuked in his efforts to abdicate in favour of his son (which was a real possibility until the treason of Marmont), Napoleon abdicated unconditionally on 11 April 1814, with the words: 'there is no sacrifice, not even that of life, which I am not ready to make for the interests of France.'[9]

Napoleon's loss of the support of the French people is summed up by his secretary Fleury de Chaboulon who wrote:

'As long as good fortune waited upon Napoleon, his most ambitious attempts commanded the plaudits of the nation. We boasted of his profound political wisdom, we extolled his genius, we worshipped his courage. When his fortune changed, then his political wisdom was called treachery, his genius, ambition, and his courage, fool-hardiness and infatuation.'[10]

The suddenness of Napoleon's fall from favour is shown in Count Dumas' observations upon his return to Paris just after the abdication: 'I found all my companions already detached from the imperial system ... it seemed as if the government that had just ceased was nothing more than an historical recollection.'[11] The terms of the Treaty of Paris that resulted from the abdication included a provision for Napoleon and his family to keep their titles and granted him a pension of two million francs. He was given the Island of Elba 'in full sovereignty and property', with a guard of 400 soldiers.[12] The treaty did not require him to remain in Elba, nor did it forbid him from ever returning to France.

On 20 April, in a scene that ranks among the most poignant in history, Napoleon said good-by to the soldiers of his Imperial Guard. Selecting his personal guard for Elba, he bid the rest an emotional *adieu*, kissed the flag, and rode away. On the 28th he embarked in the British brig *Undaunted*, and arrived at Elba two days later.

In Elba Napoleon spent much of his time in a serious effort to improve conditions there. He revised the laws, improved the collection of taxes, and initiated a number of physical improvements. He was bitterly disappointed that Marie-Louise and his son had not been allowed to join him, but other members of his family dropped in from time to time.[13] Political leaders and other important people would visit him, and he would discuss politics with them at great length. He was especially cordial to British visitors, and went out of his way to see that the British representative Colonel Campbell was made welcome at his court.[14]

All the while Napoleon was keeping an eye on events in Vienna, where the Congress of Vienna was endeavouring to divide up Europe to everyone's satisfaction. He also began to hear rumours of assassination attempts, or of attempts to move him to St. Helena or to another island prison. Furthermore, in a move of absolute stupidity, Louis XVIII failed to pay his pension, which gave Napoleon serious fear of running out of money.

Napoleon soon began to believe that the people of France were anxious for his return. With Louis XVIII came hordes of noble *émigrés*, all of whom were eager to reclaim their titles and privileges and return France to its pre-Revolutionary condition. The new king actually tried to reassure the people of France, and civil liberties were somewhat restored from their war-status restrictions. The Constitutional Charter was designed to convince the people that there would be no return to the pre-Revolutionary days, but the behaviour of the aristocracy around the king told another story.

French peasants were fearful that their land would be given back to the *émigrés* and that the system of privilege would return. Soon Napoleon became the hero of the Revolution. Some units of the *Grande Armée* were disbanded, but the troops found it difficult to assimilate into civilian society. France's economy had little room for them, and they were disgruntled at the loss of glory their defeat had brought.

On 15 February Napoleon was visited by Fleury de Chaboulon. He relayed the opinion of Hugh Maret, Napoleon's former Foreign Minister, that the people were 'clamouring for Napoleon's return'.[15] Napoleon himself had forecast the likelihood of, and the reason for, his return. Years later on St. Helena, he told Las Cases that he had anticipated this upon his departure from Fontainebleau. He explained: 'If the Bourbons said I intend to commence a fifth dynasty, I have nothing more to do here; I have acted my part. But if they should obstinately attempt to recontinue the third, I shall soon appear again ...'[16]

Only Napoleon's closest associates were told of his plans. Bertrand was pleased with the opportunity to return to France. Drouot, on the other hand, took the entirely sensible point of view that challenging the military might of France and of the Allies with some 1,100 troops involved a certain amount of risk![17] Napoleon's mother gave him encouragement with the words, 'Go my son, go and fulfil your destiny ... I see with sorrow that you cannot remain here.'[18]

On Sunday, 26 February 1815, Napoleon set sail for France in *Inconstant*, accompanied by the vessels *Saint-Esprit* and *Caroline*.[19] Together, these ships carried some 1,100 men, 40 horses, and four cannon. As he stepped aboard *Inconstant*, he exclaimed to those around him 'The die is now cast.'[20] He was quoting Caesar, of course, on *his* bid for power. Perhaps the Mediterranean was Napoleon's Rubicon! In a bulletin to his soldiers still in France, prepared prior to his departure, Napoleon was at his most eloquent:

'Soldiers! In my exile I heard your voice! ... Your general, called to the throne by the voice of the people and raised on your shields, is restored to you; come and join him ...

'We must forget that we have been masters of other nations; but we must not suffer any to interfere in our affairs ...

'Victory will advance at the charge: the Eagle, with the national colours, will fly from steeple to steeple all the way to the towers of Notre-Dame!'[21]

A similar bulletin 'To the French People' reminded them that they had been defeated as a consequence of the defection of Marshal Augereau in Lyons and Marshal Marmont in Paris, thus snatching defeat from a sure victory![22]

Finally, he prepared a bulletin for the soldiers he was most likely to face upon landing and marching toward Paris, which read in part: 'Soldiers, the drum beats the *générale*, and we march: run to arms, come and join us, join your Emperor, and our Eagles ...'[23]

These bulletins show Napoleon's understanding of what must be done if he were to have any hope of success. He has three audiences in these messages. The first, clearly, is the army. He could not succeed if he encountered any real resistance. Indeed, he predicted the necessity and the result: 'I shall arrive in Paris without firing a shot.'[24] Therefore, he appeals to the army to join him in overthrowing the treachery of others and restoring their glory. He includes references to the treachery , the glory of his soldiers, and his 'willingness' to respond to their 'calls' that he return. These bulletins were '*Tantôt lapidaires, tantôt emphatiques, toujours éblouissants.*'[25]

The second audience was the people of France, and to them the message was pretty much the same. He understood, however, that the people would not be interested in new military adventures: they had had enough of conquest and empire. With any luck, they might be willing to support him in a new role of constitutional emperor. Thus, his appeals to glory and calls for revenge were tempered with a recognition that times had changed, and control over other nations was no longer on the agenda.

This latter point was especially important for his third audience, which was the Congress of Vienna. While it is true that Napoleon misjudged their readiness to rally against him, he certainly understood that they would at least need some sort of reassurance that he no longer harboured a desire to engage in imperial conquests. Thus, while he would contact them directly later, these bulletins deliberately stress his domestic goals, and specifically renounce a return to the earlier empire. '*We must forget that we have been the masters of other nations.*'

At 4 p.m. on 1 March 1815, the Imperial Eagle landed at Golfe-Juan; the Emperor was once again on French soil. The image was great, but the reality was daunting, made even more so by a crisis earlier in the day. Captain Lamouret foolishly took a few men and demanded the surrender of Antibes. Instead, he and his twenty grenadiers were taken prisoner. Rather than make a fight of it, Napoleon decided to ignore their plight, feeling that the first shot fired would break the spell of his arrival and lead to disaster. Indeed, he told Cambronne 'You are not to fire a single shot. Remember that I wish to win back my crown without shedding one drop of blood.'[26]

Napoleon chose to take the mountain road to Grenoble rather than pass close to the large garrisons at Toulon and Marseilles. This was sound military policy, but he also remembered the frightening reception he had received in Provence while on his way to Elba. This was a Royalist stronghold, and it would have been very risky to take this more direct route to Paris.[27] This meant leaving his cannon, carriage, and sixteen supply wagons behind, and having to walk on narrow mountain roads, often in single file. Even today, the road is narrow and travel by car is painfully slow.

At Grasse, Napoleon met with a mixed reception, as most citizens were unwilling to gamble on either the Bourbon king or the returning Emperor. Stendhal tells us, 'The people allowed them to pass without giving the least sign of approval or of disapproval.'[28] This attitude would prevail until Laffrey and Grenoble.

It was a very mountainous trip, climbing to 2,500 feet, descending into a valley, climbing again to 3,000 feet, all in the first day. They actually made very good time. At some points the soldiers had to scramble along ravines covered with ice, with Napoleon following breathlessly. No one could ride, and one mule carrying 2,000 gold *napoléons* fell off a cliff.[29]

Along the route, Napoleon talked to peasants, soldiers and people in the towns. Many of them were surprised to see their Emperor, marching on foot, through the snow. While some were less than excited, others tried to encourage him. Still others simply offered him their hospitality; for example, at Escragnolles on 2 March the parish priest, Monsieur l'Abbé Chiris, offered him two eggs.[30] Along the way Napoleon also greeted the Prince of Monaco, who had been apprehended and brought to the returning emperor. Napoleon immediately released him and remarked that they were both going home!

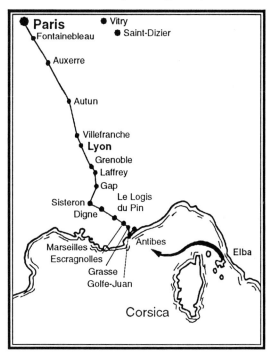

At Castellane (3 March), the villagers had not heard of his pending arrival, but provided food and drink for him and his men. He sent messages to Bonapartists in Grenoble, it being critical that he capture that city without difficulty. He also sent messages to Marshal Masséna asking for his support. These actions were very important. While on the one hand Napoleon wanted to march in advance of the news of his approach, on the other he clearly needed to have the way prepared. This was especially true with regard to supplies for his soldiers. He had Cambronne sent ahead for rations, transportation, and passports.[31]

By now the roads were much better, and Napoleon had his troops in fine marching order. As a fighting force they were still modest, but the emotional appeal was enormous. At Bras d'Or he chatted with two officials who

told him that the people would be pleased to see him on the throne provided that conscription was not renewed. Napoleon replied: 'A great many
foolish things have been done, but I have come to put everything right. My
people will be happy.'[32] Soon crowds of cheering peasants thronged the
road sides.

Up until the town of Gap it had been easy, no serious resistance had been
encountered; but Napoleon knew that eventually he would encounter regular troops. This ultimate test of his chances for success came at Laffrey,
where General Jean-Gabriel Marchand, the commanding officer at Grenoble,
had sent Major de Lessart and a battalion of the 5th Regiment to put an end
to his adventure. Napoleon's Polish Lancers actually engaged in discussion
with members of the 5th, and the general feeling was that there was little
fear that they would take hostile action.[33] De Lessart insisted that he would
do his duty, however, and this set the scene for an emotional confrontation.
As Napoleon approached, Captain Randon ordered the soldiers of the 5th to
open fire. Nothing happened. Then Napoleon spoke to the soldiers.
Accounts differ as to his exact words, but the local commemorative plaque
reads: 'Soldiers! I am your Emperor. Do you not recognise me? If there is one
among you who would kill his general, here I am!'[34] Shouts of *'Vive
l'Empereur!'* were his answer, and the confrontation was over. It was a good
day for Napoleon, as later Colonel Charles de Labédoyère surrendered the
7th Regiment of the Line, with its 1,800 men.[35]

The next challenge was Grenoble. There the commanding officer
refused to open the gates, but the people and soldiers, shouting *'Vive
l'Empereur!'*, tore them down and escorted Napoleon to the Hôtel des
Trois Dauphins. The pieces of the gate were placed under his window, with
shouts of 'For want of the keys of the good town of Grenoble, here are the
gates for you.'[36]

By now he had some 4,000 seasoned infantry, 20 cannon, a regiment of
hussars, and more men arriving all the time. More importantly, the citizens
seemed to be warming to his return; indeed, in some areas a revolutionary
fervour had arisen that had not been seen since the days of France's great
Revolution. Thus it is no surprise that he should recall: 'From Cannes to
Grenoble I had been an adventurer; in this last town I became a sovereign
once again.'[37]

While in Grenoble, Napoleon engaged in important political discussions.
He met various public officials and made it clear that he no longer wanted
to expand an empire. He acknowledged past faults and swore that he would

be a constitutional monarch: 'I have been too fond of war; I will make war no more: I will leave my neighbours at rest: we must forget that we have been masters of the world ... I wish to be less its [France's] sovereign than the first and best of its citizens.'[38] He told the people that he was there to relieve them of the oppressive policies of the Bourbons, and especially of the *émigrés*. He presented himself as the spirit of 1789 returned to do battle with the spirit of feudalism. He even allowed that the Bourbons were well meaning, but surrounded by outrageous advisers. He would never again seek to conquer others, and only desired that foreigners would treat France the same way.[39]

On 8 March he and his growing army left Grenoble for Lyons. His confidence, and his army, had improved, but there were still many potential pitfalls. The royalist forces had thus far failed, but increasingly desperate efforts to halt his march were still being made. The comte d'Artois, aided by Marshal Macdonald, was determined to defend Lyons. The soldiers, however, refused to pledge allegiance to the King, and it was clear that they were not about to fight their Emperor. The sullen refusal of the soldiers to cry *'Vive le Roi!'* told the comte d'Artois all he needed to know, and he left Macdonald to do the best he could. Macdonald's best was not much; virtually all his troops disobeyed orders and went over to Napoleon, while Macdonald himself beat a hasty retreat.[40]

While in Lyons, Napoleon began to act like a ruling monarch. He dissolved the two Chambers, and called for new laws to be passed that would make his reign more constitutional in nature. [41] He wrote to Marie-Louise, asking her to return to Paris on 20 March, their son's birthday. He re-established the imperial magistracy, and he demanded that all recently returned *émigrés* leave the country. Remembering 1814, he arranged for trials of Talleyrand, Marmont, Augereau and others.[42]

In meetings with local and military officials, Napoleon again put forth the message that the future was to be different from the past: 'I was hurried on by the course of events, into a wrong path. But, taught by experience, I have abjured that love of glory ... I have renounced forever that grand enterprise; we have enough of glory, we want repose.'[43]

One major obstacle remained. Marshal Michel Ney, the bravest of the brave, Prince of the Moskowa, had pledged to bring Napoleon back in an iron cage. A leader of the marshals' revolt in 1814, he had retired in great comfort, and could not have been particularly pleased to hear of Napoleon's latest gamble. Determined to show his loyalty to Louis XVIII and to keep France at peace, Ney began to organise a force to oppose the march on Paris. He was moved by Napoleon's proclamations, but doubted whether his old master would have forgiven him for the revolt at Fontainebleau.[44]

Napoleon was well aware of preparations being made to halt his advance. He knew, for example, that Marshal Masséna, at Marseilles, had dispatched troops against his rearguard. These troops were far from Napoleon, however, and thus provided no immediate threat. Ney, on the other hand, posed a more difficult problem. Napoleon did not really fear defeat, but wanted to arrive in Paris without having fired a shot; any other scenario would bring into question his claim to have returned at the demand of the people and with the support of the army.

Meanwhile, as he advanced through Franche-Comté and Burgundy, the support of the people was more open. These areas had prospered under the Empire, and were thus more politically supportive of Napoleon. Their enthusiasm was great, and the crowds greeted him wherever he went. At Mâcon, at Châlon, at Villefranche, he was greeted by crowds chanting *'A bas les nobles! A bas les prêtres! A bas les Bourbons!'*[45] A commemorative plaque on the spot indicates that some 60,000 people cheered him at Villefranche.

Ney's dispositions were slowed by poor organisation on the part of the government, but he made preparations as best he could. Meanwhile, Bonapartist pressures were mounting. Napoleon had Bertrand write orders to Ney, and Napoleon himself wrote a letter, which ended: 'I shall receive you as after the battle of the Moskowa.'[46]

Troops from Napoleon's entourage went forward and mingled with those under Ney's command. Conversations with his officers revealed to Ney that the cause of the Bourbons was not quite the effective rallying point that he had hoped it would be. He swore to fire the first shot if necessary, but this seemed to have little effect on his soldiers. Meanwhile he and his troops kept hearing stories of the great desire of France and all of Europe to see the Empire restored.

By 14 March Ney had made up his mind to join in Napoleon's great gamble. In a proclamation he then read to his troops he declared, in part:

'The cause of the Bourbons is lost for ever ... Liberty is at length triumphant; and Napoleon, our august Emperor, is about to confirm it for ever ... Soldiers! I have often led you to victory; I am now going to conduct you to that immortal phalanx, which the Emperor Napoleon is conducting to Paris ... Long live the Emperor!'[47]

On the 17th Napoleon arrived at Auxerre where he was greeted by the Prefect. He spent the day discussing his plans with a wide assortment of people, and later had a meeting with Ney. The scene must have been dramatic: Ney, overcome with guilt and apprehension, Napoleon relieved that this final major obstacle was removed and he once again had the services of 'the bravest of the brave'.

With Ney in hand, the remainder of the march to Paris was anti-climactic. Paris was alive with Bonapartist fervour. One banner proclaimed these words to the King supposedly from Napoleon: 'My good brother: there is no need to send any more troops; I already have enough!'[48] The hopelessness of the King's position is summed up by General Thiébault's observation that: 'I was the only person holding out for the King either around or in Paris.'[49] Perhaps there is no better illustration of the rapid growth of Napoleon's popularity than the following sequence of Paris broadsheets passed out on the streets to keep the citizens informed:

'The Tiger has broken out of his cage.

The Ogre has been three days at sea.

The Wretch has landed at Fréjus.

The Buzzard has reached Antibes.

The Invader has arrived in Grenoble.

The General has entered Lyons.

Napoleon slept at Fontainebleau last night.

The Emperor will proceed to the Tuileries today.

His Imperial Majesty will address his loyal subjects tomorrow!'[50]

While additional royalist resistance was possible – and feared – the fact was that Louis XVIII had determined to flee, which he did on the night of 19 March. The next day, street vendors celebrated the return of Napoleon by selling medals showing a bust of the Emperor and the date.[51] To add insult to injury the Paris Mint, which had so recently produced medals celebrating the reign of Louis XVIII, began to plan for a new series celebrating the return of the Emperor. By evening Napoleon had re-entered Paris, and the first phase of the 'One Hundred Days' had drawn to a close.

Napoleon had done well, so far. He had planned his moves carefully, and his plans had proved absolutely correct. He avoided battles, obtained the loyalty and discipline of the troops, and made the politically correct statements necessary to reassure a populace and a military leadership weary of war. Unfortunately he failed to wait for the Congress of Vienna to disband. Still meeting to decide the future of Europe, they were quick to declare

Napoleon an outlaw and to mobilise military action against him. That action, combined with a repeat of the political intrigue that had helped lead to his downfall in 1814, proved too much for even Napoleon to overcome, and, in the words of the comte de Mercy Argenteau:

'The cannons of Waterloo sent to a lonely death, on that rock in the Atlantic Ocean, the powerful Genius who had filled the world with the sound of his arms, and the grandeur of his fame!!!'52

NOTES

1. Houssaye, Henry. *Napoleon and the Campaign of 1814: France*, Tyne and Wear, 1994. Facsimile of 1914 edn, pp. 333-7.
2. Chandler, David. *The Campaigns of Napoleon*, New York, 1966, p.1000.
3. Montholon, marquis de. *Memoirs of the History of France During the Reign of Napoleon, Dictated by the Emperor at St Helena to the Generals Who Shared His Captivity; and Published from the Original Manuscripts Corrected by Himself*, 3 vols., London, 1823, vol. II, p. 265.
4. Hortense, Queen consort of Louis, King of Holland.*The Memoirs of Queen Hortense*, Published by arrangement with Prince Napoléon, ed. Jean Hanoteau, tr. Arthur K. Griggs, New York, 1927, vol. II, p. 78.
5. Cronin, Vincent. *Napoleon Bonaparte: An Intimate Biography*, New York, 1972, p. 361.
6. Posted at Rennes on 5 April, 1814. Found in *Original Journals of the Eighteen Campaigns of Napoleon Bonaparte; Comprising All Those In Which He Personally Commanded In Chief; Translated From The French. To Which Are Added All The Bulletins Relating To Each Campaign, Now First Published Complete.* London, n.d. (but interior title pages are dated 1817), vol. II, p. 431.
7. Houssaye, *op. cit.*, pp. 361-3.
8. Caulaincourt, General Armande de. *No Peace With Napoleon!* , New York, 1936, p. 29.
9. Napoleon I, Emperor of the French, *Correspondance de Napoléon Ier* Paris, 1869, 27, No. 21558. Translation found in Fain, Baron J. *The Manuscript of 1814. A History of Events which led to the Abdication of Napoleon. Written at the Command of the Emperor,* London, 1823, pp. 250-1.
10. Fleury de Chaboulon, Pierre-Alexandre-Edouard. *Memoirs of the Private Life, Return, and Reign of Napoleon in 1815,* 2 vols., London, 1820, vol. I, pp. 3-4.
11. Dumas, Mathieu, comte. *Memoirs of His Own Time; Including the Revolution, the Empire, and the Restoration,* 2 vols., London, 1839, vol. II, p. 480.
12. For a complete translation of the treaty, see Fain, *op. cit.*, pp. 271-82. Also, Napoleon's personal guard of 400 soon grew to more than 1,000 men.
13. A set of Napoleon's letters and orders, which reflect his activities on Elba, can be found in *Le Registre de l'Ile d'Elbe: Lettres et Ordres Inédits de Napoléon Ier (28 mai 1814 - 22 février 1815,* Paris, 1897.
14. This was not entirely for social reasons; Napoleon felt the need to keep a strong and ready link to the Allies in case there should be a threat to his personal safety. For a good discussion about this see Henry Houssaye, *The Return of Napoleon*, London, 1934, pp. 11-13.

15. Cronin, *op. cit.*, pp. 385-6.
16. Las Cases, comte de. *Mémorial de Sainte Hélène.* (Journal of the Private Life and Conversations of The Emperor Napoleon at St. Helena), 4 vols., Boston, 1823, vol. II, Part Three, pp. 30-1.
17. Thiers, Adolphe. *History of the Consulate and the Empire of France Under Napoleon,* Tr. D. Forbes Campbell and H. W. Herbert, 5 vols., Philadelphia, 1893, vol. 5, pp. 423-4.
18. Ibid., p. 423. This reminds one of Alexander the Great's father Philip who told his son 'Look thee out a kingdom equal to and worthy of thyself, for Macedonia is too little for thee.'
19. He left a letter for General Lapi in which he notified the General of his departure, expressed his satisfaction with the residents of Elba, and entrusted the care of his mother and sister to them. See *A Selection from the Letters and Despatches of the First Napoleon, with Explanatory Notes. Compiled by Captain The Honorable D. A. Bingham,* London, 1884, vol. 3, p. 361.
20. Alison, Sir Archibald. *History of Europe from the Commencement of the French Revolution in MDCCCXV to the Restoration of the Bourbons in MDCCXV,* 10 vols., Edinburgh and London, 1843, vol. x, p. 804.
21. *Correspondance,* 28, No. 21682. For a complete translation, see Fleury, op. cit., vol. I, pp. 173-7. Slightly different translations can be found elsewhere, especially *Letters and Despatches of the First Napoleon,* and Barry O'Meara's *Historical Memoirs of Napoleon, Book IX. 1815,* Philadelphia, 1820, pp. 227-30. Additionally, a reduced size photograph of this bulletin (*A l'Armée*) and the bulletin to the people (*Au Peuple Français*) can be found in René Reymond's *La Route Napoléon de l'Ile d' Elbe aux Tuileries, 1815,* Lyon, 1985, pp. 22-3.
22. *Correspondance,* 28, No. 21681. Translation found in Fleury, *op. cit.,* vol. I, pp. 177-80, and O'Meara, *op. cit.,* pp. 224-7. See also the photograph in Reymond, *op. cit.*
23. *Correspondance,* 28, No. 21683. Translation in Fleury, *op. cit.,* vol. I, pp. 181-2, and O'Meara, *op. cit.,* pp. 231-3.
24. Houssaye, Henry, *The Return of Napoleon,* London, 1934, p. 45.
25. Reymond, *op. cit.,* p. 22; 'Sometimes terse, sometimes emphatic, always dazzling.' (my translation).
26. Ibid., p. 49.
27. See Houssaye, *Return,* p. 49; Cronin, *op. cit.,* p. 389, and Alan Schom, *One Hundred Days: Napoleon's Road to Waterloo,* New York, 1992, p. 19.
28. Beyle, Marie Henri (Stendhal). *A Life of Napoleon,* London, 1956, p. 172.
29. Houssaye, *Return,* p. 57.
30. Tulard, Jean, and Garros, Louis. *Itinéraire de Napoléon au jour le jour 1769-1821,* France, 1992, p. 462. This unique book details Napoleon's daily activities throughout his career.
31. Houssaye, *Return,* p. 57.
32. Ibid., p. 63. See also his proclamation to the Hautes and Basse Alpes: 'the cause of the Nation will triumph again!', *Correspondance,* 28, No. 21684.
33. Thiers, *op. cit.,* vol. v, pp. 4323.
34. The plaque reads: '*SOLDATS. Je suis votre Empereur. Ne me reconnaissez-vous pas? S'il en est un parmi vous qui veuille tuer son général, ME VOILA!!! 7 Mars 1815*' (my translation).

35. Cronin, *op. cit.*, p, 392, and Fleury, *op. cit.*, vol. I, pp. 193-4.
36. Fleury, vol. I, pp. 195-6.
37. Aubry, Octave. *Napoleon*, London, 1964, p. 331.
38. Fleury, *op. cit.*, vol. I, pp.198-9.
39. Thiers, *op. cit.*, vol, V, pp. 434-5.
40. Saunders, Edith.*The Hundred Days: Napoleon's Final Wager for Victory*, New York, 1964, pp. 18-21.
41. Decree of 13 March 1815, *Correspondance*, 28, No. 21686.
42. Thiers, *op. cit.*, vol. 5, pp. 444-6; Fleury, op. cit., vol. I, pp. 230-50.
43. Fleury, *op. cit.*, vol. I, p. 231
44. Houssaye, *Return*, pp.100-6.
45. Thiers, *op. cit.*, vol. 5, pp. 446-7; 'Down with the nobles! Down with the priests! Down with the Bourbons!' (my translation).
46. *Correspondance*, 28, No. 21689. Translation found in Saunders, *op. cit.*, p. 33.
47. Fleury, *op. cit.*, vol. I, pp. 259-60, fn. A photograph of this proclamation is in Reymond, *op. cit.*, p. 165.
48. Chandler, David. *Waterloo, The Hundred Days*, London, 1980, 1987, p. 19.
49. Thiébault, Baron.*The Memoirs of Baron Thiébault (Late Lieutenant-General in the French Army)*, tr. A. J. Butler, 2 vols., New York, 1896, vol. 2, p. 417.
50. Chandler, *Waterloo*, p. 19.
51. Cronin, *op. cit.*, p. 394.
52. Mercy Argenteau, comte de. *Memoirs of the Comte de Mercy Argenteau, Napoleon's Chamberlain and Minister Plenipotentiary to the King of Bavaria*, tr., ed., and intr. George S. Hellman, 2 vols., New York, 1917, vol. I, p. 178.

BIBLIOGRAPHY

Bonaparte, Napoleon. *Correspondance de Napoléon 1er*, Paris, 1869.
Caulaincourt, marquis de. *No Peace With Napoleon!*, New York, 1936.
Fleury de Chaboulon, baron. *Memoirs of the Private Life, Return and Reign of Napoleon in 1815*, 2 vols., London, 1820.
Cronin, Vincent. *Napoleon Bonaparte: An Intimate Biography*, New York, 1972.
Fain, baron J. *The Manuscript of 1814. A History of Events which led to the Abdication of Napoleon. Written at the Command of the Emperor*, London, 1823.
Hortense, Queen Consort of Louis, King of Holland. *The Memoirs of Queen Hortense*. Published by arrangement with Prince Napoleon, ed. Jean Hanoteau, tr. by Arthur K. Griggs, New York, 1927.
Houssaye, H. *Napoleon and the Campaign of 1814: France*, Tyne and Wear, 1994; facsimile of 1914 edn.
- *The Return of Napoleon*, London, 1934.
Las Cases, comte de. *Mémorial de Sainte-Hélène*. Journal of the Private Life and Conversations of the Emperor Napoleon at St. Helena, 4 vols., Boston, 1823.
Saunders, Edith. *The Hundred Days: Napoleon's Final Wager for Victory*, New York, 1964.
Schom, Alan. *One Hundred Days: Napoleon's Road to Waterloo*, New York, 1992.
Thiers, Adolphe. *History of the Consulate and the Empire of France under Napoleon*. Tr. by D. Forbes Campbell and H. W. Herbert, 5 vols., Philadelphia, 1893.
Tulard, Jean, and Garros, Louis. *Itinéraire de Napoléon au jour le jour, 1769-1821*, France, 1992.

WATERLOO:
A REPUTATION DESTROYED
Andrew Uffindell

'SOLDIERS! WE HAVE NOT BEEN BEATEN.' WITH THIS PROUD proclamation to his army, Napoleon returned to France on 1 March 1815.[1] He attributed the Bourbon restoration and the allied military triumph in 1814 to treason, not defeat on the battlefield: 'two men left our ranks and betrayed our laurels, their prince, their benefactor'. Now, back on the throne of France, Napoleon needed to restore his military reputation. He had to prove that he had not been out-generalled in 1814 and so could not afford another defeat. Disaster on a battlefield in 1815 would reflect on one man alone: Napoleon Bonaparte.

His overtures of peace rejected by Europe, Napoleon prepared for war. He determined to seize the initiative and strike a pre-emptive blow before the Allied Seventh Coalition invaded France in July. While the vast Russian and Austrian armies were slowly marching towards the Rhine, he would invade the United Netherlands (an amalgamated Belgium and Holland), seize Brussels, defeat the two defending armies under Wellington and Blücher, boost French morale and possibly topple the bellicose British Tory administration. Victory in Belgium would rally France behind the Emperor and leave him in a much stronger position to sue for peace or to march against the Russians and Austrians.

Wellington's Anglo-Dutch-German composite army and Blücher's Prussians could field a combined total of 210,000 men. Napoleon's Army of the North, the strike force with which he would march on Brussels, numbered only 124,000. Hence his only hope of victory lay in a surprise onslaught to seize a central position between the two allied armies, separate them and defeat them piecemeal. The allies could not know where Napoleon would invade, so they had to guard the entire frontier from the English Channel to the Ardennes. They could only concentrate their armies for battle once they knew for sure the axis of Napoleon's main thrust. Until then, they had to cover all the potential invasion routes and Wellington, misled by Napoleon's brilliant security and counter-intelligence measures, feared for his western flank and his communications with England via Ostend.

DUKE OF WELLINGTON. ENGRAVING BY MEYER AFTER BURNEY.

BLÜCHER. ENGRAVING BY T. W. HARLAND AFTER GRÖGER.

Napoleon reckoned that the fiery Prussian Field Marshal Blücher would rush to support an ally quicker than would the cautious British Duke of Wellington: 'all my measures had therefore the objective of attacking the Prussians first'.[2] Napoleon resolved to cross the River Sambre at Charleroi, at the junction of the two allied armies, and drive back the Prussian advanced posts.

The French soldiers were experienced veterans but were undisciplined and notorious looters. They distrusted many of their commanders, who had often willingly served the restored Bourbons in 1814–15 only to rally again to Napoleon on his return from Elba. Napoleon's troops were neurotically afraid of betrayal by royalist sympathisers and were prone to panic under pressure. None the less, the French army was the best organised of the three and had strong reserves of heavy cavalry and a formidable élite, the Imperial Guard.

The Prussian troops had experience of fighting in 1813–14 and their morale was remarkably resilient. The Prussians preferred to attack and often expended their strength too quickly. In defence they were not as robust as the British infantry. Wellington's Netherlands troops and his soldiers from the German states of Hanover, Brunswick and Nassau were largely young and inexperienced and sometimes unsteady. Few of his British troops were Peninsula veterans.

From the start, Napoleon seriously under-estimated his two foes. He hardly expected them to stand and fight a major battle south of Brussels. Surely, he reasoned, Wellington and Blücher would concentrate their armies at a safe distance from the French point of attack. He anticipated that they would separate and retreat along their divergent lines of communication: Wellington westwards to Ostend and Blücher eastwards to Prussia. Anticipating a short, easy campaign, Napoleon left his best marshals behind; Suchet in Lyons to prepare to meet the Austro–Russian invasion in July, and Davout in Paris to control the empire's political opponents there.

He then made several flawed key appointments in his Army of the North. Foremost of these was Marshal Nicolas Soult as chief of staff; the reliable Berthier was dead and Soult was no adequate replacement. Napoleon entrusted him with concentrating the Army of the North south of the United Netherlands frontier. Besides giving III, IV and VI Corps wrong destinations, Soult forgot to send the Reserve Cavalry its marching orders until 12 June. This boded ill for the incipient campaign, but Napoleon failed to replace him.[3]

The French corps commanders were experienced and some, particularly Lieutenant-Generals Maurice Gérard and Claude Pajol, were brilliant. Others, such as Drouet d'Erlon and Honoré Reille, were cautious after repeated defeats in Spain at the hands of the Duke of Wellington.[4]

As his two chief subordinates, Napoleon chose Marshals Emmanuel de Grouchy and Michel Ney. Grouchy was steady but over-awed by Napoleon. Ney was hot-tempered and reckless. Napoleon gave him too little time to find his feet. 'Send for Marshal Ney,' Napoleon ordered Davout as late as 11 June. 'Tell him that if he wishes to be present at the first battles which are going to occur, he should be at Avesnes, where my Headquarters will be, on the 14th.'[5] Ney set out for the front but was not given a command, that of the left wing, until 15 June when the invasion was already under way, leaving him no time to familiarise himself with his command. This was no way to set up a command team and Napoleon deserves heavy censure for much of the faulty teamwork that ensued.

Napoleon had originally planned his invasion for 14 June but postponed it to the early hours of the 15th. The Army of the North completed its final moves into position immediately south of the frontier, from Solre-sur-Sambre in the west to Philippeville in the east. On the morning of the 14th Napoleon wrote confidently from Avesnes to his elder brother, Prince Joseph, at Paris: 'My brother, this evening I am taking my headquarters to Beaumont. Tomorrow, the 15th, I will fall on Charleroi, where the Prussian army is. This will lead to a battle or to the enemy's retreat. The army is fine and the weather quite good; the country is perfectly disposed.'[6]

In the early hours of 15 June French troops awoke to the beating of their drums. Their officers read out Napoleon's Order of the Day. He reminded his soldiers that 14 June had been the anniversary of his victories at Marengo in 1800 and Friedland in 1807. Now a coalition of the princes of Europe threatened the independence and sacred rights of France. The French army was marching to repulse this unjust aggression. It would triumph again over superior numbers. It would liberate the Belgians and then the inhabitants of the small German states from oppression. 'Soldiers!' the Emperor concluded. 'We shall have to make some forced marches, fight some battles, run some risks, but with constancy victory will be ours. The rights, the honour and the happiness of the country will be reconquered. For every Frenchman who has courage, the moment has come to conquer or die!'

NEY. PRINT AFTER GÉRARD.

Delays occurred. In IV Corps, a royalist sympathiser, Lieutenant-General Louis de Bourmont, deserted to the Prussians and this treachery shocked his troops. III Corps never received its marching orders, the officer bringing them having fallen from his horse in the night and broken his leg. The corps set off only when subsequent units were marching into its bivouacs. I Corps was also late in departing.

Following these initial setbacks, optimism began to rise in the French columns. The mist soon lifted, revealing a bright blue sky. 'It is the colour of hope,' Napoleon declared.[7] Everywhere the French received a rapturous welcome, for the inhabitants of southern Belgium were French-speaking and generally regarded Napoleon as a liberator from Dutch rule and Prussian exactions of food and lodging.

Napoleon reached Charleroi towards 11 a.m. The sappers and marines of the Guard stormed the bridge under a hail of fire and opened the way for light cavalry to ride through the town in hot pursuit of the Prussians. Napoleon had won his bridgehead over the Sambre and now established his Headquarters in the Château Puissant where he ate the lunch prepared for the commander of the Prussian I Corps.

As it reached Charleroi, the French army split into two wings and a reserve. The left wing, entrusted to Marshal Ney, was to push due north along the Brussels road towards Quatre Bras. Ney was to push back and contain Wellington's advanced units. Marshal Grouchy would lead the right wing north-eastwards to Sombreffe against the Prussians. Napoleon hoped to cut the important lateral Nivelles–Namur road at both Quatre Bras and Sombreffe to hamper communications between Wellington and Blücher.

THEATRE OF OPERATIONS FOR THE 1815 CAMPAIGN

By nightfall, Ney's leading units were 2½ miles south of Quatre Bras, but a brigade of Wellington's Nassau troops had prevented him from seizing the strategic crossroads here. Grouchy had been delayed for three hours by the presence of a Prussian rearguard at Gilly, eight miles south-west of Sombreffe. Napoleon came to inspect this rearguard's position in person, correctly estimated that the Prussians could be swept aside and ordered an attack. However, the Prussians retired without awaiting the shock. Napoleon was enraged. He ordered one of his ADCs, General Louis Letort, to charge with the four squadrons of the Emperor's escort. These horsemen crushed one battalion but were checked by another. Letort himself was shot in the stomach and died later.

Grouchy halted for the night south of Fleurus, five miles short of Sombreffe. The Nivelles–Namur road had not been cut, but Napoleon was satisfied. 'The two enemy armies were taken by surprise, their communications already considerably embarrassed,' he later wrote. 'All my manoeuvres had succeeded as I wished. I could now take the initiative of attacking the enemy armies, one by one. Their only chance of avoiding this misfortune ... was to yield ground and rally on Brussels, or beyond.'[8]

Napoleon did not expect to fight a major battle on 16 June against the Prussians at Ligny. He considered that the shock of his surprise invasion of the day before would cause Wellington and Blücher to retreat. Instead, Blücher accepted battle in the forward position of Ligny, immediately south of Sombreffe. This decision surprised Napoleon for the allies had not yet had time to mass their units from scattered cantonments. Blücher fought at Ligny with just three-quarters of his army. Lieutenant-General von Bülow, the commander of IV Corps, had misunderstood his orders and failed to arrive from Liège in time; he would not join the army until 17 June.

Blücher accepted battle at Ligny for three reasons. Firstly he wished to delay, check or even reverse Napoleon's thrust towards Brussels. Secondly he wished to gain time to enable his ally Wellington to concentrate his army, which was even more disunited than Blücher's. Thirdly Wellington had promised, over-optimistically as it turned out, that in the course of the afternoon of the 16th he would mass most of his army at Quatre Bras, six miles north-west of Ligny. Wellington intended then to overthrow Marshal Ney and the French left wing and come to join Blücher at Ligny against the bulk of Napoleon's army.

In the morning of 16 June, Napoleon, at the Château Puissant in Charleroi, received a series of intelligence reports that Prussian troops were massing around Ligny. He came to see for himself and decided to crush the Prussians at Ligny in a pitched battle before turning on Wellington and marching north to seize Brussels.

It was not until 3 p.m. that Napoleon had massed his right wing and reserve on the battlefield. By then the Prussians had managed to deploy 83,000 men and 224 guns north of the Ligny brook, which flowed all along the front line. The French were 63,000 men and 230 guns strong.

Napoleon had undertaken a personal reconnaissance of the battlefield on horseback. Now he was at the Naveau windmill in the outskirts of the town of Fleurus, on the southern edge of the battlefield. French sappers had constructed a lookout platform on the mill to provide their Emperor with a general view of the field.

Napoleon's aim was gradually to draw Blücher's reserves into the fighting along the winding Ligny brook. Fighting would increase in intensity as more French troops entered the fray, and in extent as additional French units sought to outflank the Prussian battle line to the west. Napoleon hoped to unbalance Blücher's army, to wear it down and then to break through with his Guard at Ligny village in the centre. Meanwhile, Ney was supposed to capture Quatre Bras six miles to the north-west, contain Wellington, and then to send d'Erlon's I Corps down the Nivelles–Namur road to fall on Blücher's rear. If d'Erlon and the Guard managed to link up at the village of Brye, a large section of Blücher's forces would be encircled.

Accordingly, at 3 p.m. Napoleon ordered the battle to begin. His servant, the mameluke Ali, recalled that towards the beginning of the fighting he noticed a group of young staff officers standing near the Emperor:

'In this group they roared with laughter and joked noisily about the different scenes occurring some distance in front between some Prussians and French. The Emperor, who heard the noise these officers were making, cast glances towards them from time to time to show his tedium and displeasure. At last, irritated and bothered by so much light-heartedness, he said, looking severely at the one who was laughing and chattering most: "Monsieur! You must neither laugh nor joke when so many brave men are killing each other before our eyes."'[9]

Shortly after 3.15 p.m. Napoleon sent a direct order to General d'Erlon, commander of I Corps, bidding him to march to the battlefield of Ligny.

However, d'Erlon headed in the wrong direction and by 5.30 had emerged behind the French lines, heading for Fleurus. The appearance of this as yet unidentified column caused the French left wing to panic. Napoleon had to postpone the decisive Guard attack against Ligny in order to restore the situation with troops from the reserve.

The astonished Napoleon then noticed d'Erlon turning round and retracing his steps to rejoin Marshal Ney. An incompetent staff officer had neglected to inform Ney that Napoleon had summoned d'Erlon to Ligny and thus Ney assumed that d'Erlon had marched off on his own initiative. Faced with the task of containing increasing numbers of Wellington's troops at Quatre Bras, Ney had sent a desperate recall to d'Erlon. As it was, d'Erlon was too late to intervene in either Ligny or Quatre Bras and this fiasco cost Napoleon a decisive victory. It was the single most important cause of his eventual defeat. If d'Erlon had fallen on Blücher's western flank and rear, Napoleon would never have 'met his Waterloo', or at least not in the United Netherlands. Shoddy staff work and vague orders were the chief culprits and Napoleon deserves some of the blame, although he was let down by his subordinates.[10]

Throughout the battle of Ligny, Napoleon had exercised a general control from his command post at Fleurus. Now, in the evening, he sent staff officers to the front line to act as his eyes and ears, to judge whether the situation was ripe for the intervention of the Guard. One of these officers was Major Jean-Roch Coignet. 'Go to the steeple [of Ligny] and find Gérard,' Napoleon told him. 'Wait for his orders to return.' Coignet vividly recalled what ensued:

'I galloped off. This was not an easy task; I had to make many detours. The space was covered with gardens. I did not know which way to go. However, I found the brave general at last, fighting hand to hand, covered with mud. I went up to him. "The Emperor sent me to you, General."
– "Go to the Emperor and say that if he will send me reinforcements, the Prussians will be beaten. Tell him that I have lost half my soldiers, but that, if I am supported, the victory is assured."'[11]

A tremendous artillery crossfire was devastating the exposed Prussian units on the open slopes north of the Ligny brook. Then the Guard, supported by massed cuirassiers, stormed the village of Ligny. The Prussians withdrew in disorder but managed to establish a rearguard line after some desperate cavalry counter-attacks.

The French lost 10,000–12,000 men and were too exhausted to pursue immediately. Prussian losses were between 20,000 and 25,000 plus 22 guns. The Prussians nearly lost their commander as well, for Blücher had been trapped under his dead horse during a furious cavalry mêlée. In the twilight, the 9th Cuirassiers rode past but did not recognise him. The cuirassiers' commander, Lieutenant-General Jacques Delort, regretted for the rest of his life that he failed to capture Blücher, for that might have proved decisive.[12]

Napoleon's servant Ali concluded that, 'as glorious as this day had just been for the French armies, in general we were not happy: it did not produce the results we had hoped from it, it had nothing decisive'.[13] Napoleon had broken into Blücher's battle line and forced him to withdraw, but he had not broken through or encircled the Prussian army as he had hoped in the morning.

During the night the Prussians evacuated the battlefield and slipped away to the north towards Wavre. Here they would rally and replenish ammunition. Their morale remained high and Blücher, restored by a generous dose of alcohol, was keen for another fight. By 8 a.m. on 17 June Wellington and Blücher were already exchanging messages and arranging for the Prussians to come to support the Duke at a strong defensive position at Mont St-Jean, three miles south of the village of Waterloo.

In the evening of 16 June Grouchy had requested orders from Napoleon, but the exhausted Emperor had told him to wait until morning. In any case an immediate pursuit of the Prussians would have been practically impossible because his exhausted army would have had first to dislodge a stout Prussian rearguard line in the darkness.

Next morning Grouchy returned to Headquarters at Fleurus but was told that Napoleon was asleep. Even when the Emperor awoke, he responded brusquely to Grouchy's request for orders: 'I shall give you them when I consider it convenient.'

Several commentators have argued that Napoleon's lethargy stemmed from illness.[14] But if Napoleon were ill on the morning of 17 June, his recovery by the afternoon was little short of miraculous, for he galloped after Wellington's retreating rearguard with energy remarkable for a 45-year-old. In fact, Napoleon was suffering from a far more serious malady than piles or cystitis or acromegaly: he was afflicted with supreme over-confidence. 'Once he had an idea planted in his head,' asserted his Master of Horse, General Armand de Caulaincourt, 'the Emperor was carried away by his own illusion. He cherished it, caressed it, became absorbed with it ...'[15] All

Napoleon's errors in the 1815 campaign, including his flawed appointments, stemmed ultimately from his fatal over-confidence and unwillingness to reconsider his *idées fixes.*

From the start he had believed that Wellington and Blücher would separate and retreat, not fight and unite. Now he assumed that he had dealt Blücher a resounding defeat at Ligny and knocked him out of the campaign. Napoleon intended to rest his army during the morning of 17 June before marching it throughout the afternoon and night to Brussels. Wellington, he assumed, was hastily retiring to the English Channel.

So throughout the morning of 17 June Napoleon toured the battlefield of Ligny and discussed the political news from Paris while waiting for intelligence on the military situation to come in. It was a fatal delay that allowed the initiative to slip to the Allies. If he had marched immediately to Quatre Bras he would have been able to fall on Wellington's flank, because the Duke had not been informed of the outcome of Ligny until 7.30 a.m. The Emperor's lethargy cost him his last chance of an overwhelming, inexpensive and quick victory. He had failed to live up to the proud boast a younger Napoleon had made: 'I may lose ground, but I shall never lose a minute.'[16]

Wellington, reprieved, had time to retreat to the ridge south of Waterloo while the Prussians were able to rally at Wavre and prepare to join him. Most importantly, the French lost track of the direction of Blücher's retreat. The blame for allowing the Prussians to link up with Wellington at Waterloo lies far more with Napoleon than with Grouchy.

Not until 11 a.m., after learning that Wellington had still been at Quatre Bras four hours earlier, did Napoleon give Grouchy verbal orders: the Marshal was to pursue the Prussians, catch and attack them. He was to complete their defeat and never lose sight of them. Meanwhile, Napoleon was going to take his reserve to join Ney at Quatre Bras and attack Wellington.

Towards noon, Napoleon sent Grouchy further, written, orders. He thought that the Prussians were in full retreat north-eastwards. Grouchy was to go to Gembloux and reconnoitre towards Namur and Maastricht. He was to keep the Emperor informed of Prussian movements.

For this task Grouchy was given the French right wing, a total of 33,000 men. At last Napoleon had unleashed Grouchy. But the Marshal, who had been straining at the leash for so long, advanced slowly, as if unsure of himself. He deserves censure for the tardiness and clumsiness of his movements. He marched his two infantry corps to Gembloux in a long column along a single track. Furthermore, he ordered Vandamme's III Corps to lead the march despite the fact that Gérard's IV Corps was further north. Gérard had to wait near Ligny until Vandamme had filed past from the vicinity of St-Amand.

Such tardiness would characterise all Grouchy's movements on 17 and 18 June. He would gradually realise that the Prussians had rallied at Wavre, but expected them to retreat from there to Brussels. A cross-country march to Waterloo across the marshy Lasne valley seems to have been the last thing that Grouchy expected.

Napoleon led his reserve to join Ney and the left wing at Quatre Bras. Then he pursued the retreating Wellington up the Brussels road. In torrential rain and through a sea of mud, the leading French units reached the battlefield of Waterloo towards 6 p.m. The II and VI Corps plus III Cavalry Corps and most of the Imperial Guard had halted along a 3½ mile stretch of the Brussels road, from the battlefield south to the village of Genappe. A convoy of provisions reached Genappe very late that night, but many soldiers slept without having eaten.[17]

Napoleon feared that Wellington might resume his retreat and escape under cover of darkness through the Forest of Soignes, perhaps to unite with Blücher's Prussians on the other side. This was his nightmare. He wanted a quick victory, to crush his enemy instead of forcing him back. But during the night officers returning from reconnaissance patrols confirmed that Wellington was not retreating. Two Belgian deserters brought further reassurance that their army was still in position. It was 5 a.m. Napoleon had just dictated an order to Soult:

'The Emperor orders the army to be ready to attack at 9 a.m. The corps commanders will muster their troops, will have their weapons put in order, and will allow the soldiers to make soup. They will also have the soldiers eat so that at 9 a.m. precisely each corps commander will be ready and can be in battle, with his artillery and ambulances, in the battle positions that the Emperor indicated in his order of yesterday evening.'[18]

The order of the previous evening had prescribed the positions for each French corps and had also stated that the battle would begin early in the morning. This new order of 5 a.m. postponed the opening of the attack as Napoleon realised that after a night of almost continuous rain the ground would be in no fit state to allow an army to take up battle positions quickly. In particular, the artillery pieces would sink into the mud and have to be hauled out. Furthermore some of his troops would have to march 3½ miles to the battlefield from the village of Genappe and would arrive tired and hungry only to be flung into the fight without having rested. Colonel Toussaint-Jean Trefçon stated that the postponement 'was greeted with joy for many of the soldiers were dying from hunger and usually they do not like to fight when they are dirty'.[19]

There would be plenty of time to defeat the 'Sepoy General', as Napoleon contemptuously referred to the Duke of Wellington. Through a window of his Headquarters at Le Caillou, the Emperor perceived a few rays of the morning sun peering through the clouds. 'France', he mused, 'was going to rise, that day, more glorious, more powerful and greater than ever!'[20]

But the appalling weather had made even a 9 a.m. attack doubtful. Sergeant Hippolyte de Mauduit of the 1st Grenadiers related how even companies were disunited. Groups of soldiers had wandered away from the main road, seeking shelter in distant buildings.

At 8 a.m., Napoleon held a pre-battle conference with his generals at Le Caillou. Some of his subordinates, who had harsh experience of fighting against Wellington and the British in the Peninsular War, were markedly less confident than he. Marshal Soult advised recalling Grouchy's detachment to help defeat Wellington. 'Because you have been beaten by Wellington,' sneered the Emperor, 'you think him a great general. I tell you that Wellington is a bad general, that the English are bad troops and that this will be a picnic.' Lieutenant-General Honoré Reille, commander of II Corps, disagreed:

> 'Well-posted as Wellington knows how to post them and attacked head-on, I consider the English infantry to be impregnable in view of its calm tenacity and superior firepower. Before we can reach them with the bayonet, half our attacking force would be shot down. But the English army is less agile, less supple, less manoeuvrable than ours. If we cannot conquer it by a head-on attack, we could do so by manoeuvring.'[21]

Napoleon's youngest brother, Prince Jérôme, was a divisional commander in Reille's corps. Jérôme told the Emperor that he had spoken to a waiter at an inn at Genappe. The waiter mentioned that on 17 June during Wellington's retreat through the village from Quatre Bras to Waterloo, he had overheard an English ADC say that Blücher would march to unite with Wellington in front of the Forest of Soignes. Napoleon refused to believe it: 'after a battle like Fleurus [Ligny] and being pursued by a substantial number of troops, it is impossible for the Prussians to join the English in less than two days'.

Napoleon then left Le Caillou, remarking as he did so: 'Gentlemen, if my orders are carried out well, we will sleep tonight at Brussels.' Then he rode north, to the front line.

The battlefield of Waterloo is small; Napoleon's front line extended for only 2¼ miles. The armies were separated by a shallow valley about 1,000 metres across. Wellington sheltered and concealed his troops as far as possible on the reverse slopes of his ridge while in front he occupied several farms as strong-points. In the west, British guardsmen and German light troops held Hougoumont. In the centre, a battalion of the crack King's German Legion garrisoned La Haye Sainte, and in the east, a brigade of Nassau troops guarded the farms of Papelotte and La Haye, the small village of Smohain and the château of Frischermont. This far eastern flank rested on difficult terrain, featuring sunken lanes, hedges, undulating ground and a brook. On the western horizon, Wellington placed a Netherlands division at the town of Braine-l'Alleud and 17,000 men around Hal, eight miles west of the battlefield, to guard against any outflanking moves. Indeed, Napoleon had little opportunity to manoeuvre. He was left with little choice but to launch a frontal attack on what was a naturally strong position held by a cool-headed and very experienced general.

Napoleon rode up to the French outposts to survey as much of the battlefield as possible. He also sent Lieutenant-General Nicolas Haxo, the reliable commander of the Imperial Guard engineers, ahead of the French lines to reconnoitre Wellington's position. Napoleon wanted to know if Wellington had erected any earthworks or entrenchments but Haxo reported none.

Napoleon was still waiting for the rearmost corps of his army to arrive. At 10 a.m. he ordered his troops to deploy ready for battle and reviewed his *Grande Armée* for the last time. Wellington's men watched from the ridge opposite and, as Napoleon hoped, many were intimidated. Colonel Auguste Pétiet of the French staff remembered how:

'The Emperor rode up and down the lines of the army and was received as always with cheering. He dismounted and took up a position on a quite high mound near La Belle Alliance, from where it was possible to see the battlefield and the two armies ready to come to blows. Napoleon had spread a map on his little table and while examining it, he seemed to be absorbed by profound strategic plans. I was stationed at the foot of this mound; my eyes could not leave this extraordinary man whom Victory had for so long showered with her gifts. His stoutness, his dull, white face, his heavy walk made him seem very different from the General Bonaparte I had seen at the beginning of my career during the campaign of 1800 in Italy.'[22]

Before the battle began at 11.30 a.m., Napoleon had withdrawn 1,500 metres south of the front line to a mound near the farm of Rossomme. Here at 11 a.m. he dictated an order to Marshal Soult, for the attention of all corps commanders:

'Once the entire army has been drawn up in battle order, at about 1 p.m., when the Emperor gives the order to Marshal Ney, the attack will begin to seize the village of Mont St-Jean, where the roads unite. To this end, the 12-pounder batteries of II Corps and those of VI Corps will unite with those of I Corps. These twenty-four guns [23] will bombard the troops at Mont St-Jean and Count d'Erlon will begin the

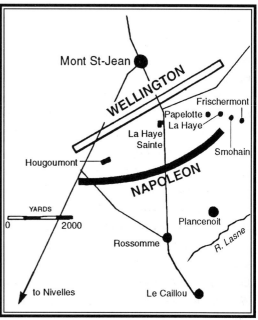

attack by sending forward his left division and supporting it, as circumstances dictate, by the other divisions of I Corps. II Corps will advance so as to keep level with Count d'Erlon. The engineer companies of I Corps will hold themselves in readiness to barricade themselves immediately at Mont St-Jean.'

Napoleon's intention was an overwhelming frontal attack in the east by d'Erlon's fresh I Corps which would burst through Wellington's left wing. Shortly after dictating this order, Napoleon modified the plan, for Marshal Ney added in pencil on a copy of the order: 'Count d'Erlon will understand that the attack will commence by the left instead of the right. Communicate this new disposition to General Reille.'

In other words, the battle would begin with a preliminary attack in the west by Reille's II Corps against Hougoumont. The operation would not be an all-out assault on the farm but a low-intensity engagement. Reille's troops were to make contact with and tie down Wellington's right wing.

The main attack by I Corps would then smash through Wellington's eastern wing while II Corps prevented Wellington's western wing from interfering with this operation. The main attack would then wheel round to the west, using II Corps as a pivot, and seize the village of Mont St-Jean. The capture of this village would cut off Wellington's line of retreat through the Forest of Soignes to Brussels and would compel him to fall back, away from Blücher and towards Ostend. The plan was reminiscent of the battle of Friedland in 1807, in that initially Napoleon's left wing would merely engage and hold the foe while a powerful right hook decided the battle.

Napoleon's dictated order of 11 a.m. outlined only the basic plan and did not specify what would happen once the main attack broke into, and hurled back, Wellington's eastern wing. As Napoleon commented, *on s'engage, et puis on voit:* 'one engages and then one sees'. But in his memoirs, dictated while in exile on St. Helena, Napoleon spoke of supporting d'Erlon's I Corps with Lobau's VI Corps and its two attached light cavalry divisions, followed by the Reserve Cavalry and the Guard.[24] As he had told his generals at the Le Caillou conference earlier in the morning: 'I shall bombard the enemy with my numerous artillery, I shall charge them with my cavalry, so that they are forced to show themselves and, when I am quite sure where the English contingent is, I shall march straight at it with my Old Guard.'[25] Once Wellington's eastern wing had been dislodged from the ridge, everything would be unleashed.

Napoleon's plan seemed simple on paper but depended for success on perfect execution, and his subordinates were not up to the task. The battle began to escalate out of control from the start, with the supposedly limited attack on Hougoumont. According to General Reille, whose II Corps assaulted the farm, his task was a matter of 'keeping in the low ground behind [south of] the wood, while maintaining in front a strong line of skirmishers.'[26]

Reille entrusted the attack to Prince Jérôme's division. His men were soon heavily engaged inside the wood and a brigade commander was among the first to be killed. To support the troops already engaged, Jérôme was forced to send in more and more infantry until his entire division was engaged. This did not worry Jérôme who, indeed, seemed determined to exceed his orders and capture Hougoumont. In vain did Reille send repeated commands to limit the attacks. One of Lieutenant-General Foy's two brigades now entered the struggle: 'the fire of the enemy was so sharp and heavy,' Foy noted. 'For us the wood was a death-trap.'[27]

Smitten by overwhelming firepower, the waves of French infantry were massacred as they vainly tried to storm the solid brick walls of the enclosed garden and the building block. At one point, a handful of soldiers of the 1st Light Infantry broke through the North Gateway into the farm courtyard but the garrison heaved the gates shut and annihilated the intruders. This was the nearest that Hougoumont came to being lost.

The headstrong French troops were too keen to attack and could not be held to limited objectives. Eagle-bearer Silvain Larreguy de Civrieux remembered advancing through the wood and being splashed with blood. Despite being surrounded by corpses, he and his comrades were elated to be in action. Wellington coolly fed in the barest minimum of reinforcements necessary to hold the farm. Thus the attack, which was intended to absorb Wellington's troops and attention, in fact unbalanced the French II Corps and tied it down. Napoleon's plan was already breaking down.

The French commanders failed to provide adequate artillery support for their infantry. 'There was but little cannonade directed against Hougoumont,' stated Major Alexander Woodford of the Coldstream Guards.[28] Instead of bombarding the farm, Reille's cannon strove unsuccessfully to neutralise Wellington's guns. Napoleon intervened by ordering up the two horse artillery batteries of III Cavalry Corps to boost French firepower.

In contrast, Wellington closely supported his garrison with artillery. He ordered Major Robert Bull's howitzers to drop a devastating hail of shells over the heads of the garrison and into the French holding the wood. This deadly and superbly accurate fire compelled the French temporarily to evacuate the wood.

At about 2 p.m. Napoleon turned his attention again to Hougoumont and belatedly ordered eight howitzers to be placed in battery to pound the building block into submission. At 2.30 p.m. the battery opened fire. 'A shell or carcass was thrown into the great barn', said Woodford, 'and the smoke and flames burst out in a terrific manner, and communicated with rapidity and fury to the other outbuildings. Some officers attempting to penetrate into the stables to rescue some wounded men, were obliged to desist, from the suffocation of the smoke, and several men perished.'[29] The fire gutted many of the buildings but miraculously died after charring the feet of a crucifix in the chapel, which remained intact surrounded by ruins. From afar it seemed that a mouse could not survive in Hougoumont but closer inspection showed British guardsmen and their German allies holding out amid the inferno. At about 3 p.m. some guns from Captain Samuel Bolton's battery managed to neutralise the howitzers before they could do further damage. The obstinate strong-point of Hougoumont would successfully hold out for the entire day.

Shortly after 1 p.m. the entire equilibrium of the battle dramatically altered. Napoleon had surveyed the battlefield with his telescope before unleashing his main attack and noticed troops on the north-eastern horizon. Confirmation soon arrived that they were Prussians. Napoleon personally interrogated a captured Prussian hussar who informed him that the whole of Blücher's IV Corps was bearing down on his eastern flank. Napoleon was forced to detach Lieutenant-General Count Lobau's VI Corps and two light cavalry divisions to meet this new threat.

Nevertheless the Emperor was not unduly worried. He had received a letter from Grouchy, written at 6 a.m. from Gembloux, stating that he was setting out instantly with the right wing to continue his pursuit of Blücher. Napoleon assumed, without justification, that only the Prussian IV Corps was advancing against him and that Grouchy would be marching on its heels. In fact three Prussian corps were marching towards Napoleon while von Thielemann's III Corps was preparing a tough rearguard stand along the River Dyle at Wavre. Grouchy had in fact left Gembloux after 7 a.m. and marched slowly; he would not reach Wavre until about 4 p.m. Thielemann would successfully hold him at bay until the late morning of 19 June, well after the battle of Waterloo was over. Napoleon did send a message to Grouchy informing him of the Prussian approach, but this message was so vague and arrived so late that Grouchy failed to see the urgency and in any case could do nothing to help.

An appalling disaster befell the French main attack. Napoleon had assembled a great battery of eighty guns in front of Wellington's eastern wing. These guns pounded the opposite ridge in a preliminary bombardment. The barrage, however deafening, was too short to have any significant effect and the soggy soil muffled shell bursts and prevented cannonballs from rico-cheting. Wellington's infantry lay down on the reverse slopes of their ridge and thus avoided many casualties.

Then, at about 2 p.m., d'Erlon's four infantry divisions advanced into the valley. One brigade assaulted the farm of La Haye Sainte on the left but the garrison held out. Napoleon should have concentrated far more artillery fire against this totally visible strong-point rather than waste shots against the troops protected by the ridge. Without such artillery fire, the French infantry were powerless in front of the solid brick walls.

To the east of La Haye Sainte, there marched four massive columns, 180 men wide and up to twenty-four ranks deep. On d'Erlon's eastern flank, skirmishers probed the defences around Papelotte, La Haye and Smohain without making much headway. West of La Haye Sainte, a cuirassier brigade rode in support.[30]

WATERLOO: FRENCH CUIRASSIERS (FOREGROUND) AND *CHEVAU-LÉGERS-LANCIERS* (RIGHT BACKGROUND) COUNTER-CHARGE THE BRITISH UNION BRIGADE. PRINT AFTER H. CHARTIER.

The massed columns were used for ease of manoeuvre and because the battlefield was so cramped. But they were a wonderful target for Wellington's gunners, who sent cannonballs tearing through the packed ranks. Once they reached the crest of Wellington's ridge, the leading columns halted to deploy so as to maximise their firepower. Major-General van Bijlandt's Dutch–Belgian infantry brigade broke and fled, leaving Sir Thomas Picton's British 5th Division to counter-attack.

A murderous infantry clash ensued as the 5th Division poured volleys into the deploying French columns. Then, out of the blue, the British Union Brigade of heavy dragoons appeared over the crest of the ridge and broke into the French ranks. The massed columns found it impossible to form defensive squares and were overrun, sustaining thousands of casualties and losing two precious Eagles. The French cuirassiers advancing to the west of d'Erlon's corps were themselves overthrown by the British Household Cavalry and could do nothing to help their defenceless infantry comrades.

Many of the triumphant British horsemen galloped wildly up to the great battery and put about fifteen guns out of action. Then French lancers swept in from the east in a decisive counter-attack; they chased and speared scores of disorganised dragoons. Napoleon sent an ADC, Lieutenant-General Dejean, to order the 6th and 9th Cuirassiers of IV Cavalry Corps to second this riposte. The valley was soon clear of fighting and, although Wellington had suffered heavy casualties, particularly in his heavy cavalry, Napoleon's plan of battle had been destroyed. Waterloo was no longer going to be a picnic as Napoleon had so confidently predicted that morning.

Napoleon had to start again and time was running out. He had decided that La Haye Sainte was the key to the battlefield. It was 3.30 p.m. Ney received orders to hurl the rallied remnant of d'Erlon's infantry against the farm in a second attempt to take it. The attack failed.

Meanwhile a fierce artillery barrage had been pounding the centre of Wellington's line and Ney noticed a retrograde movement on the ridge crest. In fact units were merely retiring slightly to gain shelter, but to Ney it seemed to be the start of a general retreat. Without informing Napoleon, Ney galloped over to IV Cavalry Corps and, overruling objections from one of its experienced generals, led it against Wellington. The Guard light cavalry followed, apparently of its own accord.

Ney should never have charged with the cavalry before La Haye Sainte fell and the French artillery had had time to shake up Wellington's troops at close range. Napoleon was taken aback. The officers around him differed as to the exact words he used but all agreed that he considered the massed charge to be premature. According to Prince Jérôme, who had rejoined him from Hougoumont, Napoleon cursed Ney: 'The wretched man! It is the second time in three days that he is compromising the fate of France.'[31] At Paris after his defeat, Napoleon told his Master of Horse, Armand de Caulaincourt: 'Ney behaved like a madman, he made me massacre all my cavalry.'[32]

Napoleon had certainly intended to hurl massed heavy cavalry at Wellington, but only after his line had been sufficiently shaken and when the French cavalry could be adequately supported by infantry and artillery. In his memoirs, Napoleon criticised Ney's cavalry charge as 'a grievous accident; my intention was to order this move – but an hour later – and to have it backed up by the sixteen infantry battalions of the Guard and a hundred guns.'[33] Napoleon had delegated too much authority to Ney and should have kept his reserve cavalry, like his Guard, under strict, personal control.

General Count Flahaut de la Billarderie, one of Napoleon's ADCs, had been with Ney at the battle of Quatre Bras on 16 June and criticised his tactics: 'nobody could have shown greater courage, I might even say greater contempt for death, than he did. But here my praise for him must end, for the affair resolved itself into a series of spasmodic attacks delivered without any semblance of a plan.'[34] The same lack of co-ordination recurred at Waterloo. If Ney had ordered infantry to follow close behind his cavalry, he might have broken into Wellington's line. In later years, Wellington's friend, Charles Arbuthnot, declared: 'I have heard the Duke say that Napoleon ... gained other victories by moving immense bodies of cavalry at a slow pace, and then following up the advantages gained by furious attacks of infantry.'[35]

As it was, Wellington's infantry assumed square formations, which bristled with bayonets all round and were practically impregnable to unsupported cavalry. Ensign Rees Howell Gronow of the British 1st Footguards described a typical experience:

'The charge of the French cavalry was gallantly executed; but our well-directed fire brought men and horses down, and ere long the utmost confusion arose in their ranks. The officers were exceedingly brave, and by their gestures and fearless bearing did all in their power to encourage their men to form again and renew the attack ... The horses of the first rank of cuirassiers, in spite of all the efforts of their riders, came to a stand-still, shaking and covered with foam, at about twenty yards' distance from our squares, and generally resisted all attempts to force them to charge the line of serried steel'.[36]

Once the luckless French horsemen had been checked by the intense cross-fire from the squares, Wellington's cavalry commander, Lord Uxbridge, charged to sweep the French off the ridge crest.

At about 4.45 p.m. Napoleon ordered General François Kellermann's III Cavalry Corps to join the charges, so as to support what Ney had so rashly begun. The Emperor later claimed, perhaps truthfully, that he did not also order the Guard heavy cavalry to charge, but none the less they followed Kellermann. In fact the slippery slopes were too crowded even for Kellermann. Napoleon should have sent infantry instead, for more cavalry only reinforced the failure. He now had no cavalry left in reserve. Nine thousand horsemen seethed and swarmed over the slippery slopes of the congested battlefield. None thought to spike Wellington's abandoned guns and so whenever the cavalry fell back to regroup, they came once more under a murderous discharge from Wellington's gunners. Colonel Michel Ordener, in command of a brigade formed of the 1st and 7th Cuirassiers, recalled how:

'The charges followed one after another without interruption. We were almost masters of the plateau. But the English, although three-quarters destroyed, seemed to be rooted in the soil; we would have had to kill them to the last soldier. Worn out by fatigue, our cavalrymen stopped [and were] exposed without shelter to the musketry and artillery fire ... Disaster began and my brigade took enormous losses.'[37]

The cavalry waited in vain for French infantry to march to their rescue and to consolidate their hold on the ridge.

At about 4.30 p.m. the leading units of the Prussian IV Corps had entered the battle. To give Wellington a breathing space, Blücher debouched dramatically from the Bois de Paris and steadily drove back Lobau's outnumbered VI Corps. If Napoleon had properly reconnoitred his eastern flank early in the morning, he would have discovered the Prussian approach far earlier and Lobau would have had time to march the three miles from the battlefield to the steep Lasne valley. Blücher had experienced immense dif-

ficulty in crossing this muddy defile, but the crossing would have been practically impossible if it had been attempted under fire. Napoleon had lost his
best chance to check the Prussians and hold them at bay until Wellington
had been overwhelmed.

The French were now fighting two battles simultaneously: an offensive
battle against Wellington and a defensive battle against Blücher.[38] Napoleon
delegated the attacks on Wellington to Ney, but he had no sector commander to check the Prussians. Consequently, he had to conduct that fight himself, and this prevented him from co-ordinating the two fronts. He had broken his own maxim: 'better one bad general than two good ones'.[39] At
Rossomme, Napoleon was only 1,500 metres from Blücher's front line but
2,500 metres from Wellington's. By 6 p.m. the Prussians were so near that
their cannonballs were falling around Napoleon on the Brussels highroad.
Blücher had carried the fight into the heart of the French army; Napoleon
could not fail to be fatally distracted by this terrible threat to his army's
right flank and rear. Blücher did not merely distract 13,000 troops from the
onslaught on Wellington, he distracted Napoleon.

Only at 5.30 p.m. did Ney belatedly remember the 6,000 infantrymen of
Reille's II Corps who had not yet been sucked into the slaughter at
Hougoumont. Ney led these troops, Lieutenant-General Bachelu's division
and one brigade from Foy's command, towards the ridge crest immediately
north of Hougoumont orchard. It was too late; the French cavalry had been
forced to abandon the crest and were too exhausted to lend any cover or
support. The infantry marched up the slope, to be met by a 'hail of death'.
Cannon belched forth canister shot; musketry volleys left the leading French
ranks in tatters.

General Foy recalled seeing the enemy squares, their front ranks kneeling
and presenting a hedge of bayonets. The rear ranks fired. Major Lemonnier-
Delafosse, Foy's ADC, noticed Bachelu's column to his right, dissolving
under the hailstorm of lead, writhing like a wounded animal, collapsing into
a triangular formation, with soldiers drifting away from the base. Foy himself was shot in the shoulder. Now everyone was running. The British firepower and iron tenacity that Reille so respected had triumphed once more.
Of 6,000 men, the French attacking force had lost 1,500 in a matter of minutes and had been swept away by the advance of Major-General Frederick
Adam's brigade of British light infantry.

At about 6.30 p.m. Ney finally seized La Haye Sainte, but only after the
garrison had practically exhausted its ammunition. Now at last Ney pushed

forward a fully co-ordinated force of infantry, cavalry and artillery acting in close mutual support. The results were devastating. Colonel Christian von Ompteda was ordered to counter-attack French infantry with a King's German Legion battalion in line, but French cuirassiers cut it to pieces.

Slaughter ensued as the French cavalry compelled Wellington's infantry to remain in squares. These small, packed formations were vulnerable targets for the French guns. A whole side of a Hanoverian infantry square was blown away. Several brigades in the centre recoiled one hundred metres. Everywhere, Wellington's line took heavy punishment from a formidable combination of swarms of skirmishers backed up by cavalry and artillery. Sergeant Tom Morris of the 73rd Foot watched helplessly as French guns fired canister at his square at close range. This fire blew complete lanes through the living walls of the square and then the cavalry dashed forward:

'But before they reached us, we had closed our files, throwing the dead outside and taking the wounded inside the square, when they were again forced to retire. They did not, however, go further than the pieces of cannon – waiting there to try the effect of some more grapeshot. We saw the match applied, and again it came as thick as hail upon us. On looking round, I saw my left-hand man falling backwards, the blood gushing from his left eye; my poor comrade on my right, by the same discharge, got a ball through his right thigh, of which he died a few days afterwards.'[40]

As the Prussians were fighting so fiercely and loomed so ominously in the east, Napoleon dared not for the moment risk sending in his Guard against Wellington's wavering line, despite a desperate plea from Ney. The opportunity passed; the Duke moved up his last reserves. Lieutenant-Colonel the Hon. Henry Murray, commander of the 18th Hussars, arrived with two fresh light cavalry brigades from the far eastern flank. He was horrified by the situation he found in the centre: 'I remember seeing wounded and deserted horses limping about in the smoke and one of these (turning in a circle) having a great wound from a cannon-shot behind his shoulder upon the flank so that the side looked open. There were helmets and fragments of arms lying about the ground.'[41]

The French gradually fell back into the valley to regroup. A pause ensued. Then French guns redoubled their fire to herald a final assault. A French deserter galloped through the valley to call out to a group of British officers: 'Long live the King! Get ready. That b****** of Napoleon will be upon you with the Guard before half an hour.' It was 7.30 p.m.

Napoleon had detached the Young Guard to check Blücher at the village of Plancenoit. When the Prussians forced even that reinforcement to fall back, he had flung two Old Guard battalions into the fray. These veterans swiftly swept the Prussians out of the village at the point of the bayonet. By efficient use of crack though numerically inferior forces, Napoleon had finally contained and exhausted the offensive of the Prussian IV Corps. Until fresh troops from Blücher's other corps arrived on the battlefield, this sector would remain stable. Napoleon had won himself a badly needed respite on his eastern flank and he used it to resume close personal supervision of the battle against Wellington.

At this stage many a general would have broken off the battle and retreated. But Napoleon could not afford a single setback for it would destroy his reputation and embolden the political opposition in Paris. He had no choice but to stake everything on an attack by his Guard against Wellington. To boost his army's flagging morale, Napoleon sent messengers around the battlefield falsely to announce that Marshal Grouchy was arriving. This ruse was risky, for if Napoleon's troops discovered the truth the sudden disillusionment would shatter the army. But Napoleon was a gambler, and the cheers of '*Vive l'Empereur! Soldats, voilà Grouchy!*' certainly galvanised his army into a renewed effort in support of the Guard attack.

The assault force comprised six Middle Guard battalions; further battalions of the Old Guard were forming a second wave in the valley ready to support a breakthrough or check a setback. The Middle Guard advanced, majestically, imperturbably, up the smoke-covered slopes. Led by Marshal Ney and a host of famous generals, these veteran warriors marched as if on parade. Napoleon himself had led them into the bottom of the valley, from where he watched the attack. If the guardsmen had marched due north, along the Brussels road, they would have struck Wellington's weakest sector. But the French could not have known this and other troops were already assaulting the area. So the guardsmen inclined slightly to the west.

The six battalions struck Wellington's line in succession, from east to west. The 3rd and 4th Grenadiers dislodged Colin Halkett's decimated British brigade but were checked and then overthrown by a powerful counter-attack by fresh Dutch–Belgian troops.

Farther west, the 3rd Chasseurs halted in dismay as the British 1st Footguards suddenly rose from the cornfields in which they had been lying and poured a devastating hail of musketry into their astounded foe. 'Those who from a distance and more on the flank could see the affair,' wrote Captain Harry Weyland Powell of the 1st Guards, 'tell us that the effect of our fire seemed to force the head of the Column bodily back.'[42] The 3rd Chasseurs broke, only to rally behind the 4th Chasseurs who surged forward in a last, desperate advance. Then Lieutenant-Colonel Sir John Colborne swung his 52nd Light Infantry decisively round out of the line to face the open flank of the luckless French chasseurs. Soon it was over and the Middle Guard was streaming in disorder back into the valley.

By then, more Prussians, the advance guard of Ziethen's I Corps, had stormed on to the north-eastern corner of the battlefield and broken through the remnant of the French I Corps. The French army cracked. The shock of disillusionment was too great; Napoleon had deluded his men into believing that Marshal Grouchy was coming to their rescue. Instead, a fresh force of ferocious Prussian horsemen now swept across the battlefield. The leading units of Blücher's II Corps had also arrived and its 5th Infantry Brigade was spearheading a final, victorious onslaught on Plancenoit. As a

NAPOLEON AND THE OLD GUARD AT WATERLOO. PRINT AFTER RAFFET.

further blow, Wellington's entire line was pouring down from the ridge crest in pursuit of the broken battalions of the vanquished Middle Guard.

The blood-chilling cry of '*la Garde recule!*' echoed round the field: 'the Guard is falling back.' Everywhere, the French army, having staked so much on this last attempt, simply melted away. 'In a few moments', recalled General Foy, 'our magnificent army was no more than a rabble of fugitives.'[43]

A few squares of the Old Guard held out against the torrent of fugitives and pursuers until, crushed by musketry and artillery fire, they disintegrated into groups which made their way southwards. Napoleon realised that he could do no more and rode off the field. He had suffered his final defeat. The genius of war, the victor of Austerlitz, Jena and Friedland, had been beaten once and for all, on the battlefield. He had been defeated by Wellington, who had developed the perfect antidote to his tactics, and by Blücher, who had inflicted on him his own favourite strategy of falling on the flank of a foe and threatening his lines of communication. For Napoleon, nothing could be more humiliating: 'death is nothing, but to live defeated is to die every day'. As David Chandler has justly concluded, 'Napoleon had lost more than just his men and one battle: he had finally forfeited his reputation.'[44]

NOTES

1. Chalfont, Lord (ed.) *Waterloo: Battle of three armies*, 1979, p. 27.
2. Chair, S. de. *Napoleon's Memoirs*, 1985, p. 504.
3. Callatay, P. de. 'L'entrée en campagne' in *Waterloo 1815: l'Europe face à Napoléon*, 1990, pp. 29-30.
4. For a comprehensive study of Napoleon's generals in 1815, see T. Linck, *Napoleon's Generals: the Waterloo Campaign*, 1994.
5. *Correspondance de Napoléon 1er*, 1869, vol. 28, pp. 314-15.
6. Ibid., pp. 322-3.
7. Barral, G. *L'épopée de Waterloo*, 1895, p. 111.
8. Chair, *op. cit.*, p. 507.
9. Saint-Denis, L. *Souvenirs du mameluk Ali sur l'empereur*, 1926, pp. 105-6.
10. For a comprehensive examination of the d'Erlon fiasco, see A. Uffindell, *The Eagle's last Triumph: Napoleon's victory at Ligny, June 1815*, 1994.
11. Coignet, J. *The Notebooks of Captain Coignet*, 1986, pp. 276-7.
12. Stouff, L. *Le Lieutenant-Général Delort*, 1906, p. 96.
13. Saint-Denis, *op. cit.*, p. 107.
14. See, for instance, D. Howarth, *A Near Run Thing*, 1968, pp. 52-6; J. Holland Rose, *The Life of Napoleon I*, 1924, pp. 484-6.
15. Fuller, J. F. C. *The Decisive Battles of the Western World 1792-1944*, ed. J. Terraine, 1985, p.163.

16. Chandler, D. *The Illustrated Napoleon*, 1990, p. 70.
17. Lévi, A. *Carnet de campagne du Colonel Trefçon*, 1914, p.184.
18. Houssaye, H. *Waterloo 1815*, 1987, p. 279.
19. Lévi, A. *op. cit.,* p. 185.
20. Chair, *op cit.*, p. 521.
21. Houssaye, H. *op. cit.*, p. 311.
22. Pétiet, A. *Souvenirs militaires*, 1844, pp. 213–14.
23. The total was increased to eighty by the time the battery opened fire.
24. Chair, *op. cit.*, p. 525.
25. Foy, M. *Vie militaire*, 1900, p. 279.
26. 'Notice historique sur les mouvements du 2e Corps', in duc d'Elchingen, *Documents inédits sur la campagne de 1815*, 1840, p. 61.
27. Foy, *op. cit.*, pp. 282–3.
28. Siborne, H. (ed.). *The Waterloo letters*, 1983, p. 264.
29. *Idem.*
30. See A. Uffindell and M. Corum, *On the Fields of Glory: the Battlefields of the 1815 Campaign*, 1996, p. 165.
31. Casse, A. du (ed.). *Mémoires et correspondance du Roi Jérôme et de la Reine Cathérine*, 1866, vol. 7, p. 23.
32. Parker, H. *Three Napoleonic Battles*, 1983, p. 207.
33. Chair, *op. cit.*, p. 546.
34. Kerry, Earl of. *The First Napoleon*, 1925, p. 119.
35. Parker, *op. cit.*, p. 165; see also H. Maxwell, *The life of Wellington*, London, 1900, vol. 2, p. 139.
36. Gronow, R. *The reminiscences and recollections of Captain Gronow, being anecdotes of the camp, the court, and the clubs, and society at the close of the last war with France*, 1900, vol. 1, pp. 70, 191.
37. Lot, H. *Les Deux Généraux Ordener*, 1910, p. 94.
38. Parker, *op. cit.*, p. 151.
39. Chandler, *op. cit.*, p. 68.
40. Morris, T. *Recollections of Military Service in 1813, 1814 and 1815*, 1845, p. 149.
41. BL Add. MS 34,706/19.
42. Siborne, *op. cit.*, p. 255.
43. Foy, *op. cit.*, p. 283.
44. Chandler, *op. cit.*, pp. 67, 159.

BIBLIOGRAPHY

Becke, A. *Napoleon and Waterloo*, 1936; reprinted London, 1995.
Brett-James, A. *The Hundred Days*, London, 1964.
Chair, S. de. (ed.). *Napoleon's Memoirs*, London, 1985.
Chalfont, Lord (ed.). *Waterloo: Battle of Three Armies*, London, 1979.
Chandler, D. *Waterloo: The Hundred Days*, London, 1980.
Cotton, E. *A Voice from Waterloo*, 9th enlarged edn., Brussels, 1900.
Haythornthwaite, P. *Uniforms of Waterloo*, London, 1979.
Houssaye, H. *Waterloo 1815*, Evreux, 1987.
Howarth, D. *A Near Run Thing*, London, 1968.
Keegan, J. *The Face of Battle*, London, 1976.
Lachouque, H. *Waterloo*, London, 1975.

Longford, Lady. *Wellington: The Years of the Sword*, 1969.

Mercer, C. *Journal of the Waterloo Campaign*, 1870; reprinted London, 1985.

Nofi, A. *The Waterloo Campaign, June 1815*, London, 1993.

Parker, H. *Three Napoleonic Battles*, Durham, N.C., 1944; reprinted 1983.

Siborne, H. (ed.). *The Waterloo Letters*, 1891; reprinted London, 1983, 1993

Siborne, W. *History of the Waterloo Campaign*, 1844; reprinted London, 1990, 1995.

Uffindell, A. *The Eagle's Last Triumph: Napoleon's Victory at Ligny, June 1815*, London, 1994.

Uffindell, A., and Corum, M. *On The Fields of Glory: the Battlefields of the 1815 Campaign*, London, 1996.

Weller, J. *Wellington at Waterloo*, 1967; reprinted London, 1992.

ST. HELENA:
CONTROVERSY TO THE END
Tim Hicks

LTHOUGH NAPOLEON'S IMPRISONMENT ON ST. HELENA IN HIS twilight years involved no battles, great affairs of state or involvement in world events, today it is without doubt the single most contentious period of his life. Dispute rages over the legality of his imprisonment, the cause of his death, whether he died of natural causes or was murdered and if so by whom. To date this question has been the subject of investigations by the FBI and various universities, debates in learned societies, books, articles in newspapers, historical, scientific and medical journals and intense speculation, both informed and uninformed.

As the title suggests, this chapter will examine the complex controversy surrounding the last six years of the Emperor's life, but to avoid confusion will narrate events from Waterloo to the Emperor's death in exile on St. Helena using accepted historical fact, then attempt impartially to draw out the various controversial aspects of this period separately for the reader to draw his own conclusions from the scientific, historical and medical evidence available. Those readers requiring an in-depth examination of the St. Helena years are recommended to read the excellent 'St. Helena Trilogy', by Gilbert Martineau, or *Assassination at St. Helena Revisited*, by Ben Weider and Sten Forshufvud, from all of which I have drawn heavily for the narrative.

Following his defeat at Waterloo on 18 June 1815, Napoleon planned to rally his wing of the army, order the northern and eastern fortresses to hold out for three months, concentrate the armies of Rapp, Brune, Suchet and Lecourbe at Lyons, link up with Grouchy and Soult, and then launch a counter offensive that would sweep the exhausted Allied armies back to Belgium. With their supply lines over-extended and large numbers of their troops tied up in siege operations and lines of communications duties, this could have presented a formidable threat to the Allies.

Remembering the events of 1814, he returned to Paris to safeguard his dynasty from political betrayal, but he was to late. By the time he arrived at Paris on the 21st the news of his defeat was well known. His Minister of Police, Fouché, had already primed the Chamber of Deputies to overthrow the Emperor and force him to abdicate. On the 22nd Napoleon abdicated in favour of his son, the King of Rome, intending to sail to America in one of two French frigates anchored at Rochefort. He moved from the Elysée to Malmaison, where he had a farewell meeting with his former mistress, Marie Walewska, and his son, Alexandre.

By the 28th, the imminent arrival of the Prussian army under Field Marshal Blücher, who h⌐d sworn to hang Napoleon at the head of the army, left Napoleon no choice. The passports and safe conducts were issued and Napoleon hid a capsule of poison on his person, to prevent the humiliation of capture by the Prussians. He bade his last farewell to his mother, Letizia Bonaparte, as she made a tearful departure to exile in Italy, and then took time to wander through the elegant rooms and apartments, no doubt remembering the happy times he had spent there. He lingered in Josephine's room, where she had died, and then at 5 p.m. he left via the East Gate, pausing only for one last glance at Malmaison before the coachman whipped up the horses to start Napoleon's second journey into exile.

Napoleon arrived at Rochefort on 3 July, hoping to make good his escape past the blockading British squadron. The plan was to hold all the shipping in the harbour and release it to sea with Napoleon in one of the frigates. The Royal Navy would be unable to search so many ships at once, and Napoleon would escape to America in the confusion.

However, on 7 July the Provisional Government handed over power to the Bourbons. Henceforth any Frenchman assisting Napoleon to escape would be committing an act of treason. This news reached him on the 9th, and he became concerned that if he delayed his departure he could be handed over to the Royalists for trial, so he ordered his staff to re-plan the escape. The 60-gun frigate *Méduse* would attack HMS *Bellerophon* (74 guns) under cover of darkness, while the latter was at anchor. Although *Bellerophon* would sink the frigate without difficulty, in the resulting confusion the Emperor would slip away in the frigate *Saale*. Preparations for the operation began at once, but the *Saale*'s captain vetoed the plan as a potential act of treason against Louis XVIII, and Napoleon had to abandon all hope of using the two frigates, or indeed any of the other shipping in the harbour. On 12 July he was rowed from the *Saale* to the Isle d'Aix, and on the 14th contact was made with Captain Maitland of HMS *Bellerophon*. Napoleon wrote to the British Prince Regent:

'Your Royal Highness, exposed to the factions which distract my country and to the enmity of the greatest powers of Europe, I have ended my political career and I come like Themistocles to throw myself on the

192

hospitality of the British people; I put myself under the protection of their laws, which I claim from your Royal Highness, the most powerful, the most constant, and the most generous of my enemies.

Napoleon

Rochefort, 13 July 1815.'

(Actually written on the 14th.)

Napoleon spent his last night in France at the Commandant's house on the Isle d'Aix. On the 15th he embarked in *Bellerophon,* only hours before a courier arrived at Rochefort from Paris with orders for his arrest. He was received by Captain Maitland and stated, 'I am come to throw myself on the protection of your Prince and laws.' This left the issue of his eventual fate in the hands of the British government. On the 20th the Prime Minister Lord Liverpool wrote to the Foreign Secretary:

'We are all very decidedly of the opinion that it would not answer to confine him in this country. Very nice legal questions might arise on the subject, which would be particularly embarrassing. But, independent of these considerations, you know enough of the feelings of people in this country not to doubt he would become the object of curiosity immediately, and possibly of compassion, in the course of a few months: and

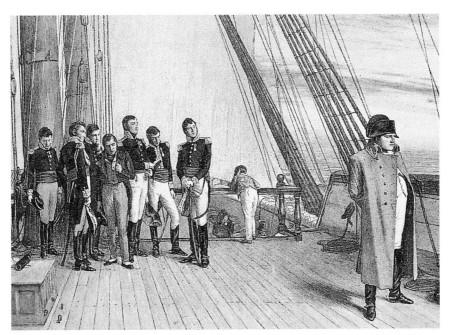

NAPOLEON ON HIS WAY TO EXILE. PRINT AFTER W. Q. ORCHARDSON.

the circumstance of his being here, or indeed anywhere in Europe, would contribute to keep up a certain degree of ferment in France ... St. Helena is the place in the world best calculated for the confinement of such a person. There is a very fine Citadel there, in which he might reside. The situation is particularly healthy. There is only one place in the circuit of the island where ships can anchor, and we have the power of excluding neutral ships altogether, if we should think it necessary. At such a distance and in such a place, all intrigue would be impossible; and, being withdrawn so far from the European world, he would very soon be forgotten.'

Napoleon's legal position was summarised by the Lord Chancellor as follows:
'The state of war between France and England authorised Bonaparte's detention as a prisoner of war, especially as, according to Captain Maitland, no undertaking had been entered into with him. Bonaparte was no longer a French subject since his abdication and accession to the throne of the island of Elba. It was therefore possible to consider him as having been defeated in the legitimate war fought against himself alone and to declare him a prisoner of war.

Lord Eldon, Lord Chancellor.'

On 26 July, Captain Maitland was ordered to sail to Plymouth and to treat Napoleon as a general officer, not a sovereign or Emperor. This no doubt was a source of concern to Napoleon and his retinue, as was their eventual fate, when he read in the newspapers that his destination was to be St. Helena. Under the Treaty of Paris signed on 28 July 1815, Napoleon was entrusted into British custody, and the three allied powers of Prussia, Russia and Austria, with France, were empowered to send a Commissioner to St. Helena to satisfy themselves of the security arrangements. Napoleon protested, but to no avail. Bowing to the inevitable, he selected those members of his entourage who would go into exile with him.

An attempt was made by a lawyer named Mackenrot to secure Napoleon's release by serving a subpoena on Lord Keith, the naval officer in whose custody Napoleon was being held, citing Napoleon as a witness in a libel case then being brought by Admiral Cochrane. To avoid the subpoena, Keith sought sanctuary aboard HMS *Tonnant* and then in another warship; embarking in a fast rowing boat, he was still pursued by the indefatigable Mackenrot, who first boarded *Tonnant* and then gave chase to Keith, in his own boat. On 4 August *Bellerophon* was ordered to sea to evade sightseers and prevent the subpoena being served, and on the 7th Napoleon said farewell to those Frenchmen he was leaving behind. With his household, he was transferred to HMS *Northumberland.* Before leaving, the exiles were first relieved of their valuables and – with the exception of the Emperor – their swords. On the 9th they were placed in the custody of Rear-Admiral Sir George Cockburn and they set sail for St. Helena.

On the morning of 15 October 1815, after an uneventful voyage, *Northumberland* dropped anchor in Jamestown Bay, where the news that Napoleon had arrived created a local sensation. Initially Napoleon and his retinue were to be accommodated at Porteous House, an inn rented for them while their permanent residence, Longwood House, was made ready. (It is interesting to note that a certain Major-General Wellesley had also stayed at

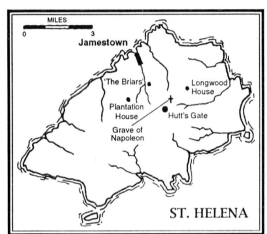

Porteous House in 1805 on his way back to Britain from India.)

Napoleon disembarked on the Middle Steps of Jamestown Quay at 7.30 p.m. on the 17th and made his way to his new lodgings. The next day he inspected Longwood, then being renovated by Admiral Cockburn's sailors and on the way back noticed a pavilion with a heart-shaped waterfall behind it. This stood in the grounds of a house called 'The Briars' which belonged to a minor official named William Balcombe. Napoleon was so taken by its beauty that he moved from Porteous House and stayed at 'The Briars' for the next two months, striking up a platonic friendship with Balcombe's daughter Betsy, while he started to dictate his memoirs.

On 20 November, Admiral Cockburn invited Napoleon and the French contingent to a ball at the Governor's Residence, Plantation House. The invitation, however, was addressed to *General Bonaparte*, not to the Emperor Napoleon. The Emperor responded, 'Send the card to the addressee. The last I heard of him was at the Pyramids and Mount Tabor.' On 10 December Napoleon was compelled to move into Longwood House, despite the fact that work was still in progress there. He entered via a flight of steps through the veranda into the billiard room, passed through the drawing- and dining-

LONGWOOD, NAPOLEON'S RESIDENCE AT ST. HELENA. UNSIGNED ENGRAVING.

LONGWOOD. PRINT AFTER R. CORDWELL, FROM A DRAWING OF 1821
BY FREDERICK ALLISON.

196

rooms with a passage to his two private apartments and a tiny passage later converted to a bathroom. These rooms were at the front of the house, in full view of the French staff and the British orderly officer. Outside was a muddy courtyard and some sheds used as offices. The Emperor's personal staff lived in the other wing of the house.

Once established in Longwood House, Napoleon soon fell into a routine. He would rise at six, have tea or coffee, wash, shave and have a rub down with eau-de-cologne. He lunched at ten and then worked on his memoirs in the billiards room, dictating them to his private secretary, Las Cases, laying his maps on the billiard table and using the balls to hold the maps open. He would then bathe, usually for about an hour but sometimes for as long as three. He would receive visitors in the late afternoon, visit the Bertrands at their villa, 'Hutts Gate', and play with their children before returning to Longwood and correcting the day's dictation until supper was served.

The new Governor, Lieutenant-General Hudson Lowe, arrived on 14 April 1816. His military career had been relatively undistinguished. Commissioned in 1787, he had commanded Corsican troops, served in Elba, Portugal, Minorca, and Egypt, and had been billeted in Napoleon's family home, Casa Bonaparte, during his Corsican service.[32] Wellington had rejected him as Chief of Staff in 1815; he received a knighthood in 1817. He was an officious, insensitive man, selected for his knowledge of French and Italian, intelligence experience and his rigid, methodical outlook. On appointment, he tightened up security, posting sentries around the walls of Longwood, creating an elaborate system of signalling stations to report on Napoleon wherever he was, censoring his communications, cutting his budget from £20,000 to £12,000 and interfering in the internal arrangements of Longwood House. In particular, he issued orders that the orderly officer was to ensure that he visited Napoleon at regular intervals. Napoleon was also forbidden to ride far from Longwood without an escort.

Napoleon resented this surveillance and therefore seldom ventured forth, spending most of his time at Longwood, which was on a particularly bleak and exposed part of the island. It had not been inhabited by any family for more than a few months in any year because of the cold climate, which was always wet, even in summer, giving rise to a humid, clammy atmosphere that was acknowledged as being unhealthy. There were also violent changes in temperature, a cause of bronchial infections that often affected the French household. The fall in temperature was particularly rapid in the evenings, and during September and August the Longwood plateau was

NAPOLEON ON ST. HELENA. PRINT AFTER HORACE VERNET.

often completely enveloped in cloud. The house had no damp course and not enough fires or dry wood to keep it warm. Very soon the furniture and floorboards carried a film of mildew. Even today, the wallpaper peels, the house smells of damp and has to be re-decorated every year.

Napoleon had gone on long rides across the island in the early part of his confinement, enjoying the exercise and a picnic lunch. However, he soon became bored with seeing the same sights and resented the extra supervision imposed on him by Hudson Lowe. He stopped riding and, apart from a period when he took an interest in renovating the gardens of Longwood, seldom ventured outside or took any exercise – although there is some evidence that the wife of one of his courtiers, Madame Albine de Montholon, was his mistress. Understandably, Napoleon took a fiendish delight in baiting Hudson Lowe, by staying indoors and out of sight to frustrate the sentries, constructing elaborate sunken paths so that he could remain hidden from view while enjoying the garden, and spying on the sentries through holes in the shutters. Napoleon had all the chairs removed from the room when they had meetings, so Hudson Lowe had to stand. He also denounced him in letters smuggled to Europe. There is no doubt that Napoleon hated Hudson Lowe, and this perhaps helps explain the allegation in his will that he had poisoned him.

In early 1820, Napoleon's health began to decline, and he became seriously ill. On 25 October he expressed the hope that, 'Perhaps Death will soon put an end to my suffering.' Hudson Lowe, concerned that Napoleon had not been seen for some time, and convinced that his 'illness' was a sham, sent a message to say that he must show himself or his door would be forced by the orderly officer.

On 16 April 1821, Napoleon expressed the wish that his ashes be scattered by the banks of the Seine 'in the midst of the people of France whom I loved so dearly'. By the 25th he was vomiting blood and was convinced that he was dying of cancer of the stomach, the same disease that had killed his father. He therefore signed the final codicils to his will.

On 27 April he suffered violent vomiting, and Hudson Lowe was told of the doctor's grave concern. In his last days he was purged with tartar emetic and drank an *orgeat*, an orange-flavoured drink that includes the oil of bitter almonds. On 3 May he received the sacraments, and the doctors administered ten grains of calomel – three times the normal dose – which caused a terrible intestinal upheaval, loss of consciousness, difficulty in breathing and the passage of tarry stools of partially digested blood.

He died in the drawing-room at 17.49 on 5 May 1821. His last words were: 'France ... The Head of the Army ... Josephine ...'

This was an agonising death, following a long illness and a humiliating captivity. One cannot help but think that it would have been better if he had been killed, sword in hand, at the head of the Middle Guard, leading the last attack at Waterloo.

On the 6th an autopsy was performed by Napoleon's physician, Dr Antommarchi, in the presence of British military and naval surgeons. Cancer of the stomach was diagnosed as the cause of death. One doctor noted enlargement of the liver (which was not diseased), but was ordered by Hudson Lowe to omit this finding because it was thought to support the cause of death being hepatitis, which, being endemic to the island, could make St. Helena – and therefore the British Government – responsible for Napoleon's premature death at the age of 51.

After the autopsy, his body was washed and dressed, the hair was shorn by his valet, Noverraz, a death mask was taken, the death certified and the coffin hermetically sealed ready for burial.

Napoleon was not to be buried on the banks of the Seine as he had wished, but on St. Helena at a beautiful little spring shaded by willows, which he had once visited and admired. The Governor attended, the garrison lined the funeral route with reversed arms, their bands playing funeral marches. Behind the hearse was led the last horse Napoleon had ridden. The contingent of exiles followed, and sentries were permanently posted at the grave. [1, 2, 3, 4, 6, 12, 19]

Having reviewed Napoleon's time on St Helena, in order to examine the various controversies surrounding Napoleon's death, it is probably appropriate to start with an examination of his medical history and autopsy. We know that in 1788 Napoleon had a liaison with a prostitute and that he contracted scabies at the siege of Toulon in 1793. He was also inoculated with scabies as a counter-irritant to gastric catarrh in 1798.[30] He suffered from dysuria (pain while urinating) for many years,[24] and there are two documented instances of his having fits which were diagnosed at the time as epileptic.[25] There is some evidence to suggest that he may have contracted syphilis[25] and suffered from brachycardia (a slow heart beat),[25] urinary gravel and cystitis.[24]

Napoleon had a history of pain in the upper abdomen from September 1812, particularly during the battle of Leipzig in October 1813. In 1815 he complained of pain after meals. In 1817 he complained of pain on the right side of his abdomen, which Dr O'Meara diagnosed as hepatitis, which was endemic to the island and for which he was instantly dismissed by Hudson Lowe, acting no doubt to evade British responsibility for any decline in his health. In January 1819 he was again taken ill with severe abdominal pain, which was again diagnosed as hepatitis and for which Hudson Lowe again dismissed the doctor. In September 1819 he was suffering with abdominal pain and vomiting, which Dr Antommarchi diagnosed as hepatitis.[20] However, in November 1819 he was able to take up gardening and his health improved.

The five post-mortem reports produced at the time have been analysed and summarised by Dr Yarrow:

'1. The stomach was ulcerated, and there was perforation.

'2. The perforation had been partially shut off by old adhesions to the liver and diaphragm.

'3. The ulcer had a rolled, everted edge.

'4. The liver was enlarged.

'5. No lumps or nodules were found in the liver, although looked for.

'6. Exudation was present in the abdominal cavity.

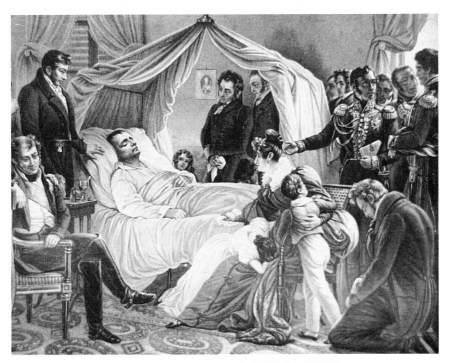

DEATH OF NAPOLEON. PRINT AFTER C. STEUBEN.

'7. Partly digested blood was found in the stomach.

'8. An abundance of body and abdominal fat was present.

'In his report, Dr Walter Henry noted that the body was feminised with hairless, white, delicate skin, well defined breasts and a mons Veneris (fat accumulating above the genitals). The genitalia were exceedingly small, suggesting testicular atrophy. Dr Robinson suggests that these characteristics were as a result of an acquired primary hypogonadism (small testicles) resulting from an orchitis which led to testicular atrophy and impotence.'[25]

Based on the autopsy reports, Dr Yarrow points out:

'If Napoleon had indeed died of cancer of the stomach, his corpse would have been wasted, shrunken and devoid of body fat. Moreover there would almost certainly have been secondary growths in the liver. That is not to say that there may not already have been early cancerous changes in the ulcer as suggested by the rolled, everted edge, but the point is that this could not have been the cause of his death.'[20]

The controversy over Napoleon's death arises from the results of tests on Napoleon's hair, which revealed the presence of massive amounts of arsenic. On 28 August 1995, the FBI's department of Chemistry and Toxicology concluded that, 'The amount of arsenic present in the submitted hairs is consistent with arsenical poisoning.'[22, 4] This was based on different, authenticated samples of Napoleon's hair taken between 1805 and 1821, all of which contained arsenic.

Conversely, in their analysis of a sample of Napoleon's hair cut after his death, Lewin, Hancock and Voynich of the Hospital for Sick Children, Ontario, did not find high levels of arsenic but did find a moderately increased level of antimony, which was present in the tartar emetic.[23]

When given in small doses over a period of time, arsenius oxide was without doubt a most effective method of assassination. Indeed, it became known as 'the inheritance powder' because it was ideal for murdering aged and infirm relatives for the purpose of inheriting an estate. Until the invention of the Marsh test in 1832 it was undetectable, the symptoms of arsenical poisoning being easily mistaken for many other ailments; it is tasteless and dissolves quickly, and half a gram per dose is enough. We know that it was freely available on St. Helena and used as a rat poison,[2] and the amount required would fit into a small envelope.[7]

This therefore poses two crucial questions:

1. What did Napoleon die of?

2. And how did the arsenic get into his hair?

With regard to the first question, Dr Yarrow's conclusion is that the findings were not consistent with death from cancer, but were entirely consistent with death from haemorrhage and peritonitis caused by an untreated perforated gastric ulcer:

'his previous medical history is highly indicative of a chronic gastric ulcer, which probably perforated in January 1819 when he had his acute attack with all the signs and symptoms of a perforation. This was delimited by the adhesions to the liver and diaphragm (found at the post-mortem) which probably saved his life on that occasion, and gave rise to the misunderstood liver symptoms. The ulcer reappeared in the spring of 1820 and there were subsequently episodes of haemorrhage as evidenced by the tarry stools and vomiting of digested blood. Finally, in the first days of May 1821, the ulcer leaked again with further haemorrhage and incipient peritonitis, as evidenced by the post-mortem findings of peritonal exudation.'

The theory that Napoleon was murdered by poisoning has been put forward by Weider and Forshufvud as follows:

'Hair grows about one inch every two months. Since the hair was cut at the scalp and was three inches long, this represented six months of Napoleon's life. By testing the hairs by section, we were able to know almost to the day when he was given high doses of arsenic. The results of the tests on the hair showed extreme highs and lows of the levels of arsenic. The lowest point was 2.8 parts per million and the highest 51.2ppm, and in each section of hair tested, the levels varied in peaks and valleys. This proves that Napoleon ingested more arsenic at specific times and less at others. Keep in mind that the normal level in the hair at the time was about 0.08ppm. Examples of the highs and lows on the Napoleon hairs that were tested are: 51.2; 45.2; 24.5; 18.8; 2.8; 7.1; 20.4; 24.1; etc. These results, which are way above normal, prove without a doubt that Napoleon was being fed arsenic at different times.'[22]

They point out that the normal level of arsenic in the hair at the time was about 0.08 ppm and that a comparison of Napoleon's symptoms on the specific dates prior to his death correlates exactly with the levels of arsenical intoxication discovered in the hair shaved off by valet Noverraz on 6 May 1821. Altogether the proponents of the poisoning theory found that

Napoleon suffered from 30 of the 34 known symptoms of arsenical poisoning, and the testing of Napoleon's hair shows that the arsenic had entered the body at intervals over a long period of time in large doses, not evenly in minute amounts over time. They also point out that the body was hairless and, when exhumed in 1840, was exceptionally well preserved, which are signs of arsenical poisoning.

Weider and Forshufvud identify the poisoner as General comte Charles Tristan de Montholon, an officer of the old aristocracy whom they state had seen no fighting in his career and had been dismissed from his post as French Envoy to Würzburg by Napoleon because he had married the twice-divorced Albine Roger against Napoleon's wishes. De Montholon benefited significantly from the will, and his stepfather was a highly influential friend of Louis XVIII. In April 1814, de Montholon was arrested for embezzling 5,970 francs of military funds being the property of the *département* de Puy-de-Dôme.[13] These charges were dropped in 1814 and again in 1822. According to the poisoning theory, de Montholon was blackmailed by the comte d'Artois, Louis XVIII's brother and head of the Bourbons' secret service, into joining Napoleon's household as a spy under the threat of a court-martial for embezzlement. All the members of Napoleon's court in exile ate the same food, but Napoleon always drank his own wine from his own bottle; so the only way that he alone could have been poisoned was by his wine. De Montholon was one of the three exiles who stayed until the end and, as Chamberlain of the Royal Household, was the only person to have access to the wine. However, although it is alleged that Napoleon was being poisoned with arsenic from 1805 onwards, de Montholon would not have had access to Napoleon until 1815.

It is not Forshufvud and Weider's belief that Napoleon died of arsenical poisoning. Weider points out that during his last days Napoleon was given several tartar emetics: 'Tartar emetic is antimony potassium tartrate; it is highly toxic and induces vomiting. Its symptoms resemble those of arsenic, and it is no longer used because of its high toxicity. Giving Napoleon the tartar emetic over a period of time ensured that mercury cyanide would not be vomited and would remain in his body in order to complete the poisoning method of the period. Calomel contains mercury chloride, and bitter almonds (from the argeat) contains hydro-cyanic acid or prussic acid. Together they combine in the stomach to form mercury cyanide.' Napoleon died of 'chronic arsenical intoxication combined with acute cyanide poisoning'.[22] In February 1820, the last surviving Bourbon male capable of fathering an heir was assassinated by a Bonapartist fanatic as he entered the opera. This effectively meant the end of the Bourbon line in France, and to prevent the Bonapartist dynasty being invited to return and rule France once the Bourbons were extinct, assassination by cyanide, a method which was known at the time and was recorded in the de Brinvilliers memoirs, was ordered in order to resolve the matter quickly.

Recent work by David Hamilton-Williams has sought to corroborate Forshufvud and Weider's findings. Certainly, he has demonstrated that de Gros, the French Commissioner's diplomatic secretary, was an agent of the Bourbon secret service, when it was previously believed that the Commissioner had maintained informants among the locally recruited servants in Napoleon's household. There is no evidence to suggest that de Gros's brief was anything other than that of surveillance, and other assertions made by Hamilton-Williams have to be treated with caution.

There are a number of inconsistencies and inaccuracies in the theory. These are that:

1. Montholon did have an active service career until 1809 and had been decorated twice with the *Légion d'honneur*. His lack of active service after that date was a consequence of wounds received at Wagram where Macdonald's corps, in which he served, was very heavily engaged indeed. He was not unique in being involved in dubious financial dealings and probably agreed to go into exile to avoid his creditors.[15]

2. No concrete evidence of a plot, e.g., letters or witnesses, has emerged. Claims have been made in the press and by Hamilton-Williams that Montholon's confession has been found, but on investigation by the author these were found to have been without basis.[11]

3. Weider and Forshufvud suggest that Napoleon was being poisoned with arsenic from 1805 onwards, but do not say how this took place.[4] It is inconceivable that any secret service of the time would have infiltrated a deep-cover agent into Napoleon's household, with the opportunity of poisoning him, in 1805 and then waited until 1821 to kill him.

An alternative explanation for the arsenic content in Napoleon's hair has been put forward by Dr David Jones of the Chemistry Department of Newcastle University, who pointed out that in the eighteenth century it was a common practice to use Schalers Green as a colouring in wallpaper. Schalers Green is produced by combining copper sulphate with sodium arsenite to produce copper arsenite, which provides the green colouring in the compound. In the damp climate of Longwood, mould would have formed on the paper, and this would have been contaminated with arsenic from the wallpaper, giving off the poisonous arsenical vapour, arsenic trimethal. Jones points out that arsenic easily forms vapours by evaporation and is highly poisonous. Many of the staff and servants were affected by quite serious bouts of illness while in Longwood and showed symptoms of arsenical poisoning which were mistaken for other illnesses. When the Emperor took an interest in his gardening in 1819 and spent long periods of time in the open, his symptoms all but disappeared. When he spent more time inside Longwood House, from October 1820, the symptoms returned, and the Emperor was fatally affected because of his age and the general decline in his health, which was accentuated by arsenical poisoning.[7]

An authenticated sample of the wallpaper from Napoleon's time at Longwood was obtained after a radio appeal and, when examined at Glasgow University using x-ray fluorescence spectography, was proven to be arsenical and in quantities that were toxicologically significant and consequently considered to have given off poisonous vapour during Napoleon's tenure of Longwood. The study of hair samples spanning 1816–21 have reported regularly fluctuating levels of arsenic, which is to be expected from a source such as a damp and mouldy wallpaper in a house as damp as Longwood. The amount of arsenic in Napoleon's hair would therefore vary with fluctuations in humidity, temperature, ventilation and the amount of time that Napoleon spent in the relevant rooms.[31]

Other explanations have been put forward for the arsenic in Napoleon's hair. It may have resulted from the medical treatments prescribed by Dr Antommarchi. Tartar emetic is a salt and was prescribed shortly before death; these salts may have been contaminated naturally by arsenic. Arsenic itself may have been administered as a medicine – it was used to treat epilepsy, syphilis and skin diseases, all of which may have been present in Napoleon's medical history. It was also used to improve appetite.[27, 29]

It has also been suggested that arsenic was present in a hair tonic that Napoleon used or as a repellent to keep insects away from the stored hairs.[27] However, if this were so, the arsenic would show as occurring evenly throughout the hair, not with massive variations. To quote Weider:

'Over the years, people have attributed the arsenic in Napoleon's hair as coming from the wallpaper at Longwood House, the water he drank,

medication he took, or from the hair cream he used. If these supposi-
tions were indeed factual, then the arsenic levels in his hair would have
been constant, as he would have taken in the same amount of arsenic
on a daily basis. The extreme highs and lows show without a doubt that
these theories are not based on fact in any manner whatsoever, and
should be dismissed'.[21]

As well as the possibility of Napoleon having been murdered, there are other
controversies.

New research on the Balcombe Collection which is now held at 'The Briars'
and at the Mornington Peninsular Art Centre by the diligent historian Bob
Elmer has revealed the existence of a note written by Lord Keith's secretary,
one James Meek, on a copy of Mackenrot's subpoena:

'The original of this letter with enclosure were received by Lord Keith
by HM Sloop *Actaeon* the 5th August 1815 at 4.40 p.m. and opened by
his Lordship on board the *Tonnant* at that time in my presence being
then off the Start and several leagues from the shore.

James Meek.

Original letter sent to Lord Melville on 6 August 1815 by Lord Keith JM.'[18]

'THE SHADE OF NAPOLEON': AN ALLEGORICAL SCENE OF NAPOLEON'S GRAVE
ON ST. HELENA. THE SPACE BETWEEN THE TWO TREES FORMS AN IMAGE OF
THE EX-EMPEROR. PRINT BY BAIRD.

At that time Napoleon was in Keith's custody, and his duty as a naval officer was to obey the law and serve the subpoena on Napoleon, who would then have had to be landed and transported to London to give his evidence in the High Court, thus delaying his departure for St. Helena, focusing public attention on him and possibly making his continued detention impossible. Instead, he handed Napoleon into the custody of Admiral Sir George Cockburn and HMS *Northumberland*, which sailed with Napoleon to St. Helena. In England, a bill of indemnity was passed to settle the legal position of Napoleon and to protect the relevant ministers from legal action.

In modern times it is accepted that only a nation state has a right to declare and wage war. Napoleon was the sovereign ruler of Elba and had never agreed to remain on that island. The Allies had broken the Treaty of Fontainebleau by failing to pay his pension, and Louis XVIII had fled France when Napoleon invaded with the Army of Elba. Although the concept of a country being at war with an individual may have been lawful by the standards of the age, the retention of Napoleon as a permanent prisoner of war after the fighting had ceased and the peace treaty had been signed appears perverse. It is perhaps for this reason that a bill of indemnity was passed to protect the relevant ministers from legal action and deprive Napoleon of the protection of Habeus Corpus, in the teeth of opposition in Parliament and criticism in the press.

Finally, in the most bizarre episode of all, Dr John Lattimer, an American urologist from New York, has been reported in the press as claiming that he has purchased Napoleon's penis. He claims that Dr Antommarchi cut the penis off during the autopsy at the behest of a Corsican chaplain, Vignali, whom Napoleon had allegedly insulted by calling him impotent. Lattimer's records show the penis as belonging to Vignali before finding its way via several owners to Christie's, where Lattimer purchased it for $4,000. This is without doubt the most bizarre and ridiculous of the controversies surrounding the Emperor's last days, particularly as there were seventeen people present at the autopsy and the body was subsequently washed and prepared for burial by valet Noverraz, all of whom would have noticed such a glaring omission.[8] This hypothesis can, I feel, be safely rejected.

The final episode took place on 15 October 1840, when Bertrand, Marchand, Saint-Denis, Gourgaud and some other members of the St. Helena Imperial Household returned to observe Napoleon's body being disinterred, examined and returned to France, where it now lies under the dome of Les Invalides. Of the seven of his surviving marshals, only Soult, Oudinot, Moncey and Grouchy attended the funeral.

The reader will have to make up his own mind about the various controversies surrounding the exile. The only sure way of resolving the poisoning controversy would be to exhume the body and perform another autopsy. For my part, I hope the Emperor is left in peace.

NOTES

1. Martineau, Gilbert. *Napoleon Surrenders*, London, 1971.
2. Martineau Gilbert. *Napoleon's St Helena,* London, 1968.
3. Horricks, Raymond. *In Flight with the Eagle.*
4. Weider, Ben, and Forshufvud, Sten. *Assassination at St Helena Revisited*, New York, 1995.
5. Weider, Ben, and Hapgood, David. *The Murder of Napoleon*, London, 1982.
6. Forshufvud, Sten, and Weider, Ben. *Assassination at St Helena – The Poisoning of Napoleon Bonaparte.*
7. Jones, David. *The Strange Case of Napoleon's Wallpaper.* Timewatch, BBC2.
8. Jenkins, Iain. Newspaper Article, 'Boney's little bit on the side'.
9. Wilsher Kim. Newspaper Article, 'Arsenic brought Napoleon to his bitter end'.
10. Hamilton-Williams, David. *The Fall of Napoleon: The Final Betrayal*, London, 1994.
11. Maury, Renee. Private correspondence with the author.
12. Chandler, David G. *Dictionary of the Napoleonic Wars*, London 1979.
13. Chandler, David G. 'On the death of Napoleon' in *Journal of the Napoleonic Association*, Second Series, No 4.
15. Coates-Wright, Philip J. C. 'An answer to "On the death of Napoleon"' in *Journal of the Napoleonic Association*, Second Series, No 5.
16. Jones and Leadingham. 'Arsenic in Napoleon's wallpaper' in *Nature*, vol. 299, 14 October 1982, p. 626.
17. Benbow, Dr. John. Conversations with the author.
18. Elmer, Bob: 'Napoleon's exile was illegal' in *Journal of the Association of Friends of the Waterloo Committee*, August 1993.
19. St Helena. *Official Guide*, 1979.
20. Yarrow, Dr. H. 'The Death of Napoleon on St. Helena' in *Journal of the Association of Friends of the Waterloo Committee*, December 1982. And remarks made during the Association of Friends of the Waterloo Committee debate: 'Napoleon on St. Helena: death or natural causes?' in October 1993.
21. Weider, Ben. Lecture to Florida State University, 17–19 September 1995.
22. Le Souvenir Napoleonien. Press release: *Last doubts about Napoleon's death resolved.*
23. Lewin, Hancock and Voynovich. 'Napoleon Bonaparte – no evidence of chronic arsenic poisoning' in *Nature*, vol. 299, p. 627.
24. Richardson, Robert G. 'How sick was Napoleon?' in *Practitioner*, January 1981, vol. 225, p. 109.
25. Robinson James O. 'The failing health of Napoleon' in *Journal of the Royal Society of Medicine*, vol 72, August 1979.

26. *The Times*, 23 June 1994.
27. Keynes, Milo. 'Did Napoleon die of arsenical poisoning?' in *The Lancet*, vol. 344, July 1994.
28. Rosenthal, Dr. J. Conversations with the author.
29. Martindale. *The Extra Pharmacopoeia*, The Pharmaceutical Press, 1941.
30. *British Medical Journal*, 1894, p. 152.
31. *Nature*, vol. 299, p. 627–8.
32. Hicks, Tim. Personal visits to Corsica and Malmaison.

BIBLIOGRAPHY

Chandler, D. G. *Waterloo: The Hundred Days*, Osprey Publishing Ltd, London, 1980.
Hamilton-Williams, David. *The Fall of Napoleon*, Arms and Armour Press, London, 1994.
Martineau, Gilbert. *Napoleon Surrenders*, John Murray (Publishers) Ltd., London, 1971.
– Napoleon's *St. Helena*, John Murray (Publishers) Ltd., London, 1968.
Weider, Ben, and Forshufvud, Sten. *Assassination at St. Helena Revisited*, John Wiley and Sons Inc., New York, 1995.

PART TWO
THE ASSESSMENT

NAPOLEON AND HIS MEN
James R. Arnold

THE WORLD HAS EXPERIENCED MANY GREAT GENERALS WHOSE dazzling displays of military leadership changed the course of history. There have been only four Great Captains, men whose combination of inspiring leadership and consummate tactical and strategic skill rank them significantly ahead of all others: Alexander, Hannibal, Genghis Khan and Napoleon. During his own time, and for more than one hundred years after, men related military theory and practice to Napoleon's concepts of warfare and measured ideas and performance against his standards. Yet, when Napoleon Bonaparte entered his headquarters in 1796 to meet his principal subordinates, no one anticipated that greatness lay ahead. Such were Napoleon's talents that before the meeting ended, two veteran generals had sensed the limitless possibilities.

Napoleon was twenty-six years old, unknown and unproven when he assumed command of the Army of Italy. He had none of the advantages – reputation, power, largess – that would later simplify his leadership duties. He summoned his three senior divisional generals: Jean Serurier, a 53-year-old officer with 34 years spent in the old Royal Army; Charles Augereau, a 38-year-old former soldier of fortune; and André Masséna, at 37 already a renowned combat leader. These are not men easily impressed, particularly when they learn that they are to be led by a mere boy general, a jumped-up Corsican with good political ties. Napoleon enters the room and they decline to doff their plumed hats. Seeing that they are slow to acknowledge his superior rank, he whips off his hat and thus by the convention of the day forces them to remove theirs. Promptly he puts his own hat back on and stares at them. His gesture is unmistakable: I am in command here.

He questions them about their forces, lays out his plan, announces that tomorrow he will hold an inspection, and the following day attack the enemy. Masséna later wrote of this experience that when Napoleon put on his general's hat he 'seemed to have grown two feet'. The hard-bitten Augereau told Masséna, 'That little bastard of a general actually frightened me!' This was one of the calculated effects Napoleon had on men. Seventeen days and two victories later he had conquered Lombardy and taken the next step towards joining the ranks of history's Great Captains.

Among the relationships that cement loyalty to a leader are friendship and love. Napoleon dismissed friendship, saying it was only a word. He acknowledged that he had no true friends. He claimed that he loved no man except his brother Joseph, and that by force of habit because Joseph was his elder brother. 'It takes time to make oneself loved,' he explained, 'and even when I had nothing to do I always vaguely felt that I had no time to waste.' Friendship and love were for women. As for himself, 'No sentimentality! One must be firm, have a firm heart ... Otherwise one has no business mixing in war and government.'

None the less Napoleon had a captivating presence. When he left France for the last time in 1815, it took him only a few hours to win over completely the officers and crew of HMS *Bellerophon* although they were hardly a group predisposed to think well of him. If on the decks of *Bellerophon* he chose charm, he also could overpower and intimidate. His personal aura did not come from his physical frame, which stood an unimposing five feet three inches. It did not come from his dress. In his early commands his neglected clothing attracted ridicule. As emperor his best-known dress was the simple, undress uniform of the Guard Chasseurs à Cheval. The aura seemed to come from his eyes. They were deep-set, large, greyish-blue, and had an almost

'*VIVE L'EMPÉREUR!*'. PRINT AFTER RAFFET.

hypnotic effect upon those who attracted his intense gaze. And this man was a consummate actor, capable of assuming whatever role the situation demanded. He controlled his personality, using it as one more tool to further his goals. Few leaders of state or men of power can or will subordinate their personality regardless of circumstances. Napoleon remarked during the Consulate, 'If I wanted a man sufficiently badly, I would kiss his arse.'

Napoleon's campaign to elevate himself from First Consul to Emperor provides a window to observe his style of leadership. At a time of transition from republican forms to imperial police state – a time fraught with potential political instability consequent on the abandonment of many revolutionary ideals – Napoleon mapped out a programme to ensure the army's loyalty to himself and to his new dynasty. He began at the top by taking a brilliant step to thwart potential rivals while simultaneously creating a high command structure for his army. Proclaimed Emperor by overwhelming public electoral support on 18 May 1804, the next day he recreated the title and rank of marshal by naming eighteen men to the rank. With this gesture he both showed his appreciation to his comrades and co-opted those who might oppose him.

He next applied himself to consolidating his personal hold over the army. The most spectacular symbol of this effort came on 16 August 1804 when he distributed the *Légion d'honneur* to selected individuals in the presence of nearly 60,000 soldiers and some 20,000 sightseers. It was a visual extravaganza with Napoleon seated on his throne surrounded by the standards taken from the enemy in past campaigns. At his side were dignitaries of every description as well as the new marshals. Around him, arrayed in a fan formation of columns, stood his soldiers. More than 1,000 drummers sounded *Aux Champs* while cannonfire reverberated in time to the music. It was a riveting, intoxicating experience.

When, on 2 December 1804, Napoleon's coronation took place in the presence of the Pope, Napoleon insisted on placing the crown on his own head. He could not help but gloat a bit, remarking to brother Joseph, 'If only our father could see us now.' Three days later he returned to business, stage-managing one more drama to complete the bonding cycle between the army and himself. He summoned the army's colonels to Paris to receive their Eagle icons from his own hands. The Imperial Eagle adorned the top of a unit's flagstaff. Napoleon intended it to be considered more valuable than the flag itself. 'Soldiers, here are your Colours! These Eagles will always be your rallying point ... Do you swear to lay down your lives in their defence?' 'We

swear!' cried the colonels. Henceforth, the defence of the Eagle was fundamental to unit pride, the role of Eagle-bearer reserved for the unit's bravest.

Simultaneous with this time of intense political scheming came Napoleonic
France's most important military refinements. Exhibiting his extraordinary
ability to wear the two hats of head of state and army commander-in-chief,
from 1803 to 1805 Napoleon created the era's most proficient land-based
military machine, the *Grande Armée*. Along France's Channel coast, the so-
called Camp of Boulogne, a force of some 160,000 men had an unequalled
opportunity to drill in all aspects of tactics. A typical corps spent one month
relearning individual and platoon manoeuvres. Then it graduated to two days
a week occupied with battalion drill and three with divisional manoeuvres.
On Sundays the entire corps manoeuvred, and twice a month it participated
in army manoeuvres complete with live musket and cannonfire at targets.
These experiences honed the soldiers to a fine edge of discipline that persisted as long as the veterans of the *Grande Armée* survived. As late as 1813
Marshal Auguste Marmont attributed certain units' proficiency to the presence of a hard knot of surviving *Grande Armée* veterans. The realistic exer-
cises also gave the brigade, division and corps generals an opportunity to
practice their trade. Meanwhile, in Paris, Napoleon comprehensively examined past and present performances and weeded the army of unfit generals.

In addition to forging a highly effective army and wedding it to his person,
Napoleon accomplished one other important objective during this time. The
months the troops spent along the coast overcame memories of France's divi-
sive past. Hitherto veterans had thought of themselves as soldiers of the Army
of the Rhine or the Army of Italy. There was considerable friction among
them. Henceforth they considered themselves as soldiers of the *Grande
Armée*. They also assumed an immense regimental pride. While an unfortunate spate of often deadly duelling ensued, there was no question that
Napoleon had instilled a powerful *esprit de corps*. Likewise, in the past there
had been tension between officers who were the sons of aristocrats, and officers who had risen through the ranks in an embodiment of France's republican ideals. These tensions now largely disappeared. Ambitious young men,
regardless of background, shared the hope of distinguishing themselves during the coming campaign, of earning glory and rapid promotion. There was
tremendous competition among keen officers – Napoleon encouraged rivalry
in the belief that it produced the best efforts – but it had a unifying goal: mak-

ing the Grande *Armée* second to none. By establishing this high standard, Napoleon obtained the machine he needed to found a dynasty.

The re-creation of the marshalate was both a grand gesture and a practical necessity. Napoleon understood that his assumption of the imperial mantle was not entirely approved of by key army leaders. Indeed, several of his atheist, republican generals could stomach his coronation's religious overtones only by fortifying themselves liberally with alcohol, cursing continually (*sotto voce*) during the proceedings, and making sardonic comments. But, by his swift stroke – today I am named Emperor, tomorrow I name you marshals – he co-opted potential opposition by offering the irresistible lure of a marshal's baton. So they may have cursed and complained, but they did so while proudly fingering their batons. Which of them – apprentice dyer Jean Lannes; Joachim Murat, an innkeeper's son originally destined for the church; would-be village baker Nicholas Soult – could have anticipated that he would rise so far?

The first creation had fourteen active marshals. The men Napoleon knew best were those with whom he had served in Italy and Egypt. From this group came Augereau, Berthier, Bessières, Lannes, Masséna and Murat. Only Augereau was past his prime. Indeed in later years people would complain about his indifferent performance only to be brought up short by the Emperor, who would recall the perilous days of 1796 and say, 'Ah, but you should have seen him at Castiglione.' The other five comrades were quite simply fine soldiers. Berthier was a model chief of staff, inimitably interpreting and transmitting the Emperor's intentions. Lannes improved constantly, displaying notable grand tactical skill. Masséna was a brilliant soldier for any era. Bessières and Murat were exceptional cavalrymen; the former possessed tactical judgement and took care of troopers and horses alike; the latter had a fine eye for terrain and a showy courage that inspired troopers to storm through any opposition. Davout, a relative unknown at the time of his selection, was another 'Egyptian'. Even though he had spent most of his time in Egypt on independent assignment, his great competency had caught Napoleon's eye. Like Masséna, Davout was a great soldier. He never suffered defeat on the battlefield. In selecting meritorious individuals from among his old comrades, Napoleon did not mis-step.

Half of his original selections came because he wanted to represent all the famous armies of Revolutionary France. He chose Brune in order to conciliate France's Jacobin/republican elements, and Jourdan and Moncey because they had led important armies during the days of the embattled republic. None of these ever contributed importantly to future campaigns. Three marshals represented the renowned *Armée de Sambre-et-Meuse* – Ney, Mortier and Soult. Napoleon knew of them only by reputation. They possessed mixed talents; Soult, a highly skilled leader capable of independent command, Ney and Mortier aggressive and useful as long as they remained within the Emperor's eyesight. All three were fighting soldiers well above the ordinary.

Then there was Bernadotte. Napoleon selected him from mixed motives. He had married the sister of Napoleon's elder brother's wife and thus was family by Corsican standards. More importantly, Napoleon knew that Bernadotte harboured high ambition and was well connected politically to a potentially dissident group. The Emperor must have thought that gratitude would bind Bernadotte to him. After all, having attained power, Napoleon was helpful to those who had helped him during his lean days. The fact that the likes of Bernadotte did not behave this way surprised and puzzled him. Napoleon entered a relationship believing the worst. He defied anyone to trick him, saying that they 'would have to be exceptional

NAPOLEON AND THE YOUNG GUARD. RAFFET.

rascals' to be as bad as he assumed them to be. Given that Bernadotte was to be the first marshal to betray him, one can only conclude that here was an 'exceptional rascal'.

In sum, both army and national politics constrained Napoleon in his original selections for the marshalate. The salient point when assessing his ability to select men is that from the marshals' ranks came the subordinates who, within four years, expanded France's borders into the greatest European empire since Roman times.

While he did utter his well-known aphorism, 'men are led by baubles', his understanding of what motivated men was far keener. He appreciated that bravery could not be bought with money: 'A man does not have himself killed for a few half-pence a day.' Nor would a petty distinction inspire courage. Napoleon worked very hard at creating an atmosphere of glory with which to engulf specifically his military and generally his nation. He told Fouché in 1805, 'One obtains everything from men by appealing to their sense of honour.' Honour could be earned by pursuing glory. 'Death is nothing,' he told his army. 'But to live defeated and without glory is to die every day.' His cult of glory persisted long after his death. Writing a campaign history almost forty years after the event, one veteran explained a setback with sadness and observed how the offending officer 'let slip the occasion to acquire immortal glory'.

Napoleon's most notable success at inspiring the cult of glory came when he created one single decoration that superseded all others. This was the *Légion d'honneur*. It was a small, white-enamelled star with five twofold rays suspended on a scarlet silk ribbon. Because the miniature star closely resembled a cross, it was by this designation that it was universally known. Anyone could earn the Cross, anyone that is who displayed exemplary service to France. It was not a mere bauble but rather a symbol of equality. Napoleon understood that under the Bourbons the old chivalric orders had strengthened caste division. In the past, regardless of a poor man's achievements, there were numerous awards he could not earn simply because of his low birth. With its military and civil branches, the *Légion d'honneur* was a universal incentive for diverse ambitions.

On countless fields men exerted themselves to earn the coveted Cross. The successful storming of Landshut in 1809 put the Emperor in a good mood. Addressing one of the victorious regiments he asked, 'Who is the bravest man in the regiment?' The colonel hesitated; some men were simply struck dumb in Napoleon's presence. The Emperor repeated the question to the other officers. Silence. Finally he spied an elderly *voltigeur* captain: 'Well, old fellow, who is the bravest soldier in the Thirteenth Regiment? 'Sire,' the captain replied, 'it is the drum-major. Everyone knows that.' Turning to the drum-major, Napoleon said: 'You have been designated the bravest of a brave regiment. I promote you to lieutenant and chevalier in the *Légion d'honneur*.' The troops responded with enormous enthusiasm. In the next battle they would fight with personal knowledge that extreme bravery could be rewarded.

During a similar review, when Napoleon was soliciting recommendations from the regimental officers and issuing gratuities and decorations upon deserving soldiers, an old *grognard*, as was his right, approached the Emperor and asked for the Cross. Napoleon asked what he had done to deserve it. The veteran of Italy and Egypt replied, 'It was I, Sire, who in the desert of Joppa gave you a watermelon.' 'I thank you for it again. But the gift of a fruit is hardly worth the Cross.'

The veteran, who had been calm until now, lost his composure, shouting, 'Well, and don't you reckon seven wounds received at the bridge of Arcola, at Lodi, and Castiglione, at the Pyramids, at Acre, Austerlitz, Friedland; eleven campaigns in Italy, Egypt, Austria, Prussia, Poland ...'

The Emperor interrupted and, mimicking the soldier's excited manner said, 'There, there – how you work yourself up when you come to the essential point! ... I make you a Knight of the Empire, with a pension of twelve hundred francs. Does that satisfy you?'

The man did not realise that becoming a knight implied receipt of the *Légion d'honneur*. He replied, 'But your Majesty, I'd prefer the Cross.'

Reviewing the 26th *Légère*, a regiment that had just successfully stormed the Ebelsberg château, Napoleon asked the colonel who was the unit's bravest officer. Taken by surprise, the unnerved colonel stammered. Napoleon snapped, 'Well! Have you heard me?' The colonel replied, 'Yes, Sire; but I know many who ... ' The Emperor interrupted, 'No pretty phrases, answer.'

The colonel nominated a Lieutenant Guyot, an officer who the previous day had stood in an open courtyard exchanging shots at five metres' range with enemy troops in a château. As the bodies of his men piled up around him – a third of his regiment fell in ten minutes – Guyot had formed a firing line by having the rear ranks pass forward loaded weapons to himself and a handful of others. Although the French fell in heaps – some chasseurs had to clamber atop their fallen comrades to get a decent shot at the château's windows – Guyot persisted until he had silenced the hostile fire. Now he stepped forward to be named by Napoleon a baron of the empire and receive a handsome pension.

Next Napoleon asked the colonel who was the regiment's bravest soldier? Up stepped the nominee, Carabinier Corporal Bayonnette. The name delighted Napoleon, who named Bayonnette a Chevalier in the *Légion d'honneur* with a fine pension.

The Emperor deliberately put on such displays to encourage officers and men to fight in the knowledge that valour could be rewarded on a colossal scale. In Corporal Bayonnette's case, his actions had an unintended consequence. Henceforth, Bayonnette avoided all combat exposure. As his comrades remarked, he was not so stupid as to get himself killed now that 'his bread was baked'.

From the beginning, Napoleon intuitively understood the minds of his soldiers. His first battles in Italy in 1796 were victories (how different the course of history if they had been defeats!). With victory came his soldiers' respect. Since he wanted his soldiers to display courage, perseverance, and unquestioning obedience, he next sought to earn their affection. In his method of military leadership he emulated Turenne (1611–75), a general he greatly admired. In the words of Colonel John Elting, Napoleon adhered to Turenne's credo 'that you must love soldiers in order to understand them, and understand them in order to lead them'. Napoleon had a genuine affection for his soldiers. He understood what motivated soldiers and French soldiers in particular because from an early age he had applied himself to studying this. Upon assuming his first command in Italy he deliberately set out to forge a bond of affection between the rank and file and himself.

Time and again during the course of his career he recognised the face of an old soldier and singled him out, recalling the days of old or perhaps, better yet, grabbing his ear lobe between thumb and forefinger and giving it a good pull. The recipient treasured such gestures and would remember them for a lifetime. It is impossible to conceive of one of Napoleon's contemporary's – Tsar Alexander, the Emperor Francis, the King of Prussia, or the snobbish, blue-blood Wellington – combining such recall of a lowly private's service with a gesture of physical affection. His easy familiarity with his men made him highly popular. 'I remember you from Egypt ... You were with me at Castiglione ... How many wounds have you suffered? ... What, you have yet to receive the Cross after so many campaigns? Why didn't you remind me?' A soldier would proudly relate such an encounter that night around the campfire and it became the stuff of legend.

By his recognition of individuals Napoleon did much to bolster army morale. He also worked to build unit pride by praising distinguished regiments. In 1807 he told the 44th *Ligne* that 'your three battalions count as six in my eyes', to which they shouted back, 'and we shall prove it'. At Graz in 1809, the 84th *Ligne*, two battalions with about 1,200 men, defended the Saint-Leonhard cemetery against some 20,000 Austrians. It lost three officers and 31 men killed, twelve officers and 192 men wounded, and 40 prisoners. These casualties, while heavy, were not atypical. What was special was the unit's ability to hold on for nearly sixteen hours against a vastly superior force. When the survivors reached Napoleon's Headquarters outside Vienna, the Emperor inspected the 84th, handed out 84 Crosses, and made the regiment's colonel a count. To honour further the regiment, he authorised it to inscribe in gold lettering the legend 'UN CONTRE DIX' (one against ten) on its standards. Napoleon well appreciated how his words affected his men. After reporting in one bulletin that 'the 32nd was there; I was tranquil', he observed that henceforth this demi-brigade was prepared to die for him.

Then there was the back of his hand: 'Quartermaster-General,' he publicly boomed before soldiers of the 39th and 85th, two demi-brigades who had recently exhibited less than stellar battle conduct, 'let it be inscribed on their Colours: "They no longer belong to the Army of Italy".' On another occasion an officer overheard the Emperor berate the 4th *Ligne*, a unit which had lost its Eagle to a Russian cavalry charge at Austerlitz. Napoleon spoke with such vehemence that the officer observed that, although he was only a spectator, 'yet I must own that my flesh crawled. I broke into a cold sweat, and at times my eyes were coursing with tears. I do not doubt that the regiment would have performed miracles, if it had been led into action at the very next instant.'

Sometimes it was his soldiers who elevated his morale. On the eve of Austerlitz he had a thoroughly disagreeable interview with an overbearing Russian prince. He had had to play-act a role of abject subservience and was angry. He walked about the French outpost line lashing at clods of dirt with his riding whip. Nearby was an old soldier, taking his ease, filling his pipe while his musket rested against his legs. Napoleon glanced toward him and spat out vehemently, 'Those Russian buggers think they can make us swallow anything.' The veteran happily replied, 'Not on your life! Not if we have anything to do with it!' Napoleon laughed appreciatively. The words restored his good humour. Regaining his composure he mounted his horse and returned to Headquarters.

Until the American Civil War demonstrated the impact of accurate shoulder firearms, the catalogue of martial leadership had included willingness to expose oneself to enemy fire. Napoleon did not shy away from such exposure. If he demanded bravery of others, he also exhibited it himself. We see him in 1809, in full view of Austrian pickets, masquerading as a simple soldier preparing for a swim in order to examine a potential Danube crossing site; in 1812, riding to within 200 yards of the walls of Smolensk with Berthier, and then proceeding another 100 yards alone to select a point to assault; the night before Waterloo he dismounts amidst an artillery barrage to scout on foot the terrain for the next day's attack. During the course of his career he had some nineteen horses shot beneath him. Throughout it all he exhibited exemplary sang-froid.

Before Ratisbon in 1809 a ball struck him in the foot, causing a nasty-looking, rapidly swelling contusion. News of the wound spread quickly and the army became anxious. Sensitive to this, the Emperor refused medical advice to retire to his carriage and instead mounted his charger, a beautiful white horse gifted him by the Bavarian king. Mounted, he provided an unmistakable target. Soon bullets came whizzing by, prompting him to turn to his retinue and comment dryly, 'Doesn't it seem as though these bullets are reconnoitring us.' Later in the same year, during a critical moment on the field at Wagram, French and allied troops were routing before a powerful Austrian attack. To steady his men Napoleon rode 'from one extremity of the line to the other, and returned at a slow pace'. So many shots flew past him that one imperial aide kept his 'eyes riveted upon him, expecting at every moment to see him drop from his horse'.

A little later a howitzer shell exploded nearby causing the Emperor's horse to shy. Alarmed, Oudinot exclaimed, 'Sire, they are firing on the Headquarters.' Napoleon replied, '*Monsieur*, in war all accidents are possible,' and calmly continued to finish his dictation. Indeed, nowhere was safe from Austrian artillery fire on the almost billiards table-flat field at Wagram. On 6 July twenty-six of Napoleon's Headquarters officers were hit during the day. Here hairbreadth escapes were common. As one courier doffed his shako to acknowledge that he understood Napoleon's orders, a cannonball knocked it from his hand. The Emperor roared with laughter, commenting, 'It's a good job you're not taller!' He remained unflappable even under the heaviest fire. He set a standard for bravery by his own example. Thus, just after the incident described, he could pose on a small mound while a division of heavy cavalry trotted by, respond to their cheers by pointing in the direction they must attack, and instruct each passing colonel to 'charge to the hilt'. Coming from someone less willing or able to display courage, the words might have rung hollow. From Napoleon, they inspired.

Shining competence was the key to Napoleon's leadership. A royal inspector observed him during his schooldays at Brienne. He reported that the youth 'has always been distinguished for his application in mathematics'. This talent led him to join the most scientific of the three military arms, the artillery. The French artillery of this time was undergoing major technical reform. Napoleon's mathematical talent and energy well matched the dynamic drive to modernise. He came under the tutelage of Baron du Teil, one of the best artillerists of the day, who encouraged him to broaden his military knowledge. Napoleon responded, proving himself an avid reader and apt pupil. He approached military history in analytical fashion. Step by step he collected strategic and grand tactical concepts and unified them into a whole. As David Chandler observes, 'Napoleon was not an original thinker where military theory was concerned.' Rather he took existing concepts and improved them. What is vitally important to his later success is that he laboured tirelessly to build a solid foundation of knowledge for his chosen career. Beginning with a technical mastery of artillery, he expanded his knowledge to encompass military history and theory. In the future, intelligent men would follow him because they recognised the power of his brain.

He described his thinking process as follows: 'Different subjects and different affairs are arranged in my head as in a cupboard. When I wish to interrupt one train of thought, I shut that drawer and open another. Do I wish to sleep? I simply close all the drawers, and there I am – asleep.'

His arrangement of his Headquarters, his carriage and much else reflected this thinking process. In September 1805, while preparing for the march east against Austria and Russia, he dictated a letter to Berthier asking him to 'let me know whether you have carried out my instructions, namely to entrust somebody who is acquainted with German to follow the march of the Austrian regiments, and file the details in the compartments of the box you were told to make for that purpose. The name or number of each regiment is to be entered on a playing-card, and the cards are to be changed from one compartment to another according to the movements of the regiments.'

No leader in recorded history worked harder in a more focused way. In 1806 he commented that the dossiers devoted to his army, with their detailed statistics of men present and absent, horses healthy or lame, and number of available cartridges for the cannon, were his favourite reading material. 'Work is my element,' he declared. At least until his marriage to Marie-Louise in 1810, at all times he worked exceptionally long hours. Twenty hour days were routine: 'I was born and made for work. I have recognised the limits of my eye-sight and of my legs, but never the limits of my working power.' He dictated orders while being shaved, conducted interviews while bathing, plotted strategy while attending the opera.

On campaign he drove himself even harder. The amount of riding he did is astonishing. In Colonel Elting's words, 'He was an able, daring, reckless horseman who rode farther and harder than any ruler and most other men of his generation.' So he is seen in January 1809, having received alarming

'THE EMPEROR IS WATCHING!': FRENCH INFANTRY ADVANCE, CONSCIOUS OF
NAPOLEON'S PRESENCE. PRINT AFTER RAFFET.

news of Austrian war preparations, galloping mile after mile along Spanish roads as he speeds back to Paris, reaching with one hand to whip his companion's horse so that they will make better time. The speed at which he travelled is likewise astonishing. He completed his 700-mile journey from Spain to Paris in six days. In 1812 he covered nearly 1,300 miles of winter road in thirteen days, departing Smorgoniye on 5 December, arriving shortly before midnight in Paris on the 18th in time to put in a full day's work on the 19th. At moments of supreme crisis Napoleon worked at a tremendous pitch. During the final planning of the Danube crossing in 1809, until mid-afternoon of the second day at Wagram, he spent 60 of 72 hours on horseback.

In order to utilise efficiently his travelling time, Napoleon had a large coach which served as a mobile office. Its seat was divided by a low partition to allow him and a passenger, generally Berthier, to work without inconvenience. Facing the seat was a cabinet neatly compartmentalised with locking drawers to hold maps, files, and correspondence as well as open cupboards for food, drink, toiletries, paper, pens, telescopes, and a library. A sliding leaf pulled out from the cabinet provided a desk. A large, silver timepiece hung from a wall. At night a lantern illuminated the working surface from behind the passenger's shoulders. A rear trunk held bedding, extra torches, clothing. Beneath the coachman's seat was one of the Emperor's folding field beds which could be used to convert Napoleon's seat to a sleeping surface (poor Berthier had to sleep sitting up!). If a courier arrived, day or night, Napoleon could read his dispatches, consult any relevant files or maps, draft a response, have Berthier prepare the formal orders, and summon a fresh courier, all without stopping.

In the field he typically adhered to a schedule well designed for a time when communications sped no faster than the pace of a hard-spurring courier. So, to his camp bed between 7 and 9 p.m. for four hours' sleep. During this time his subordinates wrote their reports and daily summaries while his staff compiled the data. By midnight most reports should have arrived at Headquarters and so Napoleon arose to digest the news. As the army slept he worked, dictating necessary replies, designing new plans based on the latest information. Couriers left Headquarters with the new orders at about 3 a.m. Chores completed, he took another nap before dawn and then rose with the sun to begin the main work of the day.

It habitually began with a summons for General Bacler d'Albe with the maps. This most valuable officer headed the Emperor's topographical office and handled all staff duties associated with planning sessions. He daily updated the situation map and maintained the *carnets*, notebooks stuffed with facts and figures, that contained information about every Imperial and enemy unit. Together the two would crawl on all fours over the maps to mark troop locations with coloured pins and to measure distances for the day's assigned marches. Unless it were a day of battle requiring his personal reconnaissance, he then granted interviews to the various important persons he had summoned or who wished to speak to him. Attention to the mountain of paperwork followed, for he was not just a field general but also the head of state of a vast empire.

Then by mid-morning to horse with his 'little Headquarters' to visit subordinates and inspect units. He firmly believed in the benefit of assessing with his own eyes his men's condition and of frequently being seen among them. Throughout military history most troop reviews have consisted of a pro-forma inspection conducted by functionaries or superior officers who have little time for and less knowledge about what they are looking at. Not so a Napoleonic troop review by the Emperor. These occasions were times of considerable anxiety for officers because a good performance could lead to the next step on the promotion ladder while a less than stellar review could end a career.

Typically on his first pass Napoleon rode at a walk across the unit's front. Next he might put the unit through some basic manoeuvres. Then came the dreaded interrogations with the rapid-fire barrage of questions: 'What is your effective strength? How many men in hospital? Sick in cantonments? Absent from any other cause?' Woe to the officer who did not have the answers pat, who stammered, or became confused. The Emperor believed that if a man could not withstand the pressure of his interrogation, he would not be able to maintain his composure on a battlefield. Among many there was the hapless Colonel Merlin of the 8th Cuirassiers who became so rattled during an inspection that his response showed an enormous difference between the total of his effectives and the amount made up by summing the sub-totals. For his blunder he received 'words of reproof and looks that did not bespeak the near approach of favours'. Perhaps Merlin recalled this humiliation when he opted to lead a brigade of light cavalry against Napoleon during the Waterloo campaign.

Officer interviews completed, the unit filed past Napoleon for the last time. Repeated shouts of '*Vive l'Empereur!*' (expressed with varying degrees of feeling depending on recent conditions) might evoke a comment directed at the unit's commander: 'Colonel, on the first action a bullet or a General's stars.'

And then the great man departed to perform the same task again or to move on to a corps headquarters to discuss pending operations with a marshal.

He refused to interrupt his business with meals, often taking a quick bite while in the saddle. Then, back to Headquarters for another review of recently received reports, another flurry of dictated orders to teams of perspiring secretaries, and another round of interviews. Dinner was a necessary nuisance, a perfunctory affair often conducted in silence and lasting a short twenty minutes. A last summons for d'Albe, a final examination of the latest maps and then to bed to prepare for another cycle of the same.

The maintenance of an uninterrupted work-flow day after day was an enormous organisational effort. To accomplish this Napoleon created history's first, all-encompassing, staff structure. It comprised two principal branches: the *Maison* (the household of Napoleon's personal staff); and the General Staff of the Army (*Quartier général de la Grande Armée*). In 1805 Imperial Headquarters numbered 400 officers and 5,000 men. To support the massive invasion of Russia in 1812 it swelled to 3,500 officers and more than 10,000 men. The *Maison* was Napoleonic France's nerve centre. Grand Marshal of the Palace Geraud Duroc supervised the *Maison*, being responsible for its administration and for the Emperor's personal safety. An intelligent, honest, and courageous officer in his own right, Duroc ran an exceptionally orderly organisation.

The Household camp comprised eight large tents erected around a 1,200 by 600 feet rectangle. There was one tent for Napoleon; one shared by Duroc and Caulaincourt; and one each for Napoleon's aides-de-camp, officiers d'ordonnance, secretaries and senior officers. More junior assistants shared the remaining three. A formal 'gate' opposite the Emperor's tent gave access to the camp, and there was a rear service entrance. Nearby were parking locations for the wagons, a picket line for the imperial horses, kitchens, camps for the escorts, and all other necessary impedimenta. At night, lanterns illuminated the entrance to each tent and also defined the camp's perimeter. The night duty officer maintained a small, mobile headquarters loaded aboard wagons and ready to move out at a moment's notice. All night another aide, a page, a sergeant of the escort and a corporal assigned to the wagon train served two-hour stints outside the Emperor's tent. Their job was to transmit instantly the order to mount up should Napoleon unexpectedly decide on a nocturnal foray. This entire arrangement was designed to permit Napoleon and his headquarters to respond to any emergency at any time.

The Russian cannonball that mortally wounded Duroc in 1813 left a void at imperial Headquarters. Napoleon had respected Duroc's ability to manage the *Maison*. More than that, contrary to his words rejecting friendship, he considered Duroc a friend. He remembered Duroc's daughter in his will.

The *Maison*'s other senior officer was Armand de Caulaincourt, Napoleon's Master of Horse. He supervised all imperial travel, had responsibility for the movement and logistical support of the *Maison*, and managed the couriers. He shared Napoleon's work ethic and like the Emperor could coherently juggle a myriad of unrelated details in order to produce a harmonious whole. Napoleon deeply trusted and respected him and Caulaincourt reciprocated with intelligent service.

A 'Cabinet' or office attached to the *Maison* performed the necessary if dull secretarial chores of transmitting orders. Far more important was the Topographical Office headed by the indispensable Louis Bacler d'Albe. He maintained the map table exhibiting the current situation and took part in the heated planning sessions that formed the basis for a campaign. An artist by profession, d'Albe possessed ample martial skills and became an invaluable assistant in all campaign planning.

Much of Napoleon's success can be attributed to a staff that in its organisation and personnel was the best the world had yet seen. In Berthier, Duroc, Caulaincourt, and d'Albe, Napoleon had selected men capable of handling a staggering work load with great competence.

When Napoleon had to absent himself from the *Maison* he was accompanied by his 'little Headquarters', a battle command group of picked assistants including Berthier, Caulaincourt (who had the additional job of carrying the appropriate local map attached to a button on his coat), a trooper carrying the entire map folio, duty officer, two aides, two orderly officers, a horse, a page to carry the imperial telescope, equerry and groom, interpreter, and Napoleon's personal servant, the mameluke Roustam. Proceeded by two orderly officers with an escort of one officer and twelve troopers, followed at a thousand metres by four squadrons of Guard cavalry, this highly mobile command group allowed the Emperor to circulate freely while maintaining control.

As the structure of his carriage and Headquarters suggests, Napoleon's combination of disciplined intellect and enormous capacity for work gave him a mastery of the details associated with land warfare. It was quite different with naval affairs. He was unable to inspire any of his sailors, largely because he failed to understand the paramount importance of wind, tides and currents upon naval operations. He complained that sailors spoke an entirely different language and it was one he did not understand. His admirals, in turn, took advantage of his ignorance. When he urged some scheme upon them which they did not approve, they explained that it was impossible because of prevailing winds or adverse currents. Napoleon suspected that they were making game of him, but he was not certain. He lamented that some great French admiral such as Suffren was no longer alive. He tried to tackle the naval challenge by doing what he understood. He worked to increase France's naval might by having every shipyard throughout his empire engage in a colossal and ultimately enormously wasteful naval construction programme. Whatever could be done on land - capturing naval bases, cutting off the Royal Navy's access to resources, restricting British trade - he did. But in the end his inability to understand the supremacy of the technical side of naval affairs made him throw up his hands in frustration.

'BAKED POTATOES!': NAPOLEON SHARES THE RATIONS OF HIS GRENADIERS OF THE IMPERIAL GUARD. PRINT AFTER RAFFET.

After his elevation to First Consul and then to Emperor, Napoleon was able to enjoy one of the traditional tools of leadership – the granting of favours. In 1806 he reinstituted a nobility. Having seen mob violence at close quarters during his impressionable youth, Napoleon retained a fear of revolution and anarchy. By dispensing privilege on a supreme scale he hoped to render his regime proof against reaction. Thus a Davout rose from Marshal in 1804 to Duke of Auerstädt in 1808 to Prince of Eckmühl in 1809; a Ney from Marshal in 1804 to duc d'Elchingen in 1808 to Prince de la Moskowa in 1813; brother-in-law Murat straight from Marshal in 1804 to King of Naples in 1808. Even a relative nonentity like Mortier became the duc de Trevise in 1808. In a remarkably short time, even former revolutionaries became very comfortable, referring to one another as 'Prince of' this or 'Duke of' that. Agreeable though it was for these sons of innkeepers and coopers to be called duke and prince, perhaps more pleasant was the fact that the titles included valuable pensions that made the marshals rich men.

Napoleon should not have been surprised if such promotion and elevation went to the heads of several of them. Few retained the perspective of Madame la Maréchale Lefebvre, the one-time charwoman, who, upon hearing herself publicly referred to as the Duchess of Danzig, winked at the footman and chirped, 'Hey boy, what do you think of that?' The danger for Napoleon was that people raised so high would grow complacent. While on military campaign Napoleon deliberately kept his staff and subordinates on edge, believing that a state of nervous tension ensured their best efforts. Perhaps unwittingly he violated this man-management style by continuing to lavish privilege and rewards upon the marshalate. Soon many of the marshals came to accept all this as their due. When a friend congratulated Lefebvre for his luck in being elevated to Duke of Danzig, the Marshal exploded, 'Luck? Come out into the garden and I'll take twenty shots at you at thirty paces. If I miss, the house and everything in it is yours! ... I had a thousand shots fired at me at much closer range than ten paces, before I moved into this!'

For the army's rank and file there were the awards: swords of honour, monetary grants, promotion, and nomination to the Guard. Admittance to the Imperial Guard was a plum assignment. Henceforth a man received extra pay, the best quarters, a rank equivalency superior to that of the line units, first call on rations and medical care. In addition, Napoleon was loath to commit the Guard to battle, preferring to retain it as an ultimate reserve. Not for nothing were some of the Guard formations known as 'The

Immortals', 'The Gods' and the 'Cherished Children'. The Emperor gave great attention to the Guard's every detail and the resulting units were without equal.

The Emperor hand-picked the Guard officers. Not only did they have to be veterans of a certain number of campaigns, they had to possess surpassing bravery. Napoleon was always on the lookout for qualified candidates. In April 1809 a cavalry officer of the 2nd Chasseurs à Cheval approached the Emperor to present two captured flags. The officer had received a slash from an Austrian sabre and blood was dripping from his face as he handed the trophies to Napoleon. The Emperor asked him his name. 'Lion,' he replied. Napoleon exclaimed, 'Lion, I will remember you and you will be grateful; you are well marked.'

When later a vacancy in the Imperial Guard Chasseurs à Cheval occurred, Napoleon rejected the names Berthier presented to him. 'No, no. Bring me my Lion!' In the midst of a complex, life and death campaign, Napoleon remembers one deserving officer and rewards him for his valour. Here was painstaking attention to detail, a genius for man management.

Particularly during the glory days of the *Grande Armée*, Napoleon convinced the soldiers that their conduct, his own conduct, and France's destiny were one. As Bourrienne put it, 'he had the secret of involving his men with him in the unbelievable activity of his affairs'. The egalitarian familiarity between Napoleon and his men was unique and goes a long way to explaining why his army achieved prodigies of valour. Successful generals are usually popular. But the *Grande Armée*'s esteem for Napoleon surpassed popularity. In its adoration it approached idolatry, revering Napoleon as a sort of father figure and demigod.

It is easier to turn the heads of young soldiers than to inspire veterans – *Grognard* does mean grumbler after all. Repeated wars tarnished the sheen of '*la gloire*'. One infantry captain recalled that only occasionally did his men shout '*Vive l'Empereur!*' with great enthusiasm. Ordered to cheer by their officers, more commonly they muttered, 'Let him give me my discharge, and I'll cheer as much as they please!' or 'We have no bread; when my stomach is empty, I cannot cheer.' Still, Napoleon had a sublime talent for circulating among his rank and file and, with a mere glance or a brief word, inflaming their spirit. 'I used to say of him,' commented the Duke of Wellington, 'that his presence in the field made a difference of 40,000 men.' Devotion to Napoleon persisted even in the toughest conditions. During the retreat from Russia a soldier remarked, 'we're cooked, but *Vive l'Empereur* all the same'. Likewise a soldier of the Imperial Guard said, 'when there's no one left but us, there'll still be plenty'.

Few were more devoted than those hand-picked officers Napoleon chose to be his aides-de-camp. They could be trusted to perform any duty, regardless of obstacles, with intelligence and bravery, or die trying. In the words of David Chandler, they were 'expected to be equally capable of leading a charge, negotiating a treaty or cooking a chicken'. An indication of their quality is the fact that he entrusted at least three of them, Bertrand, Mouton and Lauriston, with corps command. Above all, to be an imperial aide meant one was at the apex of courage in an army full of brave men. At a key moment in April 1809, when the Emperor's strategy hinged upon the capture of a bridge, Napoleon turned to Georges Mouton: 'put yourself at the head of that column, and carry the town of Landshut'. It appeared to be a near-suicidal undertaking, but Mouton did precisely that.

But the Emperor selected aides who were not simply courageous automatons. Later in the campaign at Aspern-Essling, he sent Mouton at the head of the Young Guard Tirailleurs to recapture the key village of Essling. Although Mouton soon received a wound, his counter-attack stopped the Austrian advance in its tracks. But it could not reclaim the village, so Napoleon 'committed' another of his aides, Jean Rapp, with two more Young Guard battalions. Rapp's orders were to relieve the pressure on Mouton and then retire. He marched up to Mouton's position and explained his orders. He then said, 'You have overawed those masses by your resistance; let us charge them with the bayonet ... if we succeed, the Emperor and the army will give us credit for our success; if we fail, the responsibility will rest with me.' Mouton replied, 'With both of us.'

The two aides, exhibiting a fine disregard for orders, hurled their men into a winner-take-all assault, and by the narrowest margin succeeded. When Rapp returned to the Emperor, Napoleon said, 'If ever you did well by disregarding my orders, you have done so today; because the army's salvation depended upon the recapture of Essling.'

Mouton continued to distinguish himself during the 1809 battles for Vienna. For his overall campaign conduct Napoleon elevated him to the imperial nobility by naming him Count Lobau. But he went beyond that, displaying the personal touch, the identification of the responsive chord, by commissioning the renowned artist David to create a magnificent painting depicting Mouton leading the charge over the Landshut bridge. As one aide remarked, 'This keepsake from Napoleon was worth more than the highest eulogies.'

Not only did Napoleon carefully select his aides and the members of his Imperial Guard, he perused most of the officer nominations for his entire army. Clearly he could not know all the officers personally, so he was guided by the advice of trusted subordinates and by the nominee's campaign experience. He hated to promote desk officers, commenting that he only liked officers who made war. He applauded the policy of promoting men from the ranks, a practice that became increasingly necessary as officer casualties mounted. From 1809 on, nearly one-quarter of all junior officers came from the ranks. Whereas ten of the empire's twenty-six marshals had served in the ranks before Napoleon's elevation to First Consul, during the empire few rankers rose beyond captain. None came close to becoming a marshal. The idea that each soldier carried a baton in his knapsack was illusory.

Early in his career Napoleon wrote that it was vitally important for successful government not to let men grow old in their jobs. As Emperor he generally adhered to this belief. In 1809, arguably the apex of his empire, the average age of his eighteen active marshals – the army's most senior leadership – was just under 45 years. Masséna's trials in Spain and Portugal demonstrated the peril of entrusting a prematurely aged officer with too much responsibility. Masséna's preoccupation with the good life – not the least of which was his dashing, hussar-clad mistress – superseded his attention to military matters and his campaign failed dismally.

'You must speak to the soul in order to electrify the man,' Napoleon said. In similar vein he commented to General Brune in 1800 about the power of words to inspire soldiers. He put this belief into practice by keeping a printing press at his Headquarters. He had printed Orders of the Day for issue before a battle and post-battle bulletins to describe what had taken place. He was able to find just the right words to put his soldiers on their mettle. Thus in 1796 he addresses his near mutinous Army of Italy: 'Soldiers! You are ill-fed and almost naked. The government owes you a great deal, but it can do nothing for you. Your patience and courage do you honour but give you neither worldly goods nor glory.' Having acknowledged and described their miserable situation in three sentences, he has taken a long step toward winning their trust. He pledges to lead them to Italy's wealthy provinces and great cities where they can find honour, glory, and riches. Having at least given his men a glimmering of hope that a change in their squalid condition is near, he concludes with a challenge, 'Soldiers of the Army of Italy! Could courage and constancy possibly fail you?'

Two years later in Egypt his sick, weary army confronts the mameluke cavalry at the Battle of the Pyramids. He exhorts his men by historical allusion, tapping into their sense of national and unit pride: 'Remember that from those monuments yonder forty centuries look down upon you!'

At the decisive battle of Austerlitz in 1805, he has his trusted *Grande Armée*. Accordingly, he adopts a different tone. Each company commander reads the message to his men on the eve of the battle:

'The Russian battalions are the same which you beat at Schöngraben, and the same which you have pursued without respite until now. We occupy formidable positions, and while the enemy march upon my batteries, they will open their flanks to my attack ... We cannot afford to let victory slip from our grasp on a day like this when the honour of the French infantry and the whole nation is at stake.'

Here he is inspiring confidence by reminding his army that there is nothing to fear from this new enemy and then taking the unprecedented step of sharing his strategy, foretelling his battle-winning stroke against the Pratzen heights.

Then there were the after action reports. Regiments that had distinguished themselves received a coveted mention. Praise beyond all praise were the words that the designated unit had 'covered itself with glory'. On those special occasions – epic victories that redrew the map of Europe – there were simple words of esteem: 'Soldiers! I am pleased with you! You have, on this day of Austerlitz, justified everything that I had expected of your boldness, and you have honoured your Eagles with an immortal glory ... Soldiers! When I have accomplished everything that is necessary for the happiness and prosperity of your land, I shall lead you back to France. There you will be the objects of my most tender care. My people will greet you with joy, and it will be enough for you to say "I was at the battle of Austerlitz", and they will reply "There stands a hero!"'

Napoleon's ability to inspire fighting men was not limited to French soldiers. Consider how Napoleon responded to his 1809 crisis on the Danube. This campaign began with a surprise Austrian invasion of Bavaria. It was the first great military and psychological challenge to the Confederation of the Rhine, a French-created grouping of German allies of which Saxony and Bavaria were the most important elements. Austrian propaganda challenged all German-speaking people to overthrow the French yoke. Mid-April found the Emperor in his carriage dashing towards the front. West of Munich he encountered the King of Bavaria who had been forced to flee his capital by the approaching Austrians.

235

The King is in a bit of a panic, he needs bracing up. Napoleon descends from his carriage to greet his ally. Responding to Napoleon's query for news from the front, the distraught king says, 'Sire, the Tyrol which you have given me is on fire. The Austrians are manoeuvring between the Isar and the Danube.' 'Rest assured,' replies Napoleon. 'You will return to Munich in a few days. I will have at my side your son, Prince Louis; all will be well.'

Four days later Louis is indeed at Napoleon's side when the Emperor inspects the division commanded by the Bavarian king's heir. The Bavarians will soon enter battle. It is time to bolster their leader. Napoleon pats him on the shoulder and compliments him for facing the enemy in the field. He adds, 'Here you see how one must be King! Otherwise, if you were to stay at home, each of your men would do the same; and then, good-bye to the state, good-bye to glory.'

The next day, 20 April, will be a day of battle. Napoleon's German allies must perform a pinning attack while French formations envelop the Austrian flanks. They are a potential weak link in his strategy so he works to inspire them. He begins by choosing Bavarian and Württemberg *chevaulégers* to serve as his personal escort. It is a high honour that conveys to officers and men alike the message: 'I trust you.' Then he turns his attention to the Bavarian rank and file. The Emperor summons the officers to a hillside overlooking the battlefield. He reads them the Order of the Day while an aide translates:

> 'Bavarians! Today you fight alone against the Austrians. No French are serving in your front ranks ... I am entirely confident in your bravery ... For two hundred years Bavarian flags, protected by France, have resisted Austria. We are going to Vienna, where we will know how to punish Austria for the harm she has so often done to your country. Austria wants to partition your country and disband your units and distribute you among their regiments. Bavarians! This war is the last you will fight against your enemies; attack them with the bayonet and annihilate them.'

This pre-battle fight talk is perfectly crafted. It stimulates Bavarian honour by word ('I am entirely confident in your bravery') and deed ('you fight alone in the front ranks without the French'). It appeals to traditional attachments by the reminder about past alliances between France and Bavaria. It promises delicious revenge ('We are going to Vienna') and makes grave reference to a consequence of defeat ('disband your units and distribute you among their regiments'), this in an era when unit lineage

NAPOLEON AND A SOLDIER'S FAMILY. LITHOGRAPH AFTER BELLANGE.

and regimental pride were important. Lastly, it offers the ultimate reward if the soldiers behave correctly, an end to danger and privation ('This war is the last you will fight').

Later in the day he will give a similar harangue to his Württemberg troops. Again he cites history to inspire them, reminding the Württembergers of their victories against Austria when they had fought in the service of Frederick the Great. He concludes, 'The time has come to triumph once more, and to take the fight to Austrian soil.' His words inflame and the soldiers respond like Frenchmen, cheering, raising their shakos on their bayonets, enthusiastically preparing for combat.

An important component of Napoleon's motivational skills was his belief in the offensive. Recall, when assuming his first army command in 1796, he says 'tomorrow I will inspect the army, the next day we will attack'. It is the same in 1809 when war begins with a massive enemy offensive. Napoleon's response is to mount an immediate counter-offensive. He is certain that Frenchmen perform best while on the attack and he suspects that all soldiers share this attribute. So he tells his Bavarians that they will march to Vienna, his Württembergers that they will 'take the fight to Austrian soil'.

During the height of the Cold War, when NATO planners contemplated the prospect of a massive Soviet assault into West Germany, one of their major concerns was morale. They had commissioned psychological studies that provided an almost mathematical measure of morale. It showed, to their consternation since plans called for defensive operations, that morale factors multiplied physical power when a soldier was on the advance and reduced power when a soldier was retreating. Napoleon appreciated such calculus intuitively.

The power of the offensive goes beyond a morale impact on individual soldiers; it affects entire war machines. Napoleon sought, through his war strategy, to impose his will on his opponent, to force his enemy to respond to his manoeuvres. This was most apparent with his favourite strategic manoeuvre, *la manoeuvre sur les derrières* (the advance of envelopment). Napoleon's faith in the offensive was such that over his entire career he only truly fought on the defensive three times; Leipzig in 1813 and La Rothière and Arcis in 1814. Notably he resorted to the defensive on these occasions only after the dismal failure of his initial attack.

During his Italian Campaign of 1796, when the Directory attempted to divide the Italian command into two, Napoleon replied that 'one bad commander is better than two good ones'. At the start of his career the young general embraced a concept that has since been articulated by military theorists as 'unity of command'. Adherence to this principle, particularly after Napoleon became head of state, gave him an immense advantage over his opponents. His single controlling mind directed an entire empire's resources in pursuit of his policy. When national aspirations collided and the issue had to be resolved on the battlefield, the head of state became the supreme field commander. In contrast, his adversaries either had to refer their strategy through their governmental authorities or worse, operate like Kutusov at Austerlitz with those authorities – the Russian Tsar, the Austrian Emperor – peering over his shoulder. As a field general and then a national leader, Napoleon gathered power so as to possess absolute 'unity of command'.

Napoleon's tremendous centralisation of authority worked most of the time because of his great genius. However, it had some unhappy consequences because Napoleon neither granted his subordinates much command latitude nor, with the exception of his step-son Eugène, rigorously instructed them in his art of war. These were conscious omissions and they worked against him in Spain – when he tried to run the war while remaining in Paris and thus inflicted upon his Peninsula generals outdated orders – and in Russia where the vast spaces necessitated subordinate initiative and too many subordinates proved unready.

In assessing Napoleon's leadership and applauding many of his marvellous strategic combinations, one must balance one's admiration by recalling four events. In 1799, when it became clear that his grandiose schemes had failed, he abandoned his army in Egypt. In 1809, following his defeat at Aspern-Essling, he abandoned his army on Lobau Island. In 1812, after extricating the remnant of the *Grande Armée* from a Russian trap on the Berezina, he abandoned it to return to Paris. On 18 July 1815, when his last roll of the battle dice failed at Waterloo, he left his army to fend for itself and returned to Paris. In each case there were good reasons for leaving the army, but there were also reasons to remain.

Napoleon believed that, 'Men are moved by two levers only: fear and self-interest.' When necessary he did not shy away from employing this first lever. In Egypt in 1798 he ruthlessly crushed an anti-French revolt. Each night the headless corpses of executed ringleaders adorned Cairo's walls. Bonaparte believed that this provided a good lesson to would-be dissidents. Later in his career he felt that the dictates of the state justified such measures. Moreover, he understood that small doses of quick and certain punishment obviated the need for large-scale repression. 'Nothing', he told Junot, 'is more salutary than a terrible example given at the right time.' During the 1800 revolt in the Vendée, he advised his general to burn down two or three large communities because experience proved a 'spectacularly severe act ... is the most humane method'. Likewise he advised his brothers to begin their reigns of the various puppet states he gave them by making themselves feared. He told Joseph that he must make himself feared from the start or his reign would fail.

While he readily accepted the need for stern measures – 'bloodletting is among the ingredients of political medicine' – he had nothing but contempt

NAPOLEON AND THE GRENADIERS OF HIS OLD GUARD. RAFFET.

for brutality for its own sake. A leader could not let emotion or revenge influence him. The brain, not the heart, had to be his guide. The requirements of state might necessitate some ugly things but excess – brutality without calculation or purpose – was criminal. Regarding his own reputation as a stern, hard-hearted ruler, he said, 'So much the better – this makes it unnecessary for me to justify my reputation.'

He considered public opinion a formidable although invisible power. He set out to control it, candidly telling his *Conseil d'Etat* in 1804 that, 'we are here to guide public opinion, not to discuss it'. He wanted to guide or control public opinion without the public realising that they were puppets being manipulated by a master puppeteer. Accordingly he took particular care to control the press. In 1805 he had his Chief of Police inform the nation's most widely read newspapers that the revolutionary times were over and he would never tolerate them saying or doing anything against his interests. They might occasionally publish articles 'with just a little poison in them', but they did so at the risk of finding that 'one fine morning somebody will shut their mouths'.

He used religion to advance his regime. The Revolution had witnessed an assault on the Catholic Church. To promote stability, and to the horror of some of his godless army comrades, he returned the Church to a central place in French life. It was all very calculated, as witness the official Catechism in which the correct response to the question: 'What should one think of those who would fail in their duties toward our Emperor?' was: 'According to the Apostle Saint Paul, they would resist the order established by God Himself and would make themselves deserving of eternal damnation.' Lest one think this mingling of state and Church exceptional, recall the 'Citizen's Catechism' circulated by the Spanish guerrillas: 'Question: Is it a sin to kill a Frenchman? Answer: Yes, excepting those who are fighting under Napoleon's Standards.'

As early as 1800, while struggling to achieve the First Consulship, he explained that there was no question that there were large groups hostile to him. The question, as he saw it, was 'whether in each class of the people some chord responds to me'. For some that chord might be his laws, for others his victories; but everywhere there was at least one potentially responsive chord.

When Napoleon assumed the imperial mantle, he had to weld disparate groups to his purposes. Those among the old nobility who had survived the guillotine posed a special challenge. Napoleon well understood that they considered him boorish, low-bred, Corsican. He offered them commissions in the army. They were uninterested. He offered them administrative posts in his government. They declined. Then he found the chord. He invited them to participate in the day-to-day formal life of his Court, a Court which he consciously created along traditional royal lines. This was the life the old nobility appreciated and missed. Enthusiastically they re-entered Court routine. To co-opt their children, and provide another source of cannon-fodder at a time of manpower shortage in 1813, he created four mounted regiments of *Gardes d'honneur*. Uniformed in splendid dark green and scarlet, the young sons of the old *noblesse* went to war. The army divined Napoleon's purpose; they promptly took to calling them 'The Hostages'. To rule an empire of disparate groups, Napoleon had to find and touch some chord. He did it masterfully.

On occasion he could be exceptionally boorish. Consider the case of the American Ambassador to France, John Armstrong. Armstrong would prove himself to be a man of intelligence and military skill as a Secretary of War during the war between Great Britain and the United States in 1812. But he was also outspoken and rough-spoken, and his speech included very little of the French language. When the Emperor conducted diplomatic audiences he customarily stood in the centre of a ring of ambassadors and walked around from one to the next. During his first circuit he exchanged pleasantries. During his second he engaged in duels of wit with the likes of a Metternich. Throughout Napoleon would be the consummate actor, conveying diplomatic messages with displays of affection or with diatribes. Such was not the case with poor Armstrong. Napoleon abused and insulted Armstrong, largely on the grounds that the man could not speak French. Typically he delivered a rapid-fire series of questions usually beginning with, 'Well, have you learned French yet?' It was petty and uncharacteristic, but apparently he cared not. Finally in 1810 he asked for Armstrong's recall.

Occasionally he would lose his temper entirely. Most often it was poor Berthier who received the brunt of it. Startled imperial aides came across one scene where an enraged Napoleon, the smaller man, was slamming Berthier's head against a wall! More common than physical violence was written or verbal abuse. Thus to his spoiled younger brother Jérôme, who had exhibited a decided preference to dallying with his opera star mistress over marching with his army: 'You must bivouack with your outposts, be on horseback night and day, go with the vanguard to get your intelligence at first hand – or else stay in your seraglio. You are making war like a satrap. Is it from me, good God! that you have learned this?'

Just as he could always find the right words of praise, so too was he a master of 'those extremely offensive snubs' that reduced even generals to near tears. Few could withstand Napoleon's verbal assaults; his succinct, analytical criticism reduced most men to quivering jelly. An officer such as Vandamme, who could fearlessly lead a bayonet charge against a battery, said, 'So it is that I, who fear neither God nor Devil, am ready to tremble like a child when I approach him.' A very small handful stood implacably before these attacks and their ranks notably included Charles Talleyrand-Périgord. Completely frustrated by Talleyrand's diplomatic machinations – in fact, although Napoleon did not realise it Talleyrand was betraying Napoleon to Austria – the Emperor shouts: 'Answer me! What are your schemes? What is it that you want? Do you dare tell me?' Coolly Talleyrand refuses to respond at which point Napoleon explodes, telling him he is 'shit in silk stockings'. But, and this rarely occurred, Talleyrand had the last word. As he left the room he commented, 'What a pity that so great a man should be so ill bred.'

Napoleon created a meritocracy and this was another key to his glory years. He tapped into the stifled ambitions of the French people. Hitherto France's nobility had dominated Church and state. In Napoleon's view, the Revolution's chief aim was to destroy all privilege. Its proclamation of the equality of rights opened new fields to everyone, subject only to their talents. Repeatedly Napoleon told people: 'Be successful! I judge men only by the results of their actions.' In 1802 he observed that skill in choosing men 'is not nearly so difficult as the art of enabling those one has chosen to attain their full worth'. Unlike most of history's tyrants, Napoleon did not surround himself with toadies and yes-men. He staffed both the government and the army with men of great competence, tolerating the likes of the contentious Talleyrand because he judged him the most able minister he possessed.

Throughout his reign Napoleon was keenly aware that his was a newly established government born of revolution and fire. Because it lacked hereditary legitimacy, he thought it insecure. Security could only come by continuing to 'dazzle and astonish'. In France and throughout Europe he believed that he reigned only through the fear he inspired. He thought that even his generals would desert him if he ceased to gain victories. He concluded, 'My power is dependent on my glory, and my glory on my victories. My power would fall if I did not base it on still more glory and still more victories. Conquest made me what I am; conquest alone can keep me there.'

On the basis of such comments, many writers equate Hitler with Napoleon. Such a comparison could hardly be more flattering to the former and more unfair to the latter. Napoleon left many enduring institutions as part of his legacy. While First Consul he took a keen interest in the redrafting of France's legal code, personally attending no fewer than 57 of 109 meetings devoted to the Civil Code. A participant recalls that these meetings reviewed every aspect of administration, finance and law, and that Napoleon made such profound contributions to the discussions that he astonished the experts. The progressive codification of the legal system, a system based upon toleration and equity, led to the Civil, Commercial, Criminal and Penal Codes, whose influences persist in many parts of modern Europe. Under his guidance France incorporated the best of the revolutionary principles of equality of opportunity and fraternity. How very different is Hitler's legacy of hatred and destruction. That said, it must also be noted that like Hitler, Napoleon gave his country a stable government, order, efficiency and prosperity at the price of tyranny.

Turning to his military leadership, consider Napoleon's self-description, provided in an 1805 letter to brother Jérôme: 'What I am, I owe to strength of will, character, application and daring.' Hitler perhaps shared Napoleon's will and daring, and this may also be why many writers have been led astray. But Hitler lacked Napoleon's basically decent character and came nowhere close to the Emperor's intellectual application. Hitler's triumphs came from occasional brilliant intuition; Napoleon's came from hard and brilliant work.

Over time France grew weary of war. Ebbing spirits, first noticed in the lukewarm reaction to the triumphs of 1806, deepened and spread. Sharp-eyed Laura Junot noted in 1809: 'This campaign, however, was not like that of Austerlitz, crowned with laurels interspersed with flowers: mourning followed in the train of triumph, and every bulletin plunged a thousand families in tears.'

Napoleon, as head of state, founded many enduring institutions. What he did not do, despite years of martial triumph, was achieve a lasting peace. He said that 'what my enemies call a general peace is my destruction. What I call peace is merely the disarmament of my enemies.' It proved impossible to disarm all his enemies. When he defeated one or two, another emerged. Underwriting opposition was 'perfidious Albion'; Britain, safe behind the Channel, implacably opposed to having one continental power so dominant on the mainland. In turn, as long as the Emperor was unsatisfied with anything less than a swollen, French-controlled empire, mortal struggle continued.

Consider Napoleon's strategic position in 1809 as described by his great opponent, the Austrian Chancellor and diplomat Metternich: 'Prussia is destroyed, Russia is an ally of France, France the master of Germany.' Napoleon's great victory at Wagram isolated Austria and forced the Habsburg monarchy to give the Emperor's daughter as wife for the conqueror. With nearly all of Europe either subdued or allied, Napoleon confronted Spain, Portugal, and Britain. Yet from a position of such strength he could not find peace. Efforts to attack Britain economically led to his crazy invasion of Russia three years later. How could such a great strategist fail so completely?

While any answer must consider multiple factors, foremost is his failure to appreciate how the French Revolution had unleashed nationalist spirit throughout Europe. He observed in 1808 that there were two powers in the world, the sword and the spirit, by which he meant civil and religious institutions. He concluded, 'In the long run the sword is always beaten by the spirit.' Yet the very next year, when confronted with a massive outbreak of Germanic nationalism simultaneous with a continuing guerrilla war in Spain based on Spanish nationalism, he gazed about him with a blind eye. When a candid aide observed that, 'the people were everywhere tired of us and of our victories', Napoleon snarled and refused to listen.

Napoleon believed that Europe's peoples, as opposed to their rulers, had a surpassing desire to live in a meritocracy where the peasant had the same rights and opportunities as the nobleman. He believed that such a meritocracy arrived in the wake of French bayonets when conquered or suppressed territory entered his empire. He did not understand the fundamental power of nationalism, that people would rather live under a bad ruler who was their own than under a French leader of whatever quality.

Assessing his leadership during his final exile, Napoleon concluded, 'I had to sow at a gallop, and unfortunately I often cast my seed on to sand and into sterile hands.' While this is partially true, it ignores too much. His failure to appreciate the power of nationalism, his failure to bring a lasting peace to his people, was an ultimate failure of leadership. All his life Napoleon sacrificed everything to what he considered his destiny. That destiny lay entwined with the fate of France. 'I have only one passion, only one

NAPOLEON WATCHES THE ADVANCE OF POLISH INFANTRY. PRINT AFTER RAFFET.

mistress, and that is France: I sleep with her. She has never failed me, she has lavished her blood and her treasure on me.' France made enormous sacrifices for Napoleon and in the end he failed her.

BIBLIOGRAPHY

Arnold, James R. 'A Reappraisal of Column Versus Line in the Napoleonic Wars', in *Journal of the Society for Army Historical Research*, vol. LX, 224, winter 1982, pp. 196-208.

- *Napoleon Conquers Austria: The 1809 Campaign for Vienna*, London, 1995.

Bernard, J. F. *Talleyrand: A Biography*, New York, 1973.

Blaze, Elzear. *Recollections of an Officer of Napoleon's Army*, New York, 1911.

Chandler, David G. *The Campaigns of Napoleon*, New York, 1966.

- *Napoleon*. New York, 1973.

Chandler, David G. (ed.) *Napoleon's Marshals*, New York, 1987.

Chlapowski, Dezydery. *Memoirs of a Polish Lancer*, Chicago, 1992.

Delderfield, R. F. *Napoleon's Marshals*, Philadelphia, 1962.

Duffy, Christopher. *Austerlitz 1805*, London, 1977.

Dupuy, Victor. *Souvenirs militaires*, Paris, 1892.

Elting, John R. *Swords Around a Throne: Napoleon's Grande Armée*, New York, 1988.

Gachot, Edouard. *1809: Napoléon en Allemagne*, Paris, 1913.

Gonneville, Colonel de. *Recollections of Colonel de Gonneville*, vol. I, London, 1875.

Haythornthwaite, Philip J. *Napoleon's Military Machine*, New York, 1988.

Herold, J. Christopher (ed.). *The Mind of Napoleon: A Selection from His Written and Spoken Words*, New York, 1955.

Junot, Madame. *Memoirs of the Emperor Napoleon*, vol. III, London, 1901.

Koch, General. *Mémoires de Masséna*, vol. VI, Paris, 1850.

Langsam, Walter. *The Napoleonic Wars and German Nationalism in Austria*, New York, 1930.

Marbot, Baron de. *Memoirs of Baron de Marbot*, vol. I, London, 1892.

Metternich-Winneburg, Clemens. *Memoirs of Prince Metternich: 1773-1815*, vol. II, New York, 1970.

Napoleon. *Correspondance de Napoléon 1er*, vol. XXIX, Paris, 1866.

Pasquier, Etienne-Denis. *The Memoirs of Chancellor Pasquier*, Cranbury, NJ, 1968.

Pelet, J. J. *Mémoires sur la Guerre de 1809*, vols. II, IV, Paris, 1824.

Pouget, General Baron. *Souvenirs de Guerre du Général Baron Pouget*, Paris, 1895.

Rapp, General Count. *Memoirs of General Count Rapp*, London, 1823.

Rovigo, duc de. *Mémoires du Duc de Rovigo*, vols. II, III, Paris, 1901.

Saski, C. G. L. *La campagne de 1809*, vol. II, Paris, 1899-1902.

Ségur, Philippe, comte de. *Histoire et Mémoires*, vol. III, Paris, 1873.

Seruzier. *Mémoires militaires du Baron Seruzier*, Paris, 1823.

Tsouras, Peter G. *Warriors' Words: A Quotation Book*, London, 1992.

NAPOLEON'S
ART OF WAR
Philip J. Haythornthwaite

'I USED TO SAY OF HIM THAT HIS PRESENCE ON THE FIELD MADE A difference of 40,000 men.'[1] This comment by the Duke of Wellington, himself one of the greatest of military commanders, was a generous expression of admiration for his most formidable opponent; but one which was surely the truth. Napoleon's status as one of the foremost military leaders of any period is unquestioned; his reputation as one of the 'great captains' unchallenged. That reputation, however, is founded more upon the victories and events of his career than upon any innovations in the art of war which he introduced: for although he amended and improved the French army, it was still constructed upon the basic lines which existed before his assumption of supreme power, and continued to operate upon tactical principles which Napoleon developed, without introducing any radical change. His influence on strategy or tactics on the larger scale was profound, though even here he was less of an innovator than a manipulator and perfecter of earlier theories. He was indeed fortunate to be the inheritor of the work of Lazare Carnot, who deserved his sobriquet of 'the organiser of victory', so that an almost unparalleled army and military system was handed over to Napoleon. This, however, is not to denigrate his achievements or skill; by utilising and improving the systems he found in place, he became the undoubted master of the art of war in his era. That he was finally defeated was probably the consequence of the attritional effects of years of war, political decisions and circumstances, rather than of any decisively fatal flaw in the system of operations which for so long had proved successful.

Napoleon's career was much more than just that of a military leader; indeed, it could be argued that some of his greatest achievements or influences were those unconnected with the battlefield. That he was in a position to influence other spheres of activity, however, was due entirely to his military victories. How much his success depended upon his own innate talents, and how much upon circumstances and good fortune, is debatable. Great though his abilities were, he was fortunate to begin to exercise them at a time when France was in great need of such a leader, and in the early part of his career he was not alone in attracting popular support. It has been said that if Bonaparte had not been Bonaparte, Moreau would have been; but whatever the military talents possessed by General Jean Moreau – and they were considerable – his political skill was limited, and he lacked the ruthless determination of Napoleon. If Napoleon *were* fortunate in the time and circumstances in which he came to prominence, he certainly took advantage of the opportunity thus open to him. Furthermore, this opportunity came at a time of great changes in the nature of warfare, with the concept of 'national armies' based upon mass conscription, resulting in greater numbers of troops in the field than before, and with a national war effort required for their support. All of these were in place in France before Napoleon, and worked to his advantage.

Unlike many military officers of the period, Napoleon began his career as a commanding general with the advantage of an intense study of his profession, notably during his year at the artillery school at Auxonne (1788–9). Study alone, however, was not sufficient to create a commander of the highest order; to an ability for unremitting hard work, he added a capacity for analysis and discrimination which permitted him to combine theories and doctrines into a cohesive whole, moulded by his own aptitude and mental ability. Among the treatises which exerted the greatest influence upon the young Bonaparte were the works of the comte de Guibert, one of the most influential military writers of the second half of the 18th century. He treated the art of war as more than the glorified drill-book implied by some military manuals, but considered the widest implications of warfare in the Europe of his day, economic and social as well as purely military; and predicted that as 'standing armies' were insufficient to achieve a truly comprehensive victory, success could only be gained by a state prepared to make a national effort with a 'national army', adumbrating the creation of the 'citizen armies' of the French Revolutionary period. Other important influences which helped formulate Napoleon's own system of war were the writings of Frederick the Great, and of the du Teil brothers: General Jean Pierre du Teil, commandant of the school at Auxonne, and the Chevalier Jean Beaumont du Teil, also an artillerist, whose *De l'usage d'artillerie nouvelle* ... was published in 1778. (Ironically, the elder du Teil, Jean Pierre, who was perhaps the greatest encouragement to the young Napoleon, espoused the Bourbon cause in the Revolutionary Wars and was executed after his capture in 1794.)

Napoleon's system of war, like those of his opponents, had its foundations in the 'lowest common denominator', the individual soldier with his musket or sabre, united with his fellows into sub-units of the army, rising from platoon to company, to battalion or regiment, and thence to brigade. Some mention of the techniques employed by these sub-units is necessary to form the groundwork for an account of the higher tactics and strategy over which Napoleon exercised most personal influence.

The infantry's mode of operation was determined by the limited capability of their principal weapon, the smooth-bored, single-shot musket; so little use was made of rifled firearms in Napoleon's armies that they may effectively be discounted. For all the importance placed upon light infantry tactics, which from the time of the Revolutionary Wars came into greater prominence with the French than ever before, the basic infantry deployment remained the closely packed and disciplined formation which was essential for keeping order, the drill being so practised until ideally the soldiers became virtual automata, marching and firing to order even under the most arduous conditions on the battlefield.

The two principal formations, for both manoeuvre and combat, remained the column and line, the former enabling troops to move rapidly while maintaining their order, the latter enabling the maximum number of muskets to be used simultaneously. A number of misconceptions have arisen over the use of these formations, not least the definition of what comprised a column. Columns used for action were entirely different from columns used for march; for example, a French battalion deployed in 'column of divisions' had a frontage of two companies, each company being deployed in only three ranks; so that, for example, with the six-company establishment per battalion introduced into the infantry from 1808, and a two-company frontage, the depth of the column would be no more than nine ranks, whereas the frontage would be about 75 yards. Such a battalion would have half the frontage and twice the depth if deployed in column of companies, but the fact remained that such a column was radically different from the column of march, only a few men abreast. Indeed, the appearance of a column of attack may be gauged from the fact that contemporary accounts by opponents of the French sometimes confuse columns with squares.

There were conflicting theories about the best formation for combat, but Guibert's ideas gained most support. He favoured a combination of both column and line, the former for manoeuvre and the latter for firing, and a union of the two was styled *l'ordre mixte*, which could operate at all levels from battalion upwards. In essence it involved troops in line with others in column on either flank, thus combining the offensive capability of the rapid

advance of the columns with the firepower of the line. This proved especially useful in the early stages of the Revolutionary Wars, when the infantry
formations of *demi-brigades* were composed of one regular battalion (able
to deliver controlled and effective volley-fire) and two volunteer or conscript
battalions, whose lack of training made the charge in column the most effective tactic. As Guibert stressed, however, with trained infantry it was most
important that they be able to change from column to line and vice versa
without difficulty, so as to permit them to advance at speed in column, the
rapidity of movement reducing the opportunity for the enemy to rake them
with fire; and then to deploy into line before contact was made to bring the
maximum number of muskets to bear. Guibert's system was adopted officially from 1788, with the definitive version of the theory published in 1791,
the manual remaining in use throughout the Revolutionary and Napoleonic
Wars, despite attempts to amend it.

Much has been written of the failures of the column when attacking
troops in line; of how the limited firepower of the column (effectively only
the front two ranks) was very much inferior to that of the line, in which
every musket could be targeted simultaneously on the column. Many of the
published calculations refer to attacks by French columns upon British
lines, inevitably ending in the defeat of the former by the fire of the British,
defeat being finalised by a limited counter-charge by the British once their
musketry had destroyed the composure of the French column. Such examples were accurate as far as they went, but it would suggest a remarkable
lack of aptitude on the part of French commanders in maintaining a system
which failed regularly. In fact it was mostly the positioning of the line
which caused such results (as mentioned below) more than any inherent
weakness in the system. Some notable successes had been gained by
columnar attacks during the Revolutionary Wars, when troops were so
inexperienced as to be unable to deploy into line before contact; but while
on rare occasions French commanders later in the period may have endeavoured to press home with a column instead of deploying before contact, it
was standard practice for columns at least to attempt to deploy into line
before contact with the enemy. Indeed, on those rare occasions when
deployment was not attempted it was generally so unusual as to be
remarked upon; for example, a British witness of Barrosa recorded that 'we
came within about twenty paces of them before they broke, and as they
were in column, when they did they could not get away, it was therefore a
scene of the most dreadful carnage ...'[2] The events of the battle of Maida

(in Calabria, 6 July 1806) have been quoted as an example of the 'line versus column' calculation, involving the respective merits of the two formations;[3] but it would appear that the French *did* deploy before battle was joined, seemingly proven by the official report of the French commander, General Jean Reynier.[4] The fact that the practices of one enemy army (as detailed below) caused French attacks to fail was more a consequence of the manner in which French infantry tactics were applied than of a fundamental failing in the system, which probably explains why Napoleon was content to let the principles of the 1791 drill-book remain in force.

The French continued to use a three-deep line for infantry service, even though the third rank was regarded by some as an imperfect use of resources (Britain, for example, had abandoned the third rank very early in the period). Although others thought the third rank served as a useful reserve – for example Marshal Ney – this was one of the few matters of 'minor tactics' which Napoleon tried to alter, probably partly in view of reports of casualties caused by semi-trained men in a third rank injuring those in front of them. From 1813 the two-rank line was introduced upon Napoleon's instruction, but its use was never universal. In retirement, Napoleon commented that the third rank should either be given greater consistency, or suppressed altogether.

One of the most characteristic features of the tactics of the French armies of the Revolutionary period was the huge number of skirmishers deployed to precede an attack or cover a retreat. Light infantry tactics had evolved in the earlier 18th century, but were developed in the early Revolutionary Wars to a degree unprecedented in European warfare. Previously the preserve of trained light infantry, or the light infantry companies of line regiments, it became common practice in the Revolutionary armies for whole battalions, even brigades, to be deployed in 'open order', with men firing individually instead of by volley, tactics to which the other European armies initially had few answers. The system was obviously of use to armies that had large numbers of semi-trained volunteers or conscripts, whose discipline and training were insufficient to permit them to manoeuvre in a more conventional manner, but even when this training was given the skirmish tactics remained in force by reason of their effectiveness. Although from September 1804 each French line regiment was ordered to convert one of its fusilier companies to one of *voltigeurs* (literally 'vaulters', theoretically the most expert light infantry), light infantry tactics were practised by *all* infantry, which still permitted entire battalions to be deployed in open order if necessary. (The dis-

251

tinction between the ordinary *Infanterie de Ligne* and *Infanterie Légère* – line and light regiments – in Napoleon's army was largely a matter of *esprit de corps* and distinctions in uniform: light regiments were equally capable of serving in a more conventional 'line' role, and line regiments were trained to skirmish in open order.)

The deployment of skirmishers, sometimes in very considerable numbers, which remained a feature of French tactics throughout the period, also served to conceal from the enemy the manoeuvres which were taking place behind the skirmish-screen, theoretically enabling an attack to be mounted upon the enemy with less warning than if it had not been preceded by a mass of sharpshooters.

When troops were trained adequately, the prevailing formations of column, line and a combination of the two were capable of great flexibility; but as the attrition of Napoleon's wars caused a steady decline in the quality and ability of the French infantry, from its peak at about the time of Austerlitz to the young, inexperienced and semi-equipped conscripts of 1813-14, there was a corresponding decline in tactical ability. A consequence of this was the employment on occasion of very large divisional columns or squares – for example as seen at Waterloo or in the deployment of Macdonald's corps at Wagram – which involved a reduced ability for rapid change of formation, and presented massed targets for enemy artillery.

NAPOLEON ON CAMPAIGN. PRINT AFTER RAFFET.

Greater influence was exerted by Napoleon upon the cavalry than upon the infantry, because in the first instance the cavalry of the Revolutionary Wars was in general much weaker and more ineffective than the infantry. In his organisation and employment of his mounted troops, Napoleon clearly indicated the services which they might be expected to undertake. Whereas earlier the distinctions between the various categories had not always been clear, Napoleon made a more obvious distinction between heavy and light units, while ensuring that the latter could still operate effectively on the battlefield; and provided an intermediate force which combined the attributes of the other two.

The creation of the cuirassier arm (including the two carabinier regiments, which were issued with similar body-armour from 1808) was a clear indication of Napoleon's intention to use part of his cavalry as a massed striking-force on the battlefield: heavily armoured men on large horses whose primary function was to deliver penetrating and potentially decisive charges. To facilitate this tactical function, such units could be concentrated into corps of 'reserve cavalry', and it is indicative of the specialisation of such regiments for this task that a light cavalry arm, the *chevau-légers-lanciers*, was employed with such formations to provide the heavy regiments with a reconnaissance and skirmishing facility for which the 'heavies' were not ideally suited.

The light regiments, including *chasseurs à cheval* and hussars, were especially adept at such duties, and screened the army during advances or withdrawals, tasks which enhanced their reputation for panache; yet they could act with equal facility on the battlefield. Positioned between the heavy and light cavalry were the dragoons, one of the most numerous of Napoleon's cavalry formations, troops used increasingly in a battlefield role like that of the heavy cavalry, yet retaining their original aptitude for reconnaissance and flank-guards, and when required able to act as mounted infantry. (They were used in this role in the Peninsular War, and – as occurred in 1805/6 – could even take the field without horses, as *Dragons à pied*.) In addition to forming light or 'medium' brigades of the cavalry reserve, these units, not the heavy regiments, were also deployed as 'divisional cavalry' in support of the infantry.

Under the classic Napoleonic system, the light regiments would be used in the phase of an operation leading to contact with the enemy, in reconnaissance and in shielding the army's movements from the enemy's scouts; in battle the heavy regiments would contribute to victory by delivering a series of crushing charges; and upon the withdrawal of what remained of the defeated enemy, the light regiments would again come to the fore, pursuing and harrying the beaten foe. The most effective example of the latter was probably in the aftermath of the battles of Jena–Auerstädt when columns of light cavalry completed the destruction of the Prussian army.

Unlike some of his opponents, Napoleon used his cavalry not so much as an adjunct or support for the infantry, making limited charges in reaction to the movements of the enemy, but as an independent offensive arm. Instead of reserving his horsemen until they could fall upon an already disordered enemy, at times he used them in huge numbers to deliver massed attacks, for example in the great charges at Eylau and Borodino. Such manoeuvres could be potentially decisive or could help stabilise a deteriorating situation in a manner which might have been more expected from infantry. At Aspern-Essling, for example, the cavalry occupied the centre of the French position, holding it secure by a number of more limited charges. Ideally, major cavalry attacks should have been co-ordinated with other 'arms', principally by the accompaniment of horse artillery; when this did not happen, as at Waterloo, failure and the decimation of the cavalry could occur.

Because Napoleon was trained as a gunner, it might have been expected that artillery would play an important role in his campaigns, as it did. He was fortunate to inherit a professional and well-equipped force of artillery from the period of the Revolutionary Wars, for the artillery, which had never attracted aristocrats into its officer corps under the *ancien régime*, was thus less affected by purges and emigration than the other parts of the army. Together with a well-organised and proficient corps of gunners, Napoleon also inherited some of the best ordnance in Europe, which had benefited greatly from the efforts of Jean-Baptiste de Gribeauval, whose work in reforming the French artillery had begun in 1765. Napoleon was not content to maintain the previous system, however, but instituted a number of important amendments, though not introducing an entirely new range of artillery. (A new design was introduced from 1803, the 'System of *An XI*', but it was generally inferior and never became universal, the original Gribeauval System being re-introduced in 1818.)

Napoleon's most important development was in upgrading the 'weight' of his field guns. Initially the three principal 'natures' of fieldpiece were 4-, 8- and 12-pounders, named from the weight of roundshot they fired. Napoleon's principal alteration was to replace the 4pdrs and some 8pdrs by 6pdrs (originally captured Prussian and Austrian pieces), and to increase the number of 12pdrs at the expense of the less-effective 8pdrs. One of the general changes in the late 18th and early 19th centuries was the abandonment of the concept of regimental artillery or 'battalion guns', light fieldpieces which had been attached to each infantry unit to provide immediate fire-support; it was found that these light guns had insufficient hitting-power to compensate the restrictions which they could impose upon their parent unit. Regimental artillery was thus withdrawn from most armies, the French included, and Napoleon tended to concentrate his remaining artillery, 6pdrs and 8pdrs at brigade or divisional level, with the 12pdrs in corps or army reserves. It is interesting to note, however, that as the attrition of years of warfare brought about a decline in the calibre of the infantry, Napoleon re-introduced the concept of regimental artillery in a limited manner, in the belief that the weaker troops required greater artillery support.

A further factor acting against the retention of 'battalion guns' was the general acceptance that a concentration of artillery was more effective than the sum of its parts; although this was only fully applicable in armies which, like Napoleon's, possessed a sufficient quantity of artillery. Guibert was among those theorists who regarded artillery primarily as a support arm, whereas du Teil suggested a concentration of fire upon specific points of the enemy's line to achieve a tactical purpose. Probably influenced by the latter, Napoleon transformed his artillery from a support to an offensive arm. Batteries were still deployed at divisional level for more immediate fire-support, and horse artillery with cavalry formations, but Napoleon possessed sufficient guns to create an artillery reserve which could be deployed independently to concentrate a bombardment upon a particular objective, for example the section of the enemy's line that was to be assaulted. Napoleon once compared a battle to a fist-fight with cannon-balls taking the part of fists; he said that the secret of victory was to make the artillery-fire converge upon one point, and that 'he who had sufficient address to direct a mass of artillery suddenly and unexpectedly on any particular point of the enemy's force was sure of the victory. This, he said, had been his grand secret and his grand plan of tactics.'[5]

An outstanding example of the use of artillery as a primary offensive element was the artillery 'charge' of General Alexandre Sénarmont at Friedland, which turned the course of the battle. Some other examples of the use of such 'massed batteries' were less successful largely because of failures of co-ordination, for example the barrages at Wagram and Leipzig, or to the better preparation of the enemy, as at Waterloo. Nevertheless, the ability to maintain an artillery reserve and to deploy it to greatest effect remained an important feature of Napoleon's system of warfare.

Napoleon once declared that it was important for artillery to fire incessantly after battle had been joined, regardless of expenditure of ammunition, unless there were a genuine shortage, which laid great emphasis on the facility for re-supply. (Indeed, Napoleon once claimed that he would have been victorious at Leipzig had not his ammunition run out.) Originally civilians, it was not until 1800 that artillery drivers were enrolled in the army. This greatly enhanced the artillery's mobility; henceforth guns could be driven to within range of the enemy, not manhandled by the gunners from a safe distance as before. But despite the increase in size of the artillery train, it remained insufficient for the growing demands placed upon it.

The commissariat was another problem which Napoleon never fully mastered. One of the great advantages exercised over their opponents by the French armies of the Revolutionary Wars was the ability to dispense with cumbrous supply-trains and static depots, the troops being expected to 'live off the land' by foraging. This greatly enhanced mobility, and the troops managed to fight even when half starving; but it imposed certain strategic constraints, as larger formations of troops had to spread out in order to find food and fodder when areas became rapidly denuded of their victuals. The system was not entirely the product of the simple inability of the French state to keep its troops supplied during the early Revolutionary Wars, for it was Guibert who had suggested it; and it was retained for a time by Napoleon, although he acknowledged its drawbacks, not least the need for an army to separate to live but unite to fight, necessitating the ability to recognise when a concentration of forces was required. Ideally, therefore, the army was only supplied with provisions in the immediate period before contact with the enemy when foraging would be impossible, but, after the French troops almost starved to death in the 1806-7 campaign, a more orthodox system of supply had to be instituted. Even so the commissariat organisation was never able to maintain adequate supplies for all troops throughout every campaign, and on occasion broke down entirely, so that foraging remained an important part of the French army's system.

Napoleon realised that both systems of supply were imperfect, and remarked that tactical freedom would only come when an army adopted the methods of the Romans, in which each soldier ground his own flour with a

hand-mill and baked his own bread, which would have had the effect of lib-
erating an army from much of its commissariat train, 'our monstrous train
of civil attendants'. With such a plan, 'an army might have marched to the
end of the world. But, it would require time to bring about such a transition.
It could not have been accomplished by a mere order of the day. I had long
entertained the idea of such a change; but however great might have been
my power, I should never have attempted to introduce it by force. There is
no subordination with empty stomachs. Such an object could only have been
effected in time of peace, and by insensible degrees ...'[6]

Although Napoleon's influence extended throughout his army, it was in
higher tactics and strategy that it was most marked. Central to his entire
system of warfare was the organisation of the army and its mode of command. The organisation of individual units into brigades was common
before the Revolutionary Wars, and the next step in the chain of organisation, the division, had been used as early as the middle of the 18th century.
Victor, duc de Broglie, who was appointed a Marshal of France in 1762, had
experimented with self-contained divisions as early as 1761, and although
the system had applied only in wartime and then been discarded, it was
taken up by Guibert, who at the age of 13 had accompanied his father,
Broglie's chief of staff, on campaign. Permanent divisional organisations
had been instituted in the French army in 1793, so Napoleon inherited the
nucleus of his system, but he refined it until he perfected the *corps d'armée*.
This vital component in his strategic system was in effect an entirely self-
contained miniature army, complete with cavalry, divisional and reserve
artillery, engineers and commissariat, and thus capable of operating and
fighting without support, and generally commanded by a marshal.

To co-ordinate such forces Napoleon maintained probably the most comprehensive headquarters of an army of the period, which by 1805 was considerably sophisticated, even if it did not always run as efficiently as its vast
resources might have implied. The Imperial Headquarters (*Grand quartier
général*) was divided into three main branches: the General Staff of the
Grande Armée (*Quartier général de la Grande Armée*), the General
Commissary of Army Stores (which supervised all commissariat matters,
including transportation and distribution of stores), and, most significantly,
Napoleon's personal 'Household' or *Maison*. In addition to his personal staff
of aides and servants, the centre of the *Maison* was the *cabinet*, the secretarial body responsible for the transmission of orders and Napoleon's channel of communication. Equally significant was the Topographical Bureau,

responsible for cartography and an essential aid in Napoleon's planning of campaigns. Another invaluable asset were the *carnets*, notebooks in which were stored statistical information on Napoleon's own forces and those of his opponents, meticulously detailed and updated daily. When in the field, Napoleon was accompanied by his 'little Headquarters' or battle HQ of the most vital personnel: chief of staff, Master of Horse, ADCs and orderly officers, map-bearer, interpreter and escort.

Sophisticated (in contemporary terms) though the staff organisation might be, it was basically only an administrative department which relieved Napoleon of more mundane tasks. Its members were not permitted to exercise much initiative and sometimes misrepresented his orders; there were duplications of function which led not only to waste of effort but to omissions, and although Napoleon did complain about it, it was his creation. Perhaps a fair assessment would be that despite its many imperfections the system did permit Napoleon to control forces of a magnitude that would have been quite impossible without it.

One of the advantages of Napoleon's system of warfare – and perhaps also one of its disadvantages – was the fact that all command emanated from a single individual, Napoleon himself. The disadvantage was that some tasks were so great that not even an individual of his talents could hope to do everything; and yet conversely, tasks in which he was involved could scarcely but benefit from his personal supervision. That he was prepared to supervise so closely is testimony to his energy and ability for constant work. His correspondence reveals his care for the smallest details as well as for the great affairs of state; for example, in this letter to Henri Clarke, Minister of War:

> 'Order the officer of the depot of the 28th Dragoons, who was desired to furnish 100 men to the marching regiment of dragoons belonging to the army of Catalonia ... to be placed under arrest for a month ... it was composed of men taken from the hospitals or on the point of being discharged; bad horses were substituted for good ones ... the coats, trousers, boots, &c. belonging to the dragoons were taken away, and old rags given to them instead; their pistols were without cocks or pans ... Let me know the name of the officer who dared to take such a liberty ...'[7]

Apart from reflecting the practice – by no means confined to the French army at this period – of a regiment endeavouring to dispense with its most useless men first, this demonstrates Napoleon's concern for even the most trivial matters, which with a less precise commander would have been supervised by a junior staff officer.

It was not just Napoleon's strategic or tactical aptitude that made his presence on the battlefield worth the 40,000 men of which the Duke of Wellington spoke; his effect on morale was also immense. Some enemy armies and their commanders were probably so overawed by the knowledge that they faced Napoleon in person that their actions were compromised; but it is easier to quantify the effect that Napoleon's presence had upon his own troops. At times his men certainly grumbled about him – on a particularly arduous forced march in Spain, for example, 'The soldiers of Lapisse's division gave loud expression to the most sinister designs against the Emperor's person, stirring up each other to fire a shot at him, and bandying accusations of cowardice for not doing it. He heard it all as plainly as we did, and seemed as if he did not care a bit for it'[8] – but more usual were sentiments of virtual idolatry, as in fact Lapisse's division exhibited a short time later, after the arrival of food and wine had alleviated their earlier misery.

Napoleon certainly appreciated the effect of his personal magnetism, and actively encouraged it, not least in his habit of conversing with the ordinary soldiers and at least ostensibly recognising those who had fought with him in earlier campaigns. Certainly, he had a phenomenal memory, but the ability to remember individual private soldiers (thus convincing them of his care for the welfare of his troops) was to some extent the result of careful preparation by his aides; but Adrien Bourgogne of the Imperial Guard did recount a case which demonstrated Napoleon's evidently remarkable powers of memory. A sergeant approached the Emperor and asked for the *Légion d'honneur;* the man had a face of unusual ugliness, and Napoleon remembered him precisely, recalling correctly that he had first promised the sergeant the coveted Cross at the bakery in Vilna some ten months before. As every such anecdote was repeated among the soldiers, a mythology was created of Napoleon's infallibility.

Napoleon appreciated also the electrifying value of his eloquence, and the receptiveness of the French troops to it: 'When, in the heat of the battle, passing along the line, I used to exclaim, "Soldiers, unfurl your banners, the moment is come", our Frenchmen absolutely leaped for joy. I saw them multiply a hundred-fold. I then thought nothing impossible.'[9] Las Cases, who recorded this statement, then recalled a story he had been told by an eyewitness, which exemplifies Napoleon's ability to speak spontaneously and with the effect desired. Reviewing a regiment of *chasseurs à cheval* two days before Jena, as usual Napoleon asked their commander how many men were present; '"Five hundred," replied the colonel, "but there are many raw troops among them." "What signifies that," said the Emperor, in a tone which denoted surprise at the observation, "are they not all Frenchmen?" Then, turning to the regiment, "My lads," said he, "you must not fear death. When soldiers defy death, they drive him into the enemy's ranks." He here made a motion with his arm expressive of the action to which he alluded.' The immediate and enthusiastic reaction of the troops, said Las Cases, seemed to be a precursor of the great victory two days later.[10]

Consequently, no matter how theatrical his gestures and exhortations might seem, they were calculated to produce the desired effect, and were doubtless enhanced by his undeniably imperious presence combined with the easy familiarity with which he spoke to the ordinary troops, sharing their jokes as well as their hardships, and never holding himself aloof from their concerns or remarks. The ability to retain his sense of omnipotence while at the same time implying that he was one of them must have contributed to the aura of adoration with which he was viewed by his troops. A simple but probably calculated remark such as 'I know you, brave 18th; the enemy never stands before you', or 'I was calm, the brave 32nd was there,' was sufficient to win the loyalty of a regiment forever.[11]

Despite the benefits which accrued from Napoleon's personal involvement in every aspect of his armies' concerns, his centralisation of authority in his own person also had unfortunate consequences. Many of his subordinates were admirable soldiers when operating under his supervision, but rarely having been permitted to use any real initiative in such circumstances they were inexperienced in exercising independent command. This was not so serious when Napoleon was at hand, but its consequences were greater when operating in a different theatre of war, or when campaigning over an area so large that not even Napoleon could supervise everything in person, for example in Russia in 1812. Perhaps the initial fault did lie with Napoleon in not encouraging the exercise of initiative on the part of his marshals; though his reasons for not doing so are also understandable, given that his own talents meant that his personal intervention or supervision would generally be beneficial. In his dealings with subordinates he could be unfairly critical, and formidable in the exercise of his rage; he also played off one against another, which did nothing to increase the potential of co-operation between marshals, sometimes with unfortunate effects on campaign. (Napoleon's choice of his deputies was not always beyond criticism: in 1815, for example, he appointed Davout as Minister of War and Governor of Paris, and Soult as Chief of Staff, instead of allowing them to exercise their undoubted talents in a more independent role on the battlefield, although there were some sound reasons for employing them as he did.)

His principal difficulty concerning his need to fight on two fronts simultaneously was that he was unable – probably from the lack of a subordinate truly capable of waging war successfully without reference to higher authority – to delegate as fully as would have been ideal. Partly because of mutual jealousy, co-operation between the marshals in the Peninsula was not good, and their very mixed success in the war, including regular reverses against Wellington's Anglo-Portuguese army, resulted in Napoleon endeavouring to impose his influence upon a campaign in which he was not present and of which he could not have full knowledge. The results could be seriously unfortunate for the French cause, as appears to be exemplified by Napoleon's orders regarding the fortress of Badajoz in early 1812. Marshal Auguste Marmont, as commander in the field, knew that Wellington would probably attack Badajoz, but was told by Napoleon not to worry over its fate, but to prepare instead to invade northern Portugal which, Napoleon believed, would

NAPOLEON RECONNOITRING. PRINT AFTER RAFFET.

divert Wellington from any thoughts of taking Badajoz. Presumably through lack of knowledge of local conditions (itself perhaps a comment on the failings of Napoleon's subordinates to make the true situation clear), Napoleon overlooked the fact that northern Portugal was a virtual wasteland and that Marmont could not have operated there for any appreciable time before his army starved. Then, after Marmont had made appropriate preparations to implement Napoleon's instructions, Napoleon issued contradictory orders which made Marmont responsible for Badajoz, and gave him authority to march to its relief if he thought it necessary; but by the time these orders were received it was altogether too late to support the city. It may be unjust to lay the whole responsibility for the fall of Badajoz, and the French reverses which led from it, at Napoleon's door; but it demonstrated the difficulties of attempting to exert some degree of strategic command from a distance and without a system of communication adequate to convey a true assessment of the conditions pertaining in the area of operations.

The imperfections in some of the reports sent to Napoleon by his subordinates only mirrored his own dispatches, the accuracy of which gave rise to the expression 'to lie like a Bulletin'. The deliberate inaccuracy of Napoleon's dispatches has led to criticisms of his veracity, for example: 'We have known men that could not tell a lie. Napoleon could neither speak nor write truth ... His bulletins were false to a proverb. His life was one great lie from the day of his starting into notice.'[12] At times his despatches varied from the truth in order to show his own actions in the most favourable light – his re-writing of the events of Marengo is an example[13] – but some of the falsifications were deliberate attempts at misinformation, with a strategic objective. Napoleon enunciated this in a letter to Clarke which complained about Joseph Bonaparte's publication of accurate dispatches:

'When he has occasion to speak of his strength, he ought to render it formidable by exaggeration, doubling or trebling his numbers ... on the other hand, when he mentions the strength of the enemy, he should diminish it by one-half or one-third ... in war moral force is everything ... in war feeling and opinion are more than half of the reality. The art of great captains has always been to make their numbers appear very large to the enemy, and to persuade their own troops of the enemy's great inferiority ... when I conquered the Austrians at Eckmühl I was one to five, and yet my army fancied itself at least equal to the enemy ... far from owning that at Wagram I had only 100,000 men, I try to prove that I had 220,000. Constantly,

in my Italian campaigns, when I had only a handful of men, I exag-
gerated their numbers; this served my purpose without diminishing
my glory ...'[14]

Untruths calculated to undermine the enemy's morale and to increase the
intimidating aspect of Napoleon's ability were different, however, from
attempts by his subordinates to under-rate their own reverses, giving him
insufficient information to permit a true consideration of the state of a campaign. For example, Napoleon appears to have found accounts in British
newspapers to be rather more accurate at times than was the information
derived from the reports of his own commanders, the British making no
deliberate attempts to disguise the true nature of their own operations. An
example of this is found in a short note from Napoleon to Berthier in June
1811: 'I send you the English account of the action at Fuente [*sic*] de Oñoro.
Send a copy to the Dukes of Ragusa [Marmont] and of Istria [Bessières]. You
may have copied even what is scratched out, that they may know the
whole.'[15] Evidently this was preferred to the report from the French commander at Fuentes de Oñoro, Marshal Masséna.

Even with the imperfections in his system of control of subordinate commanders, Napoleon's army and method of warfare was extremely effective,
at least until he was faced with overpowering numbers of enemies, a division of effort in having to pursue the war in the Iberian Peninsula as well
as conducting his own campaigns, and a decline in the abilities of his forces
arising from the attritional effects of years of warfare. Part of this success
was due to the abilities and determination of his ordinary soldiers, but
much resulted from Napoleon's own strategic skills.

A most important factor was Napoleon's ability to identify the objective of
a campaign, and the fact that as not only commanding general but also head
of state, he had complete freedom over the policy he adopted, with no require-
ment to submit his decisions for approval by higher authority, a restriction
which hindered some of his opponents: the unity of political and military
command was highly advantageous to him. By the same token, he was entirely responsible for the foreign policy which led to his various campaigns, and
thus ultimately responsible for the reverses as well as successes. Sir John
Seeley wrote that 'we should very much underrate Napoleon's own military
genius if we regarded him simply as a winner of battles. Compared with other
generals, he shows his superiority less in tactics than in strategy and in the
comprehensive war-statesmanship by which a campaign on a large scale is
planned'; and yet equally, it was his policy which also led ultimately to his

defeat: 'a greater strategist than any that had appeared before him, but a strategist capable of great errors and failures'.[16]

Territorial occupation was never uppermost in Napoleon's plan of campaign; he saw clearly that the key to a rapid victory was the destruction of the enemy's field army, which was always his prime objective. This was not entirely a product of his own foresight, for an exhortation towards the *Blitzkrieg* style of warfare which he favoured was expressed half a century earlier, by Frederick the Great: 'Battles determine the fate of nations. It is necessary that actions should be decisive, either to free ourselves from the inconvenience of a state of warfare, to place our enemy in that unpleasant situation, or to settle a quarrel which otherwise perhaps would never be finished ... our wars should ever be of short duration, and conducted with spirit, for it must always be against our interest to be engaged in a tedious affair. A long war must tend insensibly to relax our admirable discipline, depopulate our country, and exhaust its resources.'[17]

Napoleon's favoured practice followed this advice closely, aimed towards a rapid, devastating blow upon the enemy's army, with the occupation of cities or country largely regarded as no more than incidental, or as a means of bringing about the decisive battle. To wage war in this manner, his army needed to be able to move rapidly over considerable distances, which proved to be one of its greatest strengths. The capacity for executing forced marches was central to Napoleon's ability to manoeuvre, and the army's ability in this regard was formidable. This involved not only rapid movement over relatively short distances – Davout's corps marched towards Austerlitz covering 70 miles in just over two days – but also sustained pace exhibiting amazing endurance. For example, in 1805 the *Grande Armée* marched from the Rhine to the Danube in eleven days, Soult's corps covering 275 miles; when the 4th *Tirailleurs* and *Voltigeurs* of the Young Guard were recalled from Spain to take part in the Russian campaign of 1812, they covered 468 miles in 23 days. Junot's 'Army of the Gironde' marched from the French frontier to Lisbon, 640 miles, in 43 days, the first 300 miles over main roads in 25 days and the remainder over bad roads at almost nineteen miles per day; but in this case such an effort almost wrecked the army, the cavalry and wheeled vehicles being unable to keep up with the pace of the infantry. The ability to execute such feats of marching, however, was reduced with the declining standard of Napoleon's troops, especially in the case of the young conscripts of 1813–14.

With all Napoleon's efforts directed towards the destruction of the enemy's army, it is unsurprising that his campaigning was almost always offensive; hardly ever did he adopt a defensive posture, and then only when initial offensive moves had failed. The capability for rapid movement, both in the marching of his troops and the commissariat system which kept them supplied, permitted manoeuvres of an audacity unmatched by most of his opponents. Also important was the ability of the light cavalry to screen the movements of the army while observing those of the enemy. Reconnaissance did not always work well, however, even though Napoleon sometimes followed Frederick the Great's advice on observing in person: 'Everything should be examined by our own eyes.'[18] This was sometimes undertaken at the risk of his own life; perhaps the best-known incident was the attack on Napoleon's personal staff by Cossacks on 25 October 1812 when he was in imminent danger of being captured or killed. Napoleon him-self spoke of another occasion when reconnaissance almost cost him dear-ly, when on the eve of Jena he and a few companions advanced to within a short distance of the Prussian outposts. The reputation of the Prussians was such that the French army was especially alert, fearing nocturnal attack, and so nervous were the French outposts that on his return from his reconnais-sance Napoleon was fired on by his own sentries and had to throw himself flat until his party was safely identified!

A further vital component in Napoleon's strategy was the ability of each *corps d'armée* to operate independently of support, and if necessary to fight a holding action unaided. This meant that operations could be launched over a comparatively wide area, with corps drawing together before engag-ing the enemy by virtue of their extreme mobility; this also facilitated the supply situation, with troops relying on what they could forage, so that resources were available in direct proportion to the amount of territory tra-versed. The ability to march rapidly thus rendered the necessary dispersal of troops less hazardous, with individual formations less likely to be isolat-ed from support for any appreciable time. The ideal application of the corps system was a square- or diamond-shaped formation styled the *bataillon carré,* in which the advance would be led by one *corps d'armée,* supported by a second 'rank' of two or more corps roughly abreast, with a third 'rank' of a corps in the rear; if the enemy were straight ahead, the leading corps would be the advance-guard, the last would be the rearguard, and the oth-ers the main body. If the enemy should be contacted on one or other of the flanks, the whole formation could turn to face them, in which case one of the main-body corps would become the advance-guard, the original advance and rearguards the main body, and so on. As each corps was ideally no more than a day's march from support – which with the great power of marching could still mean that such an advance could cover a great deal of territory – the ability of a corps to fight unaided could be harnessed to hold the enemy until the remainder of the army came up.

Once contact with the enemy had been made, certain principles guided Napoleon's course of action, both in strategy and tactics. One of the most important was the attempt to gain 'local superiority' over the enemy at some point of the field of conflict, whether strategically or on the battlefield. This was especially significant when Napoleon was faced with an enemy stronger than himself, as was the case in his earlier campaigns, for example, and the tactic was still being applied during the 'Hundred Days' campaign at the very end of his military career. In essence, it depended on the identification of a vulnerable point between two enemy concentrations into which Napoleon could march with his main body of troops, thus interposing himself between two enemy forces with such speed that they would have insufficient time to react. This incurred the risk of being trapped between two enemy forces, but as Napoleon always maintained the initiative his enemies could only react to his manoeuvres. Having thus positioned himself between two elements of the enemy force, Napoleon would use one corps to fight a holding action against one wing of the enemy while he concentrated the bulk of his army against the other, enabling him to achieve the 'local superiority' in numbers advantageous to its defeat. When this was achieved he would allocate one corps of his main body to pursue the beaten enemy wing, while turning the remainder of his army to the support of the detached corps which was 'pinning' the other wing, and overwhelm that in turn. This classic Napoleonic tactic enabled him to defeat in detail larger enemy forces which if united could have crushed him by weight of numbers.

Against an enemy of equal or inferior strength, Napoleon's preferred strategy involved an outflanking manoeuvre to strike at the enemy's rear or line of communications, involving a wide sweep over considerable distances, again using the French army's phenomenal marching ability. Such a manoeuvre also depended on his ability to screen his intentions from enemy reconnaissance, so that the enemy moved against what they believed was the main French position, where an element of Napoleon's army could fight a holding action, allowing the flanking-movement to take place unopposed. The consequence of this was that either the enemy would have to fight Napoleon's main body in unadvantageous circumstances, with their line of retreat blocked by the French army, or surrender by virtue of their commu-

'VIVE L'EMPÉREUR!'. PRINT AFTER DÉTAILLE.

nications being completely cut. The most outstanding success of such a flanking movement was the trapping of Mack's army at Ulm, a strategic success achieved without the necessity for a major battle.

Battlefield tactics – or 'grand tactics', the level at which Napoleon imposed his personal influence – involved the same basic principles as his strategy. Probably the most effective was the battle which involved the manoeuvre against the enemy flank or rear, in which the enemy was occupied by holding attacks delivered along the front of their line, while a part of Napoleon's army executed a march around one flank, driving it in and threatening to roll up the enemy line, or compelling it to fall back for fear of encirclement or of being attacked in the rear. This had the potential of crushing the enemy completely, as at Austerlitz, though its success was not guaranteed: it was intended that Davout's corps should overwhelm the Russian left flank at Eylau, for example, but the plan miscarried to some extent because of the stolid conduct of the Russian army which refused to be routed even though its left flank had to be entirely re-aligned at right angles to its original position.

The most costly form of battlefield manoeuvre was the massed frontal attack, which could be used in conjunction with an enveloping movement against a flank, or on a more limited front as a way of preparing the enemy for delivery of the decisive blow. By threatening a section of the enemy line – by a more limited flanking movement, or by making an especially fierce frontal attack upon one sector of the enemy position – the enemy might be induced to commit reserves to bolster the threatened position. Then Napoleon could use his own reserves to assail a different and thus weakened section of the enemy line, preceding the attack with a massive artillery bombardment by his artillery reserve, before launching a huge attack with his *masse de décision* or *masse de rupture* which would pierce the enemy line, the French light cavalry following through the resulting gap and pursuing the retiring foe.

These tactics required the ability to judge the correct moment for the execution of each part of the plan, and the flexibility to amend or change it completely according to circumstances. Both in the strategic and tactical field, such plans could miscarry, especially as the attritional cost of years of war reduced the abilities and experience of Napoleon's forces, and as the enemy commanders began to learn from experience and to copy Napoleon's own system. In the wider field, if Napoleon were unable to bring about the rapid battle he desired, and if the enemy were prepared to fall back irrespective of the territory they conceded, his plans could be frustrated; this was probably most obvious in Russia in 1812 when his opponents denied him the decisive battle, even at the sacrifice of Moscow, and with the exception of the attempt to block the Berezina crossing, continued to avoid major conflict even during his retreat. A similar tactic was to avoid an engagement with Napoleon himself, but to concentrate on detachments commanded by his subordinates.

In the interests of achieving an advantage by virtue of manoeuvre, Napoleon was never obsessive about maintaining his lines of communication; yet his own moves against the enemy's communications were potentially decisive. If the enemy chose deliberately to ignore the threat to their communications, however, the entire plan could be undone; this occurred in the 1813 campaign and most decisively in March 1814, when Napoleon's threat to Allied communications was ignored as they pursued their objective, in the latter case their advance on Paris. The ability to ignore such a threat from Napoleon required sufficient supplies in the hands of the enemy army to counteract a temporary severing of the routes of re-supply, and a knowledge of what Napoleon was probably intending; the advantage of superior numbers was also beneficial. By this late stage of the Napoleonic Wars, however, the basics of Napoleon's system had become known, so that his enemies were able to use his own tactics against him. It has been said that the defeats of 1813–14 were the result of a decline in Napoleon's talents, but while this may have been a factor, it is also the case that he was by this time operating in a political and military climate fundamentally changed from that of his earlier successes, yet he did not evolve new methods to counter the changed tactics of his enemies.

The Waterloo campaign demonstrated how Napoleon's system could miscarry. He was able to separate the two Allied forces, Ney making his holding attack against Wellington at Quatre Bras, but Napoleon was unable to deliver a decisive blow against Blücher at Ligny; so that instead of the Prussians falling back after the latter action, pursued by the detachment of Napoleon's army commanded by Grouchy, they were able to provide assistance to Wellington when Napoleon switched his attention and led his main body against Wellington at Mont St-Jean (the best counter to Napoleon's tactic of interposing himself between two halves of the enemy force being for the defeated enemy wing to fall back in such a manner as to maintain contact with the other wing). The appearance of the Prussians on Napoleon's right flank, when he was already fully engaged against Wellington, had the effect of a Napoleonic-style enveloping manoeuvre, forcing Napoleon to denude his main effort in order to hold back the increasing pressure on his flank, and thus laying himself open to counter-attack, which duly followed the failure of his final assault against Wellington. In this sense, Napoleon was undone by his own tactics used against him; but much else also went awry in this battle. The intended diversionary attack against Wellington's left flank, which was intended to draw in Wellington's reserves, in fact had the opposite effect and drew in parts of Napoleon's force which could have been used to greater effect elsewhere; the massed cavalry attacks were delivered without the vital concern for co-ordinating the movement of the various 'arms', so that they were not accompanied by the necessary horse artillery which in conjunction with the cavalry could have devastated Wellington's line; and the great frontal attacks by infantry were unnecessarily costly.

Napoleon's greatest successes derived from campaigns based upon manoeuvre rather than upon costly frontal attacks, and it was presumably this reputation for manoeuvre and enveloping attacks on a flank which led Wellington at Waterloo to station a considerable element of his force away on his right flank to guard against such a manoeuvre (and where they remained unengaged). Wellington appreciated fully Napoleon's military talents, stating that 'Napoleon was the first man of his day on a field of battle, and with French troops', and that the Napoleonic system 'he believed to be very simple and effective – that of bullying with much noise and smoke, puzzling his cautious adversaries as to his point of attack, and massing under cover of light troops and guns his own people on one or two points... He considered Napoleon to be the greatest master on record in the art of handling large masses, and deriving the greatest possible advantage from superiority of numbers and resources; further, as the most dangerous of all commanders in front of whom to make a false movement.'[19] It is conceivable that at Waterloo Wellington was actually disappointed by the unimaginative French attempts to batter in his line, relying on frontal attacks rather than manoeuvre, as if he expected more from the greatest military commander of the age. Sir Andrew Barnard, commander of the British 1/95th Rifles at Waterloo, recalled how, upon observing the tactics adopted by Napoleon during the battle, Wellington had remarked, 'Damn the fellow, he is a mere pounder after all.'[20] He was never only that; but although Napoleon had begun the campaign by stealing a march on the Allied armies – 'Napoleon has humbugged me, by God! He has gained twenty-four hours' march on me.'[21] – the somewhat unimaginative tactics adopted at Waterloo make the Duke's comment understandable.

Wellington believed that some of Napoleon's adversaries participated in their own downfall by using unsound methods or by being overawed by Napoleon's reputation. He expressed this view before he had even taken command in the Peninsular War, remarking that he had not seen the French army since 1794, 'when they were capital soldiers, and a dozen years of victory under Buonaparte must have made them better still. They have besides, it seems, a new system of strategy which has out-manoeuvred and overwhelmed all the armies of Europe ... My die is cast, they may overwhelm me, but I don't think they will out-manoeuvre me. First, because I am not afraid of them, as everybody else seems to be; and secondly because if what I hear of their system of manoeuvre is true, I think it a false one against steady troops. I suspect all the continental armies were more than half beaten before the battle was begun – I, at least, will not be frightened beforehand.'[22] This opinion Wellington maintained in retirement, adding that another failing of Napoleon's enemies was to lay too much importance upon 'distant and ineffective cannonades' and 'the relative proportions of artillery in the field'.[23]

Napoleon's opponents were many and varied, though few posed any unique tactical problems for him to solve; indeed, some owed a considerable measure of their eventual success to the adoption of systems and organisation copied from the French. In the wider sphere it could be argued that the reason such hostility was shown to Napoleon was partly because of to his own political actions: the imposition of humiliating terms after a crushing military defeat may have removed a threat in the short term, but was hardly a way of gaining the co-operation of a potential enemy in the years ahead. Napoleon's treatment of his defeated enemies may have partly ensured that their antagonism returned to haunt him in later years, but a further factor must have been the manner in which French forces were permitted to behave in occupied countries. All armies committed excesses of looting, but the French system positively encouraged, even necessitated it, and led to great injustices and the attitude articulated by Coignet of the Imperial Guard, that when in the enemy's country, 'if you don't take anything, you feel you've forgotten something'.[24] The terrorising of civilians and the deliberate destruction of their property was at times even applied as official policy. Such widespread pillage – with some commanders of the highest rank in the fore – and accompanying brutalities perpetrated against civilians served to bring forth the antagonism of populace as well as princes. This hatred manifested itself in ways which were of great significance to the French army, in the unremitting hostility of the majority of the population in Spain and Portugal, of Russia in 1812, and of parts of Germany from 1813, for example; and as a consequence to the French population which suffered when troops from aggrieved nations invaded France towards the end of Napoleon's reign. That it was possible for an invading army *not* to antagonise the populace is proven by the record of Wellington's army in southern France in the closing stages of the Peninsular War, when the strict prohibition of looting and maltreatment of French civilians (described by one member of the army as the theft of 'not even a cabbage-stalk without its head') ensured that the British received more co-operation from the inhabitants of southern France than they accorded to their own armies. Lest this be thought a matter of limited importance, it is worth reflecting how the efforts of the Spanish guerrillas weakened the French army in the Peninsular War, and occupied the attentions of many thousands of troops who were needed urgently elsewhere. Although it might have been within Napoleon's power to ameliorate much of the popular antagonism aroused by his armies, the rulers of some states would still have remained his enemies for as long as he pursued the foreign policy which he had adopted.

271

In order to oppose Napoleon effectively, while the adoption of elements of the French system was thought necessary by several of his principal enemies (Britain being a notable exception), full emulation would have required changes in the nature of society which were not possible in the Austro-Hungarian and Russian empires; only Prussia endeavoured to create a 'national' army fired with patriotic fervour akin to that which was created by the French Revolution. Elsewhere reforms were of a more limited nature, though capable of providing problems for Napoleon.

The troops of the Austro-Hungarian empire were those against which Napoleon first came into conflict as a commanding general, and they remained among his most persistent opponents, despite a succession of defeats dating from the early Italian campaigns. These cost Austria much territory: the Austrian Netherlands were lost by the Treaty of Campo Formio (1797), northern Italy by conquest, Venice and the Tyrol by the Treaty of Pressburg (1806), and the Treaty of Schönbrunn represented the final humiliation following military defeat at Wagram. From then until 1813 Austria was compelled into an alliance with France, but even the cementing of this by the marriage of the Emperor's daughter to Napoleon only suppressed Austrian opposition temporarily. Having provided a corps to assist Napoleon in his invasion of Russia in 1812, in the following year Austria joined the coalition against him and played an important role in his defeat.

The Austrian army enjoyed a deserved reputation for discipline and stolid bravery, and was especially remarked for the competence of its artillery, but until the emergence of the Archduke Charles, brother of the Emperor Francis II (Francis I when the Holy Roman Empire was dissolved after Austerlitz), its leadership was uninspired and unable to cope with the French military system. After the defeat of Austerlitz, the Archduke Charles supervised crucial reforms which modernised the Austrian forces to a considerable extent, but he had to contend with reactionary opposition in the military establishment which prevented even greater improvements. A significant, indigenous tactical development of the column was the 'mass', a solid square of infantry which could be formed rapidly by closing-up successive lines, which appeared unwieldy but (especially over open ground) could manoeuvre at the same time as having the defensive characteristics of a square, and proved to be considerably effective against the French. The influence of French methods was evident in 1813–14 when Austria used columnar attacks screened by an increased number of skirmishers, concentrated cavalry as a primary strike-force, and massed artillery bombardment.

Throughout the defeats and reforms, the Austrian soldier remained a sturdy, professional foe, although Napoleon believed that the Austrian army behaved best at Marengo, and that in successive campaigns their quality had declined, that battle being 'the grave of their valour'.[25] Be that as it may, it was the Austrian army which inflicted the first great reverse upon Napoleon, at Aspern-Essling, and despite the ultimate French success at Wagram, there was some truth in the conclusion drawn by the Austrian account of the former action:

'For the first time, Napoleon has sustained a defeat in Germany. From this moment he was reduced to the rank of bold and successful generals, who, after a long series of destructive achievements, experience the vicissitudes of fortune. The charm of his invincibility is dissolved. No longer the spoiled child of fortune, by posterity he will be characterized as the sport of the fickle goddess. New hopes begin to animate the oppressed nations.'[26]

NAPOLEON CHEERED BY THE ARMY BEFORE RATISBON, 1809.
PRINT AFTER F. DE MYRBACH.

Following his first defeat of Austria in the Italian campaigns, Napoleon's next opponents were unlike anything he had met before or would meet in the future: the Mameluke rulers of Egypt and the forces of the Ottoman Empire. The former practised a form of warfare not far removed from that of the medieval ages, the Mamelukes themselves being exclusively cavalry, whose sole tactic was a charge in course of which they would fire their carbines and pistols or throw javelins, before closing with the sword, and although they had some steady mercenary infantry the majority of their followers were little more than impressed mobs of peasants. The Ottoman forces included Janissaries and some 'regular' infantry, but the whole army was characterised by the Archduke Charles in his *Principles of War* as comprising bold warriors adept at weapons-handling, but quite incapable of co-ordinated action on the battlefield, their principal tactic being a forward rush with neither fear nor discipline; or, as expressed by Sir John Moore, the method of an ungovernable mob. The startling tactics of the courageous Mamelukes provoked Napoleon into a rare involvement in the formulation of 'minor tactics', by the creation of his 'divisional squares'. To meet the massed charges, each French division formed a huge rectangle, with sides up to six deep, an entire *demi-brigade* forming each of the front and rear faces, and another the two shorter sides. Within these large squares there was room for cavalry and baggage to be accommodated; the vulnerable corners were protected by artillery deployed just outside the perimeter of the square and covered by detached élite companies of infantry. Howitzers, capable of indirect fire (i.e., over the heads of friendly troops) could be positioned within the rectangle. These formations, arrayed in chequer-board style like conventional battalion squares, so as to be mutually supporting, were able to drive off the headlong Mameluke charges while sustaining very few casualties.

Russian forces were the next of the principal opponents against which Napoleon was engaged personally. Although Russian forces had been considerably effective in northern Italy in 1799 under the command of the great Suvarov, the army had suffered greatly from the malign influence of the Tsar Paul I, who was generally regarded as a madman and who attempted to eradicate all the reforms of his mother, Catherine the Great, largely out of spite. The result was an army which appeared 'exactly the hard, stiff, wooden machines which we have reason to figure to ourselves as the Russians of the Seven Years War. Their dress and equipments seemed to have remained unaltered; they waddled slowly forward to the tap-tap of their monotonous drums; and if they were beaten they waddled slowly back again, without appearing in either case to feel a sense of danger, or the expediency of taking ultra tap-tap steps to better their condition.'[27] The accession of Tsar Alexander I after Paul's murder in 1801 cleared the way for radical modernisation of the Russian forces, though staff functions and higher organisation were far from perfect; even with Austrian assistance the lack of permanent higher organisation was a serious disadvantage in the Austerlitz campaign, when the conduct of the commanding general (Kutusov) was inhibited by the interference of the Tsar and the Austrian Emperor, who were both present with the army.

The defeat of Friedland and the lack of continental allies led the Tsar to accept the Treaty of Tilsit, by which Russia became France's ally; but the relationship was never regarded with enthusiasm in Russia, and broke down completely shortly before Napoleon's invasion in 1812. By that time, further re-organisations of the Russian military system (under successive ministers of war, Alexei Arakcheev and Mikhail Barclay de Tolly) had further transformed the army, with new artillery and higher organisations, but the education of the officer class remained poor, and although the new systems were copied from France, the army continued to be inferior to the French in terms of flexibility, speed of movement, and the staff system. Although more emphasis was put upon light infantry tactics and the principle of massed-battery fire was adopted, cavalry was rarely used in large concentrations for decisive action. A unique resource possessed by Russia and utilised with effect throughout the period was the force of Cossacks and similar irregular light cavalry, less formidable in regular warfare but potentially devastating in skirmishing and raiding actions.

Following the repulse of Napoleon's forces in 1812, Russian forces played an important role in the campaigns of 1813–14. While never adopting the concept of a 'national' army in the French sense, the mobilisation of militia (*opolchenie*) from 1812 accorded that campaign at least some aspects of a 'national' war, and the devotion of the ordinary Russian soldier to Tsar, officers and homeland never wavered, despite the quite wretched conditions of civilian and military life endured by conscripts before and during their military service. Napoleon believed that the Russian army was at its peak at Austerlitz and declined thereafter; but what was surely never in doubt was the mettle of the individual Russian soldier, which caused Napoleon untold problems. Marbot quoted a typical example of their almost superhuman stoicism, in the action at Golymin, shortly before Eylau: 'although our soldiers fired upon them at twenty-five paces, they continued their march ... The streets were filled with dead and wounded, but not a groan was to be heard, for they were forbidden. You might have said that we were firing upon shadows. At last our soldiers charged the Russian soldiers with the bayonet, and only when they pierced them could they be convinced that they were dealing with men.'[28]

The next of the continent's great military powers against which Napoleon came into conflict was Prussia, which had not been engaged in the later Revolutionary Wars, having made peace with France in 1795. Not until the direct challenge presented by the French satellite Confederation of the Rhine (Rheinbund) did Prussia again take the field, with disastrous consequences. Under King Frederick II ('the Great'), the Prussian army had been elevated to the foremost military position in Europe, and continued to benefit from his reputation long after his death in 1786. In practice, however, the Frederickian doctrine lasted too long, and its outdated adherents resisted the modernisations which were introduced. The members of the army were the same disciplined troops as in Frederick's time, but although King Frederick William III succeeded in introducing some limited, French-style reforms, even the creation of divisional organisation was only introduced immediately prior to Jena, without the time for the new system to become familiar. The consequence of this lack of development and the absence of an inspired commander led to the disasters of Jena and Auerstädt, and Prussia's removal from the war. These battles involved no disgrace to the Prussian troops, who behaved well in the sphere of 'minor tactics' only to be undone by failures in organisation and leadership; but there was less excuse for the collapse which followed.

The period of enforced alliance provided the opportunity for a humbled Prussia to reconstruct itself, both militarily and socially, the two aspects being reformed simultaneously. In that sense, Prussia's 'national army' was closer to that of France than any other European power, and the army was reconstructed entirely under the guidance of Gerhard Scharnhorst, although he was dismissed from office in 1810 after his sense of German patriotism began to alarm Napoleon. (He later returned to duty and was mortally wounded at Lützen.) The reforms were profound: the staff and higher organisation was totally rebuilt (the latter based upon the brigade: Napoleon's restrictions on the size of the Prussian army originally precluded the formation of divisions); skirmishing ability was enhanced greatly, with the difference between light and line troops diminishing (as in the

French army); concentration of artillery fire was advocated, and great importance was placed upon the co-ordination of 'arms'. Most importantly, a spirit of national patriotism was developed which led to the creation of volunteer *Jäger* companies and squadrons attached to many units, formed of patriotic young men from the middle and upper classes who were able to arm and equip themselves at their own expense, and of a national militia (*Landwehr*) which eventually was able to take its place in the line alongside the regular troops. The limits placed by Napoleon on the Prussian military establishment complicated the great increase in strength instituted in 1813, so that many of the new formations received only rudimentary or foreign uniforms (including even uniforms for the Portuguese army manufactured in Britain), and large quantities of foreign weapons were distributed (principally British). Until they could be equipped properly, some *Landwehr* were armed with pikes, and it is a measure of the depth of patriotic feeling that such ill-equipped and partially trained formations maintained their morale. One consequence of the patriotic sentiments which sustained the army at this period was a genuine hatred of the French for the occupation and humiliation which had been endured since 1806, and the consequences of Napoleon's treatment of the Prussians had unfortunate effects upon the French civilians whose lands the Prussians traversed in the closing stages of the war. Napoleon commented that the Prussians of 1806 did not put up the resistance which might have been expected from their reputation, and that the Allied armies of 1813–14 were 'mere rabble compared with the real soldiers of Marengo, Austerlitz and Jena';[29] but if so, they were a mere rabble whose leaders had absorbed sufficient elements of the French military system to revitalise their own armies, whose members were determined to repay the French for the indignities inflicted by Napoleon upon their countries in previous years, and to learn enough to enable them to counter his methods.

The last of the main European armies to fight against Napoleon in person was that of Britain. British opposition to Napoleon remained implacable, and although the only campaigns of any great importance fought by the British Army were those in Egypt, in the Iberian Peninsula and in the Netherlands in 1815, the British contribution to Napoleon's eventual defeat was crucial, both by maritime operations and in the support of other enemies of his, principally financial but also diplomatic and in the supply of munitions. Many of Napoleon's troubles arose from his attempts to impose the 'Continental System', an economic measure designed to cripple British

trade; in itself it failed absolutely and led Napoleon into costly and ultimately fatal campaigns arising from his attempted invasions of Portugal
and Russia. The remark made by Tsar Alexander I when he stepped ashore
at Dover in 1814, 'God be praised! I have set my foot upon the land which
has saved us all',[30] may have been partially diplomatic in origin, but it was
not entirely without foundation.

Only on rare occasions did Napoleon actually confront British troops in
person, though it is worth noting that his military career was almost concluded virtually before it had begun when in November 1793 he received
a bayonet-wound in the thigh at Toulon, conceivably from a member of the
British 11th Foot.[31] His only personal involvement in the Peninsular War
ended in late 1808, and apart from a token British presence at Leipzig, he
encountered British troops only in the Waterloo campaign. Nevertheless
British forces played a significant role in his eventual defeat, by maintaining so long and so successfully the fight against the French in the Iberian
Peninsula. As long as he persisted in pursuing it, this war presented
Napoleon with an insoluble problem: a division of resources needed elsewhere, to conduct a campaign in a country in which the majority of the
population was implacably hostile to the French, and with his own forces
commanded by subordinates who were largely unequal or under-
resourced for the tasks he set them, and who on occasion were not disposed towards mutual co-operation. Napoleon confessed that the effect
was profound:

> 'That unlucky war ruined me; it divided my forces, obliged me to mul-
> tiply my efforts, and caused my principles to be assailed; and yet it
> was impossible to leave the Peninsula a prey to the machinations of
> the English, the intrigues, the hopes, and the pretentions of the
> Bourbons ... This combination ruined me. All the circumstances of my
> disasters are connected with that fatal knot: it destroyed my moral
> power in Europe, rendered my embarrassments more complicated, and
> opened a school for the English soldiers.'[32]

The effect of the continual drain upon his resources led Napoleon to write
to his brother Joseph in December 1813: 'I do not want Spain either to keep
or to give away. I will have nothing more to do with that country except to
live in peace with it, and have the use of my army.'[33]

Despite his suggestion that he had trained the British Army, unlike those
of most other European armies, its methods of operation avoided copying
those of the French, which was probably deliberate. Wellington's comments

on the subject actually related to the introduction of uniforms resembling French styles, but might have been applied more widely: 'there is one thing I deprecate, and that is any imitation of the French, in any manner ... I only beg that *we* may be as different as possible from the French in every thing ...'[34] Consequently, the evolution of higher organisation evolved independently; the brigade remained the largest formation until the appearance of divisions in Denmark in 1807, which were continued in Moore's army and introduced permanently by Wellington for his Peninsular army from June 1809. A corps system was not implemented, perhaps because of the smaller number of troops involved, but each of Wellington's divisions was a self-supporting entity, complete with its own staff, commissariat, artillery and reconnaissance facility, companies of riflemen being attached to each formation.

The role of the commissariat was a significant factor in British success in the Peninsular War. On occasion Wellington's army went hungry, but their commander's administrative ability was superior to that of most of his contemporaries (including Napoleon), and on one occasion, when discussing the most important attributes required of a general, Wellington remarked that 'what we want ... is some one to feed our troops'.[35] Napoleon's assertion that

NAPOLEON ON THE NIGHT OF BAUTZEN. PRINT AFTER RAFFET.

an army marched upon its stomach is better-known, but the implementation of its consequences was markedly inferior.

To counter the French skirmishers, light infantry service was refined in the British Army in the years before the Peninsular War – Sir John Moore is often cited as being the originator of modern light infantry tactics, although he merely improved and expanded theories which were already current – and these skills were perfected under Wellington. British lines could throw out so many trained skirmishers that even the French were outmatched, and so many troops could be used in this role that the true location of British positions was completely concealed; at Barrosa and Busaco, for example, the number of skirmishers deployed was such that the French were convinced that they had pierced the British 'first line' when in fact they had only driven back the skirmishers.

Concealment of the British position was the key to the successful defeat of French infantry attacks. Wellington trained his troops to take shelter whenever possible – lying down under fire was a way of reducing casualties not usually practised by other armies – and notably by positioning his troops on the reverse slope of a hill. With skirmishers on the brow of the hill, or further down the other side, the location of the British line could not be discerned by the attackers. This tended to reduce British casualties from artillery-fire, but more importantly prevented the French attacks from deploying properly before contact. The French would advance in column, exchanging skirmish-fire with the British light infantry, which would retire before them; then the main British line would appear from the reverse slope, giving the French no time to deploy into line to maximise their own musketry potential, before the British would deliver volleys of their own sufficient to shake the French column, to be followed by a limited but violent bayonet-charge which drove the French back in disorder. So successful was this tactic of surprise that Wellington was able to refer to French attacks as being made in the old style and being driven off in the old style; but it was not adopted by other armies as a counter to the hitherto successful French infantry tactics.

Never being personally concerned to any great extent with 'minor tactics', Napoleon made no attempt to counter this method, and indeed seems to have somewhat underrated the British on the one occasion when he met them in person in any appreciable numbers. On the morning of Waterloo, Napoleon received the advice of subordinates who had experience of fighting against the British, notably Marshal Soult, and General Honoré Reille, the commander of II Corps who had served against Wellington from late 1812 until the end of the Peninsular War. Reille thought that frontal attacks would never succeed against British troops because of their steadiness, but he believed that they could be outmanoeuvred. Napoleon cared no more for this opinion than for the advice he had received earlier from Soult, who had counselled caution and the recall of at least part of the force detached to pursue what Napoleon thought was the defeated Prussian army. Of this advice – from a marshal who had fought the British from Corunna to Toulouse, and who was among the most loyal and capable of his subordinates – Napoleon was positively dismissive and almost contemptuous, telling Soult that he only regarded Wellington as a good general because he had defeated him (Soult), but: 'I tell you that he is a bad general, that the English are poor troops, and that this will be a picnic.'[36]

It is possible that Napoleon deliberately denigrated his opponents in this manner to put heart into his subordinates – as in the passage to Clarke quoted earlier, 'in war moral force is everything ... The art of great captains has always been ... to persuade their own troops of the enemy's great inferiority' – but in this case it may also indicate an element of self-delusion, a failing of which he was not altogether free, at least during the later stages of his career. Marmont, aggrieved at what he considered to be Napoleon's interference in a war he did not understand and for which he refused to provide adequate resources (the Peninsula), described Napoleon's habit of accepting only what he wanted to believe as a deliberate closing of his eyes from the light and his ears from the truth. Further evidence for this may be provided by Napoleon's reaction to his brother Jérôme's intelligence that Blücher and Wellington intended to rendezvous that very day: he dismissed the possibility entirely, stating that such a uniting of his enemies was impossible for two days, after the beating the Prussians had received at Ligny.

If such a capacity for self-delusion existed, it must have contributed to Napoleon's decline from the high point of his successes, combining with other factors such as some diminution in the powers of his troops, countermeasures adopted by his enemies, some reduction in his own powers and physical ability, and unwise strategic and political decisions which overstretched his resources. Nevertheless, taking his career as a whole, and without taking into account the fact that it was he who was responsible for the pursuit of the politico-military policies which ultimately led to his defeat, there can be little doubt of the veracity of the view expressed by the Duke of Wellington quoted previously: that Napoleon was 'the first man of his day on a field of battle'.

NOTES

1. *Conversations with the Duke of Wellington*, Earl Stanhope, London, 1899, p. 9. The same remark is also quoted on another occasion; see *Personal Reminiscences of the Duke of Wellington*, Francis, Earl of Ellesmere, ed. Alice, Countess of Strafford, London, 1904, p. 99.
2. *The Courier*, 9 April 1811.
3. See 'An Historical Sketch of the Battle of Maida', Sir Charles Oman, in *Journal of the Royal Artillery*, vol. XXXIV, 1907-8, pp. 541-64, reprinted in the same author's *Studies in the Napoleonic Wars*, London, 1929, pp. 37-72.
4. A facsimile is reproduced in 'More Considerations and Conclusions on the Material Available from the French Official Archives', J. A. Lochet, in *Empires, Eagles and Lions*, Paris, Ontario, No. 60, December 1981, pp. 4-5. Oman's later work accepts that the French did deploy into line, and that the action instead demonstrated the superiority of two-deep over three-deep lines: see *Wellington's Army*, Sir Charles Oman, London, 1912, pp. 77-8.
5. *Memoirs of the Life, Exile and Conversations of the Emperor Napoleon*, Count de Las Cases, London, 1836, vol. IV, p. 144.
6. Ibid., vol. IV, p. 145.
7. *The Confidential Correspondence of Napoleon Bonaparte with his Brother Joseph*, London, 1855, vol. II, p. 144; this follows the early English translation, but it should be noted that 'marching regiment' is a somewhat misleading translation of *régiment de marche* which in English military terminology would be styled a provisional regiment, or one assembled from a number of different units.
8. *Recollections of Colonel de Gonneville*, ed. C. M. Yonge, London, 1875, vol. I, p. 190.
9. Las Cases, *op. cit.*, vol. IV, p. 176.
10. Ibid.
11. These remarks were actually inscribed upon the Colours of the units in question: *Demi-Brigades* of the Army of Italy. See, for example, *Drapeaux et Etandards de la Révolution et de l'Empire*, P. Charrié, Paris, 1982, p. 33; and *The War Drama of the Eagles*, E. Fraser, London, 1912, p. 14.
12. W. Knollys, in the introduction to *A Journal of the Russian Campaign of 1812*, General duc de Fezensac, London, 1852, p. viii.
13. See the chapter on this subject in *On the Napoleonic Wars*, D. G. Chandler, London, 1994.
14. *Confidential Correspondence*, vol. II, pp. 74-5, 10 October 1809.
15. Ibid., vol. II, pp. 184-5.
16. *A Short History of Napoleon the First*, Sir John Seeley, London, 1895, pp. 253-4.
17. *Military Instruction from the late King of Prussia to his Generals*, trans. Lieutenant-Colonel Foster, London, 1818, pp. 125, 128; originally written in 1748.
18. Ibid., p. 43.
19. Ellesmere, *op. cit.*, pp. 98-100.

20. Ibid., p. 179.
21. Said by Wellington; *Letters of the First Earl of Malmesbury 1745–1820*, London, 1870, vol. II, p. 445.
22. *The Croker Papers*, J. W. Croker, London, 1884, vol. I, pp. 12–13.
23. Ellesmere, *op. cit.*, p. 98.
24. Knollys, *op. cit.*, p. 59.
25. Las Cases, op. cit., vol. I, p. 336.
26. This translation from *The Gentleman's Magazine*, July 1809, p. 664, quoting *London Gazette*, 11 July; substantially the same text appeared in *Relation of the Operations and Battles of the Austrian and French Armies in the Year 1809*, W. Muller, London, 1810, p. 34.
27. *Narratives of Some Passages in the Great War with France*, Sir Henry Bunbury, 1854; London, 1927 edn., p. 145.
28. *The Memoirs of Baron de Marbot*, trans. A. J. Butler, London, 1913, vol. I, p. 200.
29. Las Cases, *op. cit.*, vol. I, p. 336.
30. *The Gentleman's Magazine*, supplement 1814, p. 691.
31. *Historical Record of the Eleventh or the North Devon Regiment of Foot*, R. Cannon, London, 1845, p. 47.
32. Las Cases, *op. cit.*, vol. II, pp. 134–5.
33. *Confidential Correspondence*, vol. II, pp. 255–6.
34. To Lieutenant-Colonel Henry Torrens, 6 November 1811; *Dispatches of Field Marshal the Duke of Wellington*, ed. J. Gurwood, London, 1834–8, vol. VIII, p. 371.
35. Relating to Marshal Beresford; quoted in *The Wellington Memorial*, A. J. Griffiths, London, 1897, p. 308.
36. The word Napoleon actually used was *déjeuner*, which has sometimes been translated as 'easy as eating one's breakfast' or as 'a lunchtime affair', but the English colloquialism 'picnic' is probably the most accurate for the meaning intended.

BIBLIOGRAPHY

Barnett, C. *Bonaparte*, London, 1978.

Blond, G. *La Grande Armée*, trans. M. May, London, 1995.

Chandler, D. G. *The Campaigns of Napoleon*, London, 1967.

– *Dictionary of the Napoleonic Wars*, London, 1979 .

– (ed.). *The Military Maxims of Napoleon*, trans. Lieutenant-General Sir George D'Aguilar, 1831; r/p with intr. by W. E. Cairnes, London, 1901; reprinted with commentary by D. G. Chandler, London. 1987.

– (ed.). *Napoleon's Marshals*, London, 1987.

Elting, J. R. *Swords Around a Throne: Napoleon's Grande Armée*, London, 1989 (very important modern study).

Esposito, V. J., and Elting, J. R. *Military History and Atlas of the Napoleonic Wars*, London, 1964 (superb maps, covering all the campaigns in which Napoleon commanded).

Glover, M. *Warfare in the Age of Bonaparte,* London, 1980.

Haythornthwaite, P. J. *Napoleonic Source Book*, London, 1990.

– *Napoleon's Military Machine*, Tunbridge Wells, 1988.

– *Weapons and Equipment of the Napoleonic Wars*, Poole, 1979.

Horward, D. D. (ed.). *Napoleonic Military History: A Bibliography*, London, 1986 (includes valuable bibliography and commentary, especially 'Armies of the Napoleonic Period', S. T. Ross; and 'Napoleon and his Family – Lives and Careers', O. Connelly).

Hughes, Major-General B. P. *Firepower: Weapons Effectiveness on the Battlefield 1630–1850*, London, 1974.

– *Open Fire: Artillery Tactics from Marlborough to Wellington*, Chichester, 1983.

Lachouque, H., and Brown, A. S. K. *The Anatomy of Glory*, London, 1962 (Napoleon's Imperial Guard, with a large number of contemporary illustrations).

Las Cases, comte de. *Memoirs of the Life, Exile and Conversations of the Emperor Napoleon*, London, 1836.

Marshall-Cornwall, General Sir James. *Napoleon as Military Commander*, London, 1967.

Nosworthy, B. *Battle Tactics of Napoleon and his Enemies*, London, 1996.

Quennevat, J.-C. *Les Vrais Soldats de Napoléon*, Paris, 1968 (includes many contemporary illustrations).

Rogers, H. C. B.. *Napoleon's Army,* London 1974.

Rothenberg, G. E. *The Art of War in the Age of Napoleon*, London, 1977.

Seeley, Sir John. *A Short History of Napoleon the First*, London, 1895.

NAPOLEON
AND HIS WORDS

Peter G. Tsouras

I N FINDING THE MAN WITHIN NAPOLEON, NAPOLEON HIMSELF IS THE best source. Few men have left so voluminous a record of their spoken words and correspondence. Luckily it was well worth recording; Napoleon freely broadcast the gems of his military genius. The Emperor was obsessed with history's judgement, and much of what he said, especially at St. Helena, was meant for that greater, timeless audience. He also spoke and wrote with a flair and style that few soldiers have equalled; his words fairly rattled with musketry. One gets the impression that he was enjoying himself immensely. The following quotations, then, are an attempt to capture the echo of the Emperor's thunder across time.

Napoleon's private secretary and confidant from 1797 to 1803, Louis-Antoine Bourrienne, wrote, 'Bonaparte had two ruling passions, glory and war. He was never more gay than in the camp, and never more morose than in the activity of peace.'[1] From this observation, all else about the man unfolds.

Napoleon himself never uttered a more revealing statement than when he said, *'I like only those who make war.'*[2] (St. Helena, 1816) He had coolly measured himself against the game and had not found himself wanting.

War is a serious sport, in which one can endanger his reputation and his country: a rational man must feel and know whether or not he is cut out for this profession.[3] (To Prince Eugène, 30 April 1809)

He was born stamped from the mould of Mars, the perfect soldier.

I am a soldier, because that is the special faculty I was born with; that is my life, my habit. I have commanded wherever I have been. I commanded, when twenty-three years old, at the siege of Toulon; I commanded in Paris at Vendémiaire; I carried the soldiers of the Army of Italy with me as soon as I appeared among them; I was born that way. (30 July 1900)

There is nothing in the military profession I cannot do for myself. If there is no one to make gunpowder, I know how to make it; gun carriages, I know how to construct them; if it is founding cannon, I know that; or if the details of tactics must be taught, I can teach them.[5] (30 July 1800)

My memory will not store a single alexandrine verse; but I do not forget one syllable of the regimental returns. I always know where my troops are. I am fond of tragedy; but were all the dramas of the world there, on one side of me, and the regimental returns on the other, I would not so much as glance at the dramas, while every line of my regimental returns would be read with the closest attention.[6] (11 February 1809)

A singular thing about me is my memory. As a boy I knew the logarithms of thirty or forty numbers; in France I not only knew the names of the officers of all the regiments, but where the corps had been recruited, had distinguished themselves; I even knew their spirit.[7] (St. Helena, 2 June 1817)

Even at St. Helena he retained a photographic memory of his army, and spoke of it in terms of love. When asked how he could remember the details of the units engaged in one of his early battles, he replied, '*Madam, this is a lover's recollection of his former mistress.*'[8]

The profession of arms was his life. '*The military are a freemasonry ... and I am the grand master of their lodges.*' [9] (Conversation, 1809) Even the enemy were included in this freemasonry; to his gaoler on St. Helena, he was able to appeal across the enmity of nations to the very English soldiers who guarded him:

In any case, who is asking anything of you? Who has asked you to feed me? If you stopped your provisions and I were hungry, these brave soldiers would take compassion on me. I could go to the mess of their grenadiers, and I am sure they would not deny the first, the oldest soldier of Europe.[10] (To Admiral Cockburn, referring to the men of the 58th Foot, part of the garrison of St. Helena, 18 August 1816)

With the natural talent for war, Napoleon had an unshakeable belief in himself, in fortune, in his 'lucky star' as he called it.

For all the faith I have in French valour, I have equal faith in my lucky star, or perhaps in myself, and as a result I never count positively on victory unless I myself am in command.[11] (Conversation, 1803)

In warfare every opportunity must be seized; for fortune is a woman; if you miss her today, you need not expect to find her tomorrow.[12] (30 July 1808)

I feel myself driven towards an end that I do not know. As soon as I shall have reached it, as soon as I shall become unnecessary, an atom will suffice to shatter me. Till then, not all the forces of mankind can do anything against me.[13]

The invincibility of his fortune was to run before him, creating even more victories in the minds of men.

A great reputation is a great noise; the more there is made, the farther off it is heard. Laws, institutions, monuments, nations, all fall; but the noise continues and resounds in after ages.[14]

My power proceeds from my reputation, and my reputation from the victories I have won. My power would fall if I were not to support it with more glory and more victories. Conquest has made me what I am; only conquest can maintain me.[15] (30 December 1802)

Even as a young general, he was impatient with superiors. The incompetence of the Directory only fed this attitude.

It is easy enough to say to a general, go to Italy, win battles, and sign peace at Vienna. But the doing of it is not so easy. I have never paid the least attention to the plans sent to me by the Directoire. Only fools could take stock in such rubbish.[16] (Goritz, 21 March 1797)

I understand why Bonaparte is accused; it's for concluding peace. But I warn you, I speak in the name of 80,000 men; the time when cowardly lawyers and low chatterers could send soldiers to the guillotine has passed, and if you drive them to it, the soldiers of Italy will march to the Clichy gate with their general: but, if they do, look out for yourselves![17] (To the Directoire, 30 June 1797)

I had rather talk to soldiers than to lawyers. Those ... made me nervous. I am not accustomed to assemblies; it may come in time.[18] (After a stormy session with the Council of Ancients, Paris, 10 November 1799)

To his love of war and soldiering was added ambition, a deadly mix to which he would give his name – 'Bonapartism'.

But all that ... he will learn will be of little use to him if he does not have the sacred fire in the depths of his heart, this driving ambition which alone can enable one to perform great deeds.[19]

I cannot obey any longer. I have tasted the pleasure of command, and I cannot renounce it. My decision is taken. If I cannot be master, I shall quit France.[20] (To Miot de Melito before the Egyptian expedition, 1798)

If ever I have the luck to set foot in France again, the reign of chatter is over.[21] (Cairo, 11 August 1799)

Power is my mistress. I have worked too hard in conquering her to allow anyone to take her from me or even to covet her.[22] (Conversation with Pierre-Louis Roederer, 1804)

As the born soldier, he intimately understood what drove other men. He grasped the essential, '*A leader is a dealer in hope.*' He was both the slave and master of the whirlwind intoxicants of war and glory. What animated him, he knew would animate most others.

> *Die young, and I shall accept your death – but not if you have lived with-out glory, without being useful to your country, without leaving a trace of your existence: for that is not to have lived at all.*[23] (To his brother Jérôme, 6 August 1802)

He relentless exposed himself to death as the price of glory. '*One must have the will to live and be willing to die. Glory can only be won where there is dan-ger.*'[24] (To his staff before the battle of Austerlitz, 1 December 1805)

His parallel with Alexander the Great is uncanny. Napoleon could as eas-ily have said as did the Macedonian:

> *Stand firm; for well you know that hardship and danger are the price of glory, and that sweet is the savour of a life of courage and of death-less renown beyond the grave.*[25]

He treated the death of others according to his own bargain with glory,

> '*I regret the brave men you have lost, but they are dead on the field of honour.*' [26] (To Marshal Davout, the day after his victory at Auerstädt, 16 October 1806)

The alternative to glory was not death but the barren absence of glory.

> '*Death is nothing; but to live defeated and without glory is to die every day.*'[27] (Letter to General Lauriston, 12 December 1804)

Napoleon understood how to appeal to this fiery ideal by putting his hand on the heart of the French soldier.

> *A general's principal talent consists in knowing the mentality of the sol-dier and in winning his confidence. And, in these two respects, the French soldier is more difficult to lead than any other. He is not a machine to be put in motion but a reasonable man to be directed.*[28]

He did this by appealing to the soldier's manhood and sense of adventure, his avarice, and every man's need to be well thought of by his fellows:

> *A man does not have himself killed for a half-pence a day or for a petty distinction. You must speak to the soul in order to galvanise the man.*[29]

Glory made easy the transition from Republic to Empire and took tangible form in decorations, promotion, rank and titles.

> *Where is the republic, ancient or modern, that has not granted honours? Call them trifles if you like, but it is by trifles that men are influenced. I would not utter such a sentiment as this in public, but here, among statesmen and thinkers, things should be spoken of as they are. In my*

opinion the French do not care for liberty and equality; they must be given distinctions. Do you suppose you can persuade men to fight by a process of analysis? Never; the process is valid only for the man of science in his study. The soldier demands glory, distinction, rewards.[30] (Paris, 14 May 1802)

I intend to make the generals and officers who have served me well so rich that there can be no excuse for their dishonouring the most noble of professions by their greed, while drawing upon themselves the contempt of the soldiers.[31] (After his victory at Ulm, 15 November 1805)

He was incredulous at the class-ridden English system which ignored the most potent motivations, and at St. Helena speculated on what was possible with English troops:

Instead of the lash, I would lead them by the stimulus of honour. I would instil a degree of emulation into their minds. I would promote every deserving soldier, as I did in France. ... What might not be expected of the English army if every soldier hoped to be made a general provided he showed the ability? [General] Bingham says, however, that most of your soldiers are brutes and must be driven by the stick. But surely the English soldiers must be possessed of sentiments sufficient to put them at least upon a level with the soldiers of other countries, where the

'THE UPSHOT OF THE INVASION, OR BONY IN A FAIR WAY FOR DAVY'S LOCKER'.
PRINT PUBLISHED BY VERNER & HOOD, LONDON, 1803.

degrading system of the lash is not used. Whatever debases a man cannot be serviceable.[32] (Conversation on St. Helena about reforming the British Army, 9 November 1816)

You English are aristocrats. You keep a great distance between yourselves and the popolo. Nature formed all men equal. It was always my custom to go amongst the soldiers and rabble, to converse with them, hear their little histories, and speak kindly to them. This I found to be the greatest benefit to me.[33] (St. Helena, 3 April 1817)

He said, '*You know what words can do to soldiers.*'[34] (to General Brune, 12 March 1800) Bourrienne recounted the calculation with which he created this mystique:

When he reviewed the troops he asked the officers, and often the soldiers, in what battles they had been engaged, and to those who had received serious wounds he gave the Cross. Here, I think, I may appropriately mention a singular piece of charlatanism to which the Emperor had recourse, and which powerfully contributed to augment the enthusiasm of his troops. He would say to one of his aides de camp, 'Ascertain from the colonel of such a regiment whether he has in his corps a man who has served in the campaigns of Italy or the campaigns of Egypt. Ascertain his name, where he was born, the particulars of his family, and what he had done. Learn his number in the ranks, and to what company he belongs, and furnish me with the information.'

On the day of the review Bonaparte, at a single glance, could perceive the man who had been described to him. He would go up to him as if he recognised him, address him by his name, and say, 'Oh! so you are here! You are a brave fellow – I saw you at Aboukir – how is your old father? What! Have you not got the Cross? Stay, I will give it you.' Then the delighted soldiers would say to each other, 'You see the Emperor knows us all; he knows our families; he knows where we have served.' What a stimulus was this to soldiers, whom he succeeded in persuading that they would all some time or other become Marshals of the Empire![35]

The spoken word emanated from a titanic personality that commanded events and men. Marshal Masséna and the other generals recalled that when the slim, sunken-faced 26-year-old general arrived to command the Army of Italy in 1796 they thought him nothing more than the favourite of a politician. His insistence to show them a picture of Josephine did nothing to change their minds. Masséna then said:

A moment afterwards he put on his general's hat and seemed to have grown two feet. He questioned us on the position of our divisions, on the spirit and effective forces of each corps, prescribed the course we were to follow, announced that he would hold an inspection on the morrow and on the following day attack the enemy.[36]

He mastered the higher elements of war, its principles, when most of the military professionals concentrated on the petty details.

Get your principles straight; the rest is a matter of detail. Principles of military art shine in history like the Sun on the horizon, so much the worse for blind men incapable of seeing them.[37]

He had discerned these principles by a profound study of military history.

The principles of warfare are those which guided the great captains whose high deeds history has transmitted to us – Alexander, Hannibal, Caesar, Gustavus Adolphus, Turenne, Eugène of Savoy, Frederick the Great ... The history of their eighty-three campaigns would constitute a complete treatise on the art of war; the principles that must be followed in defensive and offensive warfare would flow from it as from a common source.[38] (St. Helena)

All the great captains have done great things only by conforming to the rules and natural principles of the art; that is to say, by the wisdom of their combinations, the reasoned balance of means with consequences, and efforts with obstacles. They have succeeded only by thus conforming, whatever may have been the audacity of their enterprises and the extent of their success. They have never ceased to make war a veritable science. It is only under this title that they are our great models, and it is only in imitating them that one can hope to approach them.[39]

Tactics can be learned from treatises, somewhat like geometry, and so can the various military evolutions or the science of the engineers and the gunner; but knowledge of the grand principles of warfare can be acquired only through the study of military history and of the battles of the great captains and through experience.[40] (Dictation, St. Helena)

He also learned the unparalleled value of astounding his enemies by the dramatic and unexpected.

It is a principle of warfare, that when it is possible to make use of thunderbolts, they should be preferred to cannon.[41] (Dictation, St. Helena)

He avoided any rigid fixation on these same principles.

It is true that Jomini always argues for fixed principles. Genius works by inspiration. What is good in certain circumstances may be bad in others; but one ought to consider principles as an axis which holds certain rela-

291

tions to a curve. It may be good to recognise that on this or that occa-sion one has swerved from fixed principles of war.[42] (St. Helena)

There are no precise, determinate rules: everything depends on the character that nature has bestowed on the general, on his qualities and defects, on the troops, on the range of the weapons, on the season of the year, and on a thousand circumstances which are never twice the same.[43] (Dictation, St. Helena)

He quickly organised these principles into a lethal working relationship.

These three things you must always keep in mind: concentration of strength, activity, and a firm resolve to perish gloriously. They are the three principles of the military art which have disposed luck in my favour in all my operations.[44] (Letter to General Lauriston, 12 December 1804)

Keeping your forces united, being vulnerable at no point, moving rapid-ly on important points – these are the principles which assure victory, and, with fear, resulting from the reputation of your arms, maintains the faithfulness of allies and the obedience of conquered peoples.[45]

Among these principles was the one of greatest price of all, the strategy of the indirect approach to unbalance the enemy's equilibrium.

The principles of war are the same as those of a siege. Fire must be con-centrated at one point, and as soon as the breach is made, the equilib-rium is broken and the rest is nothing.[46]

Giving direction to his skills was a sense of determination and fixation on the objective.

True wisdom for a general is in vigorous determination.[47]

Many good generals exist in Europe, but they see too many things at once: I see but one thing, and that is the masses; I seek to destroy them, sure that the minor matters will fall of themselves.[48]

When you have an enterprise at hand, concentrate on it wholly; forget that anything else in the world exists.[49]

If you start to take Vienna – take Vienna.[50]

The mind that brought about victory after victory was disciplined and organised to a degree found only in the greatest of the Great Captains. It is no wonder that the Germans, created the General Staff in order to institu-tionalise the genius they had seen in Napoleon.

I have always enjoyed the analytic process, and if I fell seriously in love I would analyse my feelings step by step.[51] (25 January 1803)

Why? and How? are questions so useful that they cannot be too often asked. I conquered rather than studied history; that is to say, I did not care to retain and did not retain anything that could not give me a new idea; I disdained all that was useless, but took possession of certain results that pleased me.

'In other words,' according to J. F. C. Fuller, 'he taught himself "how to think" which is the harvest of all true education, civil or military.'[52] Napoleon understood more clearly than anyone else that,

War is essentially a calculation of probabilities.[53]

Napoleon made sure that he might dare, and dared.[54] (On the capture of Malta in 1798, dictation, St. Helena, c.1807)

He had already out-thought his opponents before the campaigns had begun.

Nothing is attained in war except by calculation. During a campaign whatever is not profoundly considered in all its details is without result. Every enterprise should be conducted according to a system; chance alone can never bring success.[55]

Military science consists in calculating all the chances accurately in the first place, and then in giving accident exactly, almost mathematically, its place in one's calculations. It is upon this point that one must not deceive oneself, and yet a decimal more or less may change all. Now this apportioning of accident and science cannot get into any head except that of a genius ... Accident, hazard, chance, call it what you may, a mystery to ordinary minds becomes a reality to superior men.[56]

There is no greater coward than I when I am drawing up a plan of campaign. I magnify every danger, every disadvantage that can be conceived. My nervousness is painful; but not that I show a cool face to those who are about me. I am like a woman in the throes of childbirth. When once my decision is made, however, I forget all, except what may carry it through to success.[57]

If I take so many precautions it is because it is my custom to leave nothing to chance.[58] (To Marshal Murat, 14 March 1808)

If I always appear prepared, it is because before entering on an undertaking, I have meditated for long and have foreseen what may occur. It is not genius which reveals to me suddenly and secretly what I should do in circumstances unexpected by others; it is thought and meditation.[59]

Nothing appeared to escape him; everything was grist for his calculations. His almost superhuman energy devoured and processed information with unparalleled thoroughness and on a scale the many leaders and staffs of his enemies could not match.

The good condition of my armies comes from the fact that I devote an hour or two every day to them, and when I am sent the returns of my troops and my ships each month, which fill twenty large volumes, I set every other occupation aside to read them in detail in order to discern the difference that exists from one month to another. I take greater pleasure in this reading than a young lady would get from reading a novel.[60] (To his brother Joseph, 20 August 1806)

Great events hang by a thread. The able man turns everything to profit, neglects nothing that may give him one chance more; the man of less ability, by overlooking just one thing, spoils the whole.[61] (25 September 1797)

He understood the dynamic relationships of the elements of strategy.

The strength of an army, like the power in mechanics, is estimated by multiplying the mass by the rapidity; a rapid march augments the morale of an army, and increases all the chances of victory.[62]

Strategy is the art of making use of time and space. I am less chary of the latter than of the former; space we can recover, time never.[63]

Time is the great element between weight and force.[64]

Time, especially time, was the single most important element of his calculations. His writings reiterate like a quickening drumbeat the importance of time. He was constantly pushing events along, hurrying his subordinates, and gaining on his enemies.

In military operations, hours determine success and campaigns.[65] (to Admiral Mazarredo, 20 March 1800)

Go, sir, gallop, and don't forget that the world was made in six days. You can ask me for anything you like, except time.[66] (To a courier to the new Tsar, Alexander I, 11 March 1803)

The loss of time is irretrievable in war; the excuses that are advanced are always bad ones, for operations go wrong only through delays.[67] (To his brother Joseph, 20 March 1806)

It may be that in the future I may lose a battle, but I shall never lose a minute.[68]

Related to his emphasis on time was an equal emphasis on constant activity so that he and his army were making the best use of time while his opponents rested, dithered or lazed.

Rapidity! Activity! Activity! All lies with you![69] (To Marshal Masséna during the Austrian campaign, 18 April 1809)

Make war seriously. You must be up at one in the morning. Your troops must be under arms at two, and you must be on the spot to receive reports from the reconnaissances sent out in all directions. You must not turn in again until eight, when you are sure there is nothing new.[70] (To his brother Jérôme, 24 April 1807)

A general-in-chief should never allow any rest either to the conqueror or to the conquered.[71]

Rapid and frequent communication among the elements of his army was another facet of his overall direction of an operation.

Let me hear from you more frequently; in a combined manoeuvre like this it is only by very frequent communication that we can achieve the best results. We are at the crisis of the campaign; they did not anticipate what we are attempting to do; woe betide them if they hesitate and if they lose a single day.[72] (To Marshal Soult, 6 October 1806)

'TIDDY-DOLL THE GREAT FRENCH GINGERBREAD-BAKER, DRAWING OUT A NEW BATCH
OF KINGS', A SATIRICAL COMMENT ON THE CREATION OF NEW MONARCHIES IN THE
STATES ALLIED TO NAPOLEON, WHO IS SHOWN TAKING FROM THE OVEN GINGERBREAD
FIGURES REPRESENTING THE RULERS OF BAVARIA, WÜRTTEMBERG AND BADEN. ON THE
FLOOR IS A BASKET OF 'CORSICAN KINGLINGS' FOR EXPORT, WHILE DEPOSED RULERS
ARE SWEPT INTO THE OVEN'S ASH-HOLE BY A 'CORSICAN BESOM OF DESTRUCTION'.
AT THE LEFT, 'HIS MAN, HOPPING TALLEY, MIXING UP THE DOUGH' IS TALLEYRAND.
PRINT AFTER GILLRAY, 1806.

He understood the role of chance in war and regarded it as a positive factor in his favour brought about by the way he harnessed calculation, planning, time, and activity.

> *War is composed of nothing but accidents, and, although holding to general principles, a general should never lose sight of everything to enable him to profit from these accidents; that is the mark of genius. In war there is but one favourable moment; the great art is to seize it.*[73]

Risk, the gambling brother of chance, was another factor Napoleon broke to his use. He was not afraid to employ calculated risk, especially since his enemies almost never employed it.

> *Every naval expedition we have attempted since I have been at the head of the government has failed, because the admirals see double and have picked up the idea, I don't know where, that you can make war without running risks.*[74] (to Decrés, 12 September 1804)

> *If the art of war consisted merely in not taking risks, glory would be at the mercy of very mediocre talent. The torment of precautions often exceeds the dangers to be avoided. It is sometimes better to abandon one's self to destiny.*[75]

Once the armies were in motion, Napoleon was able to employ another talent, that usually reserved for the first rank of commander, the *coup d'oeil*, that ability described by Suvorov as the 'quick grasp' of the situation.

> *There is a gift of being able to see at a glance the possibilities offered by the terrain ... One can call it the coup d'oeil and it is inborn in great generals.*[76]

> *My great talent, the one that distinguished me the most, is to see the entire picture distinctly.*[77]

> *In war everything is perception – perception about the enemy, perception about one's own soldiers. After a battle is lost, the difference between victor and vanquished is very little; it is, however, incommensurable with perception, for two or three cavalry squadrons are enough to produce a great effect.*[78] (Letter to his brother Joseph, 22 September 1808)

Napoleon always placed the enemy in all his dimensions at the centre of his calculations.

> *An army of lions commanded by a deer will never be an army of lions.*[79]

> *In war one sees one's own troubles and not those of the enemy.*[80] (To Prince Eugène, 30 April 1809)

A general-in-chief should ask himself frequently in the day, What should I do if the enemy's army appeared now in my front, or on my right, or on my left? If he has any difficulty in answering these question he is ill posted, and should seek to remedy it.[81] *... the enemy is welcome to know my forces and positions, provided I know his, and he be ignorant of my plans.*[82] (To his spy shortly before the battle of Marengo, May 1800)

He had a brilliant understanding of the critical nature of military intelligence and actively sought it out.

... the most difficult thing is to discern the enemy's plans, and to detect the truth in all reports one receives: the remainder requires only common sense.[83]

To get information, it is necessary to seize the letters in the postal system, to question travellers. In one word, you have to look for it. Intelligence never comes by itself.[84]

To guess at the intention of the enemy; to divine his opinion of yourself; to hide from him both your intentions and opinion; to mislead him by feigned manoeuvres; to invoke ruses, as well as digested schemes, so as to fight under the best conditions – this is and always has been the art of war.[85]

It is an approved maxim in war, never to do what the enemy wishes you to do, for this reason alone, that he desires it. A field of battle, therefore, which he has previously studied and reconnoitred, should be avoided, and double care should be taken where he has had time to fortify or entrench.[86]

The offensive was Napoleon's preferred form of warfare for it was the only sure way to victory and glory.

In short, I think like Frederick, one should always be the first to attack.[87]

Make war offensively; it is the sole means to become a great captain and to fathom the secrets of the art.[88]

When once the offensive has been assumed, it must be sustained to the last extremity.[89]

Retreat was to be shunned for he understood how it fed upon itself.

A retreat, however skilful the manoeuvres may be, will always produce an injurious morale effect on the army, since by losing the chances of success yourself you throw them into the hands of the enemy.[90]

At the beginning of a campaign, much thought should be given to whether an offensive or defensive strategy is to be adopted. However, once the offensive has started, it must be sustained to the last extremity, for ... retreats are always disastrous. They cost more lives and matériel than the bloodiest battles, with this additional difference, that in a battle the enemy loses approximately as much as you do, while in a retreat you lose and he does not.[91] (Dictation, St. Helena)

In a retreat, besides the honour of the army, the loss of life is often greater than in two battles.[92]

This refusal to surrender the moral ascendancy of the offensive and initiative added to the strength of his forces and subtracted from that of his enemies.

In war, moral factors account for three-quarters of the whole; relative matériel strength accounts for only one-quarter.[93] (27 August 1808)

Marching on Landshut I met Bessières retreating. I ordered him to march forward. He objected that the enemy were in force. Go ahead, said I, and he advanced. The enemy seeing him take the offensive thought he was stronger than they and retreated. In war that is the way everything goes. It is moral force more than numbers that wins victory.[94] (St. Helena, 14 June 1817)

Napoleon's image of 'the commander' was a reflection of himself.

The foremost quality of a commander is to have a cool head, receiving accurate impressions of what is happening without ever getting excited, or dazzled, or intoxicated by good or bad news. The successive or simultaneous sensations that the commander receives during the course of a day are classified in the mind and occupy only as much attention as they deserve, for good sense and judgement flow from the comparison of several sensations taken into equal consideration. There are men who, by their moral and physical composition, distort a picture of everything. No matter how much knowledge, intellect, courage and other good qualities they might have, nature has not called them to command armies or to direct the great operations of war.[95]

A military leader must possess as much character as intellect. Men who have a great deal of intellect and little character are the least suited; they are like a ship whose masts are out of proportion to the ballast; it is preferable to have much character and little intellect. Those men whose intellect is mediocre and whose character is in proportion are likely to succeed in their profession. The base must equal the height.[96] (Dictation, St. Helena)

Napoleon made the concept of assembly of his forces in the area of operations and their concentration of force on the battlefield the backbone of his art.

The army must be kept assembled and the greatest possible force concentrated on the field of battle.[97]

True military art consists of the ability to be stronger than the enemy at the given moment ... Military art is the art of separating for life (feeding off the land) and uniting for battle.[98]

When you have resolved to fight a battle, collect your whole force. Dispense with nothing. A single battalion sometimes decides the day.[99]

I am debouching in Saxony with my whole army in three columns. You lead the right; half a day's march behind you is the corps of Marshal Ney, and one day's march behind you are 10,000 Bavarians; all of which totals more than 50,000 men. Marshal Bernadotte leads the centre; behind him Marshal Davout's corps is marching, with the greater part of the Reserve Cavalry and my Guard; which totals over 70,000 men. [Bernadotte] will debouch through Kronach. The V corps leads my left, and is followed by the corps of Marshal Augereau. They will come through Coburg and Saalfeld, and will make upwards of 40,000 men. The day you reach Hof, the rest of the army will be in line with you. I shall hold myself in general at the centre. With so great a preponderance in numbers, and so closely concentrated, you will realise, that my purpose is not to jump at chances but to attack the enemy,

NAPOLEON EN ROUTE TO ST. HELENA. PRINT AFTER A SKETCH BY COMMISSARY IBBETSON, DRAWN FROM LIFE ABOARD HMS *NORTHUMBERLAND*.

wherever they choose to make a stand, with double their numbers.[100]
(To Marshal Soult at the beginning of the Prussian campaign, 5 October
1806)

Battle, 'the bloody decision', was also an event of dynamic relationships that
he intimately understood and manipulated.

> *In a battle as in a siege, skill consists in converging a mass of fire on a
> single point: once the combat is opened, the commander who is adroit
> will suddenly and unexpectedly open fire with a surprising mass of
> artillery on one of these points, and is sure to seize it.*[101]

> *A battle is a dramatic action which has its beginning, its middle, and
> its conclusion. The result of a battle depends on the instantaneous flash
> of an idea. When you are about to give battle concentrate all your
> strength, neglect nothing; a battalion often decides the day.*[102] (30 July
> 1800)

> *Between a battle lost and a battle won, the distance is immense and
> there stand empires.*[103] (On the eve of the battle of Leipzig, 15 October
> 1813)

> *The issue of a battle is the result of a single instant, a single thought.
> The adversaries come into each other's presence with various combina-
> tions; they mingle; they fight for a length of time; the decisive moment
> appears; a psychological spark makes the decision; and a few reserve
> troops are enough to carry it out.*[104] (Conversation, St. Helena, 4–5
> December 1815)

> *A battle sometimes decides everything; and sometimes the most trifling
> thing decides the fate of a battle.*[105] (Letter to Barry O'Meara, 9
> November 1816)

> *There is a moment in engagements when the least manoeuvre is deci-
> sive and gives the victory; it is the one drop of water that makes the ves-
> sel run over.*[106] (St. Helena, 1820)

> *A battle is a dramatic action which has its beginning, its middle, and its
> end. The battle order of the opposing armies and their preliminary
> manoeuvres until they come to grips form the exposition. The counter-
> manoeuvres of the army which has been attacked constitute the dra-
> matic complication. They lead in turn to new measures and bring about
> the crisis, and from this results the outcome or dénouement.*[107]
> (Dictation, St. Helena)

> *In giving battle a general should regard it as his first duty to maintain
> the honour and glory of his arms. To spare his troops should be but a
> secondary consideration. But the same determination and perseverance*

*which promote the former object are the best means of securing the lat-
ter. In a retreat you lose, in addition to the honour of your arms, more
men than in two battles.*[108]

In the end, even his genius faltered against a united Europe. That genius had
taught his enemies much of the skill they used to pull him down. During the
1813 campaign, he remarked, of the Prussians. 'These animals have learned
something.'[109] (After the battle of Lützen, 2 May 1813) In the end he felt the
presence of fortune depart.

*I sensed that Fortune was abandoning me. I no longer had in me the
feeling of final success. Not to venture is to do nothing when the moment
is right, and one should never venture without being convinced of good
luck.*[110] (St. Helena)

He was, to all intents and purposes, almost buried alive on St. Helena, con-
sumed by his ruin.

*It is a pity that I did not fall at Waterloo, for that would have been a fine
ending. My situation is frightful! I am like a dead man, yet full of life!*[111]
(St. Helena)

*Had I succeeded, I should have died with the reputation of the greatest
man that ever lived.*[112] (St. Helena)

Yet even the faded memory of glory was enough to cloak his opinion of himself, echoing Alexander's words,

*My own assessment of myself is based on the extent not of my life but of
my glory.*[113]

*But with me immortality is the recollection one leaves in the memory of
man. That idea prompts to great actions. It would be better for a man
never to have lived than to leave behind him no traces of his existence.*[114] (Conversation, 1802)

*Many faults, no doubt, will be found in my career; but Arcola ... Rivoli,
the Pyramids, Marengo, Austerlitz, Jena, Friedland – these are granite:
the tooth of envy is powerless here.*[115] (Conversation, St. Helena, 1815)

After his death, a note was found in his hand.

*A new Prometheus, I am nailed to a rock to be gnawed by a vulture. Yes,
I have stolen the fire of Heaven and made a gift of it to France. The fire
has returned to its source, and I am here!*

*The love of glory is like the bridge that Satan built across Chaos to
pass from Hell to Paradise: glory links the past with the future across
a bottomless abyss. Nothing to my son, except my name!*[116]

And what a name! Even his most obdurate foe, the Duke of Wellington, when asked who was the greatest general of the age, replied in awe undimmed by the passage of decades:

'In this age, in past ages, in any age, Napoleon.'[117]

NOTES

1. Bourrienne, L. A. F. de. *Memoirs of Napoleon Bonaparte*, 1891, vol. 1, p. 313. (The author was Napoleon's private secretary and confidant.)
2. Gourgaud, Gaspard. *Sainte-Hélène: Journal inédit de 1815 à 1818*, Paris, nd, vol. I, p. 300; quoted in J. Christopher Herold, ed., *The Mind of Napoleon*, New York, 1955, p. 9.
3. Napoleon, *Correspondance*, No. 15144, vol. XVIII, p. 525.
4. Napoleon, *The Corsican: A Diary of Napoleon's Life in His Own Words*, ed., R. M. Johnston, 1910; r/p as *Napoleon: The Diaries*, The Great Commander series, New York, 1994, p. 76.
5. Johnston, *op. cit.*
6. Ibid., p. 162.
7. Ibid., p. 260.
8. Las Cases, comte de. *Memoirs of the Life, Exile and Conversations of the Emperor Napoleon*, London, 1836, vol. II, p. 349.
9. Roederer, P.-L. *Autour de Bonaparte: Journal de comte P.-L. Roederer*, Paris, 1909, quoted in Herold, *op. cit.*, p. 203.
10. Johnston, *op. cit.*, p. 255.
11. Napoleon, 1803, conversation. Théodore Iung, *Lucien Bonaparte et ses Mémoires, 1775-1840*, Paris, 1882-3), vol. II, p. 162, quoted in Herold, *op. cit.*, p. 219.
12. Johnston, *op. cit.*, p. 76.
13. Spengler, Oswald. *Decline of the West*, 1925, vol. I, p. 93.
14. Bourrienne, *op. cit.*, vol. I, p. 314.
15. Johnston, *op. cit.*, p. 88.
16. Ibid., p. 32.
17. Ibid., p. 35.
18. Ibid., p. 59.
19. *Correspondance*, vol. XXXII, p. 379.
20. Bourrienne, *op. cit.*, vol. I, p. 135.
21. Johnston, *op. cit.*, p. 55.
22. Roederer, *op. cit.*
23. Lecestre, Léon. *Lettres inédites de Napoléon Ier*, Paris, 1898, vol. I, p. 389, quoted in Herold, *op. cit.*, p. 40.
24. Ségur, Plilippe, comte de. *Un aide-de-camp de Napoléon: Mémoires de comte de Ségur*, Paris, 1894-5, vol. I, p. 249, quoted in Herold, *op. cit.*, p. 36.
25. Alexander the Great, in India when the Macedonians refused to go on. Arrian, *The Campaigns of Alexander*, tr. de Sélincourt, Harmondsworth, 1987, p. 26 .
26. Johnston, *op. cit.*, p. 130.
27. *Correspondance*, vol. X, p. 69, quoted in Herold, *op. cit.*, p. 220.
28. Chaptal, J. A. *Mes Souvenirs sur Napoléon*, Paris, 1893, p. 296, quoted in Herold, *op. cit.*, p. 215.
29. Lévy, A. *The Private Life of Napoleon*, London, 1894, vol. II, p. 293, quoted in Chandler, *The Campaigns of Napoleon*, New York. 1966, p. 155.
30. Johnston, *op. cit.*, p. 85.

31. Ibid., p. 114.
32. O'Meara, Barry. *Napoleon in Exile; or, A Voice from St. Helena*, Philadelphia, 1822, vol. I, pp. 129-30, quoted in Herold, *op. cit.*, p. 212.
33. Johnston, *op. cit.*, p. 259.
34. *Correspondance*, vol. VI, p. 178, quoted in Herold, *op. cit.*, p. 214.
35. Bourrienne, *op. cit.*, vol. II, pp. 356-7.
36. Chandler, *op. cit.*, p. 56.
37. *The Principles of Combined Arms Battle*, Moscow, 1992.
38. *Correspondance*, vol. XXXI, p. 347, quoted in Herold, op. cit., p. 224.
39. Napoleon. *The Military Maxims of Napoleon*, ed. Burnod, 1827.
40. *Correspondance*, vol. XXXI, p. 365, quoted in Herold, *op. cit.*, p. 223.
41. Ibid., p. 429, quoted in Herold, *op. cit.*, p. 219.
42. Gourgaud, G. (ed.). *Talks of Napoleon at St. Helena*, London, 1904, p. 215.
43. *Correspondance*, vol. XXXI, p. 365, quoted in Herold, *op. cit.*, p. 223.
44. Ibid., vol. X, p. 69, quoted in Herold, *op. cit.*, p. 220.
45. Napoleon, *Maxims of War*, 1831, quoted in Robert Heinl, *Dictionary of Military and Naval Quotations*, Annapolis, 1966, p. 247.
46. Ibid.
47. *Correspondance*, No. 209, vol. XXXII, p. 209.
48. Berthezène, E. F. *Souvenirs militaires*, Paris, 1855, quoted in Chandler, *op. cit.*, p. 141.
49. *Military Review*, September 1980, p. 69.
50. Carlton, James. *The Military Quotation Book*, New York, 1991, p. 71.
51. Johnston, *op. cit.*, p. 89.
52. Fuller, Major-General J. F. C. *Lectures on F. S. R. II*, London, 1931, p. xiii.
53. Burne, Alfred, *The Art of War on Land*, Harrisburg, 1947, p. 7.
54. Martel, Tancrède. *Napoleon Bonaparte*, Paris, 1888, vol. IV, p. 97, quoted in Herold, *op. cit.*, p. 45.
55. Sargent, H. *Napoleon Bonaparte's First Campaign*, London, 1895, p. 16, quoted in Chandler, *op. cit.*, p. 146.
56. Rémusat, Madame de. *Memoirs 1802-08*, London, 1895, p. 135, quoted in Chandler, *op. cit.*, p. 146.
57. Napoleon, 27 April 1800, Johnston, *op. cit.*, p. 68.
58. *Correspondance*, No. 13652, vol. XVI, p. 418.
59. Heinl, *op. cit.*, p. 240.
60. *Correspondance*, No. 10672, vol. XIII, p. 87.
61. Johnston, *op. cit.*, p. 38.
62. Chandler, David (ed.). *The Military Maxims of Napoleon*, New York, 1988, p. 58.
63. *Correspondance*, No. 140707, vol. XVIII, p. 218, quoted in Chandler, *Campaigns*, p. 149.
64. Ibid.
65. *Correspondance*, No. 4689, vol. VI.
66. Johnston, *op. cit.*, p. 89.
67. *Correspondance*, No. 9997, vol. XII, p. 204.
68. Liddell Hart, B, H, *Strategy*, New York, 1954, p. 119.
69. Johnston, *op. cit.*, p. 163.
70. Ibid., p. 142.
71. Burnod, *op. cit.*
72. Johnston, *op. cit.*, pp. 127-8.
73. Burnod, *op. cit.*
74. Johnston, *op. cit.*, p. 100.

75. Napoleon, *Maxims*, 1804-15.
76. Napoleon, *Mémoires*, quoted in Heinl, *op. cit.*, p. 70.
77. Gourgaud, *op. cit.*, vol. II, p. 460.
78. *Correspondance*, No. 14343, vol. XVII, p. 526.
79. *Correspondance*, vol. XXX, p. 176.
80. *Correspondance*, No. 15144, vol. XVIII, p. 525.
81. Chandler, *Military Maxims*, p. 58.
82. Bourrienne, *op. cit.*, vol. II, p. 7.
83. Watson, S. J. *By Command of the Emperor, A Life of Marshal Berthier*, London, 1957, p. 107.
84. Chuquet, Arthur (ed.). *Inédits Napoléoniens*, Paris, 1913, p. 266.
85. Fuller, Major-General J. F. C. *Memoirs of an Unconventional Soldier*, London, 1936, p. 272.
86. Chandler, *Military Maxims*, p. 61.
87. Fuller, Major-General J. F. C. *The Generalship of Alexander the Great*, New York, 1960, p. 297.
88. *Correspondance*, vol. XXXI, p. 209, quoted in Chandler, *Campaigns*, p. 145.
89. Heinl, *op. cit.*, p. 219.
90. Burnod, *op. cit.*
91. *Correspondance*, vol. XXXII, pp. 209-10, quoted in Herold, *op. cit.*, p. 216.
92. Heinl, *op. cit.*
93. *Correspondance*, vol. XVII, p. 472, quoted in Herold, *op. cit.*, p. 219.
94. Johnston, *op. cit.*, pp. 260--1.
95. *Correspondance*, vol. XXXII, pp. 182-3.
96. *Correspondance*, vol. XXX, p. 266, quoted in Herold, *op. cit.*, p. 220.
97. *Correspondance*, vol. XXXI, p. 418.
98. Savkin, V. Ye. *Basic Principles of Operational Art and Tactics*, Moscow, 1972.
99.   Chandler, *Military Maxims*, p. 64.
100. Johnston, *op. cit.*, p. 126.
101. Phillips, Thomas R. (ed.). *The Roots of Strategy* , Harrisburg, 1940, p. 435.
102. Johnston, *op. cit.*, p. 76.
103. Napoleon, Heinl, *op. cit.*, p. 26.
104. Las Cases, *Mémorial*, quoted in Herold, *op. cit.*, pp. 222-3.
105. Heinl, *op. cit.*, p. 26.
106. *Correspondance*, vol. XXXII, p. 82.
107. Martel, *op. cit.*, vol. IV, p. 53, quoted in Herold, *op. cit.*, p. 203.
108. Burnod, *op. cit.*
109. *Correspondance*, No. 21231, vol. XXVII, pp. 150-1.
110. Lachouque, Henry. *Waterloo*, London, 1972, p. 201.
111. Kircheisen, F. M. *The Memoirs of Napoleon I*, New York, 1929, p. 224..
112. O'Meara, *op. cit.*
113. Curtius, *The History of Alexander*, Harmondsworth, 1984, p. 226.
114. Bourrienne, *op. cit.*, vol. II, p. 77.
115. Martel, *op. cit.*, vol. IV, p. 501, quoted in Herold, *op. cit.*, p. 274.
116. Norvin, Jacques. *Histoire de Napoléon*, Paris, 1827-8, p. 501, quoted in Herold, *op. cit.*, p. 281.
117. Stevens, Joan. *Victorian Faces*, Jersey, 1969, p. 99, quoted in Longford, *Wellington: Pillar of State*, New York, 1972, p. 413.. Napoleon, *Correspondence*, No. 209, Vol. XXXII, p. 209.. Napoleon, *Correspondence*, No. 9997, Vol. XII, p. 204.. Fuller, *Memoirs of an Unconventional Soldier*, (London: 1936, p. 272.. Johnston, ibid., p. 76.

POSTSCRIPT
Philip J. Haythornthwaite

N APOLEON'S PLACE IN HISTORY IS ASSURED; THAT HE BESTRODE his age like a colossus is shown by the fact that the period in which he lived bears his name – Napoleonic. The terms 'Marlburian' or 'Frederickian' may be used in connection with military affairs, 'Nelsonian' is descriptive of naval; 'Alexandrian' may relate to the place or its school of philosophy as much as to Alexander himself; 'Augustan' may refer equally to any perceived 'golden age' as to the period of Augustus. No such limits or ambivalence attaches to the Napoleonic era: the term clearly defines the period during which Europe's most influential, most respected personality, by some the most adored, by others most feared and reviled, was the sometime Corsican captain of artillery, Napoleon I, Emperor of the French, King of Italy.

It is hardly surprising that a personality of such importance had produced so many divergent views of his merits and character. His entire career was almost the stuff of legend: a meteoric rise from obscurity, the assumption of supreme power, the triumphs, the fall, and the final, tragic years of exile. No change in circumstances could have been more complete, or more illustrative of the veracity of Napoleon's own remark, that from the sublime to the ridiculous was but a step. As a British rhyme of 1814 had it, even before Napoleon's final incarceration,

'He who gave, t'other day,
Whole kingdoms away,
Now is glad to get *Elba-Room*.'[1]

During the sad, final years on St. Helena Napoleon was once observed reading an English edition of Aesop's *Fables*, in which '... the sick lion, after submitting with fortitude to the insults of the many animals who came to exult over his fallen greatness, at last received a kick in the face from the ass. "I could have borne everything but this," the lion said. Napoleon showed the wood-cut, and added, "It is me and your Governor."'[2] Frequently he remarked that it would have been preferable to have fallen in battle, at Moscow, or Borodino, or Dresden, or Waterloo. Had he been killed at Moscow, he said, he would have enjoyed a reputation as a conqueror without parallel in history; at Borodino and he would have died like

Alexander; at Waterloo, and he would have been assured of the love and regret of his people.

Perhaps these assessments are correct; but the poignancy of his death, almost alone, exiled in one of the remotest outposts of civilisation, insulted and derided like Aesop's lion, was surely a powerful element in the legend which arose after his death. The adulation which was accorded to Napoleon, by the army during his rise to power, and by most of his subjects during his exercise of it, is unquestioned. The near-deification he experienced from his troops was quite remarkable, and was the reason why countless of his followers, far from home and having fallen in a cause not their own and probably barely understood, used their last breath on earth to raise the cry '*Vive l'Empereur!*' as he passed the dying on his way across the battlefield; and engendered the sort of respect after his death which led a faithful follower to order that when his own time came, he should be buried upright, facing a statue of Napoleon, so that he might keep guard over his Emperor for all eternity. Few indeed have been so fortunate to have been the recipients of such devotion.

The conventional view of Napoleon, by his admirers, is perhaps reflected accurately by the following introduction to an early biography, written a few years after his death:

'Lastingly exalted, is the name of Napoleon! Wherever arms shall flourish, or greatness be duly appreciated; there shall Napoleon Bonaparte be held up for high and honourable estimation. Generations yet unborn shall swell the trumpet of his fame; and "squint eyed prejudice" stand blinded in the effulgence of his glory.

'When the sword of Alexander overthrew the throne of Cyrus, and subjugated the east as far as the Indies, it was the civilisation of Athens that rose under his name ... When Caesar subjugated Parthia and Germany, and planted the Roman eagle from the summit of the Caucasus, to the hills of Caledonia ... he propagated under the protection of his personal glory, the name, the language, and manners of civilised Rome ... Of all these mighty conquerors, Napoleon stands second to none. If Alexander carried with him the age of Pericles, and Caesar that of Augustus, if they were accompanied, the one and the other in their triumphs, by the genius of Homer and of Sophocles, of Plato and Aristotle, of Virgil and Horace; Napoleon carried with him an age that the arts, sciences and philosophy have rendered equally illustrious; and his enterprise is no less than that of his predecessors.

'This is the man, whom a little aristocracy wish to denounce as an odious despot and an insatiable conqueror. But in the breasts of the Artisan, the labourer, and the soldier, he is still cherished as the "Man of the people", as the personification of that spirit of equality which pervaded both his administration and the camp, and which to this day pervades the whole European Society. This is the man whose name is religiously respected by the peasant in his cottage ...'[3]

There were even those who were unwilling to believe that Napoleon *was* gone forever. In the late 1830s a Parisian theatre presented a burlesque in which an actor, in the guise of an old soldier, purported by means of a rambling and humorous monologue to give 'The Life of Napoleon in a Quarter of an Hour'; it ended: 'they have come actually to say that Napoleon is dead! ... He dead! Never! He knows better: he is incapable of it; he feigns to be dead – that's all. But he is digging, digging, digging, and one fine morning he will jump out of his hole, with his little three-cornered hat, his hands behind his back ...'[4] It was, perhaps, the articulation of the wish of many who remembered the days of the Empire, and who reflected upon what had replaced it.

Conversely, while adored by his own supporters, Napoleon was more hated and criticised by his enemies than any foe had been for centuries. In Britain – perhaps his most intractable enemy throughout the entire span of his career – this criticism ranged from the vicious and vituperative to the humorous, the latter perhaps demonstrating the level of danger and menace with which he was viewed, a reaction being that a monstrous threat was best diffused by poking fun at it. (It is a significant reflection upon the legacy of the danger posed by Napoleon that a study of the British propaganda reaction to the Napoleonic threat was published at a time when an even greater menace cast threatening glances from across the English Channel: in *We Laughed at Boney, or, We've Been Through it all Before* (J. Werner, London, 1943), both the author's text and the book's introduction by Vera Brittain made a direct comparison between the dangers of invasion by Napoleon and by Adolf Hitler, using the Napoleonic threat to comment upon that existing at the time.)

Critics of Napoleon in his own time used no such subtle devices, as every imprecation and libel imaginable were heaped upon him:

'Insatiate fiend! whom slaughter never tires,
    Whose craft can smother fury's wildest fires ...';[5]
'Some say th' infernal Monster's eyes turn blue,
    Predictive of the mis'ries which ensue ...'[6]

Such was the dislike – and perhaps dread – engendered among his enemies that a clergyman of Skipton could wish 'with perhaps more zeal than humanity' that if Napoleon were not assassinated, he might be devoured by crocodiles.[7] In 1803 George Briton's Warning Voice ... with a true but short History of Bonaparte was reviewed as depicting 'the "foul fiend" who is here painted in his proper colours of Atheism, Blasphemy, Treachery, and Murder'.[8] Others went beyond the ordinary line of insult: in 1804 Q. Mayer's Hint to England included 'proving that Bonaparte [is] the Beast that rose out of the Earth, with Two Horns like a Lamb, and spake as a Dragon, whose Number is 666, Rev. xiii'.[9] (In 1806 another writer 'confirmed' the connection by remarking on the similarity between the name 'Napoleon' and that of the king of the locusts, 'the angel of the bottomless pit, whose name in the Hebrew tongue is Abaddon, but in the Greek tongue hath his name Apollyon' (Rev. 9, 11)![10]

Such vitriol was not even quelled by Napoleon's defeat:

'The Tyrant's downfall is the world's release,
    And panting Europe breathes once more in Peace! ...
Stript of his gaudy plumes by flattery dress'd,
    The odious, low-born Tyrant stands confess'd! ...
Strange! that we find in these capricious times,
    Some who excuse the Tyrant and his crimes;
Who call a wretch all nations ought to hate,
    That which is Virtue's bright reward – the Great!'[11]

Opinions among those who had closer acquaintance with the military events occasioned by Napoleon's career were often more balanced, although their praise generally concentrated on his martial prowess rather than his character or other aspects of his rule. In exile on St. Helena, for example, he discovered little but respect and good wishes from the ordinary British soldiers and sailors whom he encountered; as one asked to be conveyed to Napoleon by a translator, 'I wish him no harm, but all possible happiness. So do most of us. Long life and health to him.'[12] (It is true that such respect is easily accorded to a beaten foe who no longer presents a threat, but even at the height of the Napoleonic Wars there were those who acknowledged their admiration for Napoleon's military talents, even though they might make all exertions to hasten his defeat.) Perhaps typical of the separation of the admiration of Napoleon the soldier from dislike of Napoleon the politician and statesman is the opinion held of him by the Duke of Wellington. He frequently referred to him as 'Jonathan Wild the Great',[13] a humorous reference to the criminal of that name, an organiser of robberies and receiver of stolen property who was hanged at Tyburn in 1725; as the Duke observed, 'Napoleon was the first man of his day on a field of battle, and with French troops. I confine myself to that. His policy was mere bullying, and, military matters apart, he was a Jonathan Wild.'[14]

Not all of Napoleon's subjects were well-disposed towards him, especially when the period of unqualified military success was ended, and not just the irreconcilable royalists or those who resented the replacement of the system which arose out of the French Revolution by the Empire. His demise was greeted with joy by some: the Revd. Weeden Butler recounted how he met a French friend, the Baron d'Ordre, whom he had not seen since the latter's family had returned from exile to France a dozen years earlier: 'Language is inadequate to express the affecting appearance he made ... "We are *free*, Mr. Butler, we are all truly *free*, at last, my dear Sir! Oh! What happiness, what joy, what pleasure! ..."[15]

Perhaps, in Thomas Campbell's words, distance had lent enchantment, or the experiences of what followed Napoleon's fall dispelled most of those sentiments, so that by the time his body was returned to France in 1840 (and encouraged by the then monarchy which hoped to harness the Napoleonic memories in its own interest), the Napoleonic legend was immovably fixed, with his reputation in that country restored to a position of reverence. Even this aroused criticism from some of those who had been his enemies; the following comments on Napoleon's popularity in the 1840s articulate opinions perhaps not uncommon in some other countries:

'In France, besides the various public monuments to Napoleon and his victories, there is not a house without a statue or a bust of him, and his likeness stares at one from every plate and dish, every wash-hand basin and **** ... The Napoleonism of France is to me utterly unintelligible. To see a proud nation bowing down to worship a Corsican, who only made their military a tool for his own elevation and that of his family – who, after shedding the blood of her sons profusely in a hundred battles, and receiving proofs of fidelity which would have called forth gratitude from any less selfish heart – treated her with a scorn and contumely unknown to her most despotic princes ... And when his ambition had been gratified to the utmost by the efforts of his troops, repaid their devotion by leading them to slaughter; and, in return for his own elevation, worked the ruin and humiliation of his country. Yet this is the man to whom France awards an Apotheosis. Alas! poor human nature!'[16]

The Napoleonic legend – if it can be so called – was fuelled by an increasing production of books concerning the Emperor and his campaigns, which had begun even before his final defeat, and which has continued to the present day. The Napoleon of legend, whose reputation brooks no criticism, might perhaps be regarded as likely to obscure the merits and achievements of the historical Napoleon. In the final analysis, his personal career was a failure: for all his achievements and successes, he established no ruling dynasty in France even though when he first assumed power the conditions were suitable for such an establishment; as Sir John Seeley commented, 'such an object was easily within his reach, if only he could stoop to pick up a crown. He did stoop, he picked up the crown, but it dropped from his hands again.'[17] That the crown fell was probably largely the result of Napoleon's military and political miscalculations in the later stages of his reign, which somewhat detracted from the great successes of his earlier career. Certainly the circumstances were auspicious when he came to prominence, but these should not devalue his achievement, for he used those circumstances to the greatest advantage. The state which evolved did not exactly embody the revolutionary principles of liberty, equality and fraternity, but something different, more Napoleon's own creation, but something which it proved impossible to sustain.

Napoleon's foreign and military policy was the cause of his failure; it could have been the reason for his success. Wars of aggression, even if to some extent the result of economic necessity, served only to alienate other states which might, under different conditions, have posed no threat to France; it might be said that it was as if Napoleon preferred to compel states into alliance with France by virtue of conquest rather than to arrange these by more pacific diplomacy. If the external policy tended to alienate other European states, the demands placed on France by years of warfare, including the increasingly unpopular conscription, tended to alienate even some of his own people. (Napoleon was aware of the potential for the changeability of public sentiment: 'The crowd which follows me with admiration, would run with the same eagerness were I marching to the Guillotine.')[18]

To view Napoleon in purely military-political terms is to ignore a great part of his legacy, for it could be said that much of modern France, at least its institutions, evolved from the earlier part of his reign; indeed, nothing so remarks this fact than the very name of the system of civil law, the *Code Napoléon*. This was drawn up under his aegis, but at its original institution on 31 March 1804 it was entitled '*Code civil des français*', and only received the name 'Code Napoléon' in September 1807; it reverted to its former name in 1818, and 'Code Napoléon' was only restored in March 1852. Like a range of other institutions which date from this period, Napoleon's personal contribution was probably minor, and it might be said that they evolved at this time not so much from the personal enlightenment of the head of state as from the fact that the vacuum caused by the revolutionary upheavals *had* to be filled. Had he never achieved supreme authority, something similar in all these cases would probably still have been established, perhaps in a different form and perhaps not so thoroughly. The reform of both military and governmental administrations had their genesis in the revolutionary period, and while benefiting from Napoleon's energy and personal contributions, the existing work would probably have been carried forward even under a different head of state.

Napoleon's influence spread throughout Europe, and not only in the immediate and most obvious way, at the point of the bayonet and with the cost of countless thousands of lives. The creation of a sense of national identity in Germany and Italy – which led ultimately to the unification of those states – and elsewhere, as in Spain, owes a debt to the period of Napoleon, although their regeneration arose primarily from resistance against him. In Italy and parts of Germany, French rule introduced enlightened reforms which were largely beneficial, and although these arose more from the tenets of the revolutionary period than originating under the empire, it was nevertheless the case that they *were* introduced under Napoleon's regime. It has been stated that all such reforms, both inside France and elsewhere, would have been likely to have continued and expanded as a result of the liberal climate arising from the French Revolution, irrespective of who had assumed supreme power, and probably they would; but it is worth remarking that it was under Napoleon's hand that they *did* happen, and it would be as misleading not to recognise that fact and to deny him a contribution as it would to accord him sole credit for all the beneficence which occurred during his reign. Whether under another leader, perhaps a Moreau, they would have been accompanied by so many years of war and so much bloodshed is an insoluble question.

What else now remains of Napoleon's legacy, beyond the Napoleonic legend and an immovable place in history? On a more personal level, there is his reputation, but little else of a concrete nature as might have been had he succeeded in establishing a Bonaparte dynasty. (The reign of his nephew Napoleon III, and the Second Empire, while owing much to the Napoleonic legend, was hardly a direct perpetuation of a Bonaparte inheritance.) As Sir John Seeley remarked of the personal legacy of the first Napoleon, as different from his wider influence, 'All that he built at such a cost of blood and tears, was swept away before he himself ended his short life';[19] or that life would not have ended in exile.

At the very beginning of his book *Napoleon: the Last Phase*, Lord Rosebery posed the question, 'Will there ever be an adequate life of Napoleon?'[20] Prior to that date – his work was published some seventy-nine years after Napoleon's death – Rosebery believed that the period was not sufficiently distant for an objective conclusion to be reached. Others of his qualifications still remain valid: that so varied were Napoleon's talents and achievements that a comprehensive assessment would be too great a task for any one man, but would require experts in each field to assess his career as a general, statesman, administrator and legislator, and not least as a man. Similarly, and after a vast increase in the literature since Rosebery's time, it is impossible to arrive at a conclusive 'final verdict'. As Napoleon in past generations, and even in his own time, gave rise to every conceivable assessment or shade of opinion, from the creator of a golden age of enlightenment and triumph to a ruthless and aggressive tyranny, so he does to this day, and probably will in the future. It may be expected that Napoleon will be as studied during the series of 200th anniversaries of the great events of his career as he has been to date, but a unanimous verdict will surely be as elusive as it has been in the past. Greatest of soldiers, charismatic leader, national icon, visionary architect of modern Europe, flawed genius undone by his own miscalculations and betrayed by those he had raised up, ruthless opportunist, tyrant: the opinions are as many as there were facets to his personality and abilities. Each individual who studies the man and his career can produce a 'final verdict' of his own, conclusions probably as diverse as those prevalent during his lifetime. The fact that such differences of assessment exist is itself testimony to the complexities of the man and the emotions he engendered, and, surely, a mark of his unique place in history.

NOTES

1. 'Impromptu on reading Buonaparte's Abdication of the Throne', by 'J. M. E.', in *The Gentleman's Magazine*, April 1814, p. 376.
2. *Recollections of the Emperor Napoleon on the Island of St. Helena*, Mrs. Abell, ed. Mrs. C. Johnstone, London, 1873, p. 257.
3. *History of Napoleon*, P. M. Laurent de l'Ardeche, London, 1840, pp. 3-4.
4. *Chambers' Edinburgh Journal*, 29 December 1849, pp. 414-15.
5. 'To Buonaparte, on the late Victory' (i.e., Salamanca), by 'Bristoliensis', in *The*

Gentleman's Magazine, October 1812, p. 367.

6. 'Buonaparte's Eyes', anon., in ibid., February 1810, p. 160.
7. *Morning Chronicle*, 18 January 1799.
8. *The Gentleman's Magazine*, September 1803, p. 842.
9. Ibid., April 1804, p. 333.
10. Ibid., August 1806, p. 696.
11. 'The Tyrant's Downfall', W. T. Fitz-Gerald (an address for the anniversary of the Literary Fund, 5 May 1814), in ibid., May 1814, pp. 486-7.
12. Las Cases, comte de. *Memoirs of the Life, Exile and Conversations of the Emperor Napoleon*, London 1836, vol. I, p. 310.
13. *Words on Wellington*, Sir William Fraser, Bt., London 1889, p. 201.
14. *Personal Reminiscences of the Duke of Wellington*, Francis, Earl of Ellesmere, ed. Alice, Countess of Strafford, London, 1904, p. l00.
15. The *Gentleman's Magazine*, May 1814, p. 447.
16. 'England and the French Press' by 'E. W.', in *United Service Magazine*, 1842, vol. I, p. 108.
17. Seeley, Sir John. *A Short History of Napoleon the First*, London, 1895, p. 301.
18. Liancourt, G. de. *Political Aphorisms, Moral and Philosophical Thoughts of the Emperor Napoleon*, ed. J. A. Manning, London, 1848, p. 36.
19. Seeley, *op. cit.*, p. 322.
20. Rosebery, Lord. *Napoleon: The Last Phase*, London, 1900, p. 1.

INDEX

Abensberg, 73
Aboukir Bay, 37
Aboukir, 38
Acre, 38, 220
Actaeon, HMS, 207
Adam, Major-General Frederick, 184
Aderklaa, 80
Aesop, 305
Aix, Isle d', 192
Ajaccio, 13
Alba de Tormes, 101
Alexander I, Tsar of Russia, 50-1, 106, 112-15, 120-1, 125-6, 139, 221, 238, 275, 278
Alexander the Great, 37, 213, 288, 301, 305, 306
Alexandria, 38
Ali, mameluke servant, 169, 171
Alle, River, 70, 71
Alps, 42, 43
Amberg, 58
America, 85
Amiens, Peace of, 45
Andalusia, 96, 97, 101, 103, 104, 106, 108
Angleterre, Armée d', 45
Ansbach, 50, 55
Antibes, 151, 156
Antibes, Château d', 27
Antommarchi, Dr, 200-1, 206, 208
Apolda, 61, 63
Aragon, 96
Arakcheev, Alexei, 275
Aranjuez, 89, 91
Arbuthnot, Charles, 182
Arcis-sur-Aube, 140, 238
Arcola, 26, 34, 220
Armstrong, John, 241
Artillery, 254-6
Artillery, French, 19
Artillery, School of, at Auxonne, 20
Artois, Charles Philippe, comte d' (later Charles X, King of France), 154, 204
Aspern-Essling, 9, 74-8, 80-1, 233, 239, 273
Aubry, former War Minister, 29
Auerstädt, 64-5, 83, 85, 254, 276
Augereau, Marshal Pierre François Charles, duc de

Castiglione, 59, 61, 63, 66-9, 81, 116, 150, 154, 213, 216-17
Austerlitz, 51-4, 56, 64-5, 71, 80, 83, 123, 188, 220, 222, 235, 244, 252, 264, 267, 272, 275, 277
Austria and Austrian forces: defeated in First Italian campaign, 33-6; forced to make peace at Campo Formio, 36; as part of Second Coalition, 45; defeated at Marengo and Hohenlinden, 45; as part of Third Coalition, 45; army surrenders at Ulm, 47-9; defeated at Austerlitz, 50-5; make peace with Napoleon, 55; rebuild army and threaten war, 73; defeated at Abensberg, 73; defeated at Aggmühl, 74; Vienna captured by French, 74; defeat Napoleon at Aspern-Essling, 75-8; defeated at Wagram, 78-81; participation in 1812 invasion of Russia, 116, 119, 121; lukewarm support for Napoleon, 121; change sides for 1813 campaign, 135; campaign to expel Napoleon from Germany, 137; defeated at Dresden, 137; defeat Napoleon at Leipzig, 137-9; cross Rhine, 139; defeated at Montereau, 139; defeat Macdonald at Bar-sur-Aube, 140; repulse Napoleon at Arcis-sur-Aube, 140; defeat French at La Fère-Champenoise, 140; enter Paris, 140; mobilise against Napoleon after his return from Elba, 161
Autun, 15
Auxerre, 156
Auxonne, 20, 22, 248
Avesnes, 165
Avignon, 22

Bachelu, Lieutenant-General, 184
Bacler d'Albe, General Louis Albert G., baron, 226, 228, 229

Badajoz, 261-2
Bagration, Prince Peter, 55, 117, 118, 121, 123, 124
Bailén, 97, 99, 108
Balcombe Collection, 207
Balcombe, Betsy, 195
Balcombe, William, 195
Bamberg, 58
Bank of France, 41
Bar-sur-Aube, 140
Barcelona, 88
Barclay de Tolly, Field Marshal Prince Mikhail, 117-18, 121, 123, 275
Barnard, Sir Andrew, 270
Barras, Paul, 24-6, 29-32
Barrosa, 250, 280
Bastille, 24, 27
bataillon carré, 58, 265-6
Bautzen, 135, 279
Bavaria, 45, 47, 73
Bayonne, 92-5, 99
Bayonnette, Carabinier Corporal, 221
Beaucaire, Le Souper de, 22-3, 25
Beauharnais, Alexandre de, 31
Beauharnais, Eugène-Rose de, *see* Eugène, Viceroy of Italy
Beauharnais, Hortense de, 38
Beauharnais, Josephine de, *see* Josephine, Empress
Beaulieu, General Johann Peter, baron, 33
Beaumont, 165
Befreiungskriege (War of Liberation), 135
Bellerophon, HMS, 192, 194, 214
Bennigsen, General Levin, count, 50, 66-7, 69, 71
Berezina, River, 129-30, 239, 268
Bernadotte, Marshal Jean-Baptiste Jules, Prince of Ponte Corvo (later King Charles XIV of Sweden), 50-2, 55, 59, 61, 63-4, 66, 113, 137, 139-40, 218-19
Berthier, Marshal Louis-Alexandre, prince de Neuchâtel et de Wagram, 33, 61, 73, 101, 164, 217, 223-4, 226, 229, 232, 242, 263
Bertrand, 150, 155, 197, 208, 217, 233, 263

INDEX

Bessières, Marshal Jean-
Baptiste, duc d'Istrie, 96
Bijlandt, Major-General van, 181
Billarderie, General Count
Flahout de la, 182
Biscay, 88
Black Forest, 48
Blücher, Field Marshal Gebhard
Leberecht von, Prince of
Wahlstadt, 10, 137, 139-40,
161, 163, 167-74, 179, 183-4,
186-8, 192, 269
Bois de Paris, 183
Bolton, Captain Samuel, 179
Bonaparte, Carlo, 13-16
Bonaparte, Jérôme, see Jérôme,
King of Westphalia
Bonaparte, Joseph, see Joseph I,
King of Naples, then King of
Spain
Bonaparte, Letizia, 13-15, 17,
192
Bonaparte, Louis, later King of
Holland, 33, 90, 92
Bonaparte, Lucien, 22-3, 39, 88
Bonaparte, Pauline, Princess
Borghese, 23
Borodino, 111, 122-4, 126, 254,
305
Boulogne, 216
Bourgogne, Sergeant Adrien,
259
Bourienne, Louis Antoine
Fauvelet de, 232
Bourmont, Lieutenant-General
Louis August Victor de, 167
Braine-l'Alleud, 175
Bras d'Or, 152
Brazil, 86
Brienne, 15, 18, 139
Brinvilliers, de, 205
Britain and British forces: at
Toulon, 23, 25-7; occupation
of Corsica, 28; Royal Navy
destroys Napoleon's Egyptian
expeditionary fleet at Aboukir
Bay, 37; participate in Third
Coalition, 45; threatened by
French invasion, 45-7; defeat
French and Spanish fleets at
Trafalgar, 65, 85; participate
in Fourth Coalition, 57; expe-
ditionary force defeats French
in Portugal, 98; expeditionary
force enters Spain, 100;
retreat to Corunna, 100-1;
repulse French from lines of
Torres Vedras, 104;
Wellington takes Ciudad
Rodrigo, 105; forced to pull
back to Portugal, 107; invade
France, 108; achieve alliance
with Russia, 113; transport
Napoleon to Elba, 148; mobilize aganst Napoleon after his
return from Elba; dispositions,
161-4; action at Quatre Bras,

168; deal Napoleon his final
defeat at Waterloo, 171-88;
accept his surrender, 192-3;
debate fate of the ex-Emperor,
193-5; transport him to St.
Helena, 195; administration of
Napoleon's captivity on St.
Helena, 197-208
Brittain, Vera, 307
Broglie, Marshal Victor François,
duc de, 257
Brumaire, coup d'état de, 38
Brune, Marshal Guillaume Marie
Anne, 191, 217, 234
Brünn, 50-2
Brunswick, General William
Frederick, Duke of, 57, 59, 62
Brussels, 161, 164, 167-9,
172-3, 175, 177, 184
Brye, 169
Bülow, General Frederick
William von, Count
Dennewitz, 168
Bureau Typographique, 29
Burgundy, 155
Busaco, 280
Butler, Revd. Weeden, 309
Buxhowden, Field Marshal
Friedrich Wilhelm, 50

Cadiz, 95, 100, 103
Caesar, Caius Julius, 18, 150
Cairo, 38, 239
Cambronne, General Pierre
Jacques Etienne, vicomte,
151-2
Campbell, Colonel Sir Neil, 149
Campo Formio, Peace of, 36,
272
Cannes, 153
Carnot, General Lazare, 247
Caroline, 150
Carteaux, General Jean François,
24
Casa Bonaparte, 197
Castellane, 152
Castiglione, 217, 220-1
Castile, 88
Catalonia, 88, 96, 104, 106, 258
Catherine II (the Great),
Empress of Russia, 274
Caulaincourt, General Armand-
Auguste-Louis, duc de
Vincenne, 124, 147, 171, 182,
228-9
Ceva, 33
Châlon-sur-Saône, 155
Champagny, Jean-Baptiste de
Nompère de, duc de Cadore,
93
Campaigns: Italian, first, 33-6;
Egyptian, 37-8; Italian, sec-
ond, 43; Ulm-Austerlitz,
45-55; Jena-Auerstädt, 57-64;
Eylau-Friedland, 65-71;
Peninsular War, 73, 83-110,
239, 245, 253; Aspern-

Essling-Wagram, 73-81;
Moscow, 111-34; Germany
(1813), 134-9; France (1814),
139-40, 143-7; Waterloo,
161-88, 269
Champaubert, 139
Champollion, Jean-François, 37
Chandler, Dr David G., 188, 233,
224
Channel, English, 45, 47, 216
Charles IV, King of Spain, 85,
87, 89, 90-4, 103
Charles, Field Marshal Archduke
of Austria, Duke of Teschen,
47, 50-1, 72-3, 75, 77-80,
272, 274
Charles, alleged lover of
Josephine, 38
Château Puissant, 167
Château-Thierry, 139
Chiris, Monsieur l'Abbé, 152
Cisalpine Republic, 36
Ciudad Rodrigo, 105
Civrieux, Silvain Larreguy de,
Eagle-bearer, 178
Clarke, Henri, 258, 262, 281
Clary, Desirée, 31
Clary, Julie, 31
Cleves, 55
Closewitz, 61, 62
Coalition, Second, 38, 45; Third,
45, 47, 55; Fourth, 57, 71,
Fifth, 73; Seventh, 161
Cochrane, Rear-Admiral Sir
Alexander, 194
Cockburn, Rear-Admiral Sir
George, 195, 208
Code Napoléon, 15, 41-3,
310-11
Coignet, Major Jean-Roch, 170,
271
Colborne, Lieutenant-Colonel Sir
John, 187
column and line, 249-51, 280-1
commissariat, 256-7, 280-1
Confederation of the Rhine, see
Rhine, Confederation, of
Constantinople, 29
consulship, 39
'Continental System', 64, 71, 86,
113, 277
Cordoba, 96
Corsica, 13, 18-22, 28
Corunna, 101, 281
Cospeda, 61
Cossacks, 119, 121, 127-9, 146,
265, 275
coup d'etat attempt in Paris of
1812, 131
Craonne, 140

d'Erlon, Jean-Baptiste Drouet,
comte, 165, 169-70, 176-7,
180-1
Danube, River, 48, 50, 74-5, 78,
223, 226, 235, 264

315

David, Jacques-Louis, 233
Davout, Marshal Louis Nicholas, duc d'Auerstädt, prince d'Eckmühl, 51-2, 54-5, 59, 61, 63-4, 66-71, 74, 78-80, 115, 118, 122-3, 128-9, 164, 217, 231, 261, 267
Dego, 28
Dejean, Lieutenant-General Pierre François, comte, 181
Delort, Lieutenant-General Jacques Antoine Adrien, baron, 171
Deutsch-Wagram, 78
Doctorov, General Dmitri Sergeivich, 67
Dornburg, 61
Dover, 278
Dresden, 57, 137, 305
Druout, General Antoine, comte, 150
Ducos, 39
Dugommier, General Jacques Coquille, 25-7
Duhesme, General Philippe Guillaume, comte, 88
Dumas, General Mathieu, comte, 148
Dumerbion, General Pierre Jadart, 27-8
Duphin, Citizen, 27
Dupont de l'Etang, General Pierre, comte, 88, 95-7
Douro, River, 97
Duroc, General Geraud Christophe Michel, duc de Frioul, Grand Marshal of the Palace, 228-9
Dyle, River, 179

Eagles, 215-16
Ebelsberg, 220
Eblé, General Jean-Baptiste, comte, 131
Ebro, River, 98
Eckmühl / Eggmühl, 74, 262
Ecole Militaire de Paris, 18
Egypt, 37-8, 195, 220-1, 235, 239
Elba, 148-9, 151, 161, 197, 208
Elbe, River, 58
Eldon, John Scott, Earl of, 194
Elmer, Bob, 207
Elting, Colonel John R., 221, 225
Enghien, Louis Antoine Henri de Bourbon-Condé, duc d', 108
England, planned invasion of, 36, 45, 47
English Channel, 161-2
Erfurt, 58-9; conference at, 98
Escorial, Affair of the, 87
Escragnolles, 152
Espinosa, 99
Essen, General Jean Henri, Count of, 67
Eugène, Viceroy of Italy, Prince, 38, 116, 119, 126, 128, 239

Eylau, 66, 67-8, 81, 254, 267, 275

Federal Bureau of Investigation (FBI), 191, 202
Ferdinand d'Este, Archduke, 47-8
Ferdinand, Prince of the Asturias (later King Ferdinand VII of Spain), 85-7, 89-93, 96, 108
Fesch, Giuseppe (later Cardinal), 15, 22-3
Fezensac, Montesquiou, duc de, 126
Figueras, 88
Fisher, Herbert A. L., 41
Fleurus, 168-71, 175
Fleury de Chaboulon, Pierre-Alexandre-Edouard, 148-9
Foch, Marshal Ferdinand, 81
Fontainebleau, 147-9, 155-6; Treaty of, 86, 88
foraging, 256
formations and drill, 249-51
Forshufvud, Sten, 203-6
Fouché, Joseph, duc d'Otranto, 191, 219, 240
Foy, General Maximilien Sebastien, comte, 178, 184, 188
Franche-Comté, 155
Francis I, Emperor of Austria (until 1806, Emperor Francis II of Germany), 51, 56, 139, 221, 238, 272, 275
Frankfurt, 58
Frederick II, 'the Great', King of Prussia, 237, 248, 264, 265, 276
Frederick William III, 55, 57, 60, 64, 70, 131, 139, 221, 276
Fréjus, 156
Fréron, Commissioner, 23-5, 30
Friedland, 70-1, 83, 123, 165, 177, 188, 220, 255, 275
Frischermont, 175
Fuentes de Oñoro, 263

Gamonal, 99
Gap, 153
Gasparin, Stanislas, 22-3, 25, 27
Gembloux, 173, 179
Genappe, 173-4
Genoa, 27
George III, King of Great Britain, 47, 56
George IV, King of Great Britain (formerly Prince Regent), 192
Gera, 59
Gérard, General Maurice Etienne, comte, 165, 170, 173
Germany and German campaigns, 27, 38, 57-64, 134-9
Gerona, 96
Gibraltar, 88
Gilly, 168

Gioacchino Napoleone, King of Naples, see Murat
Glasgow University, 208
glory, 219, 243, 285, 288, 301
Godoy y Alvarez de Faria, Manuel, 'Prince of Peace', 85-7, 89, 90, 94
Golfe-Juan, 151
Golymin, 275
Göttingen, 57
Gourgaud, General Gaspard, baron, 122, 208
Grande Armée, creation of, 47, 216
Grasse, 151
Graz, 222
Great Redoubt at Borodino, 124
Grenoble, 151-4, 156
Gribeauval, Jean-Baptiste Vaquette de, comte, 254
Gros, de, 205
Gronow, Ensign Rees Howell, 182
Gross-Enzersdorf, 78
Grouchy, Marshal Emmanuel, marquis de, 116, 175, 167-8, 171-4, 179, 186-7, 191, 209, 269
Guadarrama, Sierra de, 100
Guard, Imperial, 2, 47, 58, 61, 66, 70, 77, 80, 89, 95, 100, 124, 148, 167, 169, 173, 175, 177, 181-2, 185-8, 218, 229, 231-4, 259, 264, 271
Guibert, General Jacques Antoine Hippolyte, comte, 249-50, 255, 257
Guyot, Lieutenant, 220-1

Hal, 175
Halkett, General Sir Colin, 186
Hamburg, 139
Hamilton-Williams, David, 205
Hanau, 139
Hannibal Barca, 213
Hanover, 47, 55-6
Haxo, Lieutenant-General François Nicolas, baron, 175
Headquarters and Staff, Napoleon's, 224, 226-9, 257-8
Heilsberg, 66, 70
Henry, Dr Walter, 202
Hitler, Adolf, 243-4, 308
Hoff, 66
Hohenlinden, 45
Hohenlohe, General Friedrich Ludwig, Prince of, 57, 59, 62-3
Holy Roman Empire, 83
'Hostages', the, 241
Hougoumont, 175, 177-9, 182, 184
'Hundred Days', 156
'Hutt's Gate', 197

Iglau, 51-2
Inconstant, 150

infantry, quality of French, 252
Inn, River, 73
Ionkovo, 66
Isar, River, 236
Italy and Italian campaigns, 23, 29, 32, 38, 43, 45, 47, 50, 83, 85, 139, 238
Italy, Viceroy of, *see* Eugène

Jaffa, 38
Jäger, 277
Jamestown Bay, 195
Jena, 59, 61, 64-5, 83-5, 188, 254, 276-7
Jérôme, King of Westphalia, 116, 118, 174, 177-8, 182, 242, 244
Joachim, King of Naples, *see* Murat
John, Archduke, 47, 51
Jones, Dr David, 205-6
Joppa, 220
Joseph I, King of Naples, then King of Spain, 31, 88, 92, 96-103, 106, 109, 115, 144, 165, 214-15, 239, 262, 278
Josephine, Empress, 29, 31-2, 38, 101, 192, 200
Jourdan, Marshal Jean-Baptiste, 106, 217
Junot, General Jean Androche, duc d'Abrantes, 26, 29, 33, 86, 88, 98, 119, 264
Junot, Laura, 244

Keith, Admiral George Keith Elphinstone, Viscount, 194, 207-8
Kellermann, General François Etienne, comte, 183
Kiev, 126
Königsberg, 70-1
Kovno, 132
Krasnoië, 118, 130
Krems, 50, 52
Kutusov, Field Marshal Mikhail Hilarionovich Golenischev, Prince of Smolensk, 48, 50-1, 120-3, 125-8, 238, 275

La Belle Alliance, 175
La Fère-Champenoise, 140
La Haye Sainte, 175, 180-2, 184
La Haye, 175, 180
La Rothière, 139, 238
Labédoyère, Colonel Charles de, 153
Lafayette, General Marie Joseph Paul de Motier, marquis de, 36
Laffrey, 151, 153
Lamouret, Captain, 151
Landgräfenberg, 61
Landshut, 74, 219, 233
Landwehr, 277
Lannes, Marshal Jean, duc de Montebello, 51, 59, 61, 63, 65, 70, 98, 217

Lansdberg, 66
Laon, 140
General Pierre Bellon, baron de Sainte-Hélène, 259
Lasalle, General Antoine Charles Louis, comte, 67
Las Cases, Emmanuel Augustin, comte, 39, 149, 259, 260, 197
Lasne valley, 173, 183
Lapisse,
Latour-Maubourg, General M., 116
Lattimer, Dr John, 208
Lauriston, General Jacques Alexandre Bernard Lawde, comte de, 233
le Beausset, 22-3
Le Caillou, 174-5, 177
Le Doulcet, Louis-Gustave, comte de Pontécoulant, 29
Le Moniteur, 27
Lecourbe, General, 191
Lefebvre, Marshal François Joseph, duc de Danzig, 99
Lefebvre, Madame la Maréchale, 231
legend, Napoleonic, 309-11
Légion d'honneur, 215, 219, 220, 259
Legrand, General Claude Juste Alexandre, comte, 52
Leipzig, 57, 59, 200, 137-9, 238, 256, 278
Lemonnier-Delafosse, Major, 184
Le Souper de Beaucaire, 22-3, 25
Lessart, Major de, 153
Lestocq, General Anton Wilhelm de, 57, 65, 66, 69
Letort, General Louis-Michel, 168
Liberation, War of (German), 135
Liège, 168
Ligny, 168-70, 172-3, 269, 281
Lisbon, 86, 98, 100, 101, 104, 264
Lobau Island, 239
Lobau, General Georges Mouton, comte de, 177, 179, 183
Lodi, 33-5
Lombardy, 47, 214
Longwood House, 195-7, 206
looting, 271
Lorraine, 139
Louis Ferdinand, Lieutenant-General Prince, 59
Louis XVI, King of France, 18, 20-1
Louis XVIII, King of France, 149, 154, 156, 192, 204, 208
Louise, Queen of Prussia, 57, 64
Louisiana, 85
Lowe, Lieutenant General Sir Hudson, 197, 199, 201
Lunéville, 45

Lützen, 135, 276
Lyons, 18, 150, 154, 156, 164, 191

Maastricht, 172
Macdonald, Marshal Jacques Etienne Joseph Alexandre, duc de Tarente, 80-1, 116, 131, 140, 154, 205, 252
Mack, Quartermaster-General Karl Freiherr von Leiberich, 47-50, 267
Mackenrot, Anthony, 194
Mâcon, 155
Madrid, 85, 89, 90, 92, 94-9, 103, 250
Maison, 228-9, 257
Maitland, Captain, 192, 194
Makov, 65
Malet, General Claude François de, 131
Malmaison, 192
Malojaroslavets, 126
Mamelukes, 274; *see also* Ali *and* Roustam
Mannheim, 47
Marbeuf, Louis Charles René, comte de, 13-15, 18
Marbot, Baron M. de, 275
Marchand, General Jean-Gabriel, comte, 153, 208
Marchfeld, 75, 78
Marengo, 45, 71, 83, 165, 262, 273, 277
Maret, Hugh, 149
Maria Luisa, Queen of Spain, 85, 87, 91
Marie-Louise of Austria, Empress, 105, 144-6, 149, 154, 225
Marie-Louises, 134
Markgräfneusiedl, 78
Marmont, Marshal August Frédéric Louis Viesse de, duc de Raguse, 29, 33, 105, 140, 143, 148, 150, 154, 216, 261-3, 281
Marseilles, 27, 31, 151
Marsh test, 202
marshals, 215, 217-18, 231, 260-1; *see also individuals*
Masséna, Marshal André, duc de Rivoli, prince d'Essling, 25, 26, 76, 78, 80, 104, 152, 155, 213, 217, 234, 263
Massy, Colonel, 126
Maudit, Sergeant Hippolyte de, 174
Medina del Rio Seco, 96
Méduse, 192
Meek, James, 194, 207
Mercy Argenteau, comte de, 157
Merlin, Colonel, 227
Metternich, Clemens Lothar Wenceslas, Count (later Prince) of, 242, 244
Millesimo, 34

Mint, Paris, 156
Mirabeau, Honoré Gabriel Riquetti, comte de, 24
Monaco, Prince Honoré IV of, 152
Moncey, Marshal Bon Adrien Jannot de, duc de Conegliano, 88, 95 6, 217, 209
Mondovi, 33
Mont St-Jean, 171, 177, 269
Montbrun, General Louis-Pierre, comte, 116, 124, 139, 146
Montholon, Charles Tristan, comte de, 144, 204-5
Montholon, Madame Albine de, 199
Montmartre, 140
Montmirail, 139
Moore, Lieutenant-General Sir John, 100, 279-80
Moravia, 50
Moreau, General Jean Victor, 45, 248, 311
Morris, Sergeant Tom, 185
Mortier, Marshal Adolphe Edouard Casimir Joseph, duc de Trévise, 70, 140, 143, 218, 231
Moscow, 9, 111, 115, 118, 121-9, 131-2, 146, 268, 305
Moscowa, River, 122
Mount Tabor, 195
Mouton, Georges, see Lobau
Mühlhausen, 57
Munich, 236
Murat, Marshal Joachim, prince et roi de Naples, 31, 33, 39, 47, 51, 59, 61-2, 65-7, 69 71, 88-9, 91-2, 115, 118, 126, 217, 231
Murray, Lieutenant-Colonel the Hon. Henry, 185

Namur, 167-9, 172
Nansouty, 116
Naples, 47, 92; King of, see Murat

Napoleon I, Emperor of the French birth and early life, 13; military education, 18-20; and Corsica, 19-21; and the French Revolution, 20-5; writes *Le Souper de Beaucaire*, 22-3; Toulon campaign, 23-7, 151, 200, 278, 281, 285; political connections, 23-5; as Inspector of Coastal Defences, 27; as Artillery Commander of the Army of Italy, 27; arrest and imprisonment, 27-8; ordered to Vendée, 29; appointed to *Bureau Typographiique*, 29; crushes revolt of *13 Vendémiaire*, 30-1; meets and falls in love with Josephine de Beauharnais, 31; appointed General of the Army of Italy, 32; First Italian campaign, 33-6, 238; plans for invasion of England, 36; Egyptian campaign, 37-8, 221, 239; *coup d'état de Brumaire*, 38-9; as First Consul, 39; institutes civil reforms, 40-1; and *Code Napoléon*, 41-3, 310-11; Second Italian campaign, 43, 45, 71, 83, 165, 262, 273, 277; coronation, 215; Ulm-Austerlitz campaign, 45-55, 56, 64-5, 71, 80, 83, 123, 188, 220, 222, 235, 244, 252, 264, 267, 272, 275, 277; re-draws map of Europe, 56-7; Jena-Auerstädt campaign, 57-64-5, 83-5, 188, 254, 276-7; Eylau-Friedland campaign, 65-71, 81, 83, 123, 165, 177, 188, 220, 254, 255, 267, 275; makes Treaty of Tilsit with Tsar, 71, 110, 113, 275; and Spain, 73, 83-110, 135, 174, 239, 245, 253, 278-9; Spanish campaign, 73, 98-100; Aspern-Essling-Wagram campaign, 73-81, 205, 223, 226, 233, 239, 244, 252, 256, 262, 272-3; marries Marie-Louise of Austria, 105; birth of the King of Rome, 105; Russian campaign, 11-34, 111, 114, 115, 118, 121-9, 126, 129-32, 146, 238, 254, 268, 305; 1813 campaign in Germany, 134-9, 200, 137-9, 238, 256, 276, 278, 279, 305; 1814 campaign of Fran⁓, 139-40, 143-7; abdicates, 148; goes into exile on Elba, 148-9, 151, 161, 197, 208; receives encouragement to return to France, 149; returns to Paris, 150-6; declared outlaw by European powers, 157; prepares for war, 161; Waterloo campaign, 114, 157, 161-88, 171-2, 174-6, 191, 223, 239, 256, 269-70, 278, 280, 305-6; returns to Paris and second abdication, 191-2; at Rochefort, 192-3; 'legal' position, 193-4, 207-8; surrenders to British, 192-3; transported to St. Helena, 195; moves into Longwood House, 195; routine and life there, 197; illness and death, 199-200; postmortem controversies, 200-7; disinterrment and return to France, 208-9; legend, 309-11
ambition, 287; attention to detail, 258; centralisation of authority, 238-9, 258, 260-3; charisma, 214, 221, 232-7, 259-60, 288, 290, 306; command and leadership, 213-15, 221, 224, 234, 244, 247; courage in battle, 223; inspecting and reviewing troops, 227, 290; memory, 286; method of thought, 293; method of working, 224-9; offensive, belief in, 237-8, 265, 297; outflanking strategy, 238, 266-7; enemy commanders overawed, 270; political beliefs, 20; ruthlessness, 239, 240; system and principles of fighting, 248ff, 253, 257-8, 263-4, 266-9, 291-9; temper, 242; and fortune, 286, 301; and frontal attack, 268; and 'grand tactics', 267-9; and higher tactics and strategy, 257; and misinformation, 262-3; and peace, 244-5; and public opinion, 240; and reconnaissance, 265; and religion, 241; and reputation, 287, 301; and risk, 296; and speed, 264, 268, 294, 295; and superiors, 287; and the press, 240; as Great Captain, 213, 247; as heir to previous military systems, 224, 247-8; as strategist, 263-7; on death, 288; on war and the profession of arms, 285-6
Napoleon II, François Charles Joseph Bonaparte, King of Rome, 105, 144-6, 149, 154
Napoleon III, Louis Napoleon Bonaparte, Emperor of the French, 311
nationalism, 244-5, 248
Nations, Battle of the, see Leipzig
Naumburg, 57, 59, 61
Navarre, 88
Naveau windmill, 169
Navy, French, 18, 45, 229, 230
Neuchâtel, 55
Neverovski, General, 118
Ney, Marshal Michel, prince de la Moskowa, duc d'Elchingen, 22-3, 61, 63, 66-7, 69, 71, 98, 115, 129, 131-3, 135, 148, 15-6, 165-70, 172-3, 176, 181-2, 184-6, 218, 231, 251
Nice, 23
Niemen, River, 114, 118, 132
Nile, see Aboukir Bay
Nivelles, 167-9
Northumberland, 195, 208
Noverraz, Abram, 200, 203, 208

O'Meara, Dr, 201
oath, national, 20
Oçana, 101

Oldenburg, Peter Frederick Louis, Duke of, 113
Olmütz, 50-2
Ompteda, Colonel Christian von, 185
One Hundred Days, 156
Oneglia, 27
Oporto, 101
Ordener, Colonel Michel, comte, 183
Ordre, Baron d', 309
organ, male, allegedly Napoleon's, 208
Ostend, 161, 164, 177
Oudinot, Marshal Nicolas Charles, duc de Reggio, 115, 119, 129-31, 209, 223

Pajol, General Claude Pierre, comte, 165
Pamplona, 88
Paoli, General Pasquale de, 13, 18, 21
Papelotte, 175, 180
Paris, 10, 20-2, 27-9, 31, 36, 38, 98, 131, 139-40, 143-4, 146-7, 150-1, 154-6, 164-5, 182, 191, 215, 225, 268; Treaty of, 148, 194
Paul I, Tsar of Russia, 274
Peninsular War, 73, 83-110, 135, 174, 239, 245, 253
Pétiet, Colonel Auguste, 175
Philippeville, 165
Picton, Lieutenant-General Thomas, 181
Pino, General, 119
Pisa, 15
plague, 38
Plancenoit, 186-7
Plantation House, 195
Plymouth, 194
Poniatowski, Marshal Josef Anton, prince, 116, 122-3
Pontécoulant, see Le Doulcet
Porteous House, 195
Posen, 58
Powell, Captain Harry Weyland, 187
Pratzen heights, 51-2, 55, 235
Pressburg, Treaty of, 272
Preussisches-Eylau, see Eylau
Pripet marshes, 117
Provence, 151
Prussia and Prussian forces: territory violated by French at Ansbach, 50; isolated and humiliated by Napoleon after Austerlitz, 55; mobilize against Napoleon, 56-7; dispositions and plan of operations, 57-8; defeated at twin battles of Jena-Auerstädt, 58-64; King refuses to accept peace, 64; forced to supply greatcoats and boots for Grande Armée, 65; lose fur-

ther territory after Friedland, 71; encouragement by British to join Fifth Coalition rebuffed, 73; participation in 1812 invasion of Russia, 116; lukewarm support for Napoleon, 121; contingent defects to Russians, 131; join coalition against Napoleon for War of Liberation of Germany, 135-9; defeat Napoleon at Leipzig, 137-9; plan of campaign for 1814, 139; forces of Blücher successively defeated and repulsed, 139-40; enter Paris, 140; mobilise against Napoleon after his return from Elba, 161; dispositions and morale, 161, 164, 167; defeated at Ligny, 168-71; army rallies at Wavre, 173; participates in allied victory at Waterloo, 183-8
Pultusk, 65
Puy-de-Dôme, 204
Pyramids, 37, 195, 220, 235
Pyrenees, 83, 87, 139

Quartier-général de la Grande Armée, 228
Quatre Bras, 167-8, 170, 172-4, 182
Quatre Bras, 209

Raasdorf, 79
Raevski, General, 118
Randon, Captain, 153
Rapp, Jean, 191, 233
Ratisbon, 233, 273
Reille, 165, 174, 176-8, 184
Reille, General Honoré Charles Michel Joseph, comte, 280-1
Revolution, French, 20, 22
Reynier, General Jean Louis Ebénézer, 116, 119, 251
Rheims, 140
Rhine, Confederation of the (Rheinbund), 56, 83, 115, 135, 137
Rhine, River, 27, 47, 50, 83, 139, 161
Rivoli, 34
Robespierre, Augustin Bon Joseph de, 24-8
Robespierre, Charlotte, 25
Robespierre, Maximilien François Isidore de, 24, 27, 32
Robinson, Dr, 202
Rochefort, 92
Roger, Albine, 204
Rome, 83
Rome, King of, see Napoleon II
Rosebery, Lord, 312
Rosetta Stone, 37
Rossomme, 176, 184
Rostopchin, General Fedor Visiljevitch, Count, 125

Roustam, Raza, mameluke servant, 229
Royal Military Chronicle, 111
Rüchel, General Ernest Philip von, 57, 62-3
Russbach stream, 78
Russia, and Russian forces: join Third Coalition, 45; plans and dispositions, 47; reverse march after Ulm, 50; rendezvous with Austrians at Olmütz, 50; defeated at Austerlitz, 51-5; refuse to make peace with Napoleon, 57; retreat in face of French advance from Germany, 65; hold French at battle of Eylau, 66-9; defeated at Friedland, 20-1; make peace with Napoleon at Tilsit and join Continental System, 71; increasing tension with France, 113; invaded by Napoleon, 115-17; armies retreat and evade Napoleon's forces, 118-22; defeated at Borodino, 122-5; abandon Moscow, 125; at battle of Malojaroslavets, 126-7; armies harry retreating French, 128; repulsed at Krasnoïe, 130; fail to hold the line of the Berezina, 130-1; defeated at Lützen and Bautzen, 135; defeat Napoleon at Leipzig, 137-9; enter Paris, 147; mobilize against Napoleon after his return from Elba, 161
Saale, 192
Saale, River, 59, 61
Saalfield, 59
Sacken, General Dmitri Osten, Count, 67, 69
Saint-Cyr, Marshal Laurent Gouvion, comte de, 15, 116, 119, 129
Saint-Denis, Etienne, 208
Saint-Dizier, 143
Saint-Esprit, 150
Saint-Hilaire, General Louis Vincent Joseph le Blond, comte de, 55, 67-8
Saint-Just, Louis Antoine de, 27
Saint-Leonhard, 222
St-Amand, 173
St-Maximin, 22
St. Bernard Pass, Great, 42-3
St. Helena, 10, 26, 39, 114, 149, 177, 191, 194-5, 301, 305; Napoleon in exile on, 195-209
St. Polten, 50
St. Roch, 30-1
Saliceti, Antonio Cristoforo, 21-6, 28
Sambre, River, 164, 167
San Ildefonso, Treaty of, 85

San Michele, 33
San Sebastián, 88
Saorgio, 27
Saragossa, 95, 96, 101, 105
Savary, General Anne Jean Marie
 René, duc de Rovigo, 51, 92
Saxony, 58
Schalers Green, 205
Scharnhorst, General Gerhard
 Johann David von, 276
Schleiz, 59
Schönbrunn, Treaty of, 272
Schöngraben, 235
Schwarzenberg, Field Marshal
 Karl Philip, Prince, 116, 119,
 136-7, 139-40
Seeley, Sir John, 263, 310, 312
Ségur, General Philippe Paul,
 comte de, 122-3
Sénarmont, General Alexandre
 Antoine Hureau de, baron,
 255
Serurier, Marshal Jean Mathieu
 Philbert, comte, 213
Seven Years War, 274
Shevardino Redoubt, 122
Sièyes, Abbé Emmanuel Joseph,
 38-9
skirmishers and light infantry,
 251-2, 280-1
Smohain, 175, 180
Smolensk, 118-19, 121-3,
 126-7, 130
Smorgoniye, 226
Soignes, Forest of, 173, 174,
 177
Sokolnitz, 54
Solre-sur-Sambre, 165
Sombreffe, 167-8
Somosierra, 98-9
Soult, Marshal Nicolas Jean de
 Dieu, duc de Dalmatie, 51,
 61-3, 66-9, 98, 100, 101, 107,
 164, 173-4, 176, 191, 209,
 217-18, 261, 264, 280-1
Spain and Spanish campaign,
 see Peninsular War
square, 274
Staël, Madame Anne Louise
 Germaine, baronne de, 29
Stendhal (Marie Henri Beyle),
 151
Strasbourg, 47
Stuttgart, 58
Suchet, Marshal Louis Gabriel,
 duc d'Albufera, 105, 107, 164,
 191
Suvarov, Field Marshal
 Alexander Vasilievitch, Count
 Suvarov-Rimnisky, Prince of
 Italijsky, 274
Sweden, 113
Syria, 37

Tabor, see Mount Tabor
Talavera, 101
Talleyrand-Périgord, Charles

Maurice de, l'Eveque d'Autun,
 prince de Benavente, 36, 57,
 147-8, 154, 242-3
Tallien, Madame, 29
Tauentzien, Generalmajor
 Bolesas Friedrich Emanuel,
 Count von Wartenberg, 61
taxes and tax system, 41
Tchitchakov, Admiral Pavel,
 117, 129-31
Teil, Lieutenant-General Jean
 Pierre, baron du, 20-3, 224,
 248
Teil, General Jean de Beaumont,
 Chevalier du, 21-2, 26, 248
Telnitz, 54
Terror, the, 27
'The Briars', 195, 207
Thermidor, Madame Notre-
 Dame de, 29
Thiébault, General Paul-Charles-
 François Dieu Donné, 156
Thielmann, General Johann
 Adolf, Freiherr von, 179
Thorn, 65
Thüringerwald, 58
Tilly, Ambassador, 28
Tilsit, 71, 109, 113, 275
Tolstoi, General Ivan, Count
 Ostermann-, 67-9
Tonnant, HMS, 194, 207
Tormassov, General, 117, 119
Torres Vedras, 104
Toulon, 9, 22-7, 151, 200, 278,
 281, 285
Trafalgar, 64, 85
Trefçon, Colonel Toussaint-
 Jean, 174
Tsar, see Alexander I
Tudela, 9?
Tuileries Palace, 21, 31, 156
Turenne, Marshal-General Henri
 de la Tour d'Auvergne, 221
Turkish (Ottoman) Empire, 29,
 38, 113, 274
Tutchkov, General, 67
Tyrol, 47, 50, 236, 272

Ulm, 47-9, 65, 71, 267
Undaunted, HMS, 148
Uxbridge, Lord, 183

Valençay, Treaty of, 108
Valencia, 95-6, 101, 105
Valladolid, 100
Vandamme, General Dominique
 Joseph René, comte
 d'Unsebourg, 55, 173
Varennes, 20
Vauchamps, 139
Vendée, 29, 239
13 Vendémiaire, 31, 285
Venice, 272
Viasma, 128
Victor, Marshal Claude Victor-
 Perrin, duc de Bellune, 70-1,
 98, 101, 116, 129-31

Vienna, 50-2, 74, 222, 233, 236,
 238; Congress of, 149, 151,
 156
Vierzehnheiligen, 61, 63
Vignali, chaplain, 208
Villefranche, 155
Vilna, 117, 259
Vinkovo, 126
Vistula, River, 65-6
Vitebsk, 118, 123
Vitoria, 92, 107

Wagram, 74-5, 78-9, 81, 205,
 223, 226, 244, 252, 256, 262,
 272-3
Walewska, Alexandre, 192
Walewska, Marie, Countess, 192
Warsaw, 65
Warsaw, Grand Duchy of, 71,
 113, 115
Waterloo, 114, 157, 171-2,
 174-6, 191, 223, 239, 256,
 269-70, 278, 280, 305-6
Wavre, 171-3, 179
Weider, Ben, 203-6
Weimar, 62-3
Wellington, Field Marshal Sir
 Arthur Wellesley, Viscount
 Douro, Duke of, 10, 83, 101,
 104, 105-8, 123, 139, 161-2,
 165, 168-75, 177-86, 188,
 195, 197, 221, 247, 259, 261,
 269, 278, 280-2, 308; on
 Napoleon, 270, 281-2, 302
Westphalia, Kingdom of, 71
Westphalia, King of, see Jérôme
Wild (the Great), Jonathan,
 308-9
Wischau, 51-2
Wittgenstein, General Ludwig
 Adolf Peter, Prince of, 119,
 128-9, 131, 135
Woodford, Major Alexander,
 178
Württemberg, 47, 237
Würzburg, 58, 204

Yarrow, Dr, 201, 203
Yorck, General Johann David
 Ludwig, Count of Wartenburg,
 131

Ziethen, General Hans Ernst
 Karl, Graf von, 187